# TAX
# PLANNING
### FOR
# SUCCESS

THE BUSINESS SERIES FOR OWNER/MANAGERS

# TAX PLANNING FOR SUCCESS

## PRACTICAL APPROACHES FOR YOU AND YOUR BUSINESS

KEY PORTER BOOKS

**Canadian Cataloguing in Publication Data**

Tax planning for success

(The Business series for owner/managers)
Co-published by Deloitte & Touche.
ISBN 1-55013-190-7

1. Small business – Taxation – Canada.
I. Deloitte & Touche.  II. Title.  III. Series.

KE5906.T3 1991      343.7106'8      C89-090759-5
KF6499.ZA2T3 1991


Key Porter Books Limited
70 The Esplanade
Toronto, Ontario
Canada M5E 1R2

Printed and bound in Canada

91 92 93 94 95 96 6 5 4 3 2 1

The information and analysis contained in this book are not intended to substitute for competent professional advice. The material that follows is provided solely as a general guide to the tax and other planning issues that confront owner-managers of small- and medium-sized businesses in Canada. No action should be initiated without consulting your professional advisors.

*Tax Planning for Success* has been created by a team of writers from Deloitte & Touche and (in Quebec) Samson Bélair/Deloitte & Touche, serving Canadian clients for more than 130 years. The firm is one of the largest firms of chartered accountants and management consultants, with more than 5,400 people, including 700 partners and 3,500 professional staff in some 70 Canadian centres. It serves more than 65,000 clients in Canada, including more than 100 of the *Financial Post*'s 500 top industrial companies. As a member of DRT International, the firm also serves clients in more than 100 countries around the world.

**Editor-in-Chief:**

John Stacey, Toronto

**Assistant Editors:**

Richard Birch, Toronto
Bill Sherman, Toronto

**Contributors:**

Luc Blanchette, Montreal
Nancy Braun, Toronto
John Budd, Markham
Graham Hoey, Hamilton
Wallace Howick, Toronto
Bruce McCarley, Vancouver
Doug McCulloch, Toronto
Len Sakamoto, Toronto

# CONTENTS

# INTRODUCTION

Pain and Prosper Inc. It's got a nice ring to it. Especially those three letters on the end. You know that running a business isn't the piece of cake many make it out to be. But it does have its rewards. And those three letters "Inc." They exude a feeling of stability and permanence. You're in business. And you mean business.

Along with the Inc., or it might be Ltd., comes the assurance of limited liability, tax savings, and the ease of dealing with creditors, suppliers, and even your customers.

But should every business be incorporated? Not necessarily. For a variety of business owners, there is little benefit to incorporating. Many prefer to operate as a proprietorship specifically to avoid the complexities a corporation can introduce. Their businesses may have few assets, perhaps because they are in the service industry, and their income may not be large enough to need a tax deferral vehicle such as a corporation.

Proprietorships and partnerships are entitled to many of the same deductions and tax credits to which a corporation is entitled. However, there is no separation of owner and business as there is if your business is incorporated. Generally, as a proprietor, you are taxed on the "profit" from your business, regardless of how much you withdraw from the business. Profit is measured by calculating income from the business and subtracting various expenses that are allowed as deductions.

Partnerships operate a little differently. Again, there is no separation between the business and you and your fellow partners. However, profit is calculated for the business as a whole at the partnership level and pre-tax profit is then allocated to the partners. You, as a partner, include the allocation in income for tax purposes. Generally, all profit must be allocated and, therefore, it is all subject to tax. In many provinces, some entrepreneurs, mainly professionals such as doctors, dentists, lawyers and accountants, are not allowed to incorporate.

Joint ventures are different again. Essentially, a group of business owners forms a joint venture to pursue a specific business without using a corporation or partnership. Each joint venturer may have other business interests that are kept distinct from the joint venture itself. A joint venturer could be an individual operating as a proprietorship, a partner or partnership, a corporation, or even a trust.

Still, most Canadians in business choose to operate as a corporation, whether at start-up or after they have proved that the business is viable. The reason why, in a word, is flexibility. With a corporation, you can plan more effectively for today, for tomorrow, and beyond tomorrow when you no longer are active in the business that you have made successful.

- A corporation makes it easier to determine ownership and share in profits.
- Financing opportunities multiply and the traditional avenues are enhanced.
- Annual remuneration can be controlled and you can even choose how and when to receive company profits.
- Growth of your business is more orderly and opportunities usually open up more readily.
- Business liability may be limited to assets in the corporation.
- Key employees stay longer and tend to contribute to the business more.
- Lower tax rates apply to the first $200,000 of business income earned by the corporation.
- Personal taxes can be deferred simply by leaving money in the corporation.
- Your options to provide for your retirement increase.
- A corporation can facilitate a major expansion, for instance, moving into the export market.
- The corporation makes it much easier for your family to participate in the business and its profits.
- It's much easier to bow out and leave the ownership and operation of your business to your family with the least amount of disruption.
- Should you decide to sell, the corporation gives you options and therefore leverage you might not have with a proprietorship.

The price you pay for these benefits isn't severe. Setting up a corporation and maintaining it each year involves a significant, but not onerous, cost. In a few situations, a corporation will be more restricting than operating as a proprietorship or partnership. For example, losses can be trapped inside the corporation, whereas losses realized as a proprietor or partner can be applied directly against other sources of personal income. However, for most owner-managers, these disadvantages pale next to the benefits that the average incorporated entrepreneur will reap over the life of his or her involvement in the business.

We'll track planning opportunities throughout the typical ownership cycle of a small incorporated business, from the start-up phase when you take the incorporation plunge, through those first heady years of growth, then to the years when you decide whether to undertake that major expansion, and finally to the period when you decide it's time to bow out and let family or even complete strangers carry on what is about to become somebody else's business.

No matter where you are in the ownership cycle, several chapters in the book should be of interest. If you've just started up your business and don't have an answer for everyone who asks why you haven't incorporated, take a look at the first few chapters. Note that the planning ideas in several of the chapters also apply to unincorporated businesses.

If you've been operating your own corporation for a number of years, glance through the chapters on expansion and succession planning. If you want your business to stay in the family, it's never too soon to begin the process of transferring control to your children. This is seldom an easy, straightforward process. It deserves as much planning as you put into your major business decisions.

And if the time is nearing to sell the business, look at Chapter 13. Selling to the first person who comes along willing to pay your price may not make the most sense, especially if you're approaching retirement age and the proceeds of sale have to get you and your spouse through the next 20 or 30 years.

This is a book of planning opportunities, not a step-by-step analysis of how to undertake certain planning. In most situations, you'll need professional help of some kind to evaluate your options and steer you through what likely is a minefield of government regulation, industry pitfalls, family problems you may not have dreamed of, and specialized knowledge that you don't have and didn't even know existed. This book is intended to make you aware of such situations. If you think about them, you'll be much better prepared to meet with your professional advisors. You'll get better advice, less expensive advice, and a plan that won't need patching up in a few months' time.

The information and analysis contained in this book are not intended to substitute for competent professional advice. Planning your tax and financial affairs, and those of your business, to reduce the amount of tax paid is a complex process – one that is unique to you and your business. The material that follows is provided solely as a general guide to assist you in understanding the main income tax provisions and business considerations that can be used in the tax planning process for you and your business. No action should be initiated without consulting your professional advisors.

Please note that the information in this book is based on the law in effect and on any proposed legislation announced by the end of February, 1991.

You know your business better than anyone else. As you sift through the planning ideas contained in the following chapters, you should be able to spot a number of opportunities that will benefit you, your family and your business this year and for years to come.

# 1/Incorporating Your Business

Should every business be incorporated? Not necessarily. But most successful businesses are these days.

You certainly have a choice, unless you're a professional and are prohibited from operating as a corporation by law. Many small businesses start out as proprietorships (you run the business yourself and retain all profits) or partnerships (you and at least one other person are involved in the business and profits are shared among the partners).

However, if your business is growing, or has become more than a one-person operation, or your needs for financing are becoming more insistent, or you want to protect what you've worked so hard to build up, it may appear that the "choice" to incorporate or not has pretty well been made for you. Operating as a corporation will enhance the business's financial security and yours. It may be financially more rewarding in the long run. And it will become less difficult to solve non-financial problems and achieve non-financial goals.

## FLEXIBILITY AND STABILITY

As many owner-managers put it, "It makes the business of running my business a lot easier." Incorporation gives you more flexibility and puts your business on a solid footing to grow and expand in the years ahead. Flexibility and stability are going to be precious commodities this decade. Increasing international competition, free trade, more difficult access to financing, seemingly endless new regulations and taxes – running your own business isn't easy. The last thing you need are more impediments. But operating in the corporate form can smooth out a few of the bumps and potholes on the rocky road of commerce.

At the same time, today's small business owner is being challenged by:

- new markets that were simply inaccessible just a few years ago;
- new technology that has made niche marketing possible for even the smallest business, and
- international markets – exporting is no longer the preserve of larger companies or those with "unique connections".

Markets exist today where they didn't yesterday. And the marketplace gobbles up worthwhile new products and services just as fast as they are developed.

To survive and grow, to take your business where you know it belongs, to ensure your business will provide adequately for you and your family, now and later in life, you need to build the business on a firm foundation and have the flexibility to react quickly in this fast-paced, changing world.

## SHERI'S A SUCCESS

Sheri Sorentino worked in advertising and public relations for over a decade. Finally, a few years ago, she decided to go out on her own. Instead of chasing big-dollar clients, she focused on smaller businesses that were either developing new products and services, or trying to break into new markets. Realizing that her clients were very cost-sensitive, she put together a no-frills public relations package that lent itself to a fair degree of computerization. She knew that success depended on putting her client's enthusiasm in front of the right audience, and her ten years in the industry gave her the access she needed to those buyers.

Sheri's business turned the corner in a year and a half, and last year she hired a junior associate. Business is booming and she now needs another associate, plus clerical help. As well, she can no longer work out of her house, her computer equipment and software need a major upgrading, and her car has seen too many better days.

Sheri's just been too busy for the last three years to think about incorporating. And there was no pressing need. Aside from initial expenditures on computer equipment, software and basic office furniture, her business needed virtually no capital. Financing, when necessary, was provided through a line of credit with her mortgage-free home as security.

Now, she's looking at three salaries to meet each and every week, rent on office space, plus significant expenditures on office furniture, computer equipment and an automobile. How will incorporation help Sheri and her business?

### FINANCING

Sheri's personal line of credit is adequate to finance her business now, but it may not be as her business grows. Being incorporated may allow her to increase her line of credit if necessary, but more importantly, it will give her access to new financing opportunities.

### INVESTING IN HER BUSINESS

Sheri's income is more than adequate to meet her personal needs. She's ready to invest in her business. The small business corporate tax rate is less than half Sheri's personal tax rate (since Sheri has been operating as a proprietorship, her business income has been taxed at personal rates). By operating as a corporation, Sheri will have roughly one-third more after-tax corporate income to reinvest in the business.

## MINORITY POSITION
Sheri expects to offer one of her associates a profit-sharing arrangement. She anticipates, quite correctly, that the plan will have a better chance of succeeding if the profit sharing is based on corporate profits, rather than business income earned personally.

## CONTINUITY
With an expanding client base, Sheri knows how important it is becoming for her business to be more than just Sheri Sorentino. Her clients depend on the on-going services she and her two associates provide. By incorporating, her employees now will act on behalf of the corporation. If Sheri falls ill, the corporation will continue to exist and, with proper management, operate in her absence.

## WHAT IS THIS THING CALLED INC.?
A limited company, that is, a corporation, is a legal entity in the eyes of the law, or as some have put it, a "legal fiction". From a financial point of view, a corporation possesses the same rights and privileges as any living person under the law. In fact, tax law refers to corporations as persons – not all that much different from you or your neighbour.

A corporation can own assets, enter into contracts, and be bound in legal obligation. A corporation can also default on its obligations, be sued, and be taxed. And a corporation can employ people, conduct business, and operate virtually anywhere. Of course, its activities are carried out by individuals who are empowered to act on behalf of the corporation.

Ownership is accomplished through a share ownership structure. Sheri Sorentino, as the owner-manager of her newly incorporated company, owns all of the voting common shares. Thus, she owns 100 per cent of her company, Sorentino Consultants Inc. The corporation owns the assets of the business and is responsible for its liabilities. Sheri is also an employee of the company, an officer, and a director. Arranging the share ownership structure is dealt with in the next chapter.

It is as a director that she empowers the company to conduct the public relations business, to employ her, and to appoint her as president. As an employee and president, she runs the company. As a director and sole shareholder, she sets her own salary, decides on dividend distributions, and determines financing arrangements. As an employee and shareholder, she negotiates favourable terms with lenders. And as a senior employee, she decides payment terms for clients and hires and fires other employees.

## SPLIT PERSONALITY

From a legal point of view, Sheri always wears two hats. She no longer "is" her business. She owns shares in a corporation that conducts a business that she used to own directly. She's the bridge between the "legal fiction" that she owns and the business world in which the corporation must conduct its day-to-day affairs. She is also an employee, separate and completely distinct from the business.

This point is often not appreciated by owners of newly incorporated companies. And in most business situations, the distinction is of no importance. Sheri carried on her business the day after incorporating in almost exactly the same way as she did the day before. Her clients, her suppliers and her employee noticed nothing more than the name change.

Sheri noticed something considerably more important. The corporation now pays her a base salary. Later she will receive dividends and perhaps bonus income. She no longer participates directly in any banking arrangements. The corporation has the line of credit; she simply guarantees it. Now she keeps her own personal records, while the corporation keeps its own. Of course she works on both, but while there was one set before, now there are two. And all business transactions now go through the corporation. The corporation writes cheques to a supplier. If she pays for taxi fare, the corporation reimburses her; she simply can't add the receipt to her "business expenses".

## CORPORATE NO-NO'S

"The hardest thing to get used to with a newly incorporated business is not being able to dip into the till – for groceries, rent, vacations, or even the morning newspaper." It's a common complaint, but most owner-managers get used to keeping their personal affairs completely separate from those of the corporation. In fact, the tax law very specifically requires absolute segregation between shareholder and corporation. If you don't follow the rules, double taxation may be the penalty. And lower taxes is probably one reason why you've incorporated in the first place.

## TAX FOR TWO, AND TWO FOR TAX

The corporation must pay tax at both the federal and provincial levels (corporate taxes are discussed in greater detail in Chapter 3). After-tax corporate income is then available for the payment of dividends to shareholders. Of course, the corporation can also pay shareholder-employees a salary, which is a deductible expense to the corporation. Owner-manager remuneration is dealt with in Chapter 5.

For small business income, the combined federal and provincial corporate tax rate is between 16.5 per cent and 23 per cent. This is less than half Sheri's marginal tax rate that she used to pay on her business income. Of course, Sheri still must pay tax on any dividends she receives from the corporation, but the combined corporate and personal tax rate is about the same as she was paying before she incorporated. With the corporation, Sheri is able to invest much larger amounts of after-tax corporate income in the business – simply by leaving it there and not paying it out as salary or dividends.

One thing Sheri will eventually notice is that her corporation almost has a life of its own. When a proprietorship ceases business, everything in effect shuts down. The business was you and if you're not conducting business any longer, nothing is left. Corporations continue to exist even though they no longer conduct business. Regulations must still be observed, tax returns filed, and all obligations must continue to be met, or dealt with in some manner if the company is in financial trouble.

More importantly, suppliers and clients are now, technically, dealing with the corporation, not directly with Sheri. Sheri and her employees are more or less agents of the corporation. If, in a few years, Sheri decides to take an extended vacation for a few months, the corporation still exists. If she has managed the company's affairs properly, the business will survive. Yes, this could also possibly be arranged if the business was not incorporated, but it wouldn't be as easy, nor as secure. The corporation allows Sheri to institute much more stringent financial controls if she is not on hand each and every day. If one of her employees suddenly leaves, her clients continue to deal with the corporation.

## CASHING IN ON COMPUTERS
For a number of years, Guy Lafontaine had been informally advising friends on their computer installations, both at home and in their businesses. Requests for expertise began to increase to the point where he was saying no more often than yes. At that point, he decided to chance going into business for himself.

Even though it made no financial sense, Guy chose to incorporate immediately under the name Worry-Free Computers Ltd. In fact, the initial expense put a big hole in his personal budget. But he knew that operating as a corporation was absolutely essential in his business. He was introducing his clients to new technology that was unfamiliar to them. In short order, his clients became dependent on that technology, because it invariably cut costs and made their businesses more competitive.

But Guy knew that not every computer installation would work out as planned. Not every client would be satisfied, and some might blame Guy for decreased profitability. He was also aware that the computer business had become extremely competitive and business failures were on the rise. He wanted to protect what he was building up in his business as well as his personal possessions from unhappy clients and disgruntled creditors. By incorporating, Guy knew that in most situations he would be limiting his liabilities to what he had invested in the corporation.

## LIMITING YOUR LIABILITIES

The liabilities of a corporation are distinct from those of its shareholders. The corporation is responsible for all debts it incurs and agreements to which it is party. You, as shareholder, are only liable for debts that you personally owe to the corporation and have guaranteed for the corporation. And, of course, you are at risk for money and other property that you have invested in the corporation.

Most owner-managers find this limited liability difficult to achieve in practice, at least when starting up their incorporated business. Major creditors, such as banks, require adequate security for loans made to the corporation. Generally, they will seek your personal guarantee in addition to any security offered by the corporation. Other than having recourse to these personal guarantees, the corporation's creditors cannot attack your personal assets to satisfy the corporation's debts.

Similarly, in the normal course of business, claimants against your business will have access only to the corporation's assets to satisfy any actions. However, situations abound where directors, and even officers and employees, can be held personally liable for a corporation's activities. The limited liability aspect of a corporation certainly offers more protection than operating as a proprietorship, which offers none, but it is no guarantee that a court action won't look through the corporate shell and deal with you personally.

---

**Caution!** If you think your business is heading for trouble, or you feel that you're taking on more risk than you are comfortable with, get professional advice immediately. The professional's job is to show you how to head off potential problems before they affect your bottom line, or how to build up effective financial walls that will stop problems in their tracks.

---

For Guy Lafontaine, incorporating his business paid off within two years. His consulting business was a roaring success, and it wasn't long before he was being courted by computer software and hardware distributors. Guy found that the corporation facilitated bringing in a partner as shareholder. An ambitious expansion program got off the ground thanks to an advantageous combination of equity and debt financing from a private source. And a year later, his company merged with a national computer equipment distributor. Guy retained 25 per cent ownership.

Share ownership is a simple and expedient method of determining ownership of an enterprise. Shareholders own the shares or stock of the company, which represent their ownership interest in the whole enterprise. There are two classes of shares, common and preferred, and several different types of each with various attributes. Share structure is discussed in the next chapter.

By causing the corporation to issue or sell more shares, ownership of the business can be changed. Guy Lafontaine's company issued his first "partner" a 15 per cent stake in the business in the form of voting common shares. The private investor was issued another 10 per cent plus preferred shares. On the merger, Guy and his partners exchanged their shares for shares in the new merged company on a tax-deferred basis.

## DON'T LOSE OUT

Guy had no problem incorporating his business immediately on start-up. He had few expenses, since he was offering a service based on his expertise. It would be very unlikely for such a business to generate any losses in the first year or two. This is certainly not the case with other types of business that require substantial expenditures before starting up. In this case, it may pay to postpone incorporating until the business is in a profitable position.

---

**Timely Tip.** If you run your business as a proprietorship, any losses incurred by the business can be written off against all other sources of income you may have. This is not the case if an incorporated business incurs losses. These are incurred by the corporation, not by you personally. There is no mechanism for transferring these losses to you (unless your business fails completely – see Chapter 3), but there are ways to minimize losses (see Chapter 8). The corporation gets credit for the losses, but can use them only to reduce income in the previous three years or the next seven years.

---

## GIZMOS ARE WINNERS

A few years ago, Ray Corcoran was successful, well-off and bored. It was time to take a risk or two. So he decided to try his hand at running his own business. After six months' research, he found a company with a good new product, but which was in bad shape. The owner simply had no idea how to market his product and control costs. For more than 15 years, Ray had made his living doing just this for a large manufacturing concern.

A deal was struck under which Ray bought a controlling interest in the struggling young manufacturing company, Gizmo Inc. The current owner retained a minority interest and stayed on in a managerial/research position. In less than a year, Ray had turned the company around and was looking forward to substantial profits.

Before consummating the deal, Ray formed a shell corporation, usually called a "holding company", with himself as controlling shareholder and his wife and two children, through a trust, as minority shareholders. This holding company then purchased the majority interest in the manufacturing company, usually referred to as the operating company. Why did Ray choose this particular structure?

### ESTATE PLANNING
Ray knew that if everything panned out as planned in the next seven or eight years, he would have enough for him and his wife to live on for the foreseeable future. The corporate structure made it easier to begin planning for how to leave his assets to his children.

### SUCCESSION
Bearing his estate planning goals in mind, Ray needed a corporate structure that would make it easier to deal with any buyouts or problems in the operating company. He also wanted a flexible structure that would allow his children to become involved in the business if they wished and even take it over eventually.

### TAX SAVINGS
Ray knew that high taxes would be the biggest impediment to achieving his goals over the next ten or fifteen years. The two-tiered corporate structure offered some significant tax deferrals, and it gave him more options to plan for his retirement.

## LOOSENING THE REINS
There are several ways to begin passing ownership of your assets to your children while you are still alive, while at the same time retaining control over the property, but minimizing tax both now and in the future. These actions and goals are at the heart of most estate and succession planning. If those assets are owned by a corporation, programs are easier to implement, it's easier to retain control, and the unexpected can be dealt with more expeditiously.

This is particularly true if you own business assets. You can retain control through one type of shares (voting preferred), while your children may participate in the capital growth of the company through another type (common). You can gradually sell or transfer ownership of shares to your children or new owners as you slowly bow out of the business. Or you can retain sufficient control to ensure that your retirement needs will be met by the corporation. Estate and succession planning are discussed further in Chapters 7 and 12.

## THE $400,000 CAPITAL GAINS EXEMPTION

One of the greatest monetary advantages a corporation offers is access to the $400,000 small business capital gains exemption. This is available on the sale of shares in qualifying small business corporations. Each member of your family is entitled to his or her own exemption, which of course multiplies the tax savings. If your business is not incorporated, you will have available only the standard $100,000 capital gains exemption and, unless other members of your family can establish an ownership interest in the business, they won't be able to use their exemptions. Using the two capital gains exemptions to your best advantage is discussed in Chapter 10.

## RETIREMENT PLANNING

As an individual running an unincorporated business, the only option open for tax-assisted retirement savings was an RRSP (registered retirement savings plan). RRSPs are no less important to an owner-manager, but you now have the option of establishing and contributing to a registered pension plan. You can also set up a deferred profit sharing plan for your employees, and you may be able to pay yourself a retiring allowance when you finally bow out of the business.

---

**Caution!** It is absolutely essential to get professional advice – both legal and accounting – when incorporating. The pitfalls are many and mistakes are expensive to fix up later, if they even can be mended. Do it the right way now. You'll save money in the long run, be able to set up the kind of protection and flexibility you want and need, and be more assured of achieving your long-range financial goals on schedule.

---

# 2/Setting Up the Corporation

Incorporating is not a "do-it-yourself" project that you can whip off next weekend. On the surface it may seem straightforward – establish the legal entity, issue a few shares, transfer business assets into the corporation, and start up fresh Monday morning – but it is a complex process that requires professional legal and tax help. Your advisors will steer you clear of the many pitfalls that face new owner-managers, start your tax planning out on the right foot, and ensure that you and your company have the flexibility to meet the demands of tomorrow.

## THE SHELL GAME

The first step in incorporating is to establish the legal entity, or corporate shell. This is a formal legal procedure that must be carefully followed. Once in existence, the corporation is able to acquire your business from you for shares in the corporation, or other consideration.

You may incorporate federally or provincially. If you expect to be operating in more than one province, federal incorporation makes the most sense, because your business then can operate in any province or territory. However, there may be fewer restrictions, and possibly less cost, if you incorporate provincially. The corporation will not be restricted to operating just in that province, but if you do set up shop in another province, or wish to combine your operation with an incorporated business in another province, additional regulatory requirements may have to be met. When Guy Lafontaine formed Worry-Free Computers Inc., he incorporated provincially. He wanted to keep his initial outlay to a minimum and he didn't expect to be operating outside his own neighbourhood, let alone outside the province.

## TAKING STOCK OF THE SHARE CAPITAL

There are essentially two types of shares that a corporation may issue, common and preferred. Different classes of each may be issued (Class A, Class B) and different attributes may be ascribed to each class of shares.

Common shares participate in the growth of the corporation and are commonly called equity shares. Their value depends on the net worth or value of the corporation.

14

Preferred shares are usually valued at a specific amount that is not dependent on the value of the corporation. However, they may also participate in the growth in the value of the corporation to a greater or lesser degree. How much their value deviates from this base value depends on a variety of factors, including their redemption or retraction value (see below) and whether dividends are in arrears. Preferred shares derive their name from the fact that they usually have a preference claim over common shares for return of capital in the event of wind-up or bankruptcy. As well, they usually have a preference claim on any dividends paid by the corporation.

---

**Caution!** In recent years, the taxation rules governing preferred shares have been significantly tightened up to prevent certain abuses. You are cautioned to talk with your professional advisor before settling on the issue of any types of preferred shares.

---

Some of the special features or "preferences" that may be attached to corporate shares include:

- **Voting rights** – entitle the shareholder to vote at shareholders' meetings and to elect directors of the corporation. Common shares generally have voting rights; preferred shares may or may not, or sometimes voting rights may be conditional, such as on the non-payment of dividends.
- **Dividend participation** – dividends on each class of shares are determined by the directors. Dividends must be paid pro rata on shares of the same class. Preferred shares may receive a fixed percentage of dividends, sometimes based on their issue price and sometimes on a fixed amount per share.
- **Participating preferred** – participate in dividends with common shares on a pro rata or other basis, sometimes after receiving a fixed-percentage dividend.
- **Cumulative** – on cumulative preferred shares, dividends accumulate if unpaid in a previous year and generally must be paid before dividends are paid on common shares.
- **Convertible** – one class of shares may be exchanged for another, perhaps with conditions attached, for example, preferred into common before a particular expiry date.
- **Redeemable** – the corporation may opt to redeem shares from shareholder.
- **Retractable** – the shareholder may cause the corporation to redeem his or her shares.
- **Stated capital** – value of the consideration for which the shares were issued.

- **Redemption or retraction value** – value for which the shares will be
  redeemed by the corporation.

There is almost no limit to the different types or classes of shares that
the corporation may authorize. However, most owner-managers will
need only two or three types at incorporation to accommodate family
involvement in the business, or other shareholders.

## DECIDING ON THE SHARE STRUCTURE

Newly incorporated companies must issue at least one common share,
and several jurisdictions require that more be issued. You can either
purchase the shares for cash, or they can be issued to you as consideration on the transfer of your unincorporated business assets into the
corporation (see below). You also may want to issue preferred shares, or
even debt, as other consideration.

Deciding on the share structure becomes more complex when family
members enter the picture. Chances are that one of the reasons you
incorporated your business was to generate some income in the hands of
your spouse and children, which will produce substantial tax savings.
We discuss these income splitting possibilities in more detail in Chapter
7. Here we just note that the attribution rules in the tax law may cause
dividends paid to family members to be taxed in your hands unless you
structure the share ownership properly. Other anti-avoidance provisions discourage a variety of actions that would cause abnormally high
amounts of income to be taxed in the hands of family members when
that income would otherwise be taxed in your hands.

However, a recent legal case heard before the Supreme Court of
Canada (the *McClurg* case) indicates that it may be possible to carefully
arrange share ownership among family members and not have any
dividend payments attributed to the owner-manager. In this particular
case, the taxpayer and his partner incorporated a company to conduct an
active business. Together, they held all the voting shares. The wives each
held a number of non-voting common shares of a different class. The
taxpayer's wife participated in the business on a part-time, but significant, basis.

Dividends were paid on the wives' shares but not on the taxpayer's
and the partner's shares. Revenue Canada included 80 per cent of the
dividends in the taxpayer's income. The taxpayer appealed this assessment.

The dispute made its way through three different courts before finally
being heard by the Supreme Court. There it was decided that a discretionary dividend clause in the corporation's articles of incorporation
allowed this type of dividend distribution. There was no evidence of tax
avoidance, but rather, the arrangement was the product of a business

contract made for adequate consideration (that is, the wife purchased the shares with her own funds).

## INCORPORATE WITH CARE

If you plan to involve family members as shareholders in the corporation, a great deal of care must be taken on incorporation to avoid potentially disastrous tax consequences. Doing it the wrong way could run you afoul of the attribution rules (see below) and possibly trigger the realization of taxable capital gains. Doing it the right way can result in substantial savings from income splitting and accomplish a tax-deferred transfer of your business assets to the corporation.

### THE WRONG WAY

You transfer the business assets that you own personally to your corporation in exchange for common shares. So far, so good. Provided that you file the necessary tax elections in time, the assets will roll over into the company tax-free.

Shortly thereafter, you give some of the common shares to your spouse and children. This is where you run into trouble. Because you transfer the shares to your family members without consideration, you are essentially diverting income to them that you would normally earn. Revenue Canada will apply the attribution rules and tax future dividends paid to your spouse and to any children under the age of 18 in your hands. In addition, any capital gain that might arise on a future sale of the shares by your spouse will be taxed in your hands.

The attribution rules do not apply to future capital gains that may be realized on the sale of shares by your children. That is the good news. The bad news is that the gift of the shares to your children will be treated for tax purposes as a sale for proceeds equal to fair market value. You may therefore be faced with tax on a large capital gain in the year you give the shares to your children.

### THE RIGHT WAY

Your spouse, your children, and perhaps you, each subscribe for common shares in the newly formed corporation. If at all possible, your family members should contribute more than a nominal amount for their shares. It is essential that the amounts they do invest come from their own funds and not from money that you have given them.

After this initial share subscription, you transfer the business assets to the corporation. In exchange, the corporation issues you voting preferred shares that are designed to reflect the full fair market value of the business assets (including goodwill). You might want to make sure that enough votes are attached to the preferred shares to provide you with sufficient control over the business. You might also take a note back from the corporation as part consideration for the transferred assets.

Now, any dividends from earnings in the business should be able to be distributed to all shareholders without fear of attribution. Also, provided that the amount of any note you take back as consideration does not exceed the tax value of the net assets, the transfer of the business to the corporation will be accomplished on a fully tax-deferred basis.

Issuing a different class of common shares to each child allows different rates of dividends to be paid on each class of shares. It also may facilitate a more equitable split of income among children who actively work in the business and those who don't. Issuing different classes of shares to family members has, in effect, been sanctioned by the *McClurg* court decision (see above). Note that it is extremely important that the proper share structure be arranged. It is expected that Revenue Canada will be closely examining all such arrangements to ensure they fall within the guidelines set out in the *McClurg* situation. It is also thought that the government may consider changing the law to prohibit share structures that appear to have been created primarily to split income and reduce the family's tax bill.

## SEPARATE CORPORATIONS
It's becoming more and more common for an owner-manager to set up more than one corporation, often at the same time, since there will be some cost savings. There are a variety of reasons why you might establish a holding company (Holdco) or perhaps a sister company (Sisterco) to your operating company (Opco).

Typically, you would own all the shares of Holdco, which will own all or part of the shares of Opco. The shares of both Opco and Sisterco would be owned by you, or if you also have a Holdco, all or part by Holdco. The arrangement would resemble the diagram below:

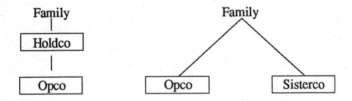

### $400,000 EXEMPTION
As explained in more detail in Chapter 10, the special $400,000 capital gains exemption is available only on the disposition of shares held by a resident individual in qualifying small business corporations (QSBCs). To be eligible, the small business must employ at least 90 per cent of the

fair market value of its assets in an active business (see Chapter 3) at the time of disposition and, for the 24 months preceding the disposition of the shares, more than 50 per cent of the fair market value of the corporation's assets must be used in an active business carried on primarily in Canada.

Holdco will be considered to be a QSBC if substantially all its assets consist of the Opco shares, assuming Opco itself qualifies. If this is not the case, a Sisterco, in which you own all the shares, may be necessary to maintain the eligibility of Opco for purposes of the capital gains exemption. Sisterco might, for instance, own real estate leasing assets and portfolio investments, which are not generally considered to be assets used in an active business. This will ensure that the $400,000 exemption remains available if you should decide to sell the business.

## Protection from Creditors

Instead of holding assets with accrued gains personally, or transferring them to your operating company at fair market value, you might consider transferring them to Holdco or Sisterco at cost (after filing the appropriate income tax election) and then arranging to lease the assets to the corporation that conducts the business. You could also opt to transfer them at a value greater than cost and perhaps trigger a capital gain that would be eligible for your $100,000 capital gains exemption. If Holdco or Sisterco owns these assets and leases them back to Opco, they should be beyond the reach of creditors of Opco in normal situations. Of course, in the early stages of your business, you may have to pledge these assets as collateral for loans to Opco.

## Preserving Losses Carried Forward

If Opco has losses that are about to expire (see Chapter 3) and is paying substantial amounts of interest on debt, it may be possible to transfer that debt to Holdco or Sisterco, which would pay the interest. The losses then could be used to reduce profits that Opco would begin to generate because it no longer has to service the debt. Of course, then Holdco or Sisterco has the loss problem and must eventually generate income; otherwise, the losses will expire unused. Note that dividends received on the shares of Opco held by Holdco will not offset the interest expense in Holdco, since they are received tax-free. This technique also may serve to extend the useful life of business losses. The carry-forward period is restricted to seven years. The loss-carry-forward clock starts ticking anew when Holdco or Sisterco begins to realize losses.

There is a possibility that Revenue Canada could attack this arrangement under the GAAR provisions (general anti-avoidance rules), since shifting debt from Opco to Holdco or Sisterco appears to have no other purpose than to extend the life of losses that otherwise would expire.

### FAMILY MEMBER INVOLVEMENT

Holdco or Sisterco will make it easier to split income among family members and effect an estate freeze. This is simply a course of action you undertake to freeze the value of accrued capital gains and limit your future tax liability. Future capital appreciation of the business generally would accrue to your children. This subject is pursued in greater detail in Chapters 7 and 12.

Generally, the more complicated your financial and family affairs are, the more complicated the corporate structure of your business can tend to become. However, too much complexity can be self-defeating. It is essential that you understand the reasons for a particular structure and are fully aware of the effect any actions you might take will have on your business.

## TRANSFERRING ASSETS TO THE CORPORATION

We've noted several times that assets can be transferred to the corporation on a tax-deferred basis. Generally a sale of assets to a business by arm's length parties takes place at fair market value. Of course, you do not act at arm's length with the company that you just incorporated. But the tax rules generally deem transactions between non-arm's length parties also to take place at fair market value for purposes of determining any tax liability.

In specific circumstances, relieving provisions allow the transfer of assets to a Canadian corporation to be treated as if the transaction had been conducted at less than fair market value, which in effect defers any potential tax liability until the assets are actually sold. Without this provision, you would be deemed to have disposed of your business assets at fair market value when you transfer them to the corporation. You could be liable for tax on capital gains, recapture of capital cost allowance (depreciation) claimed in previous years, inventory profits and recapture of write-offs for intangibles such as goodwill.

Both the corporation and you, as vendor-shareholder, must make an election on the amounts agreed on as the sale value of each asset sold. This amount then becomes your proceeds of disposition for tax purposes and the cost of the assets to the corporation. These transfers, usually referred to as Section 85 rollovers, provide for a floor and a ceiling on the elected value. In exchange for the assets, you can receive any combination of debt, preferred shares, and/or common shares. However, any excess of the fair market value over the tax value of the assets must be reflected in the shares; if the amount of debt exceeds the tax value of the assets, there will be an immediate capital gain.

---

**Caution!** A number of other criteria must be met when electing under

Section 85. Your professional advisor will ensure that all your "i's" are dotted and your "t's" are crossed.

## GST ON TRANSFER OF BUSINESS ASSETS
Generally, GST will not be payable on the transfer of most of your business assets to your corporation, provided those business assets are used exclusively in a business activity.

## WHAT TO TRANSFER?
One of the reasons you incorporated was to limit your liability. With your business inside the corporation, only those assets actually owned by the corporation can be seized by creditors; they can't go after your personal assets unless you have specifically pledged them as collateral.

**Timely Tip.** If limited liability is a major concern, it may make more sense to transfer as few assets into the corporation as possible. One solution is to retain them personally, or transfer them into a separate company, and then lease them back to the operating corporation. You, or Sisterco, would charge sufficient rental on the assets to cover your costs, including capital cost allowance (CCA).

If you own the assets personally and are leasing them, you could earn a profit that would be considered earned income for purposes of RRSP contributions. On the other hand, the income might be taxed fairly heavily if earned personally, whereas if a lower lease rate is charged, Opco's income would increase and be taxed at the much lower small business rate. If you choose, the income could then be left in Opco. Note, however, that the rental charge must approximate similar charges in the marketplace.

If the assets are transferred to Sisterco and then leased to Opco, you may want to involve family members in the ownership of Sisterco. Sufficient rentals would be charged to generate profits, which then could be distributed to your family members. They likely would pay less tax on these distributions than you might. If the rental expense paid by Opco to Sisterco is deducted against active business income (see next chapter), the rental income earned by Sisterco will likely be considered to be active business income.

## IF THE CORPORATION ISSUES YOU DEBT
It's not necessary for the corporation to charge interest on debt issued to you in exchange for the transfer of assets to the corporation from your unincorporated business. In fact, if your business is just borderline in

the early years, the interest paid by the corporation could result in the corporation incurring losses that may be difficult to use. As well, you'll receive income that is taxable.

If other family members are involved as shareholders, it will be important to attach appropriate terms and conditions to non-interest-bearing debt to ensure that Revenue Canada cannot successfully contend that the debt is worth less than the value you have assigned to it. Making the note payable on demand and providing for interest at reasonable rates in the event of default will usually be sufficient.

As you'll see in the next chapter and Chapter 5, there are only minor differences in tax payable if you receive salary, dividends, or interest from the corporation. If you don't charge interest on the loan, the corporation simply earns more profits. These can be distributed as salary or dividends.

You may not want to let that interest-free loan sit in the corporation too long. If your business falters, the corporation may have trouble generating the cash to repay you. If you run into personal difficulties, personal creditors may demand that interest be paid on the loan, which could put your company in more trouble.

There are a host of regulatory hurdles that need jumping when you incorporate. Take the time with your professional advisor to vault each and every obstacle. The penalties for taking short-cuts may not appear that severe on the surface, but they may affect other decisions you make, particularly tax and financial planning decisions.

# 3/How Your Corporation Is Taxed

Corporate taxation – it sounds formidable, but the basics, which follow a step-by-step logical sequence, are easy to master. As the owner-manager of a small business, you've got an important stake in understanding at least the fundamentals of how the government treats the income earned by your business and how much of it will be left in your hands.

Tax planning is part of the competition equation. The more you know about taxes, the better prepared you will be to make profitable business decisions. And tax planning is at the heart of personal financial planning. Virtually every decision you make has a potential tax consequence that shouldn't be ignored.

Corporate tax on business income is levied at a basic federal rate of 38 per cent (see the section "Corporate Tax Rates" below and note that investment income is treated a little differently). The actual tax your corporation pays depends on allowable deductions, surtaxes, and the amount of provincial income tax payable, which can add up to 17 percentage points to your company's tax bill. The basic 38 per cent rate applies to all corporations, including yours, which we assume is a Canadian-controlled private corporation, or CCPC. You as owner-manager have the controlling interest in the company.

A CCPC is defined as a private corporation that is neither controlled directly or indirectly by a public corporation nor by non-residents (nor by any combination of public corporations and non-residents). Thus, your company must be resident in Canada and you, as controlling shareholder, must also be resident in Canada. Generally, you will control the company if you own shares representing more than 50 per cent of the voting rights of all issued shares. If any public company or non-resident is in a position to dictate how you vote your shares, or otherwise has sufficient influence to, in fact, control your company, it will not qualify as a CCPC. However, just because your company has entered into a franchise, licence, or distribution agreement with a public company or non-resident that imposes various terms and conditions on how you operate the business, the public company or non-resident will not be considered to control your company.

## TYPES OF CORPORATE INCOME

The basic 38 per cent tax rate applies to all types of income, including what the law calls "active business income". This is simply defined as all income earned by the corporation except income earned by a "specified investment business" and a "personal services business".

A specified investment business generally is one that earns primarily investment income (interest, dividends, capital gains, rents or royalties) and doesn't employ full-time more than five persons. A business that leases assets, other than real property, is an active business, not a specified investment business. If you set up a corporation to earn investment income, chances are it will be a specified investment business (see Chapter 10). The "personal services business" definition catches employees who have incorporated but continue to offer their services through the corporation to their former employer.

## ACTIVE BUSINESS INCOME

The definition of active business income encompasses virtually every type of business except those earning investment income or income earned by incorporated employees. Incidental investment income earned in the course of conducting an active business generally qualifies as active business income. For example, your company might earn interest on overdue accounts or on temporary cash balances. Active business income also generally includes the recapture of capital cost allowance arising on the sale of assets used in the business, and the taxable portion of a gain on the disposition of eligible capital property (this is the technical term for intangibles such as goodwill).

---

**Caution!** This definition of an active business refers to an activity in your corporation, not the corporation itself. To be eligible for the special $400,000 small business capital gains exemption (see Chapter 10), your CCPC must qualify. For the preceding 24 months, at least 50 per cent of its assets must be used in carrying on an active business primarily in Canada. As well, at the time of sale, at least 90 per cent of the corporation's assets must be used in an active business. A corporation whose assets consist of shares in a corporation that meets the two tests also generally qualifies.

---

## CORPORATE TAX RATES

The basic rate of federal tax (38 per cent) is reduced by a 10 percentage point federal tax abatement for all income earned in a province or territory. This is intended to compensate for provincial and territorial taxes levied on this same income. Income earned outside Canada is not eligible for the abatement.

A surtax is imposed on corporate income tax payable, similar to the personal surtax we all pay. The surtax rate is 3 per cent of net federal tax payable, that is, federal tax net of the 10 percentage point abatement. Thus, the federal tax rate of 28 per cent (38 per cent minus 10 per cent) is increased to 28.84 per cent (28 per cent plus 3 per cent of 28 per cent). The corporation's Large Corporations Tax (LCT) liability, if any (see below), is generally creditable against this 3 per cent federal surtax.

Income derived from manufacturing and processing activities and small business income receive special treatment. The manufacturing and processing (M&P) deduction reduces the tax rate by 5 percentage points beginning July 1, 1991. For the period July 1, 1990, to June 30, 1991, it was 4 percentage points, and was 3 percentage points from July 1, 1989, to June 30, 1990. It is available to all corporations on eligible income earned in Canada. However, it applies only on corporate income of a CCPC which has not benefitted from the small business deduction (discussed below), which is generally income in excess of $200,000 each year.

## M&P DEFINED

The tax authorities consider the manufacturing of goods to involve the creation of something or the shaping, stamping or forming of an object out of something. Processing of goods generally involves a technique of preparation, handling or other activity designed to effect a physical or chemical change in the article or substance, other than natural growth.

Packaging and wrapping, if carried on in conjunction with other manufacturing and processing activities, as well as the breaking of bulk and repackaging, are activities qualifying for the deduction. Activities not eligible include farming and fishing, logging, on-site construction, operating an oil or gas well, mining, and processing or producing minerals, gas, electrical energy or steam. If less than 10 per cent of gross revenue from all active businesses carried on by the corporation in Canada is derived from M&P activities in Canada, the corporation is not eligible for the M&P deduction.

The amount of eligible M&P income is determined by a formula that relates the cost of labour and capital pertaining to M&P in the year to the total cost of labour and capital, multiplied by active business income earned in Canada in the year. For example, assume that a corporation's income is $400,000 in the year. Its total labour costs are $300,000, but those devoted to M&P activities are $250,000. Its total cost of capital is $700,000, of which $550,000 is dedicated to M&P. Thus, its eligible M&P income is:

$$\frac{\$250,000 + \$550,000}{\$300,000 + \$700,000} \times \$400,000$$

$$= \frac{\$800,000}{\$1,000,000} \times \$400,000$$

$$= \$320,000$$

The M&P deduction applies only to income in excess of $200,000 (the small business limit), which in this example is $120,000 ($320,000 minus $200,000). Therefore, the company's M&P deduction is 5 per cent of $120,000, which equals $6,000. This is deducted directly from federal tax payable.

## SMALL BUSINESS DEDUCTION
The small business deduction is set at 16 per cent on the first $200,000 of active business income earned by the corporation each year. It is available only to CCPCs. The small business deduction must be prorated if the company's tax year is less than 12 months. Note that the M&P deduction is not available on income eligible for the small business deduction.

In summary, the federal tax rate on small business income is 12.84 per cent and, beginning July 1, 1991, it is 23.84 per cent on manufacturing and processing income not eligible for the small business deduction.

### Federal Tax Rate – M & P Deduction Only

| | |
|---|---|
| Federal tax | 38.00% |
| Less - federal tax abatement | 10.00% |
| | 28.00% |
| Add - 3% federal surtax | 0.84% |
| | 28.84% |
| Less - M&P deduction | 5.00% |
| Federal tax rate on M&P income | 23.84% |

### Federal Tax Rate – M & P and Small Business Deduction

| | |
|---|---|
| Federal tax | 38.00% |
| Less - federal tax abatement | 10.00% |
| | 28.00% |
| Add - 3% federal surtax | 0.84% |
| | 28.84% |
| Less - small business deduction | 16.00% |
| Federal tax rate on small business income | 12.84% |

The table below outlines the basic tax calculation that Ray Corcoran's company goes through. The pre-tax income of Gizmo Inc. is $300,000, all of which is manufacturing income. Throughout the book, we'll assume that the provincial rate is 10 per cent on income eligible for the small business deduction and 15 per cent for other income. In fact, provincial tax rates vary from about 2.5 per cent to 17 per cent. Appendix A contains a summary of federal and provincial corporate tax rates.

### Tax Calculation for Gizmo Inc.

| | |
|---|---:|
| Income | $300,000 |
| Tax at 38% | $114,000 |
| Less - 10% federal tax abatement | 30,000 |
| | 84,000 |
| Add - 3% federal surtax | 2,520 |
| | 86,520 |
| Less - 16% small business deduction on first $200,000 | 32,000 |
| Less - 5% M&P deduction, $100,000 eligible ($300,000 minus $200,000) | 5,000 |
| Total federal tax | 49,520 |
| Add provincial tax (see later in chapter): | |
| 10% on first $200,000 | 20,000 |
| 15% on remainder | 15,000 |
| Total federal and provincial tax | $ 84,520 |

## ASSOCIATED AT THE HIP

The $200,000 annual small business limit must be shared by "associated corporations". The complex association rules prevent you from gaining access to a larger small business deduction than you are entitled to. For example, you are not allowed two separate small business deduction limits if you own two corporations. You must share the one $200,000 limit between the two companies because they are associated.

Generally, associated corporations are those controlled by the same individual, company or trust, or group of individuals, companies or trusts, or any combination. The rules are far-reaching and cover virtually any situation you care to dream up. If you are particularly inventive, the Minister of Revenue has the power to deem corporations to be associated if it is believed that their separate existence is not solely for the purpose of carrying on their businesses in the most effective manner and that one of the main reasons is to reduce tax payable.

Corporations are not necessarily associated if they are owned by members of the same family. For instance, you might wholly own a manufacturing company while your spouse owns a retail company that has no connection with your business at all. Each corporation would be eligible for the full small business deduction. However, if your spouse simply formed a company to market the goods manufactured by your company, the two corporations would likely be associated, since you and your spouse have established the two operations to double up on the small business deduction.

---

**Timely Tip.** If you and your spouse each own separate businesses, talk to your professional advisor about setting them up so that they are not associated. The extra small business deduction could be worth up to a $32,000 federal corporate tax reduction, as well as up to a $10,000 provincial tax saving ($20,000 in Quebec) if the provincial rate falls from 15 per cent to 10 per cent.

---

### CORPORATE PARTNERSHIPS

If two or more corporations are involved in a business venture on a partnership basis, access to the small business deduction generally must be shared by them to the extent of income earned from the partnership. Rules exist to prevent abuse of multiple access to the small business deduction if your corporation happens to be engaged in more than one corporate partnership.

### INVESTMENT INCOME

The taxation of investment income earned by a corporation is not quite as straightforward as the taxation of business income. But, if you have negotiated the twists and turns of reporting dividend income on your personal tax return, understanding how corporate-earned investment income is taxed is no more difficult.

The theory behind taxing investment income in the corporation makes perfect sense. Investment income earned by a corporation and distributed to shareholders as dividends should be taxed at approximately the same rate as if the shareholder had received that investment income directly. To that end, the tax law contains several mechanisms to ensure that the tax rates are about equal, but also ensure that large amounts of tax are not deferred for extended periods.

### SPECIFIED INVESTMENT BUSINESS

As mentioned above, if a corporation is earning investment income, it will generally be considered to be earned by a specified investment business. This investment business may be the only activity of a corporation you have set up specifically for this purpose (see Chapters 6 and 11). Or your operating company may also earn investment income that is not incidental to your active business income, in which case the corporation will essentially be conducting a second business – an investment income business.

A "specified investment business" is a business, the principal purpose of which is to earn investment income, which includes interest, dividends, income from real property, rents, and royalties. The leasing of property, other than real property, is excluded from the definition. Investment income includes capital gains. However, if you set up a company exclusively to buy and sell property or securities, you might be considered to be conducting an active business.

For example, your corporation might deal in land. If there is a significant amount of buying and selling activity, the corporation might be viewed as trading in land as a business, rather than investing for longer-term gains. From a tax perspective, the full amount of gains would be taxable, not just three-quarters as is the case if the gains are considered to be capital gains from the realization of investments held to earn rental or investment income over many years.

Distinguishing between business income (or losses) and capital gains (or losses) is not always an easy matter. Very often, the degree of activity is a determining factor. In the above example, the more transactions in land during the year, the more likely it is that you will be considered to be earning business income. However, if the corporation buys one piece of land, rents it out for 20 years, and then sells it, it is much more likely to receive capital gains treatment. Similarly, any assets used in your business that appreciate in value will likely be accorded capital gains treatment when they are sold.

If you transfer your portfolio of personally owned securities into a corporation, the activity of the company – the management of the portfolio, the earning of interest and dividends, and the buying and selling of securities – will likely be treated as a specified investment business. Interest, dividends and other investment income will be taxed as described below. Gains and losses realized on the sale of securities will likely be treated as capital gains or losses. However, if your company is very active in the market, frequently trading securities in the same manner that a broker or other trader or dealer in securities might, the gains and losses on such securities transactions could be taxed as regular active business income.

An investment business with more than five full-time employees throughout the year qualifies as an active business and may be eligible for the small business deduction. Similarly, a business may qualify as an active business if services are provided to it by an associated corporation and, in the absence of such an associated corporation, the specified investment business could reasonably be expected to have required more than five full time employees.

## CANADIAN INVESTMENT INCOME OTHER THAN DIVIDENDS

Canadian investment income, which includes the taxable portion of capital gains (in 1990 and subsequent years, this stands at three-quarters of the total gain), is taxed at the full federal corporate rate of 28.84 per cent after allowing for the federal tax abatement. Provincial tax is also levied on this income at rates ranging from about 10 per cent up to 17 per cent. Different rules apply to Canadian dividends (see below).

However, a portion of the federal tax is refunded when dividends are paid to shareholders. This acts to reduce the rate of federal tax and, when combined with the preferential rate accorded Canadian dividends, produces a tax rate that approximates the rate that would be paid if the income were received directly by the individual.

## REFUNDABLE DIVIDEND TAX

Only corporations that are CCPCs throughout the year qualify for refundable tax on their investment income. The tax available for refund is generally calculated as one-fifth of the income earned. The amount actually refunded to the corporation is calculated as the lesser of 25 per cent of taxable dividends paid during the year and the amount of refundable dividend tax on hand in the corporation at the end of the year.

The available refundable tax is calculated each year, whether or not a dividend is paid, and is accumulated in the refundable dividend tax on hand account. This is a notional account only, and no specific funds are allocated to it. Also included in this account is refundable tax generated on the receipt of Canadian dividends by the corporation (see below).

In the example below, Sheri Sorentino's corporation earns $1,000 of Canadian investment income. The provincial tax rate is 15 per cent.

### Refundable Dividend Tax on Hand

| | |
|---|---:|
| Investment income | $1,000.00 |
| Federal tax @ 38% | $ 380.00 |
| Less - federal tax abatement | 100.00 |
| | 280.00 |
| Add - 3% surtax | 8.40 |
| Add - provincial tax @ 15% | 150.00 |
| Combined tax | $ 438.40 |

Amount available for dividend:

| | |
|---|---:|
| Balance after-tax | $ 561.60 |
| Dividend refund (see below) | 187.20 |
| Dividend paid | $ 748.80 |

Amount available for refund – lesser of A and B:

| | |
|---|---:|
| A: Refundable dividend tax on hand (1/5th of $1,000) | $ 200.00 |
| B: 25% of dividend paid ($748.80) | $ 187.20 |
| Amount refunded | $ 187.20 |
| Refundable dividend tax remaining on hand ($200 minus $187.20) | $ 12.80 |

As explained in Chapter 5, Sheri will end up with $506.90 after paying personal tax on the $748.80 dividend she receives from the corporation. If she earned this income directly, she would have $521.50 after paying personal tax.

Typically, though, Sheri's corporation would also pay at least some dividends out of after-tax active business income each year in order to exhaust her refundable dividend tax on hand. In the example above, Sheri's company would simply declare an additional dividend in the amount of $51.20, which would exhaust the refundable tax left on hand. This would narrow the difference between receiving the investment income through the corporation and earning it personally.

However, if your corporation earns only investment income, you will, in most provinces, generate excess refundable dividend tax each year that you may not be able to recover. Generally, this will occur when the combined federal and corporate tax rate on the investment income exceeds 40 per cent.

## CANADIAN DIVIDENDS

Because dividends represent the after-tax earnings of a corporation, dividends are generally allowed to flow through a chain of corporations without further tax. However, to prevent individuals from incorporating their investment portfolios to take advantage of this tax exemption and so obtain a significant tax deferral if the dividends were left in the corporation, a special refundable tax of 25 per cent is imposed on such portfolio dividends received by private corporations. The tax is normally referred to as Part IV tax, since this is where it is found in the *Income Tax Act*. There is no provincial tax on dividends received by a corporation from Canadian sources, even if Part IV tax is paid. There is also no federal surtax added to the Part IV tax.

Part IV tax forms part of the pool of refundable tax on hand and is

completely recovered if the corporation distributes the amount received
as a dividend to its shareholders in the form of a taxable dividend.

| | |
|---|---:|
| Dividend received by corporation | $1,000 |
| Part IV tax | 250 |
| Net amount available for dividend | $ 750 |
| Dividend paid | $1,000 |
| Part IV tax refunded (25% of $1,000) | $ 250 |

If dividends are received from a corporation controlled by the investor
corporation, or if the investor corporation holds shares representing
more than 10 per cent of the votes and more than 10 per cent of the fair
market value of all issued shares, Part IV tax is not payable unless the
payer corporation generated a dividend refund on payment of these
particular dividends. This would occur if the paying corporation originally received Canadian investment or dividend income and subsequently flowed the income in the form of a dividend to a controlled or
sister corporation.

## CAPITAL DIVIDEND ACCOUNT

Certain amounts that might be received by your corporation are not
subject to corporate tax. The most common is the one-quarter of net
capital gains that escapes tax. This one-quarter also would not be taxed if
received personally.

If such an amount were to be paid as a regular dividend, it would
become subject to personal tax. To prevent such an inequity, the tax-
exempt one-quarter of a capital gain can be paid out of the corporation
as a capital dividend. These are not taxable when received personally.

These tax-free amounts are accumulated in a private corporation's
capital dividend account. If the account has a positive balance, tax-free
dividends can be paid. As far as the tax-free portion of a capital gain is
concerned, the account can go into a negative balance if capital losses are
realized. These must be netted against gains to determine the net
amount that can be paid out of the capital dividend account.

---

**Timely Tip.** If the corporation realizes a capital gain early in the year,
it makes sense to declare a capital dividend immediately, especially if
capital losses may occur later in the year. In the future, these losses
must be applied against any gains before the capital dividend account
can regain a positive balance.

---

For example, let's assume that the corporation owns two assets:

|           | Asset A  | Asset B   |
|-----------|----------|-----------|
| Proceeds  | $2,500   | $  500    |
| Cost      | 1,500    | $1,500    |
| Gain (loss) | $1,000 | ($1,000)  |

Asset A is sold some time before Asset B is sold. If no capital dividend is distributed, the loss offsets the gain. When the corporation distributes the $3,000 proceeds from the sale ($2,500 + $500) as a dividend to shareholders, personal tax must be paid on the entire distribution.

However, the corporation can pay a tax-free capital dividend of $250 (one-quarter of $1,000) as soon as the $1,000 gain on asset A is realized. This reduces the amount to be distributed to $2,750 ($3,000 minus $250). The saving is the amount of tax that otherwise would have been paid on the $250 that is distributed tax-free. Of course, the corporation's capital dividend account is now in a negative position, which will affect the next capital gain to be realized.

Other types of income that accumulate in the capital dividend account include:
- the tax-free portion of a gain on the sale of eligible capital property (for example, goodwill), subject to certain adjustments;
- capital dividends received from another corporation, and
- a portion of the proceeds of certain life insurance policies of which the corporation is a beneficiary.

Note that capital losses do not affect the ability of the corporation to pay capital dividends based on these other types of income. Such losses affect only the payment of capital dividends based on the realization of capital gains.

If a corporation ceases to be a private corporation, the capital dividend account disappears.

## CORPORATE LOSSES

Losses in a corporation are the same type that an individual might incur – business or non-capital losses, net capital losses, farm losses and restricted farm losses. Generally, the rules are the same too.

Business or non-capital losses, which would include investment losses of a non-capital nature, can be carried forward seven years and be used to reduce taxable income in those years. All types of losses, including non-capital ones, can be carried back three years.

Allowable capital losses can be applied only against taxable capital gains, and they must first be applied against gains realized in the year. Capital losses can be carried forward indefinitely.

Farm losses and restricted farm losses can be carried forward ten years. Losses of hobby farmers can be used only up to a limit of $8,750 in any one year against other sources of corporate income. The limit is calculated as $2,500 plus one-half of the next $12,500 of income earned. Losses in excess of this limit (restricted farming losses) can be applied only against farming income of previous or succeeding years.

There is no mechanism in the tax law for transferring accumulated corporate losses to individual shareholders, or for transferring a shareholder's loss to the corporation. As well, losses cannot be shared among related corporations, except in unusual circumstances such as amalgamations or liquidations. Thus, if you control two corporations, the losses in one cannot be directly used to reduce taxable income in the other corporation. Also, if the control of a corporation changes (for example, the corporation is sold to an arm's length party), there may be adverse effects on any losses available for carry over to preceding or future years.

---

**Caution!** Remember that if you incorporate your business when it is in a loss position, you will trap future losses in the company. You may be better off to use up these losses against other personal income and incorporate when profits are assured.

---

### ALLOWABLE BUSINESS INVESTMENT LOSSES
A business investment loss is the loss incurred on the disposition of shares in a small business corporation or on the disposition of most forms of debt owed to you by a small business corporation. A small business corporation is a CCPC which uses a substantial number of its assets in an active business. A business investment loss can be used to reduce income from other sources including employment income.

Shares or debt must be disposed of to a person with whom you deal at arm's length. Shares also will be considered disposed of if the corporation is bankrupt (or, in some circumstances, if it has ceased to carry on business), and debt will be considered disposed of if the debt is established to be uncollectible. If the shares disposed of were issued prior to 1972 (or were substituted for such shares), the business investment loss must be reduced by the amount of any taxable dividends received on the shares (or substituted shares) by the taxpayer, the taxpayer's spouse, or a trust of which either was a beneficiary. The amount subtracted is eligible for regular capital loss treatment. This dividend rule does not apply if you have acquired such pre-1972 shares at arm's length after 1971.

Three-quarters of the business investment loss, the "allowable business investment loss" (ABIL), is treated in the same manner as a non-capital loss, such as a business loss. This means that you may deduct the allowable portion from all sources of income in the current taxation year, rather than just applying it against capital gains. Unused ABILs may be carried back three years and forward for seven years and similarly be applied against all sources of income. Income in the loss year must be reduced to zero before these losses can be carried backward or forward, with the result that personal tax credits are lost. However, you have a choice as to how much of a loss carry over you want to claim in a carry-over year. After the seven-year carry-forward period, unused ABILs become ordinary capital losses and may be carried forward indefinitely, but can only offset capital gains.

A business investment loss for a taxation year after 1985 is treated as an ordinary capital loss to the extent of any claims made under your lifetime capital gains exemption in previous years. In addition, any capital gain realized will not be eligible for the capital gains exemption to the extent of any business investment losses realized in prior years after 1984. In effect, the government will not permit you to double up on the special deductions for ABILs and the capital gains exemption.

## LARGE CORPORATIONS TAX (LCT)

The LCT is imposed at the rate of 0.2 per cent (0.175 per cent before 1991) on a corporation's taxable capital employed in Canada in excess of $10 million. Associated corporations that are CCPCs must share this $10-million limit. Taxable capital generally includes shareholders' equity, most indebtedness and reserves that are not deductible for income tax purposes, less an allowance for investments in other corporations.

With such a large threshold, most small businesses should not be subject to the LCT. Any LCT liability can be used to offset the corporation's 3 per cent federal surtax, and unused amounts can be carried back three years and forward seven years as a credit against surtax in those years. Unlike provincial capital taxes (see below), the LCT cannot be deducted in computing income subject to income tax.

## UNEMPLOYMENT INSURANCE

Unemployment insurance (UI) premiums are becoming more and more of a factor in determining a corporation's income. Generally, you will be excluded from participating if you own or control more than 40 per cent of the voting shares of the corporation. In addition, family members who are employees may be exempt. The general rule is that UI is not applicable if the employee is dealing at non-arm's length with his or her employer. But, if the terms of employment (family member's work and remuneration) are similar to situations where employees do deal at arm's length with their employers, UI premiums must be remitted.

---

**Caution!** UI is not voluntary. If you or your employees fall within the rules, premiums must be remitted. If you are under the 40 per cent threshold, consideration might be given to rearranging the share structure to get you over the threshold.

## PROVINCIAL TAXES

All provinces and the two territories levy tax on corporate income. Four provinces also levy a tax on capital (all ten provinces tax the capital of financial institutions), and most impose special taxes, such as oil and gas royalties and mining and logging taxes.

Provincial tax is levied on corporate income determined for provincial tax purposes, which varies only slightly from income determined for federal tax purposes. Each jurisdiction has a dual-rate system which gives preferential treatment to small business income. Several offer a reduction on M&P income, and still others offer specific tax holidays to small businesses.

The federal government collects the tax for seven of the ten provinces and for the two territories by applying the appropriate provincial tax rate to taxable income as calculated for federal purposes. Alberta, Ontario and Quebec collect their own corporate income tax. Taxable income is based on the federal calculation, with certain adjustments. The various rates of provincial tax are summarized in Appendix A.

Provincial income tax is payable on the amount of income earned by the corporation that relates to the particular province. Thus, if a corporation has a permanent place of business in more than one province, income must be apportioned among those provinces. For most corporations, taxable income is apportioned on the basis of the ratios of salaries and wages paid and gross revenue earned in each province to total salaries and wages paid and total gross revenue.

## PROVINCIAL CAPITAL TAX AND PAYROLL TAXES

Generally, a corporation must have a permanent establishment in a taxing province to be liable for the capital tax. The tax is prorated based on gross revenues and wages relating to the particular province.

Taxable capital is essentially the amount required to fund a corporation's assets either internally (share capital and retained earnings) or externally (debt to third parties excluding unsecured short-term liabilities). Deductions from taxable capital may be allowed for goodwill and for investments in other corporations, which represent other taxpayers' liabilities and therefore are included in their capital tax calculations. The actual computation varies among the provinces.

The current rates for provincial capital tax are outlined in Appendix

B. Payroll taxes exist in Ontario, Manitoba and Quebec. In Ontario, the Employer Health Tax (EHT) replaced the former Ontario Health Insurance Plan (OHIP) premiums on January 1, 1991. As an example of how payroll taxes operate, Ontario's EHT is a 1.95 per cent tax on employers with gross annual payrolls over $400,000. For annual payrolls of $200,000 or less, the rate is 0.98 per cent. Graduated rates apply for annual payrolls between those amounts. Details are different, of course, in the other provinces that impose payroll taxes.

At present, provincial capital taxes and payroll taxes, those set by reference to salary, wages, or other remuneration, are deductible in computing federal taxable income, while provincial income taxes are not. The February 1991 budget proposed to limit the deductibility to $10,000, which must be shared among a corporate group. Taxes in excess of this amount will not be deductible.

However, companies will be allowed a deductible "tax allowance" equal to the amount by which 6 per cent of the company's taxable income exceeds $10,000. The system will be phased in over three years, becoming fully effective on January 1, 1994. Generally, companies in provinces with relatively low capital and payroll taxes will benefit, as will companies with a high level of taxable income relative to their capital base and payroll. Companies in the opposite situation will be disadvantaged. As well, CCPCs that pay large bonuses to owner-managers out of income subject to the high corporate tax rate will likely experience additional costs, since payroll taxes apply to these bonuses.

## CORPORATE TAX INSTALMENTS
Corporations must pay tax in monthly instalments throughout the year.

Instalments are generally based on the lesser of tax paid in the preceding year and expected tax liability this year. Interest is payable on deficient or late payments. The instalment payments are due at the end of each month in the taxation year. Payment must actually be received by Revenue Canada by the last day of the month.

Interest is charged at the prescribed rate (the rate set by the government based on T-Bill rates) plus two percentage points. This interest is not deductible for tax purposes.

If your corporation does fall behind and owes interest, the slate can be wiped clean by paying future instalments ahead of time and earning interest to the company's credit. This interest offsets any interest that is owing. This is a much better course of action to follow than letting spare cash earn taxable interest at commercial rates.

If the amount of interest owing on deficient or late tax payments exceeds $1,000 at any time, the interest rate increases by 50 per cent of the prescribed rate. Note that the interest owing as a result of this 50 per cent penalty cannot be wiped out by paying excess or early instalments later in the year. The prescribed rate of interest on overdue taxes in the third quarter of 1991 was 12 per cent, and so, to the extent a 50 per cent penalty applied, the effective rate was a whopping 18 per cent.

The final payment of tax for a taxation year must be made by the end of the second month after the end of the taxation year. A CCPC with income less than $200,000 in the previous year and that claims the small business deduction in the current year has three months to make a final payment of tax owing. Income tax returns need not be filed until six months after the end of the fiscal year.

The provincial requirements for instalments generally mirror those followed for federal tax purposes.

## THE GOODS AND SERVICES TAX (GST)

We look at the GST only very briefly. It is a tax on the consumption of most goods and services in Canada. The GST, which is imposed at 7 per cent, is a multi-stage tax imposed at each stage of commercial activity – importing, manufacturing, wholesaling, retailing and consumption. The GST is a tax on domestic consumption; exports are, in effect, not taxed.

In very basic terms, your company pays GST on its purchases, collects GST on its sales, and remits the difference to the government periodically. To determine the amount to remit, you must determine your input tax credits, that is, eligible GST paid on purchases. If input tax credits exceed GST collected in a particular reporting period, you are refunded the difference.

GST is not charged on tax-exempt goods and services, and the providers of such are not entitled to input tax credits. Tax-exempt goods and services include:

- long-term, and some short-term, residential rents;
- used housing;
- day care services;
- legal aid services;
- most health and dental services, including hospital and nursing home services;
- most educational services;
- most goods and services provided by charities;
- most domestic financial services, and
- most goods and services provided by non-profit organizations, public-sector organizations and governments.

No GST is charged on zero-rated goods and services, but in this case, providers are entitled to input tax credits, which means that they will generally be in a refund position. Zero-rated goods and services include:

- prescription drugs;

- medical devices;
- basic groceries;
- agricultural and fishery products;
- exports;
- prescribed major farm and fishing equipment purchases, and
- rental of farm land under a sharecropping arrangement between taxpayers registered for the GST.

Unless you are selling tax-exempt goods and services, your business must be registered for the GST if its sales exceed $30,000 a year. And even if you sell zero-rated goods, you should be registered in order to claim input tax credits for GST paid on your purchases.

Generally, GST must be remitted monthly and the amount collected and input tax credits claimed must be calculated to the penny. However, small businesses have been given special concessions. First, if your annual taxable sales are between $500,000 and $6 million, you may file returns quarterly instead of monthly. If annual taxable sales are less than $500,000, you may file annually, but quarterly instalments must be made. Monthly and quarterly returns must be filed one month after the month or quarter to which they relate. The annual return must be filed within three months of the end of your fiscal year, and instalments are due at the end of each fiscal quarter.

Second, grocery and convenience stores with annual GST-included sales of $500,000 or less, and other businesses with annual GST-included sales of $200,000 or less can use the quick method of determining how much GST to remit to the government. Essentially, this lets you remit a specific percentage of the GST-included sales to the government as GST, rather than computing the exact amount (i.e., GST on sales, less input tax credits). Input tax credits are still allowed on capital acquisitions. The standard percentage is 5 per cent. Specific types of businesses may be able to remit as little as 1 per cent.

Finally, streamlined accounting can be used by businesses that sell a mix of 7 per cent taxable and zero-rated taxable groceries at the retail level, and which have total annual taxable sales in the previous year of less than $2 million. With streamlined accounting, you don't have to keep tally of the exact amount of GST paid and collected on specific taxable goods. GST calculations are performed on total taxable sales and purchases.

The penalties for not collecting and remitting GST are much greater than the costs you will incur for becoming a tax collector for the government. Registering now will ward off the nightmares that are sure to haunt you in the future if you attempt to operate outside the GST system.

# 4/Financing Strategies

Most new small businesses can only look forward to the day when they will have all the financing that they need. For now, though, you'll likely have to turn to a variety of sources to ensure your business remains viable as it picks its way through the perils of those critical first few years.

Obtaining the kind of financing your business needs always involves trade-offs.

- If your company borrows, some type of security will invariably have to be posted. This may take the form of guarantees posted by the business, perhaps pledging accounts receivable, or it could be a personal guarantee you make secured by a mortgage on your home.
- Both equity and debt financing may result to some degree in a loss of control over your business. The holder of debt may want payment guarantees out of profits, or may want to be consulted before you make certain business decisions, or even put limits on your remuneration. Equity investors may want a significant minority position with seats on your board of directors. Major investors may want controlling or majority positions.
- And of course, you want to get the biggest bang out of each dollar that comes into the company. This means maximizing your tax savings and minimizing the cost of the financing.

**WHERE DO YOU DRAW THE LINE?**
All owner-managers discover eventually that there is a limit to the risk they want to incur when they borrow. Mortgaging the house may be palatable, but mortgaging the cottage that's been in the family for three generations may be out of the question. All owner-managers discover sooner or later how much control they want to give up. Some demand 100 per cent ownership all the time; others can live with being left a significant minority interest and a long-term employment contract if the new investment ensures the success and health of the business.

As well, all owner-managers must face the fact that creditors are on the other side of the fence. They want to maximize their income, which means there is upward pressure on your costs. And even though both of you want to minimize any tax impact, what is good for one party may work to the detriment of the other.

"Make money with other people's money" is certainly sound advice, but not very practical advice to the relatively new business. Most creditors and investors are going to want to see you risk a great deal, perhaps almost everything, before they get involved. And why shouldn't they? If you were in their shoes, would you expect anything different?

## THE BASIC RULES

The tax treatment of various forms of financing has become increasingly complex. As lenders and investors attempt to minimize tax costs, they have devised innovative ways of injecting and extracting cash from companies. However, the basic rules remain relatively unchanged.

### INTEREST

Interest on debt is deductible as an expense if incurred to earn business or investment income. The interest your corporation pays on the mortgage on the building out of which it operates is deductible, as is the interest on its line of credit. However, there are limits to what kind of interest is deductible. Indirect borrowing may not result in an interest deduction. For example, if you specifically borrow to finance the payment of dividends that are greater than accumulated corporate profits, chances are your company would be denied a deduction for the interest expense. But if you extended your line of credit to buy inventory or pay wages and other business expenses, but paid the dividend from cash collected from customers, the interest would likely be deductible.

### DIVIDENDS

Dividends are not deductible to the corporation. They must be paid out of after-tax funds. However, dividends are taxed at a lower rate than interest in the hands of an individual recipient.

### FINANCING EXPENSE

Certain financing expenses are fully deductible. For example, leasing costs are deductible as incurred, and the costs associated with factoring your accounts receivable (see below) are deductible, generally as interest expense.

### ISSUING COSTS

Any costs incurred on the issue of shares generally must be capitalized and deducted over five years. Certain expenses associated with the issue of debt must be amortized over the greater of five years and the term of the debt, including any renewal periods. However, costs incurred on an annual basis are deductible each year.

If the corporation borrows and is in a loss position, it may generate additional losses that it has difficulty using. It may be more appropriate for the owner-manager to borrow, deduct the interest against other sources of personal income, and invest the funds in additional shares of the corporation. Assuming that the owner-manager has sufficient personal income, this will ensure the deductibility of the interest expense.

## WHERE TO START?
Look in the mirror to find the best place to start. As noted above, unless you've put some of your resources on the line, it will be difficult to convince others to invest or loan you funds.

## EQUITY
As the owner-manager of your business, you undoubtedly own common shares and maybe preferred shares. Buying more is a simple procedure, and, on the surface, attractive. If structured properly, dividends can be paid at your discretion. You determine the dividend rate, which can be more handsome than the interest rate on debt. As well, you get to look forward to what you hope will be a significant increase in value of the shares. And if you control the company, you can cause the corporation to buy back your shares whenever you need the cash.

The ability of your corporation to pay dividends depends on annual profits and earnings that have been retained in the business. Generally, if there are no retained earnings, dividends cannot be paid. And the payment of dividends is restricted if the financial position of the corporation might be compromised. Similarly, it may not always be possible to sell your shares back to the corporation. Nevertheless, if all goes well and you receive substantial dividends from the corporation, equity financing is hard to beat.

## DEBT
Most owner-managers lend money to their companies at some point. As you'll see in the next chapter, it may be the most logical course of action if corporate income exceeds $200,000, the small business limit, and the corporation pays you sufficient salary to reduce income to the $200,000 level.

But debt also has its limitations. The loan can be non-interest-bearing, or it can bear interest that need not necessarily be paid each year, although limits do apply (see Chapter 6). The interest rate should not exceed commercial rates, although it could be a floating rate. If your company has other creditors, your loan to the corporation should be secured so that you recover these funds ahead of unsecured creditors should your business run into financial difficulty.

If you borrow personally to finance a loan to the corporation, the interest expense on the loan will generally be deductible even though the funds are reloaned to the corporation at a low interest rate or interest-free. However, to ensure the deductibility of the personal interest expense, the corporation must use the funds to earn taxable income, and the corporation must have been unable to obtain commercial financing without the personal guarantee of the owner-manager.

If the corporation pays interest on the personal loan, the interest income is taxable in your hands. However, it counts as investment income to offset any CNILs you may have amassed (cumulative net investment losses – see Chapter 5).

---

**Timely Tip.** You may be better off in some cases not charging interest on funds loaned to your company. This has the effect of increasing the corporation's income by the amount of interest it otherwise would have paid. You can receive this as an after-tax dividend, as salary, or leave it in the corporation for reinvestment (see next chapter).

---

## INVESTING BY FAMILY MEMBERS
If members of your family have their own funds, that is, money that has not been transferred to them by you, investing these funds in the business may result in substantial tax savings through income splitting (see Chapter 7 for more detail).

## DON'T FORGET YOUR RRSP
Although RRSP funds cannot be invested directly in your business, you may be able to arrange an indirect investment. Your RRSP can hold a first mortgage on your home. You must have a self-directed plan and follow the restrictions demanded by Revenue Canada. These restrictions are not onerous, but they may be costly. You could then invest the money from the mortgage in your corporation in the form of debt or equity. The interest you pay to your RRSP on the mortgage should be deductible.

## GOVERNMENT ASSISTANCE
There are literally billions of dollars available in Canada for assistance to businesses of every shape and size. Assistance may come in the form of an outright grant, loan subsidies, loan guarantees, minority equity positions, expert advice and counselling services, and specific tax breaks. Several provinces have venture capital programs in place and many municipalities offer incentives for locating in their jurisdiction.

---

**Timely Tip.** Keeping up-to-date on the government assistance available is a full-time job. Don't attempt to do it by yourself. Talk to your professional advisor who can either let you know what might be available or put you on to an expert who will lead through the bureaucratic maze.

## FRIENDS AS INVESTORS

Everyone has heard the Trivial Pursuit story. "Friends invest small amount in risky venture. Business wildly successful. Friends get rich." Perhaps your business is just as promising and your friends believe in your abilities just as much. But this is a tricky area. All too often, an owner-manager who taps his or her friends for investment funds loses both the friends and the money.

We suggest you consider friends as last-resort financing. And even then, think twice or three times. It's the times when your business is in trouble that you need your friends the most. They may not be too friendly if they are watching your business and their hard-earned money turn into dust.

## CONVENTIONAL SOURCES OF FINANCING

Creative is the word that is most closely associated with financing these days. Swaps, floors and collars, options and futures, hedges, securitization, unbundling, asset-linked, indexed-linked, and of course junk bonds – the new terminology is endless, and almost all these financing vehicles are inappropriate to the typical small business. We'll just briefly survey the common conventional sources of financing open to most small businesses – loans, equity participation, leasing and factoring.

## SUPPLIERS OF EQUIPMENT AND INVENTORY

One of the first places to turn to for short-term financing is your suppliers. You might consider negotiating for more generous terms. For instance, perhaps you can make payments in 45 days rather than 30 days, or perhaps you could agree to smaller interest penalties on late payments as long as the payments are made by a specific date. Large equipment suppliers may also offer a variety of term financing arrangements to encourage you to buy from them. These may take the form of term loans secured by the equipment, or conditional sales contracts with extended payment terms.

With inventory suppliers, you might be able to arrange to take some goods for resale on consignment, rather than having to purchase them. This may save you from having to borrow to acquire necessary inventory.

If you are a particularly valued customer, you might even find a cash-flush supplier who is willing to loan your company funds on a short-term basis, or take a minority equity position.

## COMMERCIAL LOANS

There are essentially two types of commercial loans – capital or term loans and operating loans. Term loans extend over a specific period, often have a fixed interest rate, and are generally used to finance the purchase of capital goods, such as equipment or vehicles. A mortgage is a term loan with real property used as security for the loan.

Operating loans are just that – short-term loans that provide the cash needed for day-to-day operations. They bridge gaps when, for example, payables temporarily exceed receivables. Typically, an operating loan will take the form of a line of credit. This simply permits you to borrow, often as an overdraft, up to a specific amount from the lender. The interest rate generally floats and is usually expressed as the prime interest rate plus a percentage or two or three depending on your business's credit worthiness.

It is unusual for a small business to obtain credit commercially without posting some type of security. With term loans, it is usually the assets purchased with the borrowed funds, plus additional collateral or personal guarantees. With operating loans, accounts receivable and inventories may need to be pledged, as well as other assets in some cases.

Rather than becoming subject to the vagaries of interest rate fluctuations, you might want to consider longer-term loans. If rates are bouncing around or are likely to go up, you may benefit from a lower rate of interest. As well, the certainty of knowing your interest expense each month allows you to better manage cash flow in the business. But remember that with a line of credit, you generally borrow only what you need, which does minimize cost, although lines of credit may be subject to administrative charges that could be substantial.

## PARTICIPATING LOANS COULD MEAN TROUBLE

Participating loans are becoming less common, primarily because Revenue Canada rarely allows the "participating" portion of the payment as a deduction since it is not considered to be interest. Generally, interest must represent compensation for the use of the amount borrowed, be expressed as a percentage of capital borrowed, be calculated on a daily accrual basis, and reflect current commercial interest rates. Payments cannot suggest the existence of an equity investment.

Unfortunately, this is more or less what participating loans are designed to be. A portion of the payment may be interest and fall within Revenue Canada's definition, but a portion is also based on profitability of the business or some other criteria such as gross revenues. If this is indeed the case, a deduction for the participating portion of the payment may be denied, and a deduction may also be denied for the other "interest" portion. Thus, the payment may resemble a dividend, except the recipient will not be able to treat it as a dividend. It will be looked on as business income, taxable at normal rates. And this means that the effective rate charged on the loan must be high enough to compensate the lender for this expected tax liability. Note that the government is reviewing the rules relating to the deductibility of interest in certain areas, including participating loans.

---

**Caution!** Definitely have your professional advisor review any borrowing arrangements you are contemplating that involve payments based on anything other than a stated percentage of the principal borrowed.

---

## FEDERAL BUSINESS DEVELOPMENT BANK (FBDB)

The FBDB, which is run by the government, is known as the lender of last resort. If you are unable to find conventional financing, the FBDB will consider your case. It offers term loans for capital acquisitions and operating loans. It will also act as the guarantor on commercial loans. Loans and repayment terms are structured, where possible, based on the business's ability to meet its obligations.

## EQUITY INVESTING

Attracting equity investments is usually much more difficult than finding someone willing to lend funds to your business. But once successful, equity investment offers significant benefits over other forms of financing.

### MINORITY SHAREHOLDERS

Equity investments are less expensive, at least initially. Investors generally must be willing to wait until the company is turning a profit before any dividend payments are made. This lack of pressure to be continually meeting interest payments on debt is often a make-or-break factor for many small enterprises. And often the investor can inject a degree of expertise into the enterprise that may just be the missing ingredient in what proves to be a successful formula.

However, persons investing in smaller businesses usually invest to acquire the right to an increase in value of the shares. Generally, they require a method to realize these gains on equity (for example, a guarantee of their shares being redeemed by the corporation); rarely do regular dividend payments offer the returns that investors expect.

## VENTURE CAPITAL

Venture capital corporations offer one source of equity financing, but from the many seeking, only a few are chosen. In fact, not every business would welcome this kind of financing. The venture capitalist will demand to be actively involved in the corporation's business and will want to sit on the board of directors. Venture capitalists look for investments that promise an annual return in the 30 per cent to 50 per cent range. They are willing to assume a great deal of risk, but only if the rewards are spectacular.

If your business fits the mould, venture capital investment may be worth pursuing. On paper, you retain nominal control of your business, but you probably have to relinquish a great deal of power to make unilateral decisions. In return, you probably get expert management from the venture capitalist, as well as expertise on how to expand successfully. If the profits do indeed materialize, you could end up considerably better off than you are now.

## FBDB

The FBDB will, in some circumstances, consider taking up a temporary equity position in certain small businesses. This participation is intended to benefit companies that have high growth potential but little access to capital markets.

## PROVINCIAL ASSISTANCE

A more suitable source of financing may be a provincially run match-up service, like the ones operated by the Ontario and Quebec governments. Prospective investors are matched with companies looking for funding. In theory, this should put a business together with an investor who understands the nature of the business and has a good idea of the risks that must be taken and the rewards to expect.

## EMPLOYEE FINANCING

Although not often used, you could consider instituting a stock purchasing program among employees (see Chapter 9). The drawback to these types of plans is that employees generally want to be able to sell their shares, which probably means you or the corporation will have to be the buyer, since shares in private companies are not readily marketable. Bear in mind also that minority shareholders have distinct rights that, if exercised, could interfere with how you run the company. If you have held absolute control of your company and have never had to share the decision-making, introducing minority shareholders may be a complication you wish to avoid. As well, employees may not have the necessary access to capital to make a meaningful investment.

## GOING PUBLIC

The time may eventually come for you to think about going public. By that time, however, your business will likely have grown to a substantial size and have a good track record of sustained earnings over a period of several years.

Turning your business into a public company is not a step that should be taken lightly. First, many of the tax benefits that you have enjoyed as a CCPC disappear. No longer will your corporation be eligible for the small business deduction on its first $200,000 of taxable income each year. As well, access to R&D investment tax credits is reduced significantly.

When you go public by offering securities for sale by listing them on a public stock exchange in Canada, your company will lose its status as a CCPC. Your shares will therefore no longer qualify for the $400,000 small business corporation capital gains exemption. However, recent amendments to the tax law will permit you to elect to realize a gain on your shares at the time you go public to take advantage of the exemption. In effect, the gain is capitalized into the cost base of your shares and will therefore reduce the amount of the gain you will have to recognize for tax purposes when you actually sell your shares in the future.

Going public can be expensive – extremely expensive unless you are planning to raise tens of millions of dollars. And to add insult to injury, most of the costs associated with a public issue of shares can no longer be written off immediately. They must be amortized over a period of five years. But this may be a small price to pay for the infusion of the new capital.

## LEASING

Is leasing all it's cracked up to be? If you listened closely to your parents when you were younger, your first inclination may be to pay cash and get title to the asset you are acquiring. But this course of action may actually cost you in the long run.

In theory, buying should be more cost-effective than leasing. After all, you are adding a middleman's profit to the equation and that money has to come from somewhere. But consider the following facts:

- Lessors can borrow more cheaply than you can, simply because they borrow more.
- Lessors can often buy more cheaply because they buy more.
- Lessors can offer services related to the asset much more cheaply than you might pay if bought from another source.
- You may be able to lease seasonally, which lowers cost, rather than purchasing an asset that sits useless most of the year.
- Short-term agreements may offer protection against obsolescence or the agreement may guarantee upgrades to the equipment.

Still, everything may break even, except for the fact that your cash flow can be greatly improved by leasing rather than owning. Lease payments are deductible in full, whereas annual CCA (capital cost allowance or depreciation on assets that the corporation has purchased) claims, plus any interest expense relating to the purchase, may be lower than lease payments. And lease payments may actually be smaller than loan payments. Finally, your company may be entitled to certain tax breaks that the lessor is not, and vice versa. These would be negotiated into a favourable leasing rate.

And perhaps most important, it may be easier to lease than to borrow because of the financial condition of your business. Also, leasing may not affect existing credit lines, whereas a purchase with borrowed money would.

There are essentially two types of leases – operating leases and capital leases. With an operating lease, you rent the asset for a relatively short period of time and then return it to the lessor. With a capital lease, you rent the asset for a longer period, and generally the lessor receives the rent plus the end value of the asset. You, the lessee, often guarantee a certain minimum end value and you may have an option to purchase.

## PITFALLS OF LEASING

In some situations, the tax authorities may deem you to have purchased the asset even though you are actually leasing it. This will generally occur if ownership is transferred to you at the end of the lease, if you have an option to purchase it on favourable terms, or if you must guarantee that the lessor will receive the full option-to-purchase price. In this case, you will be entitled to claim CCA, investment tax credits, and any related interest expense, but you will not be able to deduct the full amount of your lease payments.

Recent restrictions on leasing may affect some owner-managers. The proposed rules restrict the amount of CCA that may be claimed by the lessor, which in some instances will reduce the attractiveness of leasing compared with purchasing. Most assets with a value less than $1 million are exempt, including automobiles, office furniture and equipment, computers and buildings. All items valued at less than $25,000 are exempt. Generally, the rules affect sale-leaseback transactions for major items.

Under the new rules, you may jointly elect with the lessor to be considered to have purchased the asset, in which case you can claim CCA and interest expense. However, you will be subject to recapture of CCA previously claimed, but you may be able to deduct a terminal loss, that is, the amount by which the undepreciated capital cost of the asset exceeds the sale price.

One recent change may work to your benefit. Each major purchase of

Class 8 assets, which include office equipment and furniture (depreciable at 20 per cent), will now be added to a separate class, which makes it more likely that you'll be able to claim terminal losses. When these particular assets are sold, recapture or a terminal loss will result because the class is empty. Generally, when assets are replaced, the new assets are added to the class and recapture or terminal losses are rare.

---

**Caution!** There still may be advantages to leasing in a sale-leaseback situation, but you should consult with your professional advisor before signing an agreement.

---

## FACTORING

Factoring your accounts receivable can be expensive, but it should be considered if you are chronically short of working capital and are finding it difficult to extend a line of credit. With a factoring arrangement, the factoring company purchases your accounts receivable at a discount. You instruct your customers to pay the factoring company. Generally, you receive cash for the receivable up front, rather than waiting the usual time to clear your accounts. The factoring company may take on the risk of late or non-payment, which of course is one of the many ingredients that go into determining the discount rate charged. Or the factoring company may leave you with the problem of bad debts, but charge you a more favourable rate. In either case, the factoring company will certainly research your receivables before purchase.

The advantages to the small business owner are many. If you have numerous small clients, you are relieved of the expense of processing your receivables, which can be substantial compared with other expenses. While certainly paying for the privilege, you receive your cash immediately and know exactly when you will receive it each time you enter into an agreement with a factoring company. And with that cash, you will be able to take advantage of early payment discounts from suppliers, which can act to reduce the cost of factoring.

# 5/Getting Earnings Out of the Corporation

As the owner-manager of a corporation, you have the luxury of determining how you'll be compensated and the challenge of figuring out the compensation mix that's best for you, your family and your business. Deciding to receive salary and/or dividends is central to your planning and is the focus of most of this chapter. But we'll also look at interest payable on debt owed to you by the corporation, loans made to the shareholder by the corporation, assets leased by you to the corporation, and repayments of capital that you originally invested in the corporation.

Other more indirect elements of compensation – company-owned automobiles, stock options and various benefits – are dealt with in Chapter 8, since several of these may also be made available to other employees and be effective tax planning techniques.

## DOCUMENTATION A MUST
Getting funds out of your corporation involves formal procedures that are absolutely necessary if you want to avoid tax penalties. If you operated an unincorporated business, you may have simply opened the till or written a cheque from your business bank account. Now, the corporation must set your salary (of course you do it, but the procedure must be formalized). The directors of the corporation (you may be the only one) must formally declare dividends at an appropriate directors' meeting (yes, you may actually have to record that you attended your own director's meeting and you were the only attendee). And the corporation, through its principal officers (you may be the only one) must declare any year-end bonuses to be paid.

---

**Caution!** Even though these procedures may sound a bit odd, the penalties for stepping off the straight and narrow are not to be taken lightly. For example, if a bonus is not paid within the 180-day limit after the fiscal year end (see later in this chapter), the corporation will not get the deduction in the year intended (bonuses or salaries are a deductible expense to the corporation). If you receive a bonus that has not been properly documented, declared and paid, your company could lose the deduction entirely, and you will still have to include the full amount of the bonus in your income for tax purposes. Double taxation is a steep price to pay for ignoring a few rules and the advice of your accountant.

## INTEGRATION THEORY

When the after-tax profits earned by your company are distributed as dividends, they are included in your taxable income. The company does not receive a deduction for these dividends. Consequently, profits generated through a corporation are taxed twice: once when earned by the company and again when distributed as dividends to the shareholders.

To alleviate this double taxation of income earned through a corporation, the corporate and individual tax systems are integrated. For small business income, integration theory says that, from a tax perspective, it shouldn't matter whether an owner-manager receives a salary from his or her corporation, which is deductible to the corporation and fully taxable in the owner-manager's hands (the tax results would be the same if the owner-manager earned the business income directly), or receives dividends from the corporation out of after-tax small business income. This integration theory works for investment income, but it falls short of achieving tax equality for business income which is not eligible for the small business deduction.

The dividend gross-up and tax credit mechanisms on the personal side of the tax ledger are part of the integration process. Dividends received by the shareholder are grossed up on his or her personal tax return to approximate the amount earned before tax at the corporate level. A tax credit is then granted in an amount designed to give the shareholder a credit for the amount of tax already paid by the corporation. Like many theories, integration does not work perfectly. The different provincial rates of tax on both the corporate and personal levels, payroll taxes, and the corporate and personal surtaxes mean that the system provides only rough justice.

Let's look at a straightforward example in which you have a choice of receiving salary or dividends from your corporation. We'll make the following assumptions:

- Corporate income before tax is $100.
- Corporate small business tax rate is 22.84 per cent.
- Quebec corporate small business tax rate (combined) is 16.29 per cent.
- There are no payroll taxes, except Quebec Health Insurance.
- You are in the top tax bracket.

- Provincial rate of personal tax (outside Quebec) is 55 per cent.
- Quebec rate of personal tax is 24 per cent.

|  | Provinces Other Than Quebec | | Quebec | |
|---|---|---|---|---|
|  | Salary | Dividend | Salary | Dividend |
| *Corporate income* | $100.00 | $100.00 | $100.00 | $100.00 |
| Quebec Health Insurance (3.45%) |  |  | 3.45 | – |
| Salary to owner-manager | 100.00 | – | 96.55 | – |
| Corporate tax | – | 22.84 | – | 16.29 |
| After-tax profits | $ 0.00 | $ 77.16 | $ 0.00 | $ 83.71 |
| *Owner-manager's income* |  |  |  |  |
| Salary | $100.00 | $ – | $ 96.55 | $ – |
| Dividend | – | 77.16 | – | 83.71 |
| Dividend gross-up (25%) | – | 19.29 | – | 20.93 |
| Taxable income | $100.00 | $ 96.45 | $ 96.55 | $104.64 |
| Federal tax @ 29% | $ 29.00 | $ 27.97 | $ 28.00 | $ 30.34 |
| Dividend tax credit (2/3 of gross-up) | – | 12.86 | – | 13.95 |
| Basic federal tax | 29.00 | 15.11 | 28.00 | 16.39 |
| Federal surtax (10% of tax) | 2.90 | 1.51 | 2.80 | 1.64 |
| Quebec tax abatement (16.5% of tax) |  |  | (4.62) | (2.70) |
| Federal tax | 31.90 | 16.62 | 26.18 | 15.33 |
| Quebec tax @ 24% |  |  | 23.17 | 25.11 |
| Quebec dividend tax credit (8.87% of $104.64) |  |  | – | (9.28) |
| Quebec tax |  |  | 23.17 | 15.83 |
| Provincial tax (55% of basic federal tax) | 15.95 | 8.31 |  |  |
| Total individual tax | 47.85 | 24.93 | 49.35 | 31.16 |
| Add corporate tax from above | – | 22.84 | – | 16.29 |
| Total tax on $100 | $ 47.85 | $ 47.77 | $ 49.35 | $ 47.45 |

## SALARY OR DIVIDENDS OR BOTH – IT ALL DEPENDS

In our example, distributing a dividend is favoured very slightly over paying a salary. The difference in our hypothetical province outside

Quebec is only 8 cents on each $100 earned by the corporation. The actual differences can be much more dramatic, depending on the province in which the income is earned by the corporation and received by the shareholder.

There is one general rule of thumb, although it is not always applicable. You should consider withdrawing at least as much from the company as possible until the net amount of tax you pay is equal to the tax the company would have paid had you not withdrawn the funds. Depending on your particular circumstances, the best way to do this may be by taking all salary or a combination of salary and dividends. You can always loan funds back to the company, and at any time in the future the company can repay the loan to you on a tax-free basis (see below).

As for a hard-and-fast rule on the salary versus dividend question, there isn't one. The numbers have to be worked out for each company and shareholder. But tax savings are certainly not the end of the story when determining how to distribute corporate earnings. A variety of other factors come into play when deciding whether to distribute corporate income eligible for the small business deduction in the form of salary or dividends.

Directors' fees are considered to be employment income and are treated in the same manner as salary. They are deductible to the corporation and should be included in any determination of a salary and dividend mix.

As discussed later in this chapter, corporate income in excess of $200,000 should always be paid out as salary or a bonus.

## RETIREMENT SAVINGS

We look at the pros and cons of using registered retirement savings plans (RRSPs) and registered pension plans (RPPs) to save for retirement in Chapter 9. Here we just note that to contribute to an RRSP, you must have earned income. Salary counts, as do bonuses and directors' fees; dividends do not since they are investment income. Similarly, you must be remunerated by a salary in order to qualify for benefits from a defined benefit RPP, which means you must earn a salary in order for you or the corporation to make contributions to the plan. Owner-managers are not allowed to benefit from deferred profit sharing plans (DPSPs). Neither are family members nor other persons who are not dealing with the corporation at arm's length.

To make a maximum RRSP contribution of $11,500 in 1991, you must have earned income of almost $64,000 in 1990 (beginning in 1991, your limit is based on the previous year's income). For a maximum contribution to be made to a defined benefit RPP, your wages received as an employee in 1990 may have to be as high as $86,111. A variety of factors besides current salary determine how much can be put into an RPP.

## YOUR BUSINESS AS YOUR RETIREMENT FUND

There are, of course, other ways to plan for your retirement years. Many owner-managers figure that their business will eventually provide them with all the retirement funds they are likely to need. Instead of using RRSPs or RPPs, they opt to use after-tax funds to reinvest in the business. It is difficult to make comparisons between the two methods. With an RRSP or RPP, pre-tax corporate or personal funds are invested to eventually provide a fully taxable retirement income.

To invest in the corporation, after-tax dollars must be used. These could be as high as 80 to 85 cents for each dollar earned by the corporation. Income may eventually be received in the form of dividends, which are taxed more lightly than RRSP or RPP income. If you sell your business, the earnings on the reinvested funds also may eventually be realized as a tax-free capital gain under your $500,000 lifetime capital gains exemption ($100,000 general exemption and special $400,000 small business exemption – see Chapter 13).

Taking the comparison any further means developing assumptions about earnings in an RRSP or RPP and in your business. You would also have to take into account the risk factor. Will your business survive 20 or 30 years? Will you be around to manage it successfully? Will the capital gains exemptions still exist by the time you want to use them? These and myriad other questions need to be answered, or at least considered, as you map out your retirement planning strategy.

## CPP/QPP AND UIC

You must earn qualifying income to make Canada/Quebec Pension Plan contributions. To make a maximum contribution of $1,265 (combined employer and employee) in 1991, you must receive a salary of at least $30,500. Again, dividends do not count as qualifying income.

It becomes more and more expensive to contribute to the CPP/QPP each year. The plan is underfunded and the shortfall must be made up some way. Whether you will ever receive a pension from the CPP/QPP that reflects your total contributions is certainly open to question. Although the pensions are indexed, they are not designed to put you on Easy Street.

As an owner-manager, you can opt out of contributing to the CPP/QPP. Simply don't pay yourself a salary. Receive dividends instead. Unfortunately, this works only if corporate income is below the $200,000 small business threshold (salary or a bonus is a virtual necessity if corporate income is above this level, because of the tax savings). And by paying out only dividends, you cut yourself off from RRSPs and RPPs, as well as the government tax assistance that goes along with these retirement plans.

## OTHER SHAREHOLDERS

If you are not the only shareholder in the corporation, there may be little choice but to pay a base level of dividends. Depending on the amount paid, you may have little room to determine the most advantageous mix between dividends and salary.

This will likely not be a problem if you control the corporation. When setting it up, you created the share capital to give you maximum flexibility for a variety of purposes, including compensation. Thus, even though other family members may be shareholders, they may own a different class of shares from your controlling shares, so dividends can be determined accordingly.

The situation will not be as straightforward if you and at least one other person unrelated to you share ownership of the company. Each of you might own the same type of voting shares on which dividends may have to be paid. If each shareholder is also a full-time employee, negotiating appropriate remuneration packages should be possible. However, if one of the shareholders is not active, other ways to compensate this person must be found.

One possible solution may be to issue shares of different classes, but with similar rights, so that ownership and control are not altered in any way. You could own 100 Class A common shares, and your partner could own 100 Class B common shares. These shares would be similar but not identical. Then you would determine an equalization formula for compensation that satisfies both of you.

---

**Caution!** The shares in this type of arrangement must be different enough to warrant paying different amounts of dividends. Otherwise, the payment of the dividends might be attacked under the general anti-avoidance rules (GAAR).

---

A corporate partnership may provide solutions to many of these difficulties. Corporate partnerships are addressed in Chapter 11.

## TAX DEFERRAL

If you decide to defer receiving compensation in the year and instead reinvest profits back in the business, you can, in theory, receive these amounts at any point in the future as dividends and the earnings on the reinvested funds as salary. However, before committing yourself to such a course of action, you should look forward a few years and consider the consequences if everything does not work out as planned.

Your corporation can pay dividends at any time, as long as there are sufficient retained earnings in the company. Generally this means that you cannot take out more than your equity investment, especially if it means that the corporation may not be able to honour its debts. However, there is no guarantee that your business will always be profitable and have sufficient capital to pay dividends.

There is also the possibility that the after-tax earnings on the reinvested funds could be received tax-free under your lifetime capital gains exemption if you happen to sell the business. Again, there is no guarantee that you will have a profitable business to sell at some point, nor that the capital gains exemption will be around in future years.

You must be an employee to receive a salary. Generally, a salary paid out of active business income to an owner-manager who is actively involved with the business must be reasonable. There are no strict guidelines for reasonableness in this case. However, paying yourself a salary in a particular year could be questioned by the tax authorities if, for instance, you take a lengthy sabbatical, or are disabled and unable to work in your business, or you bow out and leave the running of the business to your children. These may be the years when you would especially like to receive a salary in order to make RRSP or RPP contributions, but it won't be possible. As well, a salary paid out of investment income could be questioned, unless there is a significant amount of activity involved in managing the investments.

The ability of the corporation to delay paying you a salary, on the other hand, is limited. For services performed during the year, the salary generally must be paid in that year, or within 180 days of the year end, for the corporation to get the appropriate deduction in that year.

## DO YOU HAVE A CNIL PROBLEM?
Occasionally, you will want to pay dividends to cure a problem you may have with cumulative net investment losses (CNILs). These develop when your investment expenses, such as interest and a variety of tax losses, exceed your investment income for the year. When this happens, your use of the capital gains exemption is restricted until you eliminate your CNILs by earning more investment income.

Dividends from your corporation qualify as investment income and can wipe out very quickly any CNIL you might have. However, there could be a cost if you must reduce the size of your salary, which in turn cuts into the amount that can be contributed to an RRSP or RPP.

If you have loaned funds to your corporation (see below), you probably won't have to make this choice, since the interest received on any loans also qualifies as investment income.

---

**Timely Tip.** CNIL problems can by avoided by some owner-managers if their corporation owns their tax shelters. The corporation incurs any losses, and corporations do not have CNILs.

---

### DO YOU HAVE AN AMT PROBLEM?

The alternative minimum tax (AMT) may come into play when you realize capital gains and/or claim sizeable RRSP deductions and tax shelter losses that reduce your taxable income. If your AMT adjusted income is too high for the amount of tax actually payable, you are assessed additional tax – AMT. Any AMT paid can be credited against your tax over the following seven years, assuming you don't have an AMT problem in the particular year.

Since dividends are taxed personally at a lower rate than salary, they do little to ease an AMT problem. You can increase the amount of personal tax payable in the year by receiving salary instead of dividends. And the more personal tax payable, the smaller your AMT liability.

Paying extra salary could, of course, result in a tax cost. For instance, if your corporation is eligible for a provincial tax holiday, the tax savings are usually substantial if dividends are paid instead of salary.

### ARE FAMILY MEMBERS EMPLOYEES AND SHAREHOLDERS TOO?

If members of your family are employees of the corporation and also shareholders, you certainly want to give some consideration to the best way of remunerating them and how such remuneration fits with the total compensation package from your business.

If your children and spouse are shareholders, but not employees, salary is not a possibility. Of course, they can receive dividends. Chances are you have set up the corporation's share structure so that sufficient dividends can be paid to them, while not interfering with the flexibility you need to set your own remuneration. These family members will suffer the same limitations that you do if only dividends are paid. The dividend income does not entitle them to make RRSP contributions or contribute to the CPP/QPP.

Any salary paid by the corporation must be reasonable in the circumstances. This means that family members must perform some duties on behalf of the corporation in their role as employees to qualify for the payment of salary, and that salary must reflect the fair market value of the duties performed. You cannot pay your youngest child $10,000 for polishing the paperweight on your desk once or twice a year. And you can't pay your spouse $100,000 for minimal accounting duties that might require the expenditure of $5,000 if you were to bring in an outsider.

As long as the salaries are reasonable and providing they are paid within 180 days of the corporation's year end, there is no restriction on the deductibility of such salaries by the corporation. Excess amounts are another story. Generally they will be looked upon as shareholder appropriations (see end of this chapter). The corporation will not be allowed a deduction for the expenditures and you, as controlling shareholder, will probably have to include them in your income for personal tax purposes. This double taxation penalty should be avoided at all costs.

Generally, the more money channelled into the hands of your family, the lower your overall family tax bill will be, both now and in the future. How your family interacts with your corporation is discussed at length in Chapter 7.

---

**Timely Tip.** You might consider arranging for your spouse and grown children to be directors of the corporation. Reasonable directors' fees can be paid to them for acting as directors, attending board of directors' meetings, and taking on the risks associated with being a director. These fees are treated in the same manner as employment income.

---

## EXHAUSTING THE CORPORATION'S REFUNDABLE DIVIDEND TAX

If your corporation has earned investment income and therefore has generated refundable dividend tax (see Chapter 3), there may be times when you should consider having the corporation pay sufficient dividends to reduce the balance in this account to zero. In some provinces, tax can be deferred by leaving investment income in the corporation rather than paying the after-tax proceeds out as a dividend. However, this applies only if the recipient is in the top tax bracket.

If dividends can be received and be taxed at less than the maximum personal rate, refundable dividend tax on hand in the corporation can be looked upon as an asset that is not earning income. Or put another more unpalatable way, by not claiming the dividend refund, you could be making an interest-free loan to the government.

Recalling the investment income example from Chapter 3, there was $12.80 of refundable dividend tax that could not be used. To use it up, a dividend of $51.20 would have to be paid ($12.80 of refundable tax plus after-tax corporate income of $38.40). For a shareholder in the middle tax bracket, assuming a 50 per cent provincial tax rate, the after-tax proceeds of the $51.20 dividend amount to $32.00, and for a shareholder in the lowest tax bracket, the after-tax proceeds are $47.68.

There is no doubt that sufficient dividends should be paid to lowest bracket shareholders to exhaust refundable dividend tax each year. If the dividend is not paid, $38.40 remains in the corporation to be invested. If the dividend is paid, the low-rate shareholder has $47.68 to invest.

The situation is not quite so cut and dried with middle tax bracket shareholders. However, the shareholder will generally be taxed at a lower rate than the corporation on any investment income earned, so generally a dividend should be paid. In some provinces, the difference may be too small to make paying the dividend worthwhile.

---

**Timely Tip.** If you are not in the top tax bracket in any particular year and you have built up refundable dividend tax in the corporation, you should consider paying out a dividend. The corporation also might be able to pay out the dividend to family members who could receive the amount with little or no personal tax.

---

## INCOME NOT ELIGIBLE FOR THE SMALL BUSINESS DEDUCTION

Income not eligible for the $200,000 small business deduction is taxed at full corporate rates (except in Quebec for active business income exceeding $200,000). Using a provincial tax rate of 15 per cent, that produces a combined federal and provincial tax rate of 43.84 per cent, including the federal surtax. If your business is earning manufacturing and processing income, the tax rate is reduced by 5 percentage points to 38.84 per cent (effective July 1, 1991).

If you were to receive dividends out of this after-tax corporate income, the combined federal and provincial tax could exceed 60 per cent (56 per cent for M&P income). Receiving such income as salary from the corporation results in much less tax. So, the rule of thumb for owner-managers in the top tax bracket is always to pay out corporate income in excess of $200,000 as salary or a bonus (for tax purposes, a bonus is taxed the same as salary or wages, but there are a couple of special rules).

First, owner-managers can generally receive bonuses in any amount, as long as they are full-time employees. The amount paid does not have to be tied to corporate income to pass a reasonableness test. This will not be the case if bonuses are paid to minority shareholders, to senior employees who are not shareholders, or to family members who are not controlling shareholders.

## TAX DEFERRAL WITH ANNUAL BONUS

Second, bonuses can be declared at the corporation's year end, but they do not have to be paid immediately. The corporation receives the deduction for the bonus as long as the amount is actually paid within 180 days of the year end. You do not have to include the amount in income for personal tax purposes until you actually receive it, which may give you up to a six-month tax deferral. However, tax must be withheld from the bonus by the corporation when it is paid out.

If the bonus is not paid, the corporation does not receive the deduction in the year the bonus is accrued. However, if the bonus is paid subsequent to the 180-day time limit, the deduction again becomes available to the corporation in the year of payment.

Third, bonuses must be formally declared in writing before the fiscal year end of the corporation. However, it is not necessary to state the exact amount to be paid, as long as there is a formula for payment in place, that, for example, depends on the corporation's post-year-end financial information.

It follows that if your corporation has substantial income in excess of $200,000, you will have little or no trouble meeting any salary requirements you may have (typically for RRSP or RPP contributions). It then becomes much easier to determine how to distribute corporate income below the $200,000 level. Of course, you might choose to leave the income in the corporation for reinvestment.

## LOANING THE BONUS BACK TO THE CORPORATION
One of the most popular ways for shareholders to reinvest in their corporations is to receive a bonus and then loan the funds back to the corporation. They would then receive a steady stream of interest income, if this is the arrangement they make with the loan. This interest income may solve any CNIL or AMT problems they might have.

Generally, bonuses are paid out of income subject to the high corporate tax rate. If they are paid out of income subject to the small business deduction and loaned back to the corporation, considerable cost could be attached to this course of action. Applying the tax rates we used in the flow-through example above, the bonus or salary would attract tax at the rate of 47.85 per cent (49.35 per cent in Quebec), leaving $521.50 ($506.50 in Quebec) to loan back to the corporation for every $1,000 of bonus received. A much larger amount, $771.60 for each $1,000 of corporate income, can be reinvested if corporate income eligible for the small business deduction is retained in the company. And looking at the longer-term perspective, after-tax small business income that is reinvested may come back as a tax-free capital gain if you sell your corporation. With the loan, you are essentially committed to receiving interest or to having your loan capital returned to you.

Ontario, Quebec and Manitoba levy employer health taxes (payroll taxes) that are based on total payroll of the corporation. The more salary or bonus that you pay, the higher your health tax levy. Only a portion of these levies will be deductible to the corporation beginning in 1992 (see

Chapter 3). Provincial health taxes are not levied on dividend distributions.

## INTEGRATION OF INVESTMENT INCOME

In Chapter 3, we looked at how investment income earned by a corporation is taxed and how that income generates refundable dividend tax. This refundable tax serves to increase the size of the dividend being paid out. The personal dividend tax credit mechanism then kicks in so that, in theory, no more tax is paid by an individual receiving investment income through a corporation than would be paid if the individual were to earn the investment income directly. The example below shows how $100 of interest income would be taxed if earned personally or flowed through a corporation. The same assumptions we have used in our other examples are used here.

### Integration in Practice

| | Flowed Through Corporation | | Received Personally | |
|---|---|---|---|---|
| | Other Provinces | Quebec | Other Provinces | Quebec |
| Interest earned by corporation | $100.00 | $100.00 | | |
| Corporate tax | (43.84) | (43.84) | | |
| After-tax income | 56.16 | 56.16 | | |
| Refundable dividend tax (25% of dividend paid $74.88) | 18.72 | 18.72 | | |
| Available for dividend | $ 74.88 | $ 74.88 | | |
| Dividend received | $ 74.88 | $ 74.88 | | |
| Interest income | | | $100.00 | $100.00 |
| Dividend gross-up (25% of $74.88) | 18.72 | 18.72 | | |
| | $ 93.60 | $ 93.60 | | |
| Tax @ 29% | $ 27.14 | $ 27.14 | $ 29.00 | $ 29.00 |
| Dividend tax credit (2/3 of gross-up) | (12.48) | (12.48) | | |
| | 14.66 | 14.66 | | |
| Federal surtax @ 10% | 1.47 | 1.47 | 2.90 | 2.90 |
| Quebec tax abatement (16.5% of tax) | | (2.42) | | (4.79) |
| Provincial tax @ 55% (24% in Quebec) | 8.06 | 14.16 | 15.95 | 24.00 |
| Total personal tax | 24.19 | 27.87 | 47.85 | 51.11 |
| Add corporate tax | 25.12 | 25.12 | – | – |
| Total tax | $ 49.31 | $ 52.99 | $ 47.85 | $ 51.11 |

| | | |
|---|---|---|
| Less excess refundable dividend tax still on hand in corporation | (1.28) | (1.28) |
| Net tax | $ 48.03 | $ 51.71 |

Once again, integration is less than perfect. Using our tax rates, it's less expensive to earn investment income directly than flow it through a corporation. There is a $1.46 difference if total tax cost is compared, and an 18-cent difference if it is assumed that all refundable dividend tax can be used. For Quebec residents, it's also less expensive to earn investment income directly, rather than flowing it through a corporation. There is a $1.88 difference.

If you have established a corporation that earns solely investment income, it may not be possible to get all the refundable tax out of the corporation. If this is the case, the extra tax cost would have to be considered carefully to determine how worthwhile the corporation is in your overall financial planning (see Chapter 10 for more discussion on investment corporations).

If the investment income is earned in the corporation and active business income is also earned, you will have little trouble paying out all refundable dividend tax each year. Still there is a small tax cost in our example. This may not be the case in each province. Once again, you should do the calculations that fit your particular situation to see what tax cost or savings are involved.

Note that the corporate tax rate on investment income is lower than the personal rate if you are in the top tax bracket. These tax deferral possibilities are discussed in the next chapter.

## PORTFOLIO DIVIDENDS

If portfolio dividends are received by the corporation, integration theory works perfectly. The corporation must pay the 25 per cent Part IV tax when the dividend is received (see Chapter 3) and this tax is fully refunded when a dividend is paid out. Thus, the same amount of tax is paid whether you receive the dividend personally or flow it through a corporation.

Dividends received by a corporation from a "connected" corporation do not attract Part IV tax. One corporation is connected to another if it owns more than 10 per cent of the voting shares and more than 10 per cent of the fair market value of all issued shares. Corporations are also connected if one controls the other.

Investment income is always taxed at a lower rate in the corporation than if received directly by a shareholder who is in the top tax bracket. Therefore, tax can be deferred if the income is left for reinvestment in the corporation (see the next chapter).

## FAMILY MEMBERS

Often, other family members who are not in the top tax bracket are shareholders of the investment corporation. In this case, it may be worthwhile flowing the investment income out to these family members, which reduces the amount of tax currently payable.

One problem with holding capital investments in a corporation is that the company is not eligible for the $100,000 lifetime capital gains exemption. If gains are realized, the income that flows out to shareholders loses its identity as a capital gain. Capital dividends of course can be paid, but these represent only the tax-free one-quarter of capital gains. These should be paid out as soon as they are realized.

Generally, there is little point in holding capital properties in an investment corporation unless the shareholders have exhausted, or plan to exhaust shortly, their lifetime exemptions. This tax break may not be with us much longer. Using it now assures you of tax savings.

## SALARIES FROM INVESTMENT CORPORATIONS

In some situations, it may be possible to pay a salary out of investment income. Controlling shareholder-employees should be able to receive one, depending on the degree of activity involved in managing the investments, and of course part-time employees could also be paid a salary. Other shareholders are out of luck and even the controlling shareholder may not be able to justify a large salary if little effort is put into the running of the investment company.

In a number of provinces, a salary paid by the investment corporation will be taxed more lightly than flowing investment income (other than Canadian dividends) through the corporation. This will almost always be the case for shareholders who are not in the top tax bracket. Note that refundable dividend tax is generated only when the investment income is actually taxed. If a salary is paid, the corporation receives a deduction and, therefore, no tax is paid on the investment income.

## LOANS TO THE CORPORATION

It's common for the owner-manager to loan funds to his or her new corporation in addition to making an equity investment. And as noted above, you may want to loan the after-tax portion of bonuses back to the corporation. Depending on the terms of the loan, repayment can be made at any time.

Generally, it is advisable to charge the corporation interest on the funds it has borrowed from you, but it is not necessary from a legal or tax standpoint. If the loan does carry interest, it should generally be charged at prevailing market rates. As we noted above, this interest may solve a CNIL or AMT problem. If the interest is not paid in a particular year, the corporation still gets the deduction for the expense, as long as it is paid by the end of the second taxation year following the one in question. This deferral opportunity is discussed in the next chapter.

Note that interest income earned by you is taxed annually on the accrual basis. Thus, if the corporation takes the deduction, you will be considered to have earned the interest, even though you haven't received it, and you must include it in income for tax purposes in that year.

---

**Timely Tip.** You may want to loan the funds to the corporation interest-free. For example, you may not know if the company will be taxable in the year or suffer a loss. If profits do indeed materialize, you can always pay out a bonus to recover the "lost interest".

---

As well, if the business is extremely short of working capital and finds it difficult to borrow elsewhere, not charging interest will certainly increase the funds with which the corporation can operate. This approach may also reduce the cost of reinvesting in the company. Since the corporation does not pay any interest on the loan, its income will be larger than it otherwise would be. You would then leave the after-tax funds in the corporation. As explained above, this is very cost-effective if the corporate income is eligible for the small business deduction. If you borrow personally to finance the loan to the corporation, the interest expense paid personally will be deductible in most circumstances (see Chapter 4).

If you structure the loan as a demand loan, repayment can be made at any time, which gives you a reasonable degree of protection over your capital. In addition, the loan may be secured by a pledge of specific corporate assets or by a floating charge on all assets. Your security will probably have to rank behind other secured creditors of the corporation, but it would rank ahead of unsecured creditors.

## SELLING ASSETS TO THE CORPORATION

Often the owner-manager will sell assets to the corporation and have a choice of taking back debt or equity, which would typically be in the form of preferred shares. The transfer can take place at cost, in which case there are no immediate tax consequences, or the assets can be sold to the corporation at fair market value. There is little point making the transfer at fair market value unless you are anxious to use up your capital gains exemption.

Assuming that the dividends on the preferred shares are paid out of small business income or investment income, integration ensures that there is little difference in the tax cost of receiving interest on debt or dividends on the shares. The debt could also be non-interest-bearing, assuming that the loan is properly structured (see Chapter 2), and you could simply receive salary, which may provide more flexibility than an interest-bearing loan.

As well, preferred shares may give you more flexibility than interest-bearing debt. Dividends can accumulate on the preferred shares and be paid whenever the company has sufficient cash. Both shares and debt can be structured so that there is little problem getting your capital out of the corporation.

## RENTING OR LEASING ASSETS TO THE CORPORATION
As explained in Chapter 2, many owner-managers choose to rent or lease many of their business assets to the corporation in order to protect them from potential creditors. Generally, you will charge rent on these assets that reflects fair market value rents. The one drawback to leasing is that you generally won't be able to create losses by claiming depreciation on the leased assets, whereas full CCA could generally be claimed if the assets were purchased by the corporation and the corporation was not in a loss position.

## REPAYMENT OF CAPITAL
At some point you may decide to redeem some of your equity investment in the corporation or cause the corporation to repay debt that it owes you. One of the major reasons for doing so is to protect from potential creditors capital that is in the business.

It is not always possible simply to withdraw your investment from the company. If the company is in financial trouble, creditors may have claims that require the capital to stay put until the claims are satisfied. As well, there may be legal restrictions that prevent you from leaving the corporation excessively short of working capital.

## SHAREHOLDER APPROPRIATIONS
As we have noted several times, you simply can't take money out of the corporation without documenting it properly. The withdrawal must show up as salary or dividends in the corporation's records or as one of the other methods of receiving legitimate amounts from the business. As well, the corporation cannot confer certain benefits on you without tax being paid. Severe penalties apply in a variety of situations.

If the corporation simply gives you funds, they will immediately be included in your income for personal tax purposes and the corporation will not receive a deduction for the expenditure. The penalty here is double taxation, an extremely steep price to pay for neglecting to document the payment as either salary or dividend.

Similarly, if the corporation lends you funds, the amount will be included in your income, and the corporation denied a deduction, unless the loan is of a particular type sanctioned by tax law. This rule is extended to include virtually all forms of indebtedness to the corporation. For example, you might buy one of the corporation's assets, say a building, from it and give back to the corporation a non-interest-bearing promissory note. The value of the building will be included in your income.

## SHAREHOLDER LOANS

Several types of loans are allowed. First, if the corporation loans you funds and the principal is repaid within one year after the end of the corporation's tax year, you are not taxed on the amount. However, such a loan cannot be a series of loans and repayments, which would act as a permanent deferral device. Moreover, you will be taxed on a benefit equal to a prescribed rate of interest applied to the loan for the period it is outstanding.

Secondly, a shareholder loan does not attract tax if the loan is documented as such and bona fide terms for repaying the loan within a reasonable period of time are arranged, and the loan is made:
- in the course of the lender's ordinary business, which means it must lend funds to individuals as a major business activity;
- so the employee owner-manager can acquire a home (vacation homes count, as do live-aboard yachts; but major renovation or refinancing of an existing home does not count);
- so the employee owner-manager can purchase treasury shares of the employer corporation or a related corporation, or
- to assist the employee owner-manager in the purchase of a car to be used in his or her employment duties.

However, the imputed interest rules in the tax law now take effect. These say that if interest is not charged on the loan at least at the rate prescribed by Revenue Canada or at the prevailing commercial rate on such loans, the employee owner-manager will be in receipt of a taxable benefit. This benefit is generally determined as the difference between the amount of interest actually paid on the loan and the amount Revenue Canada deems should have been paid. The interest must be paid within 30 days of the end of the company's fiscal year for it to reduce or eliminate a taxable benefit.

Note that you will be allowed a deduction for the taxable benefit if a deduction would have been allowed if you had actually paid the interest. For example, if you use the proceeds of the loan for investment purposes, the taxable benefit will be deductible if you would normally have been allowed a deduction for any interest actually paid.

Generally, low-interest or interest-free loans are valuable to employees, since they are much less costly than regular commercial loans, even though the benefit must be included in income for tax purposes.

However, since the owner-manager also controls the company, what is beneficial on the employee side of the equation may not look as attractive from the corporation's point of view. If the corporation borrows the funds itself and deducts the interest expense from small business income, the loan could cost considerably more than if the owner-manager had personally borrowed the funds.

The apparent advantage of a shareholder loan is the fact that the corporation can lend you more after-tax funds than would be available if the funds were distributed to you. Using the numbers from the example in the section "Integration Theory" above, on each $100 of income earned, the corporation could lend you $77.16 ($83.71 in Quebec), whereas if you received a salary, you would have cash of only $52.15 ($50.65 in Quebec). With the loan, you get the use of those extra after-corporate-tax dollars without having to pay personal tax. This is the main reason why there are very restrictive rules about shareholder loans.

Note that if the corporation advances you funds in anticipation of dividend payments that won't be made until at least the year end, you are considered to be in receipt of an interest-free loan from the corporation and the taxable benefit rules will apply.

## THE COMPANY CAR
Corporate-supplied automobiles have been a traditional way to compensate owner-managers of private corporations. Unfortunately, the tax rules are no longer so liberal. It has become much more difficult to determine how vehicles should be supplied to the owner-manager – owned or leased by the company or by the owner-manager – and luxury cars need special attention. Autos are discussed in more detail in Chapter 8.

# 6/And If You Don't Need the Income Right Now?

A tax dollar deferred may not be quite the same as a tax dollar saved, but it will do in a pinch.

It has become difficult for individuals to defer tax except through statutory retirement plans. Owner-managers are not faced with the same limitations. In fact, incorporating provides you with a legitimate and easy way to defer significant amounts of tax to future years.

The reasons for deferring the payment of tax are straightforward. Why pay $1 of tax now when you can pay it, say, ten years from now when that $1 will be worth perhaps only 50 cents, or even less. By keeping that dollar in your pocket, you can put it to work for you. Otherwise it goes to work for the government. That's why much tax planning focuses on minimizing tax now, even though those tax chickens will come home to roost eventually.

## DEFERRING TAX IN THE CORPORATION

As you'll remember from Chapter 3, income eligible for the small business deduction is taxed at a maximum of 22.84 per cent in the corporation. If the income is received as salary or a dividend, your total tax bill can jump to 50 per cent or more, depending on your province of residence.

With the corporation, deferring tax is as easy as leaving the after-tax income in the company and postponing the distribution of it as a dividend. For example, you will have $7,716 from each $10,000 of corporate income left to "invest" if the income is not distributed, but only $5,215 left over after tax if a salary is paid.

## LEAVING BUSINESS INCOME IN THE COMPANY

How worthwhile is this tax deferral? Let's assume that you either leave the after-tax income ($7,716) in the corporation for ten years, or you pay it out immediately as salary. You are in the top tax bracket, so the 47.85 per cent tax rate applies. By leaving the funds inside the company, you get to retire $7,716 of bank debt that was costing your business 13 per cent a year. Personally, you can invest the $5,215 at 10 per cent a year, although the interest is taxable each year.

69

At the end of ten years, your $5,215 will have grown to $8,670 after paying tax each year. The calculations at the corporate level are a bit more complex. By paying down the debt, the corporation is no longer paying out $1,003 of interest in the first year. This has the effect of increasing corporate income by $1,003, which attracts tax at the rate of 22.84 per cent, leaving the company with $774. This is used to pay down more debt in year two. A similar calculation is performed each year, until by the end of year ten, the company has reduced its bank debt by $20,068.

Essentially this has freed up $20,068 of after-tax corporate income that can now be paid out as a dividend. The tax rate on this dividend is 32.31 per cent, which leaves the owner-manager with $13,584. Compare this with the result when salary is paid – $8,670. If the $20,068 is left in the corporation, it may eventually be realized as a tax-free capital gain under your $400,000 small business capital gains exemption (see Chapter 10). Note that we have made two important assumptions in these calculations. First, the 3 percentage point spread in interest rates may actually be generous or just about right, depending on your business. And second, we've assumed that the increase in business income each year, which results from paying down bank debt, is eligible for the small business deduction throughout the ten-year period.

## INVESTING THE INCOME,
## RATHER THAN REDUCING DEBT

Let's look at another situation where the after-tax corporate income is actually invested in interest-bearing securities. The advantage here lies in the corporate deferral available on income taxed at the small business rate, plus the deferral resulting from investment income being taxed at a lower rate (43.84 per cent) in the corporation than if it is earned personally by an owner-manager in the top tax bracket (47.85 per cent). This time, both the owner-manager and the corporation earn 10 per cent on amounts invested.

Once again the owner-manager accumulates $8,670. The $7,716 left in the corporation grows to $13,326. As you'll remember from Chapter 3, this interest income generates refundable dividend tax that can also be paid out as a dividend. In this case, the refundable dividend tax amounts to $1,870, so a dividend of $15,196 is paid at the end of ten years. This attracts tax of $4,910, leaving you with $10,286, which is still superior to receiving the corporate income initially as salary and earning investment income personally.

## SOLVING A PROBLEM WITH INVESTCO

The major disadvantage to earning investment income in your operating company is that it could shortly no longer qualify as a small business corporation (SBC). This is defined as a CCPC (Canadian-controlled private corporation) which is using all or substantially all of its assets in an active business; that is, it must meet the 90 per cent test. This investment income is not active business income. It is extremely important to remain an SBC for two reasons:

- Income splitting opportunities and the resulting tax savings are greatly enhanced if your corporation is a qualifying SBC (see Chapter 7).
- To claim the $400,000 small business capital gains exemption, your corporation must be a qualifying SBC.

The solution is to earn the investment income in another corporation, which we will call Investco, not in your operating company, which we'll call Opco. Harking back to Chapter 3, you'll recall that connected corporations can pay dividends to each other without attracting the 25 per cent Part IV dividend tax. Thus, you would incorporate Investco and transfer some of your common or preferred shares in Opco to Investco. In exchange for the shares, you would receive shares in Investco, that could be either preferred or common. This transaction can be undertaken on a tax-deferred basis. Structuring the share ownership might be somewhat more complicated if family members are to be involved with Opco and/or Investco, so we'll assume you own all the shares.

Now, rather than Opco earning the investment income, the after-tax corporate income of $7,716 is distributed to Investco as a dividend. Such dividends would be paid up to Investco whenever the cash becomes available. Investco puts the money into securities and earns the investment income each year. The results are identical to those above where Opco earned the income. However, you now have no worries about Opco continuing to qualify as an SBC.

If necessary, you may be able to transfer investment assets from Opco to Investco on a tax-deferred basis so that Opco continues to earn a minimum of investment income. However, you should consult with your professional advisor before undertaking such a transfer.

## WHY NOT PUT PERSONAL FUNDS INTO THE COMPANY?

If the deferral results are so attractive when reinvesting corporate income, you are probably asking why not put personal savings into the corporation, retire existing corporate debt, and get the same benefits. Many owner-managers do exactly that by lending funds on an interest-free basis to the corporation. Such loans were discussed earlier in Chapter 4.

---

**Caution!** It is important to note the distinction between loaning funds to the corporation to retire commercial debt, and loaning funds to the company specifically to earn investment income. With the former technique, you are taking advantage of the low corporate rate on small business income. However, as we've seen in Chapter 3, there is no significant advantage to simply earning investment income in the corporation compared with earning it personally.

---

## EARNING PORTFOLIO DIVIDENDS IN THE CORPORATION

As we saw in Chapter 3, Part IV tax at the rate of 25 per cent is payable on the receipt of portfolio dividends. These are dividends received from companies with which your company deals at arm's length. In most situations, these will be dividends from public companies in which your company has invested. The Part IV tax is refunded when your company pays out this income to its shareholders as a dividend.

As we saw in Chapter 3, the effective tax rate on dividends for a shareholder in the top tax bracket is 32.31 per cent (36.5 per cent in Quebec). Therefore, there is a deferral opportunity if portfolio dividends are earned in a corporation and are not immediately distributed to shareholders.

If a shareholder is in the middle tax bracket, the personal tax rate on dividends is between 24 per cent and 32 per cent, depending on the province. Appendix C details the dividend rates in the ten provinces and the territories, so you can determine whether there is an opportunity for deferral in your province.

---

**Timely Tip.** Note that an individual can receive more than $23,000 of dividends and not pay any tax in 1991, assuming no other income is earned (about $10,500 in Quebec). If family members are eligible to receive dividends and they have little or no other income, portfolio dividends should be distributed. This of course assumes that attribution is not a problem (see Chapter 7).

---

Another advantage to receiving portfolio dividends is that Part IV tax, unlike income tax, does not have to be paid in instalments. It is due three months after the corporation's fiscal year end when the balance of the company's income tax must be paid. This could provide up to a 15-

month deferral depending on the fiscal year ends of your corporations.

The same techniques as are used above can be used for holding portfolio investments and deferring tax on portfolio dividend income. As well, the same restrictions and warnings apply. Let's look at the Opco and Investco example again, except this time portfolio dividends are earned in Investco. We'll assume that the dividend rate is 8 per cent and that all after-tax amounts are reinvested in dividend-bearing securities. If $100 of corporate income is distributed as salary, you'll have $52.15 left to invest. The after-tax rate of return on the dividends is 5.42 per cent. After ten years, you'll have accumulated $88.37.

If the funds are left inside the corporation, $77.16 will be available to invest. This is first distributed to Investco as a tax-free dividend. The after-tax rate of return on the dividend paying securities is 6 per cent annually. In ten years, $138.18 will have accumulated in the corporation. If this is paid out as a dividend, you will end up with $107.30 in your pocket, compared with $88.37 if you invested personally.

## CONVERTING SALARY AND DIVIDENDS TO EXEMPT CAPITAL GAINS

While the deferral opportunities are attractive, most owner-managers eventually wonder if they can convert after-tax income in their corporations to tax-free capital gains under their $400,000 capital gains exemption on qualifying small business corporation shares.

The answer is yes, but you must be careful that you do it so as not to disqualify the corporation from being eligible for the exemption. And of course, it depends on your plans for your business whether you actually see $400,000 of tax-free cash.

If after-tax corporate income is not paid to you as dividends, it is essentially added to the value of the corporation. Thus if you don't receive salary or dividends of $400,000 over a period of years, your company should, in theory, be worth $400,000 more, all other things being equal. That means a buyer should be willing to pay an additional $400,000 for your shares, all of which would be a capital gain, and tax-free under the exemption. Ignoring the side effects of perhaps having to sell your business to actually see the cash, this tactic is definitely superior to paying out the $400,000 as a dividend and paying at least 30 per cent tax on the distribution.

However, if your qualifying SBC, Opco, is debt-free, it may not take long before investment assets exceed 10 per cent of total assets as you continue to reinvest in the business. Your company will no longer meet the 90 per cent test (substantially all its assets must be employed in an active business) and you will not be eligible for the $400,000 exemption on the transfer or sale of your shares in the business. You will remain eligible for the general $100,000 lifetime capital gains exemption, however. If you and your spouse each have a $400,000 exemption, the problem is magnified.

The quick and easy solution to this dilemma is to invest the spare cash in active business assets rather than investments. However, this may not be to every owner-manager's liking. It may not be the right time to expand, and some might not like the increased exposure to potential creditors.

Transferring the investments to Investco to keep Opco within the 10 per cent limit is also a sound idea, although the value of Opco may grow more slowly as a result. All distributions for your personal needs could be made from Investco. You could even continue to pay a salary from Investco and make RRSP or RPP contributions. However, the salary you receive from Investco must be reasonable in the circumstances.

## SIX-MONTH DEFERRAL ON BONUSES

For your corporation to receive a deduction for salaries or bonuses accrued, they must actually be paid within 180 days of the fiscal year end of the corporation. However, you would include the amount in your income for tax purposes only in the year you actually receive it.

This six-month deferral is routinely used by most owner-managers. Typically, dividends are paid during the year, and any salary is accrued and paid after the year end, assuming that this does not interfere with RRSP or RPP contributions (see Chapter 9). Note that tax must be withheld from the salary or bonus payment.

This deferral can be valuable to average your tax burden over more than one year, particularly if the profits of your corporation fluctuate. For example, assume that your company earns $300,000 this year but only $200,000 next year. To reduce the income of the company to $200,000, you arrange for a bonus of $100,000 in the first year. However, only $50,000 is paid in the first year and $50,000 is accrued to be paid within 180 days after the year end. No bonus is accrued by the corporation in the second year.

By following this strategy, you maintain the corporation's income at the $200,000 level by deducting the $100,000 bonus in the first year. As well, the corporation remains eligible for the low rate of tax in both years. However, you will realize significant tax savings by spreading receipt of the bonus over two years.

If the salary or bonus is not paid within 180 days, the corporation is denied a deduction for the amount. Only when it is actually paid will the corporation be able to claim a deduction.

---

**Caution!** If corporate income exceeds the $200,000 small business limit, it is important to distribute any excess as salary or bonus. Of course, the 180-day deferral can be used. Be aware that the tax consequences of failing to make the payment within the prescribed time are onerous.

# 7/GETTING YOUR FAMILY INVOLVED

An owner-manager involves members of his or her family in the business for a variety of reasons – they are reliable, trustworthy, hardworking, knowledgeable, and in the early stages of the business, it may be less expensive to hire family than outsiders. Many owner-managers bring their children into the business with a view to turning it over to them some day. We look at succession in detail in Chapter 12. In this chapter, we look at some of the tax savings that can be achieved by involving family in the business.

## THE LESS YOU PAY, THE MORE YOU KEEP
It doesn't take long before the successful owner-manager is earning enough income to propel him or her into the top tax bracket. Tax at rates of up to 51 per cent, depending on your province of residence, take effect when your taxable income exceeds about $58,000 (1991). Throughout the book, we've assumed a hypothetical top rate of 47.85 per cent. On the other hand, there is no tax if taxable income is lower than about $6,200, and the lowest rate (25 per cent to 28 per cent) applies on taxable income up to about $29,000. In 1991, you can receive up to about $23,000 of Canadian dividends and pay no personal tax, if you have no other source of income (about $10,500 in Quebec). Of course, dividends are paid out of a corporation's *after-tax* profits. The corporate tax therefore becomes a concern when you own the corporation and are thinking of paying dividends.

Arranging your affairs so that income is "split" with one or more of your family members can produce significant tax savings, provided that you do it right and don't run afoul of a number of anti-avoidance rules in the tax law. Saving up to 25 cents in tax for each dollar earned is nothing to be sneezed at. Besides putting more money into the family coffers, you'll be able to put more aside for your children's education, for their first home, or even to start up their own business. Income splitting also may help your business. If less is paid out because less tax is paid, more can be retained in the business, which should reduce its financing needs.

And these benefits pale next to the tax savings that your family might enjoy if each of you get to use all your $400,000 small business capital gains exemption. This tax break is discussed further in Chapter 10. Here we just note that each individual is entitled to his or her own exemption on the sale of shares in a qualifying small business corporation. The regular $100,000 lifetime exemption also applies on such a sale. Small business tax planning shouldn't lose sight of the possibility of doubling up on this exemption, and even making sure each and every child gets a crack at it. Being able to wipe out literally hundreds of thousands of dollars in tax deserves your, and your professional advisor's, best effort.

Bear in mind that ownership of assets usually must be irrevocably transferred to the family member in order to enjoy any income splitting benefits. To some with shaky marriages or children who aren't "turning out" quite as expected, this might seem unpalatable. However, family law in all provinces may dictate how you split up assets on divorce, so it may not make too much difference if your spouse actually owns something that you used to own.

However, even where family law (matrimonial regime in Quebec) provides for some form of 50-50 split upon the break-up of a marriage, there are circumstances where the ownership of assets between husband and wife can affect the amount of the equalization payment. You should consult with your lawyer before transferring assets to your spouse if this is a concern to you.

Giving assets to your children is another matter. You can use a trust to exercise control over the assets. This is usually desirable if your children are under the age of 18. However, employing a trust immediately introduces another potential problem. You might want to design the trust so that the assets could be distributed back to you or your spouse if you decide in the future that your children shouldn't eventually receive them. Be aware that there are potential tax problems with this sort of reversible income splitting arrangement.

Generally, if you are going to use a trust, it is best not to include you or your spouse as potential beneficiaries; otherwise certain attribution rules (see below) may deny you the tax savings you are attempting to achieve.

---

**Caution!** Talk to your tax and legal advisor before plunging into a comprehensive income splitting plan. What you see in the future is an important part of the equation. There is no point in jumping into something unsuitable if future costs will wipe out all the tax you been so careful to avoid paying.

---

## DON'T LET ATTRIBUTION TRIP YOU UP
Income splitting is a tax reduction strategy that ought to be considered by anyone who earns investment or business income. The objectives of

income splitting are straightforward – arrange your affairs so that income that would normally be taxed at high rates in your hands is taxed in the hands of another person with a lower tax rate, usually your spouse and/or children.

The benefits are obvious. If your spouse can earn $100 and pay $27 tax, whereas you would pay $50 tax if you earned that income, you've saved $23. Looked at another way, if that $100 were investment income, you've improved your after-tax rate of return on the investment by 46 per cent – $50 to $73.

The numbers speak for themselves. Any time you can put 46 per cent more dollars in your pocket, it's worthwhile investigating what you have to do. Unfortunately, it's not as easy as giving your spouse and children a handful of cash and letting them report the interest or dividends. Tax law contains provisions, called the attribution rules, that are designed to discourage income splitting. These rules, which have been tightened considerably in recent years, have the effect of attributing income back to you so that it is taxed in your hands, despite the fact that you have not personally received it.

The attribution rules apply if you lend or transfer property to, or for the benefit of, your spouse or minor children (under 18) with whom you don't deal at arm's length. The rules also apply for transfers to a trust established for a spouse or children. "Property" includes money, shares, bonds, a right of any kind, a home, land, etc. It does not include business income. The rules are wide-ranging and catch most types of direct or indirect transfers.

For transfers to a spouse, the attribution rules catch all investment income as well as capital gains. Only investment income is hit by the attribution rules for transfers to children and only if they are under 18. However, there are two other rules that should be noted. First, attribution may apply on loans you make to any non-arm's length party, including children over age 17. Second, there is the possibility that Revenue Canada will attempt to block your income splitting strategy under the general anti-avoidance rule (GAAR). However, this would probably happen only if you entered into a convoluted or "tricky" arrangement that represented a misuse or abuse of the rules in the tax law.

## CORPORATE ATTRIBUTION

The attribution rules in all their complexity have not ignored owner-managers and their private corporations. Specific rules apply to loans and transfers made after October 27, 1986. In very broad terms, they operate as follows. First, the individual must loan or transfer property to a corporation. One of the main purposes of the loan or transfer must reasonably be considered to be to reduce the individual's income and to benefit a "designated person". An individual's spouse or minor child (including a nephew or niece) is a "designated person" if he or she owns at least 10 per cent of any class of shares of the corporation.

Unless the individual receives (as a minimum) an annual prescribed return on the debt or shares received on the loan or transfer of property, there will be deemed attribution of interest income to the individual lender or transferor. The attributed income is reduced by any amounts actually received by the transferor or by five-fourths of any dividends received. The prescribed interest rate is set by the government each quarter and is the rate payable on late tax instalments (not including the 2 percentage point penalty).

For example, assume that your spouse and children are shareholders of the corporation. You lend the corporation $50,000 interest-free, but Revenue Canada considers that the loan enabled the corporation to pay dividends to your spouse and children that otherwise would have been paid to you, or not paid at all. If the prescribed rate is 10 per cent, you must receive $5,000 interest on the loan annually; otherwise, $5,000 will be attributed to you for tax purposes.

If you use the $50,000 to acquire shares, dividends of at least $4,000 would have to be distributed on the shares to avoid any attribution. The dividends are grossed up by one-quarter of any dividends actually paid to determine if attribution applies. If $4,000 of dividends are paid, the gross-up is $1,000. This is equal to the prescribed interest of $5,000 (dividend of $4,000 plus gross-up of $1,000) that would be charged on the $50,000, so attribution does not apply.

The corporate attribution rules do not apply to any period during which the corporation is a small business corporation (SBC). These are Canadian-controlled private corporations (CCPCs) that primarily carry on an active business in Canada and that meet the 90 per cent test mentioned in Chapter 3. Thus, if your company holds investments representing more than 10 per cent of the value of the company's assets (other than shares in an SBC), it will not qualify and thus will be subject to the corporate attribution rules.

The corporate attribution rules also do not apply when the shares of the corporation are held in trust, and under the terms of the trust, the individual may not receive any of the capital or income of the trust while he or she is a designated person. For example, such a trust for a minor child would provide that the income is accumulated until the child turns 18. It then can become payable because the child is no longer a designated person.

And finally, the attribution rules would generally not apply if a family member uses his or her own funds to acquire assets, such as shares in your company, or to transfer assets that he or she owns into the company in exchange for shares. As well, your spouse or children can acquire assets from you, such as shares in your business, at fair market value if he or she pays cash or reasonable consideration for the shares. If debt forms part of the consideration, the debt must bear interest at the lesser of the current commercial rate or the prescribed rate, and the interest must be paid within 30 days of the end of the calendar year.

## INHERITANCES
In the event that your spouse or your children receive money under someone's will, the attribution rules will not apply if these funds are invested in the recipient's own name. Thus, inheritances are ideal "untainted" funds for income splitting purposes. Rather than use such funds to pay living expenses, you should consider having your spouse or children use their inheritance for investment purposes. The interest or dividend income will be taxed in their hands, not in yours.

## GIFTS FROM NON-RESIDENTS
If you have generous relatives who reside outside Canada, gifts that they might make to your spouse or children are not subject to the attribution rules. If large gifts are involved, it may be desirable for the donor to establish an offshore trust for the benefit of you and your family. This is a complex area of tax planning. Professional advice is a must.

## SALARIES TO FAMILY MEMBERS OR "GET A JOB"
If your spouse or children are involved with the day-to-day operations of the business, it is likely that they can be looked on as employees and be paid a salary. This salary will be a deductible expense to the corporation, if it is reasonable in relation to the duties performed by the family member.

There are no specific guidelines to "reasonableness" in this situation, but you can't go wrong paying them the same amount you would pay a complete stranger to perform the same duties. As noted previously, you can't pay your spouse $100,000 for signing a few cheques just because he or she is referred to as the company's comptroller. Nor can you pay your seven-year-old $10,000 for straightening the pictures in your office, however much this might help with education expenses.

One of the factors to consider in setting the salary of a spouse or child is the applicability of unemployment insurance premiums. These were discussed in Chapter 3.

## GETTING AROUND THE CORPORATE
## ATTRIBUTION RULES
As we have noted in several chapters, you probably have set up the share ownership structure of your corporation to include participation by your spouse and even your children (if they are under 18, you would

likely have done this through a trust). We have assumed to this point that you are running an active business (investment companies are discussed in Chapter 10).

The obvious way to avoid running afoul of the corporate attribution rules is to ensure that your company is at all times a small business corporation, that is, at least 90 per cent of its resources are devoted to an active business. This is also, by the way, the key to remaining eligible for the $400,000 small business capital gains exemption.

As an SBC, dividends can be paid to shareholders with relative impunity, as long as you haven't contravened the general attribution rules. These state that your spouse and children must use their "own" funds to subscribe for shares. You cannot give or lend them the money. This is seldom a problem since, at the time of incorporating, you would have properly structured the ownership of the shares and the transfer of the assets to the corporation (see Chapter 2).

## REORGANIZING YOUR COMPANY

What happens if you incorporated before reading this book and you are the only shareholder? Now you want your spouse and children to be involved so your family can begin to realize some of those tax savings. You could reorganize the structure of the business. There are a variety of ways to do this, some more complicated than others, but these methods may achieve other goals you have in mind. Let's look at relatively simple restructuring plans that involve you, your spouse and your two children.

You can simply issue more common shares of your company (Opco) to your family. This has serious drawbacks, however. The value of your shares would be diluted and the family members would have to pay fair market value for their shares from their own funds to avoid attribution. This may not be a problem, and may even be desirable, if your spouse or children have their own funds. For example, your spouse may be earning his or her own money, or perhaps the funds were brought into the marriage or were inherited. Generally, your children will have to have inherited the money; gifts from you or any adult who resides in Canada will trigger the attribution rules, although they will apply only to the gift giver.

Reorganizing the share structure as part of an "estate freeze" (see Chapter 12) may be more appropriate. You would exchange your common shares for voting preferred shares that reflect the fair market value of the business. This can be done on a tax-free basis. Your family then would subscribe for common shares using their own funds. Dividends could be paid to family members on the common shares as soon as the appropriate amount of dividends, if any, is paid on the preferred shares, and your income splitting objectives would be achieved.

## ADDING ANOTHER CORPORATION TO YOUR LIFE

Another way that arrives at the same end is to form another company, Holdco. Your family would own common shares in Holdco, and you would transfer your Opco shares to Holdco in exchange for preferred shares. Dividends received by Holdco from Opco could then be distributed to the shareholders of Holdco. Note that Holdco would still qualify as an SBC if its assets consisted primarily of shares in Opco, which is an SBC. As you'll see later in the book, forming another company gives you considerably more flexibility as you design an estate plan, or begin earning more investment income, or begin to prepare to bow out of the business.

What can you do if your business doesn't qualify as an SBC? Perhaps the company is earning too much investment income or is leasing out a sizeable piece of real estate and earning rental income.

### THE 9.9 PER CENT RULE

One possible way of avoiding the attribution rules is for you to reorganize the company by issuing yourself preferred shares for all the corporation's assets and then issuing common shares to family members and yourself. There should be no attribution when dividends are paid, as long as each family member's shareholding is kept to 9.9 per cent or less of the total number of shares issued in that class, and the family members paid for the shares with their own money.

This solution is seldom satisfactory, however, since dividends must be paid on a pro rata basis. For each $100 of dividends paid by the corporation, your spouse and two children receive $29.70 ($9.90 each) while you receive $70.30, since you own the remaining common shares.

---

**Timely Tip.** Often, the company may not be able to support dividend payments of this magnitude and still pay you and working family members an adequate salary to support RRSP or pension plan contributions. However, if you have your own holding company which owns the shares in Opco, the dividends can be paid up to your own Holdco and be left there to invest with no immediate tax consequences.

---

### USING A TRUST TO OWN HOLDCO SHARES

Another technique that is sanctioned by the attribution rules involves creating Holdco and having a trust, of which your children are the beneficiaries, subscribe for the common shares. You could transfer your shares of Opco to Holdco in exchange for preferred shares. Under the terms of the trust, your children could not benefit in any way from

Holdco's earnings, whether through income or capital distributions, while they are designated persons. Of course, they cease to be designated persons upon turning 18, at which time Holdco could begin to distribute accumulated income to the trust's beneficiaries. In this situation, there would probably not be any immediate tax savings. The tax benefits would be realized in the future when you are able to distribute earnings to your children.

## WILL EVERYTHING WORK OUT AS PLANNED?

Family-held corporations occasionally encounter stormy seas. Despite establishing separate classes of shares and doing your best to distribute dividends equitably, somebody will as often as not think he or she has ended up with the short end of the stick.

One child may work for the company while the other doesn't, but both have equal rights to dividends. One child may turn his or her back on you, but getting those shares back won't be an easy matter. And it will be expensive reorganizing your corporate structure to disinherit the black sheep. You and your spouse may discover that all your financial orchestrations have hit a sour note and not left you enough to enjoy your retirement. And then there are the potential problems of divorce (yours or your children's), marriages of which you don't approve, or untimely deaths.

These are very real problems that many owner-managers eventually face. Don't think that they can't possibly ever happen to you. We can't stress too strongly the need for competent professional advice as you consider the various methods of restructuring your business to accommodate family members.

## PUT YOUR FAMILY IN BUSINESS FOR THEMSELVES

The attribution rules don't apply if you loan or transfer money or assets to a family member and they earn business income with the assets or money. Thus, if your spouse is considering starting up his or her own *unincorporated* business (other than as an essentially passive investor in, or limited partner of, a partnership) that is separate and distinct from yours, you can loan your spouse funds, give him or her funds or assets, guarantee bank loans, or even pay off your spouse's current bank indebtedness. All income earned by your spouse from his or her business will be taxed in the spouse's hands and not in yours.

As described in Chapter 1, Ray Corcoran set up his business by purchasing a controlling interest in Gizmo Inc. Ray's wife operates her own sculpting business. Now she is planning to open a small shop with a friend to exhibit her work and that of a few local artists. Ray plans to lend his wife a substantial amount interest-free to partially finance the venture. The attribution rules will not apply.

## ESTATE FREEZES

Several of the possibilities outlined above put a stop to you participating in the future increase in value of your business. If your children own the common shares and you own the preferred shares, the common shares will increase in value as your business prospers, while the preferred shares will more or less maintain their current value. This is one of the objectives of an estate freeze, which we discuss in more detail in Chapter 12.

There is no point in cutting off your capital appreciation until you have at least $400,000, or perhaps $500,000, of accrued capital gains built up in the shares of the business that you own. This gain can be realized free of tax under your exemption. And if you have involved your spouse in the ownership of the business from the outset, he or she will also want to realize up to $400,000 in tax-free small business gains.

If you want to put some income into the hands of family members, a simple reorganization may be sufficient. After converting your common shares to preferred shares, you could issue several different classes of common shares. In this manner, you would retain control over which shares should receive dividends.

---

**Caution!** It does happen that an owner-manager and his or her family end up with too many corporations and too much expense, primarily because they failed to integrate current planning with future expectations. We have presented various planning opportunities in different chapters, simply to take you through the planning process one step at a time. Ideally, when you do visit your professional advisor, you will have already deliberated over deferrals, income splitting, estate and succession planning, expansion, retirement planning and the "problem" of investment income. Your professional advisor can help you determine the correct mix of these various strategies in order to come up with the best overall tax planning recipe to suit your particular circumstances. Your advisor will be able to transfer the priorities you have set and the future you expect to unfold into an integrated but flexible plan that should serve you well.

# 8/Planning for Today

Owner-managers almost always find it difficult to separate their personal and business expenses. Sometimes the distinction is not all that clear. And frequently, it simply is more convenient to pay some business expenses personally or have the company pay certain personal or family expenses.

But the tax consequences can be substantially different, and sometimes punitive, depending on whether the expenditures are tax-deductible and whether the company or the owner-manager bears the cost. Careful planning and record keeping are a must. However, with the owner-manager's top tax rate potentially more than double the corporate rate, there are opportunities for substantial savings.

Although there are a host of special rules, the deductibility of most expenditures under Canada's tax laws is governed by certain general principles. To be deductible, an expenditure must:

- be made or incurred for the purpose of earning income from a business or a property;
- not be of a capital nature;
- not be a personal or living expense, and
- be reasonable in the circumstances.

While capital expenditures are not permitted as deductions when incurred, capital cost allowances (tax depreciation) are permitted to write off the cost of depreciable property over time. Certain other capital expenditures, such as the cost of purchased goodwill, may also be amortized in part and over time.

Specific deductions are available for a variety of expenditures that might not be permitted under the general principles outlined above. For example, interest on borrowed money, although perhaps capital in nature, may be deducted, provided specified criteria are satisfied.

On the other side of the coin, certain expenses that might otherwise be deductible under the general principles are specifically disallowed. The most common examples include dues paid to dining and sports clubs and 20 per cent of meal and entertainment expenses.

Personal or living expenses paid by a corporation on behalf of the owner-manager are not deductible by the company. In addition, such amounts will generally be included in the owner-manager's income as taxable benefits.

An owner-manager is not allowed to deduct personally any expenses related to his or her incorporated business except those that most employees are able to deduct, the most common being eligible travelling expenses, automobile expenses and professional dues related to employment.

## HANDLING BUSINESS AND PERSONAL EXPENSES

Let's look at some examples of expenses in different categories and how they might be handled on the most tax-efficient basis.

### EXPENSE NOT DEDUCTIBLE BUT NO TAXABLE BENEFIT

The most common example is club dues, whether for a golf or tennis club, or the downtown business club which is used for business lunches. The company cannot claim a deduction for the fees paid, but you will not be in receipt of a taxable benefit (see below) if it is principally to the advantage of your business for you to be a member of the club.

Let's assume that the club dues are $1,000. If your company is taxed at 22.84 percent, it has to earn about $1,296 to pay this $1,000 non-deductible expense, after first paying tax of $296 on the earnings. On the other hand, you would have to receive a salary from your company of about $1,918 to be able to pay the $1,000 non-deductible expense, after you pay tax of $918 at your 47.85 per cent tax rate (top tax bracket). It's obviously preferable for the company to pay the expense. It has to use about $622 less pre-tax income to pay the dues ($1,918 minus $1,296).

If your company earns more than the $200,000 limit and is therefore taxable at top corporate rates, it will not make much difference whether the company pays the club dues or you do. But, as a general rule of thumb, expenses in this category, that is, those that are not deductible and are not considered taxable benefits in your hands, should be paid by the company if its marginal rate of tax is lower than yours, and by you if your marginal rate is lower than the company's.

---

**Caution!** – It is extremely important that you scrupulously document the business use of clubs. Company expenditures on club dues, even though not claimed as a deduction, are prime targets for Revenue Canada to add to your income as a taxable benefit.

---

### EXPENSES DEDUCTIBLE BY BOTH OWNER-MANAGER AND CORPORATION

The best example here is automobile expenses (more on business automobiles later in this chapter). Essentially there is no difference whether the expense is claimed by the owner-manager or by the corporation. If the corporation pays and deducts a $1,000 expense, it must earn $1,000. If the owner-manager pays and deducts the expense, the corporation earns $1,000, which is paid to the owner-manager as salary. This $1,000 is then used by the owner-manager to finance the expense.

### EXPENSE DEDUCTIBLE BY CORPORATION
### BUT NOT BY OWNER-MANAGER

There are a variety of expenses in this category. Some do not result in the owner-manager being assessed a taxable benefit, while certain others do. We looked at the benefit that results from low-interest or interest-free loans and shareholder loans in Chapter 5. Later in this chapter, we examine the taxable benefit that may result from using a car owned or leased by the corporation.

Where an expenditure paid by the company is deductible but results in a taxable benefit to you, the tax impact is the same as if the company had paid you additional salary and you had paid the expense personally. Depending on your particular circumstances, you may be better off to pay these kinds of expenses personally, obtaining the necessary funds from the company in the form of dividends, repayment of loans or a partial return of capital. If you expect to incur significant expenses that fall into this category, you should take them into account when planning your overall remuneration strategy. We examined the key elements of remuneration planning for the owner-manager in Chapter 5.

There are certain other expenditures that may appear to pertain more to the owner-manager than to the business, but which are not considered to be employee or shareholder benefits for tax purposes. Expenditures in this category are generally deductible by the corporation and include such amounts as:

- health care plan premiums paid to a private health services plan;
- group term life insurance, but only on the first $25,000 of coverage;
- sponsorship of minor league teams, even if your children are involved (deductible as promotion expenses), and
- service club dues, as long as there is some business justification to the corporation incurring the expense.

If these expenses are incurred to earn business income, they are deductible and should be paid by the corporation. They are not deductible if borne personally by the owner-manager.

The costs of meals and entertainment are not fully deductible, even if it can be clearly demonstrated that such expenses are necessary in carrying on the company's business. Twenty per cent of meal and entertainment expenses are arbitrarily disallowed and must be added back in calculating the company's taxable income. Included in this category are items such as business lunches and tickets to shows and sporting events where customers or clients are entertained. Even though not deductible in full, the company should pay such expenses in order to obtain the tax deduction for 80 per cent of the costs.

## EXPENSE NOT DEDUCTIBLE AND TAXABLE BENEFIT

Generally, personal expenses are not deductible by either you or the corporation. If the corporation pays such expenses, you will have a taxable benefit that must be included in your income. As well, the corporation will not be entitled to a deduction if the amount was not spent to earn income.

A taxable benefit will result if, for example, you combine a pleasure trip with a business trip. The personal portion of the trip financed by the corporation must be included in your income as a taxable benefit. If your spouse travels with you, a portion of his or her expenses may be deductible if your spouse was primarily engaged in business activities on behalf of the corporation during some or all of the trip, but in most cases, your spouse's expenses will also be included in your income as a taxable benefit.

Disallowing the expense to the corporation and including the amount in your income as a taxable benefit is a double whammy. You should always arrange to pay personal expenses yourself or to reimburse the corporation for such expenses paid by it.

## PERSONAL PROPERTY OWNED BY THE COMPANY

Where property owned by a corporation is made available for the personal use of the owner-manager, the appropriate value to be placed on the taxable benefit often is an extremely contentious issue. For example, suppose that your company purchases a luxurious vacation home for the exclusive use of you and your family. You arrange personally to pay or to reimburse the company for all the operating and maintenance costs.

Provided that the company retains the ownership rights, the tax authorities should not be able to include the entire purchase price of the property in your income. Rather, the benefit to be valued is the right to the exclusive use of the property. This might be determined as the fair market rental value of the premises.

However, in many cases, a comparable rental value may be difficult to determine, and even if one can be estimated, Revenue Canada is not prepared to accept such value as the true measure of the benefit if it does not reflect a reasonable return to the company on its investment in the property.

The tax authority's approach in these situations has been to assess a benefit determined by taking into account a normal rate of return (for example, the prescribed interest rate) on the greater of the cost or fair market value of the property, plus related operating costs paid by the company, less the consideration paid to the company by the shareholder.

Does it make sense to have the corporation purchase such properties, if a taxable benefit of this magnitude is included in the owner-manager's income? Probably not. But if the funds to be invested in the property are taxed only at the low corporate rate, it may still be more tax-efficient to have the company purchase the property rather than buying it yourself, if you have to withdraw the necessary funds from the company as salary or bonus taxed at your top marginal rate. As well, remember that an investment in non-business assets by the company may mean that you cannot claim the enhanced $400,000 capital gains exemption on a future sale of your shares.

### Managing Your Cash Flow

The tax consequences resulting from various expenditures will be determined not so much by whether you or the company initially pays a particular expense, but by who ultimately bears the cost. If you personally pay an expense that is deductible only by the company, it can reimburse you and obtain the tax deduction. Make sure you fully document your expense reimbursements and keep supporting evidence on file.

If the company pays personal expenses on your behalf, you may wish to reimburse the company to avoid a disallowance to the company and a taxable benefit to you. In situations where the company has a debt owing to the shareholder, any personal expenses paid during the year can simply be charged to this account, reducing the amount due. Periodic salaries and bonuses can also be credited to the account as they accrue. In effect, the owner-manager maintains this as a drawing account to withdraw cash from time to time as the need arises.

However, if you follow this practice, take care not to let your account become overdrawn. Overdrafts will generally be treated for tax purposes as a loan to you, the shareholder. Interest at prescribed rates will be calculated on any outstanding balance receivable from you and will be included in your income as a taxable benefit. If you don't repay the amount within one year after the end of the tax year in which the indebtedness arose, the full amount may be included in your income. For further details on the tax consequences of shareholder loans, see Chapter 5.

### BUSINESS AUTOMOBILES

Over the last few years, the tax rules have changed substantially, sometimes at the rate of once a month. It appears that the government is now reasonably satisfied with the current version, but that doesn't mean it is any easier to decide whether you or your corporation should own or lease an automobile that is used for either business or pleasure and who should pay the operating costs. And those are not all the variables that must be considered when trying to solve the business auto problem.

The introduction of the GST has complicated the issue even further. Restrictions are imposed on the amount of GST input credits available on the purchase or lease of luxury autos. As well, GST is payable by the company on the amount of the taxable benefits included in the employee's or shareholder's income.

Let's quickly review the rules, and then offer one or two guidelines. Generally you will profit from professional advice, especially if you have a company fleet that is growing.

## DEDUCTION LIMITATIONS

Your company is allowed CCA (capital cost allowance or depreciation) deductions on a maximum total cost of $24,000 including provincial sales tax and unrecoverable GST for automobiles it purchases. For autos acquired after June 17, 1987, and before September 1, 1989, the limit is $20,000. CCA can be claimed at the rate of 30 per cent per annum on the declining balance. Only half the normal amount of CCA can be claimed in the year the auto is purchased. Cars costing in excess of $24,000 are each put in a separate CCA class and the terminal loss and recapture of depreciation rules do not apply. GST input credits are not allowed for amounts on which CCA cannot be claimed. As well, no GST input credit is allowed if the automobile is purchased exclusively for the personal use (that is, 90 per cent or more) of the employee or shareholder.

If the company borrows to finance the purchase of a car, the interest expense is deductible to a maximum average of $300 a month ($250 for cars acquired before September 1, 1989) for the period that the loan is outstanding.

If the car is leased, your business may deduct the least of:
- the actual lease cost, exclusive of GST;
- $650 per month ($600 for leases entered into after June 17, 1987, and before September 1, 1989), or
- the actual lease cost times $24,000 and divided by 85 per cent of the manufacturer's suggested list price plus provincial sales tax, but excluding GST (minimum $28,235 or $23,529 for leases before September 1, 1989).

If the car's suggested list price including provincial sales tax is $34,000 and the monthly lease payment is $700, the three alternatives will be $700, $650, and $581 ($700 x $24,000 / 85 per cent of $34,000). Thus, the maximum lease payment that is deductible is $581. Input credits for the GST are generated only on the $581 amount.

Reimbursing the company for the non-deductible portion of the lease cost, in the expectation that the company will be no worse off if a luxury car is leased, will not solve the problem. The tax law requires that any reimbursement by an employee of the company's lease expense reduces the deductible portion of the company's cost. For example, if the company pays $900 a month for the lease, its maximum deduction before any reimbursement might be $650. If the employee reimburses the company the $250 spread, this simply has the effect of reducing the company's deduction to $400 ($650 minus $250 reimbursement).

### EMPLOYEE'S STANDBY CHARGE

The company must also compute a standby charge for automobiles supplied to employees, including the owner-manager. This is a rough measure of the benefit to the employee of having a car available for personal use and is included in the employee's income for tax purposes. For vehicles owned by the company, the standby charge is 2 per cent based on the original cost of the car, including provincial sales tax, but not unrecoverable GST, for each month the car is available to the employee (24 per cent for a full year). GST is payable by the company on the amount of the standby charge included in the employee's income. This amount is also added to the employee's income as a taxable benefit.

The standby charge is reduced if the car is used at least 90 per cent for business, based on kilometres driven, and personal use is under 1,000 kilometres a month. In this case, the standby charge is calculated as follows:

$$\text{Standby charge otherwise calculated} \times \frac{\text{kilometres for personal use in the year}}{1,000 \times \text{number of months in the year the car is available to the employee}}$$

For instance, if personal use is only 200 kilometres a month and this equals 5 per cent of the total use, the employee is taxable on only 20 per cent (2,400 km/12,000 km) of the full standby charge. The GST payable by the company and the related benefit to the employee are also reduced proportionately. Note that commuting to the office and back is personal use, not business use, of the car.

If the vehicle is leased, the standby charge is two-thirds of the lease cost, including provincial sales tax and any amount included in the lease cost for repairs and maintenance, but excluding any amount for insurance. Here again, GST is payable by the company on the amount of the standby charge, exclusive of provincial sales tax, and the taxable benefit is increased by this amount.

As is the case with a purchased auto, the standby charge for a leased vehicle may be reduced where the car is used at least 90 per cent on business and personal use is less than 1,000 kilometres a month.

## OPERATING COST BENEFIT

If the company pays for operating costs, such as insurance, licence, fuel, and repairs and maintenance, an additional taxable benefit may be included in the employee's income. This benefit is measured by the amount of costs paid by the company times the ratio of personal to total kilometres driven. Any amounts reimbursed to the company by the employee are deducted from the amount of the benefit so calculated.

Instead of determining the operating cost benefit with reference to the actual costs incurred by the company, the employee may elect to include in income an additional one-half of the standby charge, provided that the car is used primarily for business (that is, more than 50 per cent).

GST is payable by the company on the amount of the operating cost benefit, excluding provincial sales tax and any exempt costs, and this amount is added to the employee's income as an additional taxable benefit.

## LUXURY CARS

With both owned or leased cars, the standby charge is calculated on the full cost, exclusive of GST not recoverable, not the amount available for deduction by the company. Thus, if you buy or lease a luxury car, a large portion of the cost, either the leasing cost or CCA on the purchase price, cannot be deducted for tax purposes. As well, your income and hence your tax bill will be increased by the large standby charge benefit.

So, the question still remains – should your car be owned or leased by the company, or be owned or leased personally by you or a family member? As we noted at the beginning of the chapter, you're financially better off if the company makes expenditures on goods or services that you use personally, whether or not the outlay is deductible or can be capitalized, assuming that the corporation's effective tax rate is lower than your tax rate.

However, this rule doesn't apply when the standby charge has to be figured into the calculations. Besides earning enough income to finance the purchase or lease, a significant portion of which may not be deductible if a luxury car is being contemplated, your company also has to earn enough income to provide you with the funds to pay the tax on the standby charge benefit. Rarely will it be worthwhile for the company to own or lease a luxury car when the full standby charge applies.

If an auto that falls within the deductibility guidelines is to be purchased or leased, the answer is not so cut and dried. Several choices can be made, and a number of variables must be considered for each choice, including your tax rate and the company's tax rate, how the lease or purchase is structured, and what arrangements are made if funds have to be borrowed.

**Timely Tips.**
- Arrange for an interest-free loan from the company so that you can purchase the car personally. You will be assessed a taxable benefit on the loan, equal to the interest that otherwise would be payable based on the government's prescribed interest rate, but this will likely be much lower than the standby charge benefit. You then will be entitled to claim a deduction for the benefit and claim CCA on the auto (up to the maximum cost of $24,000), prorated, of course, for business use of the car. The loan must be properly documented and terms for repayment within a reasonable period of time must be spelled out.

  Instead of claiming any deductions, you could also receive a non-taxable allowance from the company based on business kilometres driven. The allowance must be reasonable, which means 31 cents for the first 5,000 kilometres and 25 cents for any excess (4 cents of additional allowance is permitted for the Yukon and Northwest Territories). The company receives a deduction for the allowance.
- In many cases, there could be advantages to the company leasing a car rather than purchasing it. Often, the standby charge of two-thirds of the lease cost will be less than the standby charge for an identical car that is purchased. As well, some service costs can be included in the lease contract and hence be taxable benefits to you only to the extent of two-thirds.
- Either you or the company might consider leasing a car initially, and then purchasing it at some later date. Deductibility of the lease costs may be restricted during the lease period, but when the car is purchased the standby charge will be based on the used car price, which should be much lower than the original purchase price.
- You might consider transferring a personally owned luxury car to your company once its fair market value is down to the $24,000 limit. The company would get its full deduction for CCA and your standby charge would be based on the $24,000 cost amount.

It won't be easy to get a handle on your business automobile situation. Your employees may have other needs, fleet discounts may be available that will affect your calculations, you may have other family members who are employees who may benefit if the company owns or leases their autos, or you might even have operations outside Canada that affect how you deal with automobiles.

---

**Caution!** It will certainly pay to discuss your business auto situation with your professional advisor. The rule changes, the introduction of the GST, and the myriad considerations that go into any final decision are not easy to keep up with.

---

## CAPITAL PURCHASES AND CAPITAL COST ALLOWANCE (CCA) CLAIMS

Businesses are permitted to claim depreciation (capital cost allowance, or CCA, is the technical term) on most capital expenditures. Generally, expenditures to acquire assets such as buildings, manufacturing and office equipment, and vehicles, are capital in nature. Land, however, is not depreciable. Depreciable assets are, in theory, written off over their useful lives by claiming CCA each year.

Capital expenditures are distinguished from expenses made in the course of conducting your business day to day. These are deductible in the year the outlay is made. Generally, an item is expensed if it is consumed over a short period in your business activities, or is used in some fashion immediately, or will be used in the near future. Items expensed generally do not have any extended useful life.

CCA claims are usually limited to one-half the standard claim in the year a depreciable asset is purchased. Generally, no CCA claim is allowed in the year an asset is sold.

---

**Timely Tip.** If your business is planning to acquire depreciable assets, try to buy them before the end of your fiscal year. If selling assets, delay the sale until after the end of the fiscal year.

---

**Caution!** Note that if your business is purchasing an asset before the year end, it must be available for use in order to make any CCA claims in that period.

---

To claim CCA, it is not necessary that the asset actually be used, but it must be capable of being used. For example, if you buy a truck just before the year end, but take delivery early in your next fiscal year, no CCA may be claimed in the year of purchase for that truck. The rules for buildings are more complicated, since they may be available for partial use during construction.

Depreciable assets are classified according to type and rates of CCA. When your business disposes of assets, a terminal loss or recapture of CCA already claimed may result. Usually a terminal loss will be tax-deductible if all the assets in one class are sold and net proceeds are less than their undepreciated capital cost. Recapture occurs and must be included in taxable income when proceeds exceed undepreciated capital cost, that is, you claimed too much depreciation while the asset was owned. The amount of terminal loss or recapture is determined only at the end of the tax year. Consequently, if you purchase another asset during the tax year that belongs in the particular class where a terminal loss or recapture has arisen, its cost is added to the total undepreciated capital cost of the class, which may result in the effective elimination of the terminal loss or recapture.

---

**Timely Tips.**
- If a terminal loss will be realized on the sale of an asset, consider delaying replacing the asset or buying other assets of the same class until after the end of your tax year. The loss is deductible from corporate income. On the other hand, if a terminal loss on the sale of a specific asset will create or add to a loss that you might not be able to use, you might consider acquiring an asset of that class of sufficient value to offset the loss, assuming of course there is a business reason for acquiring the asset.
- If recapture of CCA is likely on the sale of certain assets, consider whether this recapture may be deferred by buying replacement assets in Canada within the allotted time period. The cost of all assets of the same class acquired before the end of the tax year will offset the amount of recapture. A one-year replacement period is allowed for buildings used in a business, provided the replacement building(s) is (are) used for that same purpose. For assets that are involuntarily disposed of (for example by fire, loss, expropriation), recapture may usually be deferred if the asset is replaced within the following two years.

---

CCA rates vary depending on the type of asset acquired. In some situations, it may be advantageous to lease assets rather than acquire them if lease payments will afford faster write-offs than CCA claims that otherwise could be made. The new leasing rules (see Chapter 4) may affect decisions on whether to lease or purchase.

## USING LOSSES

As you will recall from Chapter 3, business losses can be carried forward seven years and back three years. There are several techniques that can be used to increase corporate income and therefore use up accumulated losses more quickly.

---

**Timely Tip.** Consider not claiming CCA in a profitable year in order to increase corporate income against which losses can be applied. In a loss year, you might also choose not to claim CCA in order to minimize the loss if you felt there was a chance that you might not be able to use the losses.

---

Depending on the circumstances, you may be able to amend prior years' income tax returns to revise your CCA claim if it is advantageous to do so. Also, if you anticipate losses that might not be used, consider deferring certain other discretionary expenses, such as the allowance for doubtful accounts. Certain research and development expenses can also be deferred to future years, which will increase income and allow losses to be used. As well, you can choose to reduce the amount of any reserves you might be claiming in the year, which also increases income. However, there is a drawback to claiming a smaller than normal capital gains reserve. In any succeeding year, you are not allowed to claim a reserve larger than the one claimed in the previous year.

The easiest way you have of increasing income and ensuring that losses are used is to distribute dividends to yourself rather than a salary. Wages are deductible expenses that reduce income, while dividends are paid out of after-tax income. However, this may upset other planning you are undertaking on an on-going basis with pension plans or RRSPs.

## R&D INCENTIVES

The federal and provincial governments view the need to allocate more of Canada's resources to research and development (R&D) as critical. Significant tax benefits and other financial assistance have been made available to companies undertaking R&D by both levels of government.

### Tax Benefits for R&D

The definition for tax purposes of R&D, or more specifically "scientific research and experimental development", includes basic research to advance scientific knowledge generally, applied research that has a specific, practical application in view, and development, which is using the results of research to create new or improve existing materials, devices, products, or processes. As this definition is probably broader than a strict scientific or engineering definition, many taxpayers may be missing out on the maximum benefits available through the tax system for R&D expenditures.

The tax incentives available to R&D performers generally include:
- immediate write-offs for current and capital expenditures made in Canada;
- immediate write-off for current expenditures outside Canada;
- federal investment tax credits (ITCs) on current and capital expenditures made in Canada ranging from 20 per cent to 35 per cent;
- for qualifying Canadian-controlled private corporations (CCPCs), cash refunds of investment tax credits (ITCs), and
- various provincial tax incentives offered by Quebec, Ontario and Nova Scotia.

## INVESTMENT TAX CREDITS FOR CCPCS

For CCPCs, the applicable investment tax credit is 35 per cent of the first $2 million of qualifying R&D expenditures. To be eligible for this top rate, the CCPC (together with all associated corporations) must not have earned taxable income of more than $200,000 in the preceding tax year. In addition, the $2-million expenditure limit must be shared among the associated corporations. For individuals and corporations not qualifying for the top rate, the ITC rate is generally 20 per cent (30 per cent in the Atlantic provinces and the Gaspé peninsula).

The annual limit of investment tax credits earned by a CCPC that may be used to offset taxes is equal to 75 per cent of its federal tax payable (except surtax) plus 3 per cent of the company's small business deduction base for the year. Any ITC not used in the year in which it is earned may be carried back three years and forward ten years.

CCPCs that qualify for the 35 per cent ITC may also be eligible for a cash refund if they cannot otherwise use the ITC to offset federal tax payable. The tax credits earned on current R&D expenditures are fully refundable; those earned on capital expenditures are 40 per cent refundable.

---

**Timely Tip.** If you have incurred qualifying R&D expenditures, you may want to keep the taxable income of the company and all associated companies below the $200,000 threshold to ensure that the company will earn ITCs at the 35 per cent rate and qualify for cash refunds.

---

# 9/PLANNING FOR TOMORROW

As employee and employer, you need look no further than in the mirror to discover who will be providing for your tomorrows. The government will cough up a bit in the form of Canada or Quebec Pension Plan (CPP/ QPP) benefits and Old Age Security (OAS), but these plans aren't designed to leave you in the lap of luxury on retirement. You've got to plan for that yourself.

Essentially, you have three choices.

- You can invest in your business and assume that its success will see you and your family comfortably through your retirement years.
- You can participate in retirement plans – registered pension plans (RPPs) and registered retirement savings plans (RRSPs) – and enjoy the government's tax assistance in the form of contributions that are deducted from income (within certain limits) and the compounding of investment income on a tax-deferred basis.
- You can invest outside your business and the government-sanctioned plans, trusting to your private savings to see you through retirement.

All three eventually have a place in any owner-manager's financial planning. During the early years of your business, you probably won't have any choice but to invest as much as possible in your enterprise. Credit will be hard to come by and too much debt, even if you could find it, might put you out of business. Private investing, the third option, will naturally happen as your business matures and you find yourself with excess cash. But you probably won't follow this course until you are maximizing the opportunities under the second option – retirement savings plans provided for by legislation.

## TAX ASSISTANCE IS HARD TO RESIST

There is just no point in turning your back on the large tax write-offs available if you contribute to RPPs or RRSPs (owner-managers are not permitted to benefit from DPSPs – deferred profit sharing plans). The trade-off is, of course, a certain lack of flexibility once you have made the contributions. In return for its assistance, the government demands a

98

little – restrictions apply to investments made by the plans, and funds are generally tied up in an RPP – but not that much. This is a small price to pay for being able to participate in two of the best tax shelters available today.

We'll focus on RPPs and RRSPs in this chapter, examining the pros and cons of each so you can decide which is better to use. Neither type of plan is necessarily better than the other in all circumstances. There is, however, one very general rule of thumb that you can use as a starting point when trying to come to a decision. The emphasis here is on the words "very general". To shelter the most income from tax and provide the best retirement benefits, you should generally use RRSPs until about your mid-forties if you plan to retire at age 65, and then consider using defined benefit RPPs until you actually retire. That's the general rule. The practical rule is do what's best for you in your particular situation.

Before looking at the reasons why RPPs might be better than RRSPs, and vice versa, let's look at how these plans work from the owner-manager's point of view. With the passage of the pension reform tax legislation in June, 1990, the rules have changed considerably.

## RRSPs

Whole books have been written on RRSPs. We'll just touch on a few highlights here. Allowable contributions made to an RRSP are fully tax-deductible and income earned on your contributions accumulates free of tax. When funds are eventually withdrawn from the RRSP, they must be included in your income, where they become subject to tax.

The value of the tax deferral on both your contributions and earnings in the plan should not be underestimated. Many business owners will discover that the assets accumulated in their RRSPs may even eventually surpass the worth of their businesses, if they maximize their contributions each and every year.

Beginning in 1991, the maximum you are allowed to contribute is 18 per cent of your earned income, as defined below, in the previous year to a specific dollar maximum, which increases from $11,500 in 1991 to $15,500 in 1995. However, if you accumulate benefits from an RPP or DPSP in the year, the amount you can contribute to an RRSP is reduced.

Your earned income includes salary, wages, income from a business (whether as a proprietor or active partner), net rental income, alimony and maintenance, less any losses from business or rental or any payments of alimony and maintenance. Note that dividends, interest and capital gains are not included.

To make the maximum RRSP contribution in 1991, your earned income must have been $63,889 in 1990. The salary levels in future years are as follows:

|      | Contribution | Earned Income in Prior Year |
|------|-------------|------------------------------|
| 1991 | $11,500     | $63,889                      |
| 1992 | 12,500      | 69,444                       |
| 1993 | 13,500      | 75,000                       |
| 1994 | 14,500      | 80,556                       |
| 1995 | 15,500      | 86,111                       |

Beginning in 1996, the $15,500 maximum is indexed according to increases in the average industrial wage, which is the same increase reflected in the yearly maximum pensionable earnings (YMPE) figure that is used to determine maximum CPP/QPP contributions.

### SEVEN-YEAR CARRY FORWARD
In a year when the full allowable contribution has not been made, there will be unused RRSP deduction room. Beginning in 1991, you can carry forward unused RRSP deduction room for up to seven years. This simply means that if you didn't contribute to an RRSP but were entitled to, you can make your allowable contribution for that particular year in any of the following seven years. In most cases, the carry-forward period will be seven years. In practice, the carry-forward period will usually be longer, since any future contributions will first be considered to have been made in respect of that carry-forward deduction room, not in respect of your current year's deduction limit.

### PA ADJUSTMENTS
If you are a member of an RPP or DPSP, your RRSP contribution is reduced by an amount called the pension adjustment or PA. The PA for members of money purchase (also called defined contribution) RPPs and DPSPs is simply the amount contributed to such plans by you and your employer in the previous year (owner-managers and persons related to them cannot join DPSPs sponsored by their corporations). If you are a member of a defined benefit RPP, your PA is a dollar figure that measures the benefits you accrued in the previous year under the plan, minus $1,000. Generally, if the RPP provides for maximum lifetime retirement benefits, your PA will equal your RRSP contribution limit, minus $1,000. Therefore, the maximum RRSP contribution will be $1,000.

### DEFINED BENEFIT RPPs
Under pension tax reform, the rules have been relaxed considerably for owner-managers who wish to consider setting up a pension plan. The concept of a "designated defined benefit registered pension plan"

(DRPP) has been introduced. Essentially, these are registered pension plans where more than 50 per cent of the retirement benefits accruing in the plan go to connected shareholders (persons owning at least 10 per cent of the shares of any class), persons related to connected shareholders, persons not dealing at arm's length with the corporation and highly paid employees of the corporation. Highly paid means earning at least 2 1/2 times the current year's YMPE, which in 1991 is $30,500. Under this definition, an employee earning an annual salary of $76,250 would be "highly paid".

You can set up a plan just for your own benefit, or for the benefit of any particular group of employees you choose. Fortunately, the more restrictive rules that apply to designated plans should be relatively easy to live with.

With a defined benefit RPP, the pension benefit to be received at retirement is spelled out in the plan. The employer is then responsible for contributing sufficient amounts today to fund the benefits promised for tomorrow. Employee contributions may be made, but generally the employer must fund at least one-half the benefit.

The maximum pension benefit that can be accrued by a member of a designated plan is the aggregate of all amounts, each of which is computed for each year of eligible service provided by the owner-manager. These amounts are determined each year as the lesser of:

- $1,722, and
- 2 per cent times the updated earnings for the member for the particular year.

The following should be noted:

- The maximum amount of $1,722 will be indexed for increases in the average wage after 1994.
- An "updated earnings" calculation, not a "best average earnings" calculation, is applied. This means that the owner-manager must receive remuneration in each year for that year to qualify for a retirement benefit.
- "Updated earnings" for this purpose means that earnings are adjusted to reflect the increase in the average wage index from the particular year in which they are earned, to the year in which the owner-manager's pension commences to be paid.

Once retirement benefits have commenced to be paid, such benefits can be indexed to reflect changes in the Consumer Price Index (CPI), thus providing a measure of inflation protection to the owner-manager.

## DESIGNATED RPP RESTRICTIONS

A number of restrictions apply to DRPPs, primarily to prevent abuse.

In the past, owner-managers used these types of plans, called "top-hat" plans back then, to shelter large amounts of income, primarily based on years of service before the plan was instituted. Now, past service benefits can be provided to a connected person in respect of years before 1991 only if Revenue Canada is informed in writing of the provision of such benefits and only if the present value of all benefits provided to the owner-manager or related persons does not exceed the present value of all benefits provided to all other employees who are active members in all the registered pension plans sponsored by the employer. For years of service after 1989, past service benefits can be provided only after considering the amounts of contributions that the owner-manager has made to all RRSPs, RPPs, and DPSPs in those years. If these contributions do not exceed a certain amount, then Revenue Canada will certify that these pension benefits can be funded.

Other restrictions include:

- If an owner-manager establishes a DRPP in 1991 and benefits accrue in that year, no RRSP contribution is allowed in the year he or she joins the plan.
- Disability and reduced service benefit funding is restricted.
- Retirement is assumed to be at age 65, so early retirement benefits cannot be funded.
- Surviving spouse benefits are limited to 66 2/3 per cent of the member's pension that was being received at the time of death.
- No benefit guarantees are allowed if the surviving spouse option is chosen.
- Guarantee period is limited to 15 years.
- No funding of discretionary pension increases, such as ad hoc cost of living increases, is allowed; these must be part of the benefits under the plan.

Generally, the funding for the benefit to be paid out of the DRPP will be the responsibility of the corporation. There is provision for employee contributions; however, note that most provincial pension standards legislation and the proposed tax rules require that the employer fund at least one-half of the benefits to be paid. The main deciding factor in whether to make employee contributions will be the rate of tax levied on corporate income versus the owner-manager's marginal rate of tax. Ideally, the corporation will be one that must be paying bonuses to reduce its active business income to $200,000 or lower, in order to avoid the high corporate rate of tax.

Once the retirement benefits have been calculated, it is necessary to calculate the deductible contributions presently required to fund the benefits. In draft regulations that were released in July, 1991, the Department of Finance made this process relatively easy by dictating the method and actuarial assumptions that had to be used when computing the required contributions. These rules impose a maximum contribution limit that is primarily based on the age of the DRPP member.

---

**Caution!** Defined benefit RPPs may not come cheaply. Costs might run as high as several thousand dollars to set one up. Annual costs will be several hundred dollars, and the actuarial valuation report, which is required every three years, may be as high as $1,000. RRSPs, on the other hand, cost next to nothing to establish and maintain.

---

## DEFINED CONTRIBUTION RPPs

Under a defined contribution plan, the employer and, depending on the terms of the plan, perhaps the employee, contribute according to a formula each year. At retirement, the best pension possible is purchased with the accumulated funds. The plans are very similar to RRSPs, except they are more expensive to start up and maintain, although cheaper than a defined benefit RPP. Contribution limits are almost the same as RRSPs, except the RRSP maximum lags behind the defined contribution RPP maximum by one year. In 1991, a maximum of $12,500 can be contributed to a defined contribution plan. This rises to $15,500 in 1994 and is indexed in following years. Remember that the RRSP limit hits $15,500 in 1995 and is then indexed.

Defined contribution plans have their place in an owner-manager's plans in some circumstances.

## RRSP OR DESIGNATED RPP – THAT IS THE QUESTION

As noted above, the general rule of thumb for choosing between an RRSP and a DRPP is straightforward, if maximizing the tax deferral is paramount: RRSP in your early years, DRPP as you get closer to retirement, with the cross-over occurring within a few years of your mid-forties. For individual owner-managers, there are no hard and fast rules. Let's look at the various factors that will influence your choice.

### SIZE OF THE TAX DEFERRAL

Contributions to both plans depend on your earned income, which we'll assume is exclusively salary. RRSP contributions depend on current income (actually income in the immediately preceding year) and DRPP contributions depend on future income projected from current levels. A comparison of the DRPP contributions with the RRSP contributions is provided below for owner-managers of various ages who join a DRPP in 1991. The calculations reflect the following broad assumptions:

- The owner-manager is a male.
- The maximum pension benefit is to be accrued in each year of service (currently $1,722, indexed after 1994).
- The owner-manager will provide services until he turns age 65, at which time he will retire.
- The benefits will be indexed to increases in the CPI minus 1 per cent.
- The retirement benefits will be guaranteed for at least five years.
- After the death of the owner-manager, his widow will receive survivor's benefits calculated at 66 2/3 per cent of the annual benefits received by the owner-manager immediately before his death. Survivor's benefits will also be increased annually for increases in the CPI.
- The owner-manager will receive salary in excess of $86,000 in each of 1990 and 1991.

| Age | Allowable RRSP Contribution | Allowable DRPP Contribution |
| --- | --- | --- |
| 30 | $11,500 | $11,464 |
| 35 | 11,500 | 12,593 |
| 40 | 11,500 | 13,832 |
| 45 | 11,500 | 15,394 |
| 50 | 11,500 | 16,690 |
| 55 | 11,500 | 18,333 |
| 60 | 11,500 | 20,138 |
| 65 | 11,500 | 25,975 |

More can be contributed to the DRPP at, for instance, age 60 than to the RRSP alone for the simple reason that there are only a few years available to accumulate the necessary funds to buy the promised pension benefits at age 65. When the plan has 40 or more years to generate the funding, smaller amounts need be contributed. Note that with the DRPP, owner-managers can contribute $1,000 to an RRSP each year.

### Cost of RRSPs vs. DRPPs

There is almost no cost to opening and maintaining an RRSP. Self-administered plans typically charge $100 annual administration fees, which are deductible for tax purposes if paid outside the plan.

DRPPs are costly in comparison. Establishing even the simplest plan will cost several thousand dollars and maintaining it each year could cost several hundred dollars annually. All these costs are tax deductible if paid by the corporation.

## CREDITOR PROTECTION

Funds vested in a DRPP are not accessible to creditors of the corporation or the owner-manager. The pension benefits can be attached by creditors, but not until they are actually paid out of the plan.

Depending on the province in which you reside, RRSPs may not be protected from your personal creditors. The only general exception occurs if you have a plan that is invested in a life insurance policy (or with a trust company in Quebec). Since an RRSP is a personal asset, creditors of the corporation do not have access to the funds.

## INTEREST EXPENSE

Interest on money borrowed after November 11, 1981, to make an RRSP contribution is not deductible for tax purposes, but it is specifically allowed as a deduction for employers borrowing to make RPP contributions. Therefore, since most DRPPs will be designed to require the employer to make most, if not all, contributions, any related interest expense should be tax-deductible.

However, employers can borrow to pay a salary to the owner-manager. The resulting interest expense would be deductible, giving the owner-manager an indirect interest deduction for an RRSP contribution.

## INVESTMENTS

Both plans can invest in essentially the same types of securities and both are prohibited from investing directly or indirectly in your business. However, under certain conditions, you can arrange for your RRSP to hold the mortgage on your home. You could then use the proceeds from the mortgage to invest in your business. If the transaction is structured properly, the mortgage interest should be deductible.

When properly structured, the DRPP can allow the owner-manager to dictate the investment policy of the plan. Consideration will have to be given to tax regulations and the appropriate provincial pension legislation. The result is that the owner-manager can treat the pension plan in the same manner as he would a self-administered RRSP.

Note that if the investment performance of the DRPP is not up to expectations, a deficiency will arise and the corporation will be required to fund the deficit so that the benefits promised on retirement can be paid. Such funding is a deductible expense to the corporation. Contrast that with a self-administered RRSP that suffers from poor performance. No additional funding is permitted, so the annuitant ends up with the reduced capital and reduced retirement income at the time he begins drawing upon it.

## ALTERNATIVE MINIMUM TAX

When an individual makes a deductible contribution to an RRSP or RPP, such contributions will be added back to income for purposes of computing any alternative minimum tax (AMT) liability. The new higher contribution levels may create or increase an AMT liability. With a DRPP, the employer company will make most if not all the contributions on behalf of the owner-manager. Therefore, the AMT will not be a problem, at least as far as pension contributions go.

## FLEXIBILITY

Under the current rules, you c in withdraw funds from an RRSP at any time (except for locked-in plans), as long as you are prepared to pay the tax in the year of withdrawal. The amount withdrawn is simply added to your income, which means tax could be payable on the entire amount at the top marginal rate in your province.

Note that the financial institution will be required to withhold income tax on an RRSP withdrawal at prescribed amounts. You will still have to report the full amount paid out of the RRSP but you can claim a credit for the taxes withheld and remitted to Revenue Canada on your behalf.

The funds in the DRPP are locked in and can be used only to provide pension benefits. The DRPP can provide for a pension before age 65 (although funding levels must be based on retirement at age 65) and it can also provide for disability benefits. You can also transfer a lump sum from the DRPP to an RRSP within certain limits, but these amounts may become locked in, depending on the province in which you reside, and can be used only to provide a lifetime annuity.

---

**Timely Tip.** The terms of a DRPP can be amended within the constraints of the tax rules and regulations. For example, you might want to improve the retirement benefits at some point. Generally, additional contributions for prior years' service after 1989 would be allowed to fund any such amendments, if you had not made maximum RRSP contributions in those past years.

---

If your company is sold, you have several choices of what to do with your DRPP. One of the easiest might simply be to transfer the plan, lock, stock and barrel, to another corporation that you own. You can also transfer amounts in the plan to another DRPP in most cases and then wind up the original plan. As well, amounts can be transferred to an RRSP, but limits do apply. If your DRPP is overfunded, for example, the excess cannot be transferred to the RRSP, except to the extent of the

$8,000 RRSP overcontribution limit. You would have to receive this overfunding directly, in which case it would become taxable.

## CONTRIBUTIONS

Contributions, as recommended by the plan's actuary, must be made to the DRPP unless the plan is overfunded and is in a surplus position. Payments cannot be simply deferred and made up later. Although maximizing contributions will likely be your objective, this may not always be the best course for your business to steer each year. Leaving the business chronically underfunded while making maximum contributions to your DRPP may be toxic to everybody's financial health in the longer run.

Contributions to RRSPs are entirely voluntary. If you or the corporation don't have the funds, simply wait until you do. The new carry-forward rule for RRSP contributions gives you even more flexibility. However, to enjoy the benefits of the carry forward, you must have received earned income in each year. In most cases, it will be worthwhile receiving a salary to generate this earned income and then loaning the funds back to the corporation to top up its funding requirements. You can then make an RRSP contribution in respect of this earned income any time over the eligible carry-forward period.

---

**Caution!** To some owner-managers, having this much flexibility may actually pose a hazard. Good intentions don't always lead to good deeds, such as ensuring you make that RRSP catch-up contribution. With the DRPP, the corporation has no choice but to make the contribution each year.

---

## BENEFITS

It is impossible to compare the size of potential benefits from an RRSP and DRPP. If the earnings in the RRSP are spectacular, you should have little trouble arranging for a retirement income far more attractive than that promised in the DRPP. If the earnings are less than average, the DRPP may provide the better pension, although your corporation must still provide the funding for the pension.

If your DRPP becomes underfunded because of abnormally low investment earnings, the plan's actuary will recommend that sufficient contributions be made to correct the underfunding problem, all of which will be deductible to the corporation. No such extra contributions are allowed with an RRSP. Of course, it's your corporation that is making up for the funding with your money.

## SPOUSE NOT COVERED BY PENSION PLAN

If your spouse is not employed by the corporation, he or she cannot be a member of the DRPP. However, if you choose to use an RRSP, you can make spousal contributions to a plan of which your spouse is the annuitant. These contributions belong to your spouse irrevocably and are included in his or her income when funds are eventually paid out after retirement. If your spouse is likely to have little retirement income, making spousal RRSP contributions may result in a smaller family tax bill during your retirement years.

## ESTATE CONSIDERATIONS

The pension that can be paid from a DRPP is the same that can be paid from any RPP. However, with a DRPP, funding is limited to providing only a base lifetime pension with a 66 2/3 per cent survivor benefit, or if you have no spouse at retirement, a regular pension with a single life guaranteed for 15 years.

Still, the DRPP should be compared with an RRSP that is converted to a RRIF on retirement. If you have plenty of income during your retirement without depending on a DRPP or RRSP, you can arrange to receive minimum RRIF payments, which would be much lower than payments received from a DRPP. If your spouse survives you, he or she can become the annuitant of your RRIF on a tax-free basis. Otherwise, all amounts remaining in the RRIF go to your estate after the payment of tax upon your death.

Contrast this with the DRPP that provides for a guarantee of, say, five years. If the owner-manager retires and dies shortly thereafter, the payments he or she would have received will continue to be paid to his or her named beneficiary until the expiry of the five-year period, and then all payments cease. The total of the retirement benefits paid in a period under a benefit guarantee must not exceed the retirement benefits that would have been paid to the member in the period had the owner-manager lived. The plan can also provide that in the event of death occurring after the guarantee period, survivor's benefits can be paid to his or her spouse (up to 66 2/3 per cent that the member would have received), or a lump sum equivalent of the commuted value of the owner-manager's pension could be paid to the surviving spouse.

Bear in mind, however, that there may be more effective ways to provide for your heirs than through a DRPP or RRSP (see Chapter 12). Generally, you should plan on using your DRPP or RRSP benefits during your retirement years.

## OVERFUNDING

Strictly speaking, RRSPs cannot become overfunded. In fact, you are permitted to overcontribute up to a cumulative maximum of $8,000 without penalty, but no tax deduction is allowed. If the earnings history in the plan exceeds your expectations, you receive a better retirement income. A DRPP can become overfunded if wise investment choices have been made. Generally, up to 20 per cent overfunding is allowed. If this overfunding is in the plan at retirement, it may be possible for the amount to be withdrawn over time, which will then provide additional retirement income.

Once the 20 per cent level is exceeded, further contributions must be halted until the overfunding gets below the 20 per cent level, or the excess must be returned to the employer corporation. If your company is forced to take a contribution holiday, you will still be considered to be earning benefits from the plan in those particular years. Thus, your ability to make RRSP contributions in those years will not be improved. Consideration will have to be given to the appropriate provincial pension standards legislation that deals with the issue of pension surplus, as well as the exact wording of the plan document.

Depending on your point of view, an overfunded plan may be looked on as one of the potential advantages of DRPPs. Or you may regret the inability to shelter income during the years when the contribution holiday is in effect.

## CONCLUSIONS
If, after considering the above points, you still feel that the general rule of thumb may apply, the next step is to look at the potential funding levels a DRPP would require, given your age. Your professional advisor should be able to come up with some numbers on which you can base your decision.

## EMPLOYEES AND FAMILY MEMBERS
The psychology of employees has changed drastically in the last two or three decades. "Lifers" have gone the way of the dodo bird and many senior employees look suspiciously at any benefit that resembles the proverbial golden handcuffs. That's not to say such benefits still don't encourage employee loyalty and longevity. But there is every possibility that you will encourage just as much loyalty by providing employees with the ultimate in flexibility.

Pension plans, whether defined benefit or defined contribution, have always been considered advantageous to both employer and employee. Employer contributions might not vest for two years (depending on the province), so the employer doesn't get burned by job hoppers. Yet once those benefits are vested, the employee might look forward to the employer funding most if not all the benefits in the plan. And with defined benefit plans, the employee has the luxury of knowing just what his or her pension will amount to and of knowing that the employer is ultimately responsible for funding that pension.

On the other hand, providing the employee at all times with sufficient salary to make maximum RRSP contributions gives the employee maximum flexibility over his or her retirement funding and pension benefits. Of course, the onus is now on the employee to actually make the contributions, obtain reasonable investment returns, and arrange for the best possible pension.

Cost to the corporation will probably be the deciding factor when choosing which route to take. With an RRSP or defined contribution plan, you know almost exactly what the corporation's pension funding liability will be each year. This kind of certainty should make it easier to set prices and deal with creditors.

With a defined benefit plan, the corporation's costs will be quite low if the average age of employees is low, and correspondingly higher as the average age of your employees rises. If all members happen to be age 58, you'll pay considerably more for the defined benefit RPP than the other two money purchase plans. On the other hand, if they are all 28, you may pay considerably less.

There is also the potential of reduced funding with a defined benefit plan if investment earnings in the plan are above average. The corporation need only fund the plan sufficiently to pay the promised pension benefits. If the plan is overfunded, no contributions need be made. Again, make sure you give consideration to the appropriate rules regarding surplus contained in your provincial pension legislation.

The costs of establishing and maintaining an RPP will likely not increase if a few more members are added to the plan, which means that the costs of the plan may then not fall entirely on the shoulders of your company. For the owner-manager, this may have the effect of making an RPP competitive with an RRSP one or two years earlier than would otherwise be the case.

## YOUR BUSINESS AS YOUR PENSION PLAN

Many owner-managers wonder why they should even bother contributing to an RRSP or DRPP, when they could be investing those funds in their business. If a small business is successful, 20 per cent or 30 per cent returns on invested capital certainly are not uncommon. However, a return of this magnitude in a pension plan or RRSP would be unusual, even over the relatively short term.

---

**Timely Tip.** If your business is profitable, the company shouldn't have any trouble borrowing when financing is required. And this means that the amount you invest in the company by not contributing to an RRSP or DRPP simply replaces borrowed funds. Why not have your cake and eat it too – borrow for the company and contribute to your pension plan.

---

Generally, you will be better off if your return in the RRSP or DRPP is higher than the corporation's after-tax cost of borrowing. Historically, one might expect the two rates to be very close, if the company is claiming the deduction for the interest expense against small business income. If the deduction is taken against regular corporate income, the RRSP or DRPP wins hands down.

Not every owner-manager has the luxury of contributing to a pension plan or RRSP, as well as always having adequate financing for the business each and every year. And when push comes to shove, the business usually wins out; the pension or RRSP contributions are not made. This brings us to our second general rule of thumb. Don't worry – a successful business almost always will, in any given year, generate more retirement income than any statutory plan. As well, many owner-managers are more comfortable investing in themselves and what they know best, rather than in the usual pension investments. This kind of seat of your pants investing theory shouldn't be ignored when deciding how to prepare for the future.

## KEY EMPLOYEES

It's probably safe to say that when you see something that's good for you, your employees will likely see the same thing as good for them. They will probably be more interested in RRSPs if they are relatively young and in defined benefit RPPs if they are older. From the employer's point of view, you know that this could prove to be more expensive than offering, say, a defined benefit RPP to everyone. Providing a 30-year-old employee with sufficient income to make a maximum RRSP contribution will cost considerably more than making the appropriate contribution to a defined benefit RPP, even one with extremely generous benefits.

But keeping key employees is a problem every small business owner must come to grips with. Offering them a combination of retirement plans similar to that which you've chosen may be a key element. Stock option purchase plans may be another.

## EMPLOYEE STOCK OPTIONS – CCPCs

Employees of CCPCs who are granted stock options receive special treatment, compared to employees of public companies. (In Quebec, employees of public companies may receive the same special treatment as employees of CCPCs.) To qualify, the following conditions must be met:

- The employer corporation must be a CCPC, and the stock must be issued by either the employer corporation or a CCPC that doesn't deal at arm's length with the employer (usually they are the same company).
- The employee is dealing at arm's length with the corporation immediately after the option is granted and continues to be at arm's length after the option is exercised. This excludes employees who are owner-managers, or their families.
- The employee has not disposed of the shares within two years of acquiring them (except in the case of death), or the exercise price of the option was not greater than the fair market value of the company's shares at the time the option is granted.

If these conditions are met, a taxable benefit from employment, equal to 75 per cent of the difference between the exercise price of the shares and the fair market value of the shares when the option was exercised, will arise in the year the shares are actually sold by the employee.

For example, assume that:

- the option price is $4 a share (this is also the fair market value of the shares at the time the option is granted);
- the fair market value is $12 a share when the option is exercised, and
- a subsequent sale of the shares produces proceeds of $16 a share.

A taxable benefit of $8 ($12 minus $4) per share must be included in the employee's income in the year the shares are sold for $16. However, if the shares have been owned by the employee for at least two years prior to the sale, a deduction equal to one-quarter of the benefit ($2) is allowed in arriving at taxable income, even if the exercise price ($4) had been less than the fair market value at the time the option was granted. The remaining $4 gain ($16 minus $12) is a capital gain, three-quarters of which is included in income. This portion of the gain is eligible for the employee's $100,000 lifetime capital gains exemption, and possibly the $400,000 small business capital gains exemption (see Chapter 13). The taxable benefit portion of the gain – $6 ($8 minus $2) – is not eligible for the exemption.

Chances are that your key employees will want some type of buy-sell agreement if they are going to participate in a stock option program. Minority interest shares in small businesses are not readily marketable. Such a buy-sell agreement would be entered into by the new shareholders of the corporation with the controlling shareholder or the corporation. Under the agreement, a shareholder who leaves employment with the company, or who dies, is guaranteed that his or her shares will be purchased by the controlling shareholder or the corporation itself. The purchase price is pre-determined in the agreement, or is determined by a formula outlined in the agreement.

# 10/MID-LIFE CRISIS: AN EMBARRASSMENT OF RICHES

You now have been in business for a few years and have met with much more success than setbacks. Success has meant accumulating a little capital and earning more investment income. But that means paying more tax, sometimes on income you don't even need right now. In this chapter, we'll recap our discussions so far on investment income and delve a little further into ways to defer and in some cases even eliminate tax.

## FINDING A PLACE FOR YOUR INVESTMENT INCOME

With recent changes in the tax law, investment income has proved to be a bit of a nuisance in the small business planning equation – not the money or securities themselves, of course, just the problem of fitting them into a coherent, integrated planning package that satisfies the typical owner-manager's needs throughout his business and personal life.

As you will recall from Chapter 5, there is a slight bias to earning investment income (interest, dividends, rents, etc.) personally, rather than flowing it through a corporation. Similarly, you are slightly better off realizing capital gains personally, and much better off if you have not yet used up your $100,000 lifetime capital gains exemption.

However, as we saw in Chapter 6, there are deferral opportunities if investment income is earned and retained in a corporation rather than earned personally. Using the numbers developed in Chapter 5, the corporate tax rate on interest, for instance, is 43.84 per cent while the personal rate for an individual in the top tax bracket in 1991 is 47.85 per cent (51.11 per cent in Quebec). The corporate rate on portfolio dividends is 25 per cent, while the personal rate is 32.31 per cent (36.84 per cent in Quebec).

Still there are drawbacks. The refundable dividend tax generated upon earning the investment income may not be fully recovered when a dividend is paid by the corporation. However, if the income is earned in your operating company (Opco), you may be able to trigger a refund of all this tax as you distribute the business earnings to yourself and other shareholders in the form of dividends.

But this introduces another major problem. To qualify for the enhanced $400,000 small business capital gains exemption, Opco must be a qualifying small business corporation (QSBC). This means that at least 90 per cent of its assets must be employed in an active business. Securities held to earn investment income don't qualify as business assets.

As we discovered in Chapter 7, investment income doesn't lend itself readily to very many income splitting strategies with family members, although the attribution rules don't apply if family members are involved in the share ownership of a QSBC; otherwise they do. Until you and your spouse have used the $400,000 special exemption, there may be little point in tainting Opco just to save a few income splitting tax dollars.

## OPCO AND INVESTCO

On the assumption that you want Opco to remain a QSBC, but you want to take advantage of the opportunities to defer tax on investment income, it will be necessary to form another company to operate as the investment holding company (Investco). Also, assuming that you want to split income with your spouse and children, it makes sense to arrange the shareholdings so that your family participates in the income earned in Opco while you hold the shares of the investment company. As long as Opco qualifies as a small business corporation, there will be no attribution of Opco income distributed to family members, assuming that they have acquired Opco shares with their own funds and you have followed the advice offered in Chapter 7.

To achieve these objectives, you might take the following steps:

1. Incorporate Investco. You would hold the common shares. Family members could also own shares, but the attribution rules will be triggered if your spouse or a child owns at least 10 per cent of the shares in any class.

2. Transfer the investment assets from Opco to Investco and issue preferred shares or debt of Investco to Opco which reflects the fair market value of the assets transferred. This can generally be done on a tax-deferred basis as long as the amount of debt taken back does not exceed the tax cost of the investments transferred.

3. Any time after Investco is incorporated, you can transfer personally held investments to the corporation in exchange for consideration, either shares or debt, having a value equal to the value of the investments transferred. A transfer price can be elected for tax purposes at any value between cost and fair market value. But remember that, if you want the transfer to take place on a tax-deferred basis, the amount of debt taken back cannot exceed the tax cost of the investments transferred into Investco.

4. Reorganize Opco. You would convert your common shares to

voting preferred shares (this allows you to retain control) that reflect the current fair market value of the company. Common shares, perhaps of different classes, would be issued to your spouse and children. If desired, you could also continue to participate in the future growth in value and earnings of Opco by taking some new common shares yourself.

5. Transfer your preferred shares in Opco to Investco and take back additional preferred shares or debt in Investco. Here again you can elect to fix the sale price that will be taken into account for tax purposes at any amount between the cost and the fair market value of the Opco preferred shares. However, remember that the amount of debt issued to you by Investco cannot exceed the tax cost of the Opco preferred shares if the transfer is to be fully tax-deferred.

This basic structure offers a number of advantages:

- Opco earnings can be distributed as dividends to family members who are shareholders without the attribution rules applying.
- Opco earnings can be distributed to Investco when dividends are paid on the preferred shares that Investco now owns. No Part IV tax is payable by Investco on these dividends, except to the extent that Opco was entitled to a refund of tax on the payment of the dividend; so the full after-tax amount remains available for investment.
- After-tax investment income can be deferred in Investco without tainting the status of Opco. Even though the two corporations are associated for tax purposes, Opco remains a QSBC, even though Investco is not.
- On the other hand, dividends can be distributed from either Opco or Investco if the income is necessary to reduce your cumulative net investment losses (CNILs) so that you can make a claim under your capital gains exemption.
- If it is likely that you'll be subject to the alternative minimum tax (AMT) because of the nature of income you earn on tax-shelter investments, these can be rolled over into Investco, which should solve your AMT problem.
- Personal funds can be loaned to either corporation for investment purposes or to reinvest in the active business.
- When your Opco preferred shares are transferred to Investco, you can trigger the $400,000 small business capital gains exemption (see comments below under "Triggering the $400,000 Exemption").
- If the family members own all the common shares in Opco, they now participate in any future increase in value of Opco. The value of your holdings is frozen based on the value ascribed to the preferred shares. However, as mentioned earlier, you may wish to continue to hold some common shares so that you too can participate to some extent in the future increase in value. We'll look at this type of asset freeze further in Chapter 12.

- You might consider selling assets with accrued gains to Investco. This disposition will trigger gains that will be eligible for your $100,000 capital gains exemption. As we mentioned earlier, there is no guarantee this tax break will be around forever.

One of the drawbacks to earning investment income in your company is that corporations are not entitled to the $100,000 lifetime capital gains exemption. When the corporation realizes a gain, the after-tax proceeds are distributed to shareholders in the form of taxable dividends and capital dividends, or perhaps as salary and capital dividends to the owner-manager. The amounts lose their identity as capital gains. An individual must realize capital gains personally to qualify for the tax saving from the capital gains exemption. If you and your family members have already maximized your use of the exemption, this will not be a concern.

---

**Timely Tip.** If you still have all or a portion of the capital gains exemption left, you should consider retaining sufficient assets to make use of it eventually. You also might consider using the exemption sooner rather than later. The exemption presents an inviting target to a government that is running a large deficit and is constantly on the lookout for revenue-generating measures.

---

There is one slight problem with using Investco to earn interest or other types of investment income: you may end up with refundable dividend tax in the corporation that you cannot recover because the integration mechanism is not perfect. Recalling the numbers from the flow-through example in Chapter 3, there was $12.80 of refundable dividend tax still on hand in the corporation after paying out the maximum dividend from $1,000 of interest income earned. It will be difficult to get this final bit of refundable tax out of Investco, unless the company earns active business income of some type. There is no point in paying excess dividends, since they would just come out of capital that can be returned to you tax-free.

---

**Timely Tip.** You can probably solve the problem of non-recoverable refundable tax by transferring sufficient business assets to Investco from Opco and leasing them back to Opco at market rates. The income will qualify as active business income, and any dividends paid out of this income will use up any refundable dividend tax on hand.

---

## TRIGGERING THE $400,000 EXEMPTION

One of the most critical advantages of establishing Investco is your ability to use the $400,000 small business capital gains exemption. When you convert your common shares of Opco to preferred shares, ordinarily you will do this at cost. Chances are that you were issued those common shares for a nominal value, say, $1.

When you transfer your Opco shares to Investco, you have the option of electing a value for the transfer anywhere between your cost and fair market value. If you elect to transfer them at, say, $400,001, you must recognize the resulting gain of $400,000 ($400,001 minus nominal cost of $1) in your personal tax return. However, since Opco qualifies as an SBC, you are entitled to claim the $400,000 exemption.

We are assuming here that Opco has been a QSBC at all times during the preceding 24 months, which means that at least 50 per cent of its assets have been devoted to an active business, and at the time the shares are transferred, at least 90 per cent of Opco's assets are used in an active business. If the investment assets that you transferred to Investco would have disqualified Opco, you will have to wait 24 months before you can trigger the $400,000 exemption. During this 24-month period, Opco must meet the 50 per cent test at all times.

If your spouse was also a shareholder of Opco since inception, he or she should be able to follow in your footsteps, that is, convert Opco common shares to preferred, roll over those shares to Investco, and claim his or her own $400,000 exemption. This also solves any attribution problem that you might have with Investco. Your spouse's investment in Investco would now total $400,000, and any earnings distributed to him or her that relate to that $400,000 will not be attributed to you. As well, your spouse could establish his or her own Investco and roll over his or her shares in Opco to the new company.

---

**Caution!** Note that if your spouse has little income other than this gain, he or she could have a serious minimum tax problem. It is essential that you review all the potential implications of the transaction, including the possible impact on your alternative minimum tax position, with your professional advisor to ensure that the capital gains exemption does indeed result in tax-free income.

---

As you can appreciate, there is no immediate monetary advantage to claiming the exemption now. No cash changes hands and your pockets are no heavier after the transactions. However, the cost base of the shares in Opco that Investco owns have been stepped up by $400,000. If they are sold in the future or transferred to your children, this is the cost base that will be used to determine any capital gains, not the nominal value of $1.

---

**Caution!** The cost base of the preferred shares issued to you by Investco on the transfer of the Opco shares will also generally reflect the $400,000 gain triggered on the transaction. However, if these shares are transferred by you (or by any other person with whom you do not deal at arm's length) at any time in the future to a corporation in a non-arm's length transaction, the $400,000 addition to the cost base may not be recognized. If this were to happen, the tax consequences could be disastrous. Make sure that you thoroughly investigate the potential tax impact before you dispose of the preferred shares of Investco to any corporation or any other person with whom you do not deal at arm's length.

---

### TO DEFER OR NOT TO DEFER
Based on 1991 tax rates, there is a slight disadvantage in every province to flowing investment income (other than dividends) through a corporation, rather than earning it personally. However, the corporate tax rate on investment income is lower than the top personal tax rate, which sets up deferral opportunities. The question is, does the small tax cost of flowing income through the corporation offset the tax deferral benefits. There is no pat answer. Much will depend upon how long the investment income is left to accumulate in the corporation; the longer the deferral period, the greater the deferral benefit.

#### INTEREST INCOME
The top marginal tax rate on interest flowed through a corporation in 1991 is 49.31 per cent. We'll assume that, after the after-tax interest income is distributed as a dividend, the small amount of refundable tax remaining ($1.28 for every $100 of interest income) cannot be recovered. If it could, the tax rate would drop to 48.44 per cent. The corporate tax rate on interest is 43.84 per cent.

Let's look ahead ten years. Assume that interest of $100 is earned and reinvested, compounding at an annual rate (before tax) of 10 per cent. If you earn the interest personally, you will accumulate $86.70 at the end of ten years.

If the interest is earned by the corporation, initially there will be $56.16 left after paying corporate tax. This grows to $96.99 after ten years. A dividend, including refundable tax, of $129.32 is then distributed. After paying tax of $41.78, you will be left with $87.54. Therefore, in this example, the net benefit of deferring tax on interest income by investing through a corporation amounts to 84 cents for every $100 of interest earned over a ten-year period.

Differences in provincial tax rates could tip the balance in favour of earning the income personally, no matter how long the deferral period.

### PORTFOLIO DIVIDENDS

In the case of portfolio dividends, the deferral advantage is more pronounced. The top personal tax rates on Canadian dividends are between 32 per cent and 37 per cent. The corporate rate on portfolio dividends is 25 per cent, which is fully refundable when dividends are flowed through to individual shareholders.

Let's look at a ten-year holding period again for $100 of portfolio dividends received. All after-tax amounts earn interest at 10 per cent annually.

If the dividend is left in the corporation, $75 is available to invest. This grows to $129.53 in ten years. A dividend, including refundable tax, of $172.70 is then distributed. After paying tax of $55.80, you would be left with $116.90.

If you receive the dividend personally, only $67.69 is left to invest after you pay tax. This grows to $112.54 in ten years. The net deferral benefit over ten years, therefore, amounts to $4.36 for every $100 of dividends.

For capital gains, using the same assumptions, the net deferral benefit over ten years is marginal – only about 47 cents for every $100 of capital gain realized.

### SUMMING UP

The chart below summarizes the advantages for the three types of investment income, assuming a ten-year holding period.

### After-tax Accumulation on $100 of Investment Income Compounded at 10% over 10 Years

|  | Held Personally | Held By Corporation |
|---|---|---|
| Interest | $ 86.70 | $ 87.54 |
| Dividends | 112.54 | 116.90 |
| Capital Gains | 106.59 | 107.06 |

# 11/Expanding Successfully

If your business has been a success to this point, is there any reason why you shouldn't consider expanding? Certainly not, but plan carefully, be ready to work harder than ever and look forward to continued success and prosperity.

But don't assume that tomorrow will be much the same as yesterday. "If it was that easy getting sales up to $1 million, how much harder can it be to reach $2 million or even $5 million?" What some owner-managers fail to appreciate is that doubling or tripling sales often introduces a whole new range of complications with which they've never had to deal. However, if your business has been built on a solid foundation and you have concentrated on the fundamentals, you need not fear expanding your horizons.

Growing your business internally is a long and challenging process. Gaining increased market share, developing new products and product lines, expanding sales and distribution networks, and building increased production or service capacity are all activities that you will aggressively pursue day in and day out as you expand your business. With growth, the business becomes much more complex and requires a more sophisticated management and administrative infrastructure to operate effectively. All of this takes time and money.

As your business expands, you will no longer be able to "do it all by yourself". You will need the help of others with specialized skills and you will need investment capital.

For most small businesses, the best, and sometimes the only, source of investment capital is the earnings of the business that are ploughed back to finance expansion. Your banker and other sources of debt financing can help. But beware of excessive leverage. The bankruptcy courts are littered with tragic tales of promising businesses that tried to grow too fast. In overextending themselves, they failed to build a strong foundation to support the desired growth and expansion.

Carefully planned, controlled growth is the key to success. Gradually building the business from within, while following a focused, long-range plan, is fundamentally a sound strategy.

However, in many cases, a major expansion means some basic restructuring of your company. Frequently, your growth objectives can be achieved more effectively or can be achieved only through acquiring or merging with another business. In this chapter, we look at some of the structural issues and tax implications that you should carefully consider as you head down the expansion trail.

## BUYING A BUSINESS

The reasons you might consider the purchase of an established business are many and varied. For example, the target business may be:

- an important supplier that you want to ensure survives for the long term;
- a key customer with a foothold in a new and expanding market;
- the manufacturer or distributor of a complementary product or product line;
- a company with modern equipment and production capacity that you need in order to expand, or
- a competitor challenging your business in key markets.

Buying an established business is a bit like buying a used car. "Caveat emptor", buyer beware, is a sound warning to heed when you enter into negotiations to buy a business. You can run a serious risk of inheriting somebody else's problems, of assuming undisclosed liabilities, or of failing to realize that the business is otherwise in trouble. Make sure you "kick the tires"; perform sufficient due diligence tests so that you know exactly what assets you are buying and what liabilities you are assuming. Just as important, know what assets you are not buying and what liabilities you are not assuming.

Sound legal counsel is essential in drawing up the agreements of purchase and sale. Take the time to discuss thoroughly your objectives and the details of the business deal with your legal advisor. He or she will then be in a much better position to draw up the legal documentation that truly reflects your desires and protects your interests.

## THE TARGET

Once you have identified your target, perhaps the toughest decision you have to make is how much to pay for the acquisition. The basic question is what value will the target business add to your present operations. What impact will the acquisition have on your future earnings? It is important to assess the expected increase in *sustainable* earnings over a prolonged period of time.

For example, let's assume that you expect your business to generate an annual return on invested capital of 20 per cent. If you project that the acquisition will result in an increase in your average annual earnings of

$200,000, you should be able to pay up to $1 million for the business and achieve your required rate of return.

Projecting the sustainable future earnings from any target business is an extremely difficult task. You know how tough it is to forecast future earnings from your present business that you know so well. The difficulties compound when you are dealing with a business with which you are not as familiar and one that will undergo a dramatic, and perhaps traumatic, change upon your acquisition of control. You are well advised to engage the services of a professional business valuator to help guide you through the process of determining a price range for your prospective acquisition. The price you actually pay will, of course, be set by negotiation between you and the vendor.

## THE BOTTOM LINE – AFTER TAX

As you go through the process of forecasting earnings and evaluating various options for structuring the purchase of the target business, focus on the bottom line – earnings after tax. The effective tax rate that will apply to future earnings will not always be readily apparent. It will depend on factors such as whether the income after the date of acquisition will qualify for the low rate of tax on the first $200,000, the extent to which the earnings will qualify as manufacturing and processing profits eligible for a reduced rate, and the impact, if any, that the acquisition may have upon the allocation of income to the various provincial jurisdictions.

The availability of prior years' losses carried forward in the target company and the differences between the tax values and the purchase cost of the assets may also have a significant impact on the effective rate of tax applied to future earnings. The tax burden on post-acquisition earnings is not carved in stone, but may be substantially influenced by the manner in which the acquisition is carried out. Essentially, you could buy the target business by buying the shares of the target company that operates that business (the share alternative) or by buying the assets of the target business (the asset alternative).

## THE ASSET ALTERNATIVE

If your company purchases all the assets of the target business, the purchase price is specifically allocated among the assets acquired, generally as agreed by you and the vendor. Amounts allocated to inventory represent the tax cost of the inventory, which is deductible in computing income when the inventory is sold. Amounts allocated to depreciable property, such as buildings, machinery and equipment, are deductible for tax purposes over time through claiming capital cost allowance. Amounts allocated to non-depreciable capital property, such as land and shares in other companies, are not deductible, but represent the tax cost of such assets to be taken into account in calculating the capital gain or loss on any future sale of the assets.

Amounts allocated to goodwill (generally the excess of the purchase price over the fair value of all other assets acquired) are tax-deductible in part over time. Generally, 75 per cent of the amount allocated to goodwill may be amortized as a deduction in computing income at the rate of 7 per cent per annum applied on a declining balance basis.

As a general rule, when you buy the assets of the target business rather than the shares of the target company, a greater portion of the purchase price will be reflected directly in the tax cost of business assets. A large part of such costs will be deductible either immediately or over time in computing the taxable income of the acquired business.

## THE SHARE ALTERNATIVE

If your company buys the shares of the target company, rather than the assets, the purchase price quite simply becomes the cost of the shares for tax purposes. There is no adjustment to the tax values of the assets owned by the target company. Consequently, little or no tax relief is available to the purchaser for any premium reflected in the share price over the tax values of the assets of the target company. If the newly acquired subsidiary is wound up, such premium, subject to various restrictions, may be allocated to certain assets acquired by the parent company on the liquidation. But this allocation may be made only to non-depreciable capital property. It does not therefore become a factor in determining taxable income derived from the operation of the business.

Remember that a corporation is an entity, separate and distinct from its shareholders. When your company buys shares, the target company may become a wholly owned subsidiary, but it still maintains its separate existence. The taxable income of the two companies is determined separately - not on a consolidated basis. If the parent company is profitable and the subsidiary is not, the loss suffered by the subsidiary cannot be offset against the income earned by the parent.

In many instances, it will be desirable to merge the two companies after the shares of the target company have been acquired. This will more effectively combine the two business operations and avoid some of the tax problems that may arise from their continued separation. Such a merger ordinarily can be accomplished under specific amalgamation provisions of the governing company law or by liquidating the newly acquired subsidiary into its parent company. In either case, the merger generally can be achieved without adverse tax consequences.

## TARGET COMPANY LOSSES

In some cases, the company you identify as an acquisition candidate will be going through, or will have gone through, troubled times. You may be looking at a turnaround situation – a basically sound business that has suffered losses in the past because of poor management or inadequate financing. But with the management expertise in your company or a new financing package, you feel that the business can become very profitable. You also may be looking at a business just coming out of its start-up period. Significant start-up losses have been incurred but the target company has turned the corner and the future looks rosy.

Whatever the reason, frequently the target company will have incurred in prior years a substantial amount of tax losses that are available to carry forward and offset future taxable income. The amount of the prior years' tax losses and whether or not they will continue to be available to offset income after you buy the business are key issues in determining the price you may be willing to pay for the business and how the acquisition should be structured.

If your company buys the assets, the tax losses are left behind in the target company. To the extent that the sale of assets generates income in the target company, the losses will shelter that income from tax. Because of these tax savings for the vendor, you should be able to negotiate a lower price for the business assets and thus indirectly benefit from the tax losses of the target company.

If your company buys the shares, the tax losses come with the target company. But the tax law imposes severe restrictions on the utilization of losses after control of a company is acquired.

---

**Caution!** The rules restricting the deductibility of losses after an acquisition of control are extremely complex. Before taking any action, you should consult your professional tax advisor to ensure that you fully understand their impact on the proposed acquisition.

---

### STOP-LOSS RULES
Upon the acquisition of control, the target company's taxation year then in progress is deemed to end. This establishes a cut-off date for purposes of calculating the amount of the various losses of the target company that will be subject to the "stop-loss" restrictions. The income or loss of the target is calculated in the normal manner for the period up to the date control is acquired. If a loss results, it is added to other losses suffered in prior years. If income is earned, it may be offset by losses carried forward from prior years or it is taxable in the usual way.

The rules also impose restrictions on the amount of certain unrealized losses. For example, where the fair market value of an asset has declined below its tax cost, the decline in value generally will not be recognized as a loss for tax purposes until such time as the asset is sold and the loss is actually realized. For purposes of the stop-loss rules, however, the excess of the fair market value over the tax cost of each non-depreciable capital property will be treated as a realized capital loss as at the date control is acquired.

In a variety of circumstances, a taxpayer is given some discretion as to when certain deductions may be claimed in computing taxable income. Capital cost allowances, amortization of the purchased cost of goodwill and other intangibles, allowances for doubtful debts, and the write-off of R&D expenditures are examples of such discretionary deductions. Ordinarily, taxpayers claim the maximum deductions to which they are entitled. However, if claiming a deduction will only add to a loss and there is a risk that the loss may not be able to be used in the carry-over period, the taxpayer may postpone claiming these discretionary deductions. The stop-loss rules, in essence, are designed to determine the amount of the losses that will be subject to the restrictions as if the target company had claimed most discretionary deductions during its last taxation year ending on the date control is acquired.

The restrictions imposed on the carry over of losses after an acquisition of control are:

- Capital losses realized before the acquisition date cannot be carried forward to offset gains realized after that date.
- Similarly, capital losses realized after the acquisition date cannot be carried back to offset gains realized before that date.
- Non-capital (generally business) losses suffered before the acquisition date may be carried forward to offset income earned thereafter only if the business in which the loss was sustained continues to be carried on with a reasonable expectation of earning a profit, and only to the extent of the income earned from that business and any other business that deals substantially in similar products or services.
- Non-capital losses suffered after the acquisition date may be carried back to offset income earned before that date subject to these same conditions.

## USING PRE-ACQUISITION LOSSES

More often than not, you will want to make substantial changes to the business operations of the target company after you acquire control. If major surgery results in the reorganized business bearing little resemblance to the one previously carried on, the stop-loss rules may prevent the carry forward of losses suffered prior to the change of control. These rules can be very difficult to apply with certainty in particular circumstances. The tax authorities may be prepared to issue advance income tax rulings in specific cases, but they are generally reluctant to do so because so much depends on facts and circumstances that are subject to significant change.

In the majority of cases, you should be able to determine, with a reasonable level of comfort, whether the losses of the target company will survive the acquisition. But plan ahead. Address the issue before you do the deal and make sure you understand the risks involved, especially if the value placed on the tax losses is a potential deal breaker or an important factor in the negotiation of the purchase price.

### POST-ACQUISITION MERGERS

Frequently, the business presently carried on by your company will be similar to the business carried on by the target company. Prior years' losses incurred by the target company may therefore be available to offset income generated by the business carried on by your company after the acquisition. However, to accomplish the desired offset, it will generally be necessary to combine the business operations in one corporate entity. This may be achieved either by amalgamating the two companies or by liquidating the target company after your company acquires the shares. In either case, the tax losses will flow through and be available to the continuing corporation, subject to the same restrictions as were applied to the target company.

It may also be possible to cause your company to transfer all its assets and business to the target company after buying the shares, in order to combine the business operations in the target company. A transfer of the business by your company to its wholly owned subsidiary generally can be carried out on a tax-deferred basis.

If you decide to continue to operate the businesses in separate companies, perhaps to preserve limited liability or for a variety of other reasons, there may be other steps you can take to effectively shift losses from the target company so they can be absorbed by your company.

For example, your company might refinance all the existing bank debt of the target company. To do this, your company would borrow the necessary funds from the bank and invest in additional shares of the target company. These funds would then be used to pay off the target's bank loan. This transaction has the effect of shifting the tax deduction for the interest expense from the target company to your company. The resulting increase in the target company's income would be sheltered from tax by the application of its prior years' losses.

### LEVERAGED BUYOUTS

In Chapter 4, we examined a variety of financing strategies available to the owner-managed business. These same sources may provide some or all of the funds you need to purchase a target business. In addition, the target itself is often an important element in the financing package.

Leveraged buyout techniques, that is, using the target company's asset base and earnings stream to support and service debt incurred to purchase the business, became all the rage during the merger mania of the 1980s. But the spectacular failures of some of the largest takeovers in North American history are powerful object lessons for us all on the dangers of excessive leverage. Even the strongest businesses can be hamstrung and doomed to failure if they are forced to operate under huge debt loads. Used in moderation and in conjunction with other more conservative financing, borrowing on the security of the target company's assets and relying on its cash flow to service the debt can be very effective in particular situations.

Where you borrow to purchase a business, you may have to restructure to place the acquisition debt in the same company as the target business. You do not want to be left in the position where interest on the acquisition debt is creating tax losses in one company, while the income from the purchased business is currently being taxed in another company.

If your company borrows to buy the assets of the target business, this will not be a problem; the acquisition debt and the newly purchased business operations will be in the same company. However, if your company borrows and buys the shares of the target, the acquisition debt will be in one company and the newly purchased business will be in another. Your company may not earn sufficient taxable income to fully absorb the interest on the acquisition debt. Tax losses incurred by your company cannot be offset against taxable income earned by its subsidiary.

Merging the two companies might solve the problem. Combining the operations through a statutory amalgamation or by liquidating the newly acquired subsidiary usually can be accomplished on a tax-deferred basis. After the merger, interest on the acquisition debt will be available to offset the income of the purchased business.

However, it is not always desirable or possible to merge. In such situations, it may be possible to cause the new subsidiary to borrow for the payment of a dividend to its parent. These funds are then used to pay down the acquisition debt. The subsidiary, in effect, refinances the acquisition debt of the parent. As a general rule, provided that the amount of the dividend does not exceed the subsidiary's accumulated earnings, interest on the money borrowed to pay the dividend should be tax-deductible.

Another approach is frequently used when it is desirable to operate the purchased business in a separate company. A new company is established to make the acquisition. For example, your company forms a new subsidiary (Purchaseco). Purchaseco borrows the required funds and buys the shares of Target. Purchaseco and Target are then merged. The acquisition debt is moved into the same company in which Target's business will be carried on, but that company is maintained as a subsidiary of your company.

---

**Caution!** Because of a decision of the Supreme Court of Canada in the *Bronfman Trust* case in 1987, the application of the tax rules governing the deductibility of interest and other financing costs are in a state of some confusion and uncertainty. The comments in this book reflect the law and administrative practices of Revenue Canada as at the end of March, 1991. However, changes are in the wind. Make sure to check with your professional advisor before committing to any financing arrangement for the acquisition of a business.

---

## TWO TO TANGO

The price you ultimately agree to pay for a target business will be determined by the fine art of negotiation. Be prepared. Understanding your own position and conducting a thorough "due diligence" investigation of the target business are only part of the homework you should do. Also, find out as much as you can about the present tax position and future plans of the vendor.

You may be able to structure the acquisition in a fashion that will substantially improve the tax position of the vendor but have little or no adverse impact on your tax position or that of your company. In Chapter 13, we look at the key issues that you should consider if and when you sell your business. Many of these same issues may face the vendor of the business you are proposing to buy. The tax benefits or costs that a vendor may realize from structuring the transaction in a certain way are not necessarily the mirror image of the tax benefits or costs that you will enjoy or bear if you accommodate the vendor's wishes. You may be successful in negotiating a lower purchase price for the shares if the vendor stands to pay less tax on the sale.

For example, assume that the value of the target company's shares is substantially represented by accumulated earnings retained by the company. On an outright sale of shares to you, the vendor may realize a large capital gain and have substantial tax to pay immediately.

However, suppose that, working with the vendor, you restructure the sale to take place in the following way. The vendor transfers his or her shares into a holding company on a tax-deferred basis. The target company then pays a stock dividend to the holding company, effectively capitalizing the full amount of its retained earnings. As a general rule, as long as the dividend does not exceed the retained earnings, the cost base of the stock dividend shares will be increased by the amount of the dividend without the holding company having to pay any tax.

Your company then purchases the target company shares from the vendor's holding company. The capital gain arising on the sale will be reduced or eliminated by the step-up in the cost of the shares resulting from the stock dividend. The vendor benefits from a substantial tax deferral. Little or no tax is payable on the sale of the shares, but tax will arise if, as, and when the vendor withdraws funds from the holding company, when the shares of the holding company are sold, or upon the death of the vendor.

Your tax position is not affected at all by structuring the purchase in this fashion.

## CHOOSING AMONG THE MANY OPTIONS

Almost every prospective business acquisition can be structured in many different ways. Comparing the alternatives and selecting the best option in your particular situation can be a daunting task. The key to making the right choice is to make sure you establish a common basis for comparison.

When you are considering the economics of the deal, you may find the best approach is to focus on the most straightforward way to structure the transaction and use that as the bench-mark to evaluate alternative structures. Let's assume that you have identified the target company and have had a formal valuation of the shares done. You are comfortable with the projections of sustainable earnings and decide that you are prepared to pay $2 million cash for all of the shares of the target. This $2-million price now becomes your reference point for assessing the various different ways you might actually conclude the transaction.

For example, suppose that you buy all the assets of the target company instead of its shares. The vendor will likely demand a higher price for the assets because the tax cost of selling the assets will probably be greater than selling the shares.

No capital gains exemption is available on the sale of assets by the target company, and it will be fully taxable on recaptured capital cost allowances and inventory profits. Three-quarters of capital gains and goodwill proceeds will also be included in the target's income and be fully taxed. As well, the vendor will be concerned about the tax payable in future when the proceeds on the sale are withdrawn from the company.

From your perspective, the tax cost of the assets acquired may be substantially increased under the asset alternative. This will reduce the tax on your company's future earnings through greater inventory deductions, capital cost allowances and the amortization of the cost of purchased goodwill. But remember, you will lose the benefit of any tax losses in the target company if you buy assets rather than shares.

If the additional cost you will have to pay for the assets is less than the present value of the additional tax write-offs that become available, it may be cheaper to buy the assets rather than the shares. However, you will find that an asset purchase is much more complex than a share deal from a legal standpoint, which will result in higher transaction costs.

This process of comparing incremental costs and benefits will be useful in identifying the best way to structure the deal from a financial perspective. However, the financial aspect is only one of a number of other business factors that will come into play in deciding how the deal finally gets done.

## OTHER INDEPENDENT SHAREHOLDERS

Expansion frequently means bringing in other significant shareholders who will play major roles in running the business. They may be key employees who decide they want a piece of the action. They may be individuals who have provided the capital you so desperately needed to expand. They may also be the former owners or key employees of businesses that you buy.

One of the most critical issues you will face when considering the purchase of an owner-managed business is the question of the ongoing involvement of the owner after you buy the business. Often, it will be extremely important to retain the former owner's services, at least for a transitional period, to ensure the continued profitability of the business. The former owner may also be a key player in the financing package you put together to buy the business. By continuing to hold shares that will be redeemed or purchased over a period of years, the former owner has a stake in the continuing success of the business and eases the financing burden on you.

You may also wish to consider involving the former owner as a shareholder in your company and not in the target company. This can usually be accomplished on a tax-deferred basis by a relatively simple share exchange.

## SHAREHOLDERS' AGREEMENT

Before you involve other shareholders in your company, you may want to lay down a few ground rules for how the company will operate, how the shareholders will be remunerated, how policies will be set and what happens when a shareholder wants to sell his or her shares. These and other matters affecting the relationship between the shareholders can be set out in a formal agreement to be signed by the parties.

We list below some of the issues that might be covered in a share-holders' agreement. Always consult your lawyer for advice when drawing up such an agreement. As well, the agreement should be reviewed periodically and updated to reflect changes in personal or financial circumstances and new government legislation.

### REMUNERATION

This provision may cover the basis on which the shareholders, family members and even employees will be paid salaries, commissions and dividends, or participate in company benefits, such as automobiles and loans.

### RESPONSIBILITIES

The agreement may define in relatively general terms each shareholder's ongoing responsibilities, including specific activities, how performance is evaluated, how inadequate performance is to be handled, how family members might participate and what limits there are on their involvement, and how the company is to be organized and administered.

### DISPUTES

Procedures for settling or arbitrating a variety of types of disputes may be outlined, including last-resort measures.

### CANADIAN-CONTROLLED PRIVATE CORPORATION (CCPC) STATUS

A provision may be inserted in the agreement to ensure that the new company retains its status as a CCPC and qualification as a small business corporation. This is important for claiming the small business deduction and remaining eligible for the $400,000 small business corporation capital gains exemption.

### PROVINCIAL FAMILY LAW

Under the family law in most provinces, a person's business investments may indirectly, through equalization claims, become subject to distribution to a spouse on the breakdown of a marriage or on death. Provisions are generally included to ensure that the distribution of one shareholder's property will not cause a serious disruption in the operation of the business.

## BUY-SELL PROVISIONS

This part of the shareholders' agreement will contain the most important provisions in succession planning. They describe how a shareholder goes about selling his or her interest in the business. They may provide the departing shareholder with a buyer and a fair market price for his or her shares. Typically, the remaining shareholders retain control of the company and determine whether there will be any new shareholders and, if so, whom.

### WHEN A SALE MUST OCCUR

The buy-sell provisions specify when a sale must occur, for example, because of death, disability, retirement, or dispute. The agreement can indicate how the shares are to be transferred to an outsider (usually only if the existing shareholders approve). It can also describe the type of transfers that are exempt from the provisions.

### HOW THE PURCHASE PRICE WILL BE PAID

Extending payment over a fixed time, such as three to five years, can reduce the cash strain on the business or other shareholders.

### WHO WILL BUY THE SHARES

The agreement usually gives existing shareholders a right of "first refusal". This means that the existing shareholders must be given the first opportunity to buy the shares of a departing shareholder before they are offered to others. The right to acquire the shares is almost always given to each remaining shareholder in a predetermined proportion based on the number of shares already owned. Alternatively, the agreement may state that the corporation can redeem the shares.

### SHARE VALUE

The agreement should specify how the value of the shares is determined (for example, by expert appraisal at the date of the sale or by a valuation performed every few years with the revised value agreed upon by the shareholders) and how tax costs and tax postponements and savings are shared.

One method of determining share value is to include a shotgun clause in the buy-sell agreement. In a dispute, a shotgun clause allows one shareholder to set the price for a transaction and allows the other shareholders to decide whether to be a buyer or a seller at that price.

The greater the number of shareholders, the more complex the situation is likely to be. This can limit the effectiveness of a buy-sell clause in the shareholders' agreement. Also, a shotgun clause can place a shareholder who might be in financial difficulty at a serious disadvantage, forcing him or her to accept an offer at a price far below the fair value of the shares.

## BUY-SELL AGREEMENT ON DEATH

A buy-sell agreement is also frequently used in estate planning to ensure, for instance, that surviving shareholders have the right or obligation to purchase the shares of a deceased shareholder. It is advantageous both for survivors, who may not want an outsider to buy into the corporation, and the family of the deceased, who might otherwise have difficulty selling the shares.

The spousal rollover rules (see Chapter 12) are not applicable to shares that are subject to a compulsory buy-sell agreement and tax would be paid by the deceased shareholder on any resulting capital gains if the lifetime capital gains exemption has been fully used. However, if the buy-sell agreement is structured in such a way that the surviving shareholder has an option to buy, and the surviving spouse has an option to sell, the shares can first pass to the spouse on a rollover basis. Any capital gain arising on the subsequent sale of the shares by the spouse would be recognized in his or her hands and be eligible for the spouse's own lifetime capital gains exemption.

## FINANCING THE BUY-SELL

Whichever buy-sell method is employed, one thing remains certain - unless there is some method of funding the transaction, the agreement may not be consummated. There are three common methods of employing life insurance as the funding mechanism for a buy-sell agreement.

### CRISS-CROSS INSURANCE

This is an insurance arrangement where each shareholder of a corporation acquires a life insurance policy on the life of each other shareholder. On the death of one shareholder, the survivors receive the tax-free proceeds of the policy and use the funds to purchase the deceased's shares from his or her estate or beneficiaries. One disadvantage of this method is that the cost of the insurance to each shareholder can vary widely depending on the ages and health of the other shareholders.

### CORPORATE-OWNED INSURANCE

With this type of policy, the corporation insures the lives of each shareholder and receives the proceeds on their deaths. The corporation pays all the premiums; consequently, the cost to the shareholders is shared in proportion to their shareholdings. The proceeds are used by the corporation to purchase the deceased's shares, either from the deceased's estate or from the surviving spouse.

### SPLIT-DOLLAR INSURANCE

Split-dollar insurance is a combination of both criss-cross and corporate-owned insurance. Each shareholder purchases a whole-life type of policy on the other and assigns the cash value of the policy to the company. On the death of a shareholder, the company receives the cash value of the policy while the surviving shareholders receive the face value less the cash value and use these proceeds to purchase the shares. The advantage of this method is that the company pays most of the premiums.

## CORPORATE PARTNERSHIPS

It happens every day. Two successful entrepreneurs join forces and in the process watch their new combined business grow by leaps and bounds. This is what happened to Sheri Sorentino a few years after she started up her consulting business. She had all the business she could handle, but the company just wasn't big enough to provide a full service to most of her clients.

Enter Ashley Atkinson. Her background was advertising, including the creative side. Sheri's strength lay in public relations. Ashley also ran a successful small business and had the same problem as Sheri – lots of business, but she couldn't provide a complete service to her clients.

The two had worked on several accounts together over the past two years, found that they operated well together and began exploring the possibility of combining their businesses. They discussed a merger under which the shares of one corporation would be transferred to the other on a tax-deferred basis. The subsidiary company (the one transferred) would be wound up into the parent or purchasing company. Sheri and Ashley would each own 50 per cent of the shares of the surviving company.

Then they began discussing the possible provisions that should be included in their shareholders' agreement. They quickly discovered that, although they were in substantial agreement on how the business should be operated, their needs and desires as to how their respective share of the profits should be dealt with were quite diverse.

Sheri's only source of income was the business. At least for the next few years, she would need to withdraw all of her share of the profits in the form of salary or dividends. Ashley, on the other hand, was the income beneficiary of a trust established by a wealthy aunt and did not have an immediate need for cash from the company. Ashley also expressed the desire to involve other family members as shareholders in the company. Sheri did not.

Although they explored a number of very sophisticated capital structures that the new operating company might establish to resolve their conflicting interests, Sheri and Ashley thought that these would become extremely complex and cumbersome. Finally they agreed to form a partnership of their corporations.

The business assets were transferred by their corporations to the newly formed partnership. Each corporation was entitled to 50 per cent of the future earnings of the partnership. After an independent valuation, it was decided that the partnership would credit an additional sum to the capital account of Sheri's corporation to compensate for the value of her new computer installation.

A partnership agreement was signed by the two corporations to document various policies governing the operation of the business. The agreement also established how the profits and losses were to be shared and dealt with capital withdrawals and contributions.

A partnership is not a taxable entity per se. The annual business income, although determined at the partnership level, is allocated to each of the corporate partners. After charging the desired salary or bonus for the respective shareholders, the balance of the income is taxed in the separate corporations. The after-tax income is then available to distribute, or not, as dividends.

Structuring the business as a partnership of their individual corporations offers Sheri and Ashley a great deal of flexibility. Each is able to set the remuneration package that best suits her particular needs. All the advantages of incorporation are maintained and many of the problems of conflicting needs and objectives between the shareholders are solved.

Where a business is carried on as a partnership, the income still qualifies for the low rate of tax on the first $200,000. The limit is shared by the partners in the same proportion as they share partnership income. Each of Sheri's and Ashley's corporations is entitled to pay the low rate of corporate tax on $100,000 of business income derived from the partnership each year.

The corporate partnership format also facilitates personal and family tax planning for the shareholders. Ashley can make whatever arrangements she may desire to involve family members as shareholders of her corporation without in any way affecting Sheri's rights.

Corporate partnerships also offer a great deal of flexibility in establishing and varying arrangements among the principals for the sharing of profits and losses. For example, if Ashley decided in a few years that she wanted to reduce her day-to-day involvement in the business but wished to retain her equity interest, it would be a simple matter to amend the partnership agreement to alter the profit and loss sharing ratio in whatever manner was desired to reflect the new relationship. Such changes to the partnership agreement would not have any adverse tax implications for either Sheri or Ashley.

Individuals owning shares in an operating company face the potential realization of a capital gain on the sale of any part of their shares to other shareholders. Transfers of ownership interests in a partnership, however, can usually be arranged on a tax-deferred basis, even where the consideration on the transfer is cash. These techniques may be particularly beneficial if either Sheri or Ashley was to leave the business and her interest was to be purchased over a period of time.

If Sheri and Ashley were to decide to sell their business in a few years' time, it would also be possible to reorganize the partnership as a corporation just before the sale so that Sheri and Ashley could each take advantage of the $400,000 capital gains exemption.

## EXPANDING INTO INTERNATIONAL MARKETS

Sooner or later, the lure of the international marketplace is likely to beckon. Here again, careful planning is the key to success. You know what you went through developing a market and expanding in Canada. Breaking into international markets is almost always more difficult, time consuming and expensive. But if you are successful, the rewards will justify the effort. Increasingly, the world is becoming one global marketplace. Even the smallest business will be venturing abroad in the 1990s.

Take the time to study and understand your new marketplace. It will be different. The legal system won't be the same; corporate, commercial and tax laws will all be different from what you are used to in Canada. The way you conduct your business in other countries may have to change. It may mean adapting to the local economic and cultural conditions. Be sensitive to these cultural issues. Seemingly subtle variations in the local business environment can mean the difference between success and failure if you fail to recognize and react to them.

You may have to look beyond your regular sources of financing to expand internationally. Like you, Canadian lenders and investors don't understand foreign markets as well as the domestic ones. They will be more cautious about taking a chance in financing your international expansion.

### FIRST STOP

The first place to go for help is the federal government. A number of programs are in place to help Canadian business finance international trade and develop export markets. Check out your provincial government, too.

As you expand into the international arena, the tax environment becomes enormously complex. Not only do you have to take into account the domestic tax laws of Canada and the particular foreign jurisdiction, but you also have to be aware of the potential implications of the international tax treaty that Canada has probably signed with that country. As well, the interaction of the two domestic tax laws on particular structures and transactions can be a minefield, even if a tax treaty for the avoidance of double taxation has been negotiated.

---

**Caution!** Before expanding into the international marketplace, consult with your professional advisors both in Canada and the foreign jurisdiction. Working in close co-operation, they can advise you on the best way to structure your new international activities now and also with an eye to the future.

---

## U.S. Bound

Because of the proximity of the huge market south of the border and the advent of free trade, the first foray of most owner-managers into international trade is to the United States. There are many different ways to do business in the United States. But your options will fall into basically four categories:

- simply sell products into the United States either directly or through an independent agent located there;
- license a U.S. company to manufacture and/or sell your products and services in the United States;
- establish a business in the United States, operating as a branch or subsidiary of the Canadian company, or
- acquire an existing U.S. business.

Both commercial and tax considerations will be important in deciding on which way to go and when. We offer some brief comments on each of the options.

## Exporting to the United States

Instead of establishing a branch or subsidiary in the United States, your company can simply sell directly to U.S. customers from its Canadian locations. Or you might decide to contract with U.S. wholesalers, distributors, or other independent agents to handle your products in the United States.

Operations such as these can generally be carried on with little legal formality and should not expose your company to U.S. tax liabilities. However, to stay outside the U.S. tax net, your company must avoid creating a "place of business" or a "permanent establishment" in the United States. These are terms of art to the taxman; make sure you check with your tax advisor to stay on side.

Exporting to the United States may be a good beginning, but it may not enable you to gain the market presence that you desire.

## Licensing

You may be able to increase your market penetration by licensing a U.S. business to manufacture and distribute your products in the United States. A typical licence agreement would call for a royalty based on a percentage of sales. Generally, royalties received from the manufacturer will be subject to a U.S. withholding tax of 10 per cent. No further U.S. tax will be payable as long as you do not have a permanent establishment in the United States.

In most circumstances, your company will be able to claim a credit for the U.S. withholding tax against the Canadian tax imposed on the royalty income. If you are in a service industry, a franchise arrangement with an independent U.S. party will achieve much the same result.

## BRANCH OPERATIONS

A licensing or franchise arrangement may not give you the control you desire over day-to-day operations in the United States. You are now ready to take the plunge and set up your own operations across the border. One of the first decisions you must make is whether to establish a branch of the Canadian company or a separately incorporated U.S. subsidiary.

If your company simply opens an office or a plant in the United States, that location will be a U.S. branch of the Canadian company. The branch will have to register to carry on business in particular states, pay certain fees, and comply with local laws and regulations. But generally, the branch will be able to conduct business freely throughout the United States.

From both the U.S. and Canadian tax perspective, the branch is considered a mere extension of the Canadian company, not a separate entity. Income of the Canadian company, which is considered to be "effectively connected with the conduct of a trade or business within the United States", is subject to U.S. tax at normal U.S. corporate rates. Such income is also subject to tax in Canada. However, a credit for U.S. taxes paid may be claimed against the Canadian tax payable on income considered to have been earned in the United States.

While, in theory, this foreign tax credit mechanism should ensure that the branch profits are not taxed twice, once in the United States and again in Canada, this does not always work in practice. Disputes frequently arise between the U.S. and Canadian taxation authorities over the proper allocation of taxable income between the two countries. Most of these are ultimately settled without double tax, but the settlement process can drag on for years.

The United States also imposes a special branch profits tax on the after-tax earnings of the branch that are not re-invested in the United States. Under the Canada/U.S. tax treaty, the branch profits tax is restricted to 10 per cent, and the first $500,000 of accumulated branch profits is exempt.

## U.S. SUBSIDIARY

If you expect to be profitable in the near term, you will likely be better off to incorporate a U.S. subsidiary to carry on the business there. The income earned by the subsidiary will be subject to U.S. tax, but at rates that are generally lower than Canadian rates. When you operate as a branch, the income is effectively taxed at the greater of Canadian and U.S. rates.

The after-tax business income of the U.S. subsidiary is subject to U.S. withholding tax, generally at the rate of 10 per cent when distributed as a dividend to the Canadian parent. But no further tax is payable in Canada.

Operating as a branch may be advisable if you anticipate start-up losses. Such U.S. losses incurred by the branch will be available to reduce your Canadian company's taxable income. Losses incurred by a U.S. subsidiary will be trapped inside the corporation and be available only to reduce future income earned in the United States.

### U.S. ACQUISITION

Purchasing an existing U.S. business can provide market presence very quickly. It's an effective way to acquire plant and equipment, technological and management expertise, and additional distribution networks.

Make sure you get plenty of professional help before embarking on the U.S. acquisition trail. The planning and execution of cross-border acquisitions can become extremely complex. Designing an appropriate structure, putting the financing package together, reconciling your tax position with that of the U.S. vendor, and establishing the form of consideration and terms of payment are all vastly more complicated when dealing with two separate jurisdictions.

Don't be daunted by the seemingly overwhelming complexities facing you as you consider expanding your business. With proper planning and a sound understanding of exactly what you want to accomplish, the complexities will melt away. After all, you faced the same problems when you started up your business, and all that is now old hat.

# 12/ESTATE AND SUCCESSION PLANNING

If you've punched up variations of "The Dream" on your cerebral VCR as you drive to or from work, you're certainly not alone. The owner-manager dream plays out in three acts: your business is wildly successful, your number one child eventually becomes number one honcho in the family business, and not long after you slip into a leisurely retirement in the sun-drenched south, preferably a tax haven.

Not everyone, however, calls it The Dream. After you've been in business for awhile, you may begin to call it the results expected from astute long-range planning. Successful owner-managers say that prosperity depends on looking ahead at least five years. If you don't know where you're going, you'll have a tough time getting anywhere. Planning for The Dream demands that you look ahead a lifetime, your lifetime. That lifetime could be 30 or 40 years down the road, or it could extend no further than tomorrow.

## FACING THE HARD QUESTIONS

That's why small business advisors say that it's never too soon to begin planning for your eventual withdrawal from the business. And that means you'll have to start asking yourself the really tough questions. Not the ones about potential competitors, or can you survive a year or two of losses on a major expansion, or what happens if we go through a recession. But the ones that don't have any immediate answers:

- Can your business run itself without you so your family doesn't suffer a serious income loss?
- What happens if you die tomorrow?
- What happens if you are permanently disabled?
- Can your children run your business? Do they want to?
- Can your spouse run the business?
- Is there a buyer for your business?
- What are the financial consequences if you have to fold up your tent and start afresh?

These are only a few of the questions you'll have to ask, and continue to ask, yourself as you go through this long-range planning procedure. It's called succession planning – the process of formally determining how you will transfer your business to others and what needs to be done to prepare for the transition. An integral part of succession planning includes making decisions on what to do, both before and on your death, with assets you have accumulated. This process is called estate planning, which is loosely defined as the ongoing process of creating and maintaining a program designed to preserve your accumulated wealth and ensure its most effective and beneficial distribution to succeeding generations, according to your wishes.

When addressing business assets, it's apparent that both succession and estate planning come into play when developing any comprehensive program. Choosing a successor to take over your business, which is probably your most valuable asset, also likely means deciding who is to be your major beneficiary and when your assets are to be distributed. As well, retirement planning cannot be ignored as you put your program together.

This chapter deals only with your business assets and planning related to your business. Your professional advisor can offer direction in dealing with other assets.

## OBJECTIVES
Estate planning has three primary goals:
- ensuring that you and your family are provided for adequately now and in the future, that is, during your retirement, and that your heirs are adequately provided for after your death;
- distributing your assets according to your wishes, both during your lifetime and on your death, while ensuring that the maximum benefits available accrue to your beneficiaries, and
- minimizing various forms of wealth erosion, taxes being the most prominent, both now and in the future.

Focusing on succession planning, a number of concerns must be addressed:
- The most important is picking and grooming your successors in the business, whether they be family members, outsiders, or employees.
- Once you have made a decision, you want to ensure that you and your family continue to generate sufficient income to maintain your lifestyle and that all family members are treated fairly.
- Assuming the business will remain in the family, you definitely want to ensure that they will be able to realize the business's value through a sale if they cannot operate it without you.
- And you want to ensure that your business continues to run smoothly as you put your program into action, no matter how the future unfolds.

A comprehensive succession and estate planning program is not something that is developed overnight. In fact, it is an on-going process that needs to be updated and re-evaluated periodically. Hence the need to develop a flexible plan, firmly rooted in realistic, achievable goals. Your business will evolve and may perhaps become unrecognizable in only a few years, your personal circumstances will surely change over time, legislation will put new demands on any plan you have constructed, and your objectives will probably change to some degree as everything around you changes.

## FUNDAMENTAL ISSUES
As you develop your long-range plan, you'll discover three fundamental issues that you'll find yourself returning to over and over again as your comprehensive program matures over the years.

**1. Who Gets What?** Will your spouse or children run the business, or simply be inactive shareholders? Will you sell the business? Should you split the business up to ensure an equitable distribution?

**2. How Much Control Should You Retain?** Is it better to let new owners get their feet wet quickly or slowly? Should you maintain control to ensure a steady flow of retirement income?

**3. Where Does the Funding Come From?** Insurance may solve problems on your death, but what if you are disabled? What happens if you retire and your children don't have the cash to purchase the business?

Later in this chapter, we'll watch Ray Corcoran confront a variety of issues as he goes through the initial steps of developing a succession and estate planning program. This should give you some insight into the process and help you begin to address some of the issues and formulate answers to some of the bigger questions.

## WHERE DOES RAY STAND TODAY?
Ray Corcoran bought a controlling interest in Gizmo Inc. five years ago. The company was in financial difficulty before Ray got involved. He has managed to turn the business around and sees a bright future for it. Now that he is no longer spending all his time putting out fires and worrying about the company's survival from one payroll to the next, he is able to think about the future and even dream about the day when he will turn over the reins to someone else.

Ray is still only in his late forties. He plans to be at the helm of his business until he is at least 60, but he knows that if he wants one or both of his children to become involved in the business, he has to get them started early enough to give them a chance at running it successfully. After all, Ray "jumped" in with more than 15 years of experience behind him, which is the major factor he attributes to his being able to turn around an unhealthy enterprise.

Ray's daughter, Suzanne, is 22 and his son, Whit, is 20. Suzanne has worked part-time and summers at Gizmo Inc. since she was 17. This summer she will work with the sales force expanding the retail market for the new GIZMO II. This will be her fifth job in five years with Gizmo Inc. Suzanne is engaged to be married to Adrian, Gizmo Inc.'s brightest young light on the research side of the business.

Whit has never worked for Gizmo and has never expressed the slightest interest in the company, other than suggesting it could do a little better dealing with its waste products. In fact, this summer he has accepted a position with a conservation association to watch whales from an isolated island off the Nova Scotia coast.

Ray's wife, Gloria, is a moderately successful sculptress. Her closest involvement with the company occurred last year when she incorporated a number of GIZMO IIs in a series of works which, after walking off with several prizes, were subsequently sold to an industrial plaza developer. Her attitude to the business hasn't changed since Ray bought it: "You do your thing. I do mine."

Gizmo Inc. has thrived under Ray's ownership. He turned the company around in the first year and it became profitable the next. Two years ago, he expanded the company's markets and last year introduced the revolutionary GIZMO II. Two years ago, he bought out the original owner, a research genius and entrepreneurial failure, in exchange for cash and a long-term management contract with profit sharing.

## STRUCTURE OF GIZMO INC.
Currently the share ownership structure is as follows:

| | |
|---|---|
| Ray | 51% |
| Gloria | 29% |
| Suzanne | 10% |
| Whit | 10% |

The shares are held in a holding company, Corcoran Inc. The only assets of Corcoran Inc. are common shares in Gizmo Inc. These are the only shares outstanding. Suzanne's and Whit's shares are held in a trust of which Ray and Gloria are the trustees. The accrued capital gain on Ray's shares exceeds $700,000 and is almost $400,000 on Gloria's. However, there is very little in the way of liquidity in the company. Any attempt to generate excess cash in Gizmo Inc. would leave it seriously short of working capital and impair its ability to operate, especially when it has just launched a new product and is extending its markets nationally. Neither Ray nor Gloria has used the special $400,000 capital gains exemption. Gizmo Inc. is a qualifying small business corporation (QSBC).

Ray's will, which was overhauled five years ago when he bought the business, leaves everything to Gloria, and if he outlives her, to the two children equally. Gloria's will leaves everything to Ray, and alternatively to the children equally. But now that Suzanne has shown a decided interest in the business and is engaged to Adrian who also appears committed to Gizmo, while Whit has been making noises lately about trying to get his hands on his shares so that he can sell them and contribute to the cause, Ray is rethinking the terms of his will.

## A TYPICALLY CLOUDY FUTURE

Typically, Ray hasn't discussed his succession problems with Gloria, or with the children. In fact, he is only now beginning to come to grips with some of the thornier issues. These can be divided into three major areas: personal, family and business. In each case, Ray must ask what happens if he were to die tomorrow or become seriously disabled, and he must try to look forward a decade or two and make some reasonable predictions.

Ray definitely intends to be out of the business by the time he reaches his mid-sixties. However, he wants the option of being able to retire early, perhaps within ten years. He doesn't think that his and Gloria's retirement needs will be outrageous, but they will be substantial, certainly more than the company can afford currently. If the business continues its pattern of success, there should be no trouble financing an extremely comfortable retirement. Once retired, Gloria will have no money problems should Ray die first. The only major problem they might face is guaranteeing that the business will provide them with a good portion of their expected retirement income. If Ray is no longer at the helm, he wants to minimize the risk of some of their retirement income not materializing.

## SOME QUESTIONS ARE TOUGHER THAN OTHERS

But what happens to everything when both Ray and Gloria are gone? When Ray bought Gizmo, he thought everything had to go to the two children eventually. That's what he had always worked toward. Now that his children are older and obviously will be able to take care of themselves, he is no longer so sure that everything automatically ought to go to the next generation. After lengthy discussions with Gloria, Ray has come to the conclusion that the first priority is giving Suzanne a chance to become involved in the business to whatever level she desires. If this leads to a controlling interest and the presidency, all the better. But neither Ray nor Gloria is assuming that this will happen.

And then there is Whit to consider. Again, after lengthy discussions with Gloria, Ray is not convinced that equal treatment of the children is absolutely necessary in the long run, and Gloria agrees. They have been treated equally to date, but it may be time to begin to let them have control over their holdings and deal with them as they see fit. Naturally,

Ray would do everything possible to ensure that the two children are dealt with fairly.

Of course, all Ray's and Gloria's planning depends on the long-term health of Gizmo Inc. The company's prospects are certainly handsome. GIZMO II has been well-received; Western markets have developed as anticipated; Ray has assembled a young, creative and committed management team; and the small research staff headed by the old owner already has a prototype of GIZMO III up and working. But Ray keeps asking himself that one nagging question. Will the business survive if he drops out tomorrow for some reason or other? In the early days, Ray couldn't be certain that Gizmo would survive. Today, the answer is more likely to be yes – probably – but with a little help.

That still leaves other questions unanswered. If everything goes to Gloria on Ray's death, would it be better to dispose of Gizmo and see that she gets enough cash to see her through the rest of life, rather than be saddled with a business she knows nothing about? But if Gizmo is sold, what happens to Suzanne's aspirations? What if Gloria remarries? Would Ray want her new husband to be in a position to take over the business? Would Suzanne still get a crack at running it if she proved capable? What would whale-watching Whit get out of it?

What happens if Suzanne marries Adrian, gets divorced, and Adrian ends up with a substantial interest in the company? How will Ray and Suzanne react to Adrian? If Ray is no longer around, how will Gloria fare in a situation like this? Is Adrian capable of running Gizmo, or do his strengths lie strictly in research?

Let's look at the various elements of Ray's plan issue by issue. But first, we briefly look at the tax rules on death, which figure into some of Ray's planning.

## TAXATION ON DEATH

Tax considerations are always important. They become doubly so on the death of an owner-manager because poor tax planning or no planning can quickly bury a business. If you understand how taxation applies on death, you should be better equipped to decide how to plan for your successors in the business and how to distribute business assets during your lifetime to achieve your succession, estate and retirement planning objectives.

There are no Canadian death taxes, federal or provincial, levied on the value of the assets that pass to beneficiaries. Only income amounts received or deemed to be received by the deceased and capital gains realized (or deemed to be realized) are subject to tax. It is this last point that is crucial when planning for your business assets.

Note, however, that the recently elected Ontario government promised during the election that they would consider succession duties for estates over $1 million. At the time of publication, no proposals for the introduction of such taxes had been released.

In the year of death, the deceased is deemed to have disposed of all capital property immediately before death. This of course includes your shares in the corporation and any business assets that you may hold personally and lease to the corporation. "Non-depreciable" property, such as land or shares of corporations, is deemed disposed of at its fair market value immediately before death. "Depreciable" capital property, such as machinery and equipment, is deemed disposed of at a value midway between its undepreciated capital cost and its fair market value. These deemed dispositions can result in capital gains and losses, as well as a terminal loss or recapture of depreciation already claimed.

There does not have to be an actual sale of the capital property. Tax is calculated in your final income tax return as though all your property had been sold just prior to the date of your death. If capital assets have appreciated significantly from the time of their acquisition, a large tax assessment on the "profit" from these deemed dispositions may result. Since there has been no actual sale of assets, the estate may have difficulty paying any taxes that are levied. The only source of cash to pay the taxes may be the business, which could put its viability in jeopardy. Note that the alternative minimum tax (AMT) is not applicable in the year of death.

## TAX RELIEF

There are three specific relieving provisions in the tax law that prevent or postpone unduly harsh tax consequences on death. We discussed the first in Chapter 10 – the special $400,000 lifetime capital gains exemption on the disposition of shares in a qualifying small business corporation. And of course the standard $100,000 lifetime capital gains exemption would also apply, if it hasn't already been used.

For the owners of a farming business, all tax can be deferred if the business (shares in a corporation, or an interest in a farm partnership, or the family farm itself) is bequeathed to a child, grandchild, or great-grandchild of the deceased. The child inherits the cost base of the parent and becomes responsible for any tax that might eventually become payable. Of course, the transfer should be made at a value that uses up the full $500,000 capital gains exemptions.

Finally, and most importantly, a tax deferral is available if the capital property is bequeathed to your spouse or a spousal trust (we'll discuss trusts later in the chapter). The property is transferred at your cost, so your spouse or the spousal trust would inherit this cost base and become responsible for any tax payable in the future. An election can be made not to have this spousal rollover rule apply. If such an election is made, property is bequeathed at fair market value and tax may apply.

Despite the value of the rollover, it should be ensured that the deceased has made full use of his or her lifetime capital gains exemptions. Unfortunately, assets must be transferred, on an asset by asset basis, to your spouse on death at cost or fair market value. Making a transfer at fair market value may open up the capital gains exemptions but it could also expose the estate to a great deal of unnecessary tax. However, this should not be too troublesome when dealing with the shares of a corporation. Each share is treated as a separate asset. Consequently, an election can be made to transfer some shares at fair market value and others at cost. Careful advance planning will help you avoid running into these kinds of problems.

Much estate planning focuses on using up the $500,000 capital gains exemptions before the death of the owner-manager and ensuring taxes are kept to a minimum when business assets pass to children. We have already seen examples of the two main techniques that are used to accomplish both these goals. In Chapter 10, a holding company was used to step up the cost base of shares in the operating corporation and use up the special $400,000 exemption. In Chapter 7, several of the income splitting techniques involved freezing the value of the owner-manager's shares in the active business so that all future gains accrued to the children.

## THE BUSINESS

The future of Gizmo Inc. looks extremely promising. The fair market value of the family's shares has grown to more than $1.5 million in about five years, from less than $200,000. Slower, but still handsome, rates of growth are expected over the next decade at least. As noted above, Ray has created a vibrant, forward-looking company with a young and increasingly knowledgeable management. From a financial point of view, Ray should have no trouble achieving any of his longer-term goals.

And if growth continues at the current rate, Ray should have no trouble instituting a generous profit-sharing program that rewards both short-term and long-term performance.

## FAMILY

Decisions concerning his family were the most difficult of all. But Ray finally decided that he would like to begin a slow transfer of ownership to Suzanne, assuming she retains her interest in the business. At the same time, he doesn't want to leave his management team out in the cold if Suzanne decides she wants to pursue another career. If he decides to sell Gizmo when he is closer to retirement age, he wants his employees to have first crack at the business and be in a position to afford to buy him and Gloria out.

Ray also concluded that if Suzanne is in, Whit should probably be out.

Therefore, Ray wants to set the wheels in motion for Whit to get his hands on his interest in Gizmo – not as shares, but as cash with strings attached. Of course Ray wants to be fair and ensure that Whit gets what should be coming to him.

Having decided that Suzanne and Whit should be treated equally but also be given some say in the future of their shareholding in Gizmo, Ray considered putting a program in place under which Suzanne could gradually purchase Whit's shares at fair market value. Suzanne would have to finance the purchase of the shares herself from accumulated income on her own shares, loans and perhaps notes payable to Whit if that could be arranged. Ray would help both of them where he could, if it became necessary.

The children's current shareholdings would continue to be owned by the trust, and Ray would continue to act as trustee and exercise control over the shares.

At the same time, Ray wanted to set the wheels in motion for Suzanne to be able eventually to take control of Gizmo when Ray finally was ready to bow out of the picture. Several possible techniques are discussed below under tax considerations.

## DIFFICULT DECISIONS

Giving one child the chance to opt out of the family business at the tender (or, in many cases, not so tender) age of 20 is a difficult process. Making the initial decision is only the first arduous step. Chances are the children agree with the decision, or you probably wouldn't have made it in the first place. But ensuring that both understand it completely and understand the long-term consequences is another matter.

And Ray's concerns don't end there. Should Whit be compensated if Suzanne ends up owning most of Gizmo's shares? Ray's professional advisor pointed out that Suzanne will likely be earning those shares through her commitment to Gizmo and her desire to take it over from Ray one day. Sitting on an isolated island watching whales may be admirable, but it doesn't automatically entitle Whit to an equal number of shares – or any shares or compensation for that matter. He will be reimbursed for his shares at fair market value and is free to invest or spend the funds in any way he sees fit. Suzanne has made it clear that she is willing to reinvest everything in Gizmo as long as she sees a career as owner set out unquestionably in front of her.

This was the first, but not the last, time that Ray realized succession planning is almost always marked by compromise. To get something, you've got to give up something else. Ray has chosen Gizmo and financial prosperity over strict, unwavering equal treatment of his children. As his advisor sagely noted, familial equity and stability of a business are often on the opposite sides of the fence. Strict adherence to one can often lead to the demise of the other.

## TAXES

It comes as no surprise that Ray wants to keep taxes to a minimum now and in the future. In fact, he would like to take advantage of the special $400,000 capital gains exemption on small business corporation gains as soon as possible. He thinks that it is a tempting target for a government facing a $30-billion-plus deficit.

So the next step in Ray's deliberations was to consider an estate freeze of his and Gloria's shares. This will trigger capital gains eligible for the special $400,000 small business corporation (SBC) exemption. It also ensures that more future appreciation in the value of Gizmo Inc. accrues to the remaining owners of the common shares.

## ESTATE FREEZES

An estate freeze can be defined in general terms as a method of organizing your affairs so as to permit any future appreciation in the value of selected assets you currently own to accrue to others, usually your children. Under an estate freeze, you retain, or at least have access to, the current value of the frozen assets; only the future increases in value are transferred to the child. With a partial freeze, you retain an interest in part of the increasing value of the asset, while your child also participates. It is also possible for you to retain control over those assets. Ideally, a freeze will not have any current tax implications, other than using available exemptions.

### CORPORATE FREEZE

A corporate estate freeze is usually undertaken only if there is an expectation of continued growth of the business. Of course, a freeze may also be used to take advantage of the special $400,000 SBC exemption.

### DIRECT SALE

There are various ways to implement a freeze. You might consider a direct sale to your adult children. You would sell them your shares in the company and take back a non-interest-bearing note payable for the fair market value of the shares. This method has a number of disadvantages. The attribution rules could apply on any dividends paid on the shares, because interest is not paid on the note. You would have disposed of your shares on the transfer and be subject to tax on any resulting capital gain, minus any exemptions to which you are entitled. And finally, you could lose control of the company unless you retain control by other means, perhaps with sufficient voting preferred shares that you continue to own.

## HOLDCO FREEZE
A more common method is to use a holding company, Holdco. We have examined this type of transaction previously. The children would incorporate a company, Holdco, and acquire all its common shares for a nominal value. You would transfer your shares in the operating company to the newly incorporated Holdco on a tax-deferred basis and take back voting preferred shares in Holdco as consideration for the transfer.

## INTERNAL FREEZE
The other method commonly used is the internal freeze, which we first examined in Chapter 7. When the applicable provincial or federal companies act permits, you may exchange all your existing common shares for voting preferred shares. Subsequently, a new class of common shares is created that the children purchase.

Under these last two methods, future appreciation of the company accrues to the children. You retain control through the voting preferred shares. And the sale or reorganization can be undertaken at fair market value to use up the $400,000 SBC exemption. On the negative side, any money owed to you is still tied up in the corporation and therefore exposed to some risk.

## INVESTCO FREEZE
All of the above freeze methods work with a corporation that holds primarily portfolio investments, but there are additional complexities. Of course, no $400,000 special SBC capital gains exemption is available, and unless certain precautions are taken, the attribution rules will apply if children under the age of 18 are involved.

To avoid attribution, the children's shares in Investco must be held by a trust, and the terms of the trust must specify that the children cannot receive or use any income or capital of the trust while they are under 18. The result of these restrictions is that all trust income is taxed in the trust at the top marginal rate of tax, since a preferred beneficiary election cannot be made. If children are near the age of 18, this may not be a serious concern, since the income would have been taxed in your hands at the top rate in any case.

## DIVORCE
Over the past few years, changes in family law in certain provinces could affect the distribution of shares on divorce. If assets are acquired by a couple during their marriage, the increase in their value during the marriage is factored into the 50-50 equalization payment that, according to some provincial law, must be made after the marriage break-up.

To ensure that assets remain in the hands of the child in the event of divorce, the parent in both the Holdco and internal freezes should acquire the common shares and then gift the common shares to the child. This will generally exclude the common shares from the matrimonial property of the married child in most instances, since assets inherited or received by way of gift are usually excluded from matrimonial property. In Quebec, shares of a private or public corporation are not included in the matrimonial property.

## ASSET FREEZE

You also might want to consider an asset freeze. In this situation, some or all of the underlying operating assets of the company, Opco, are sold to a new corporation, Newco, incorporated by the children. You retain control of Opco and take back debt or preferred shares in Newco to retain control of the operating assets. Future increases in value of the business now accrue in Newco, not Opco. This type of freeze can be expensive and complex, although it may be suitable if you want to break up your corporation into several different businesses. This could also be the best method of separating real estate from the business operations. The real estate could be left behind in Opco and the operations could be transferred on a "freeze" basis to Newco.

## PARTIAL FREEZE

Ray leans toward a partial freeze because he isn't satisfied that his current wealth can provide the level of retirement income that he suspects he and Gloria will need. He wants to trigger sufficient capital gains to use the special $400,000 SBC exemption, but he also wants to continue to participate in the capital appreciation of Gizmo. He thinks prospects for the company are exceptional.

To begin the freeze, Ray incorporates another company we'll call Investco. He and Gloria are the only shareholders. Next, he exchanges some of his common shares in Corcoran Inc., the holding company, for special voting preference shares. The exchange is conducted at fair market value so that he triggers a capital gain eligible for the $400,000 special exemption. Finally, the preference shares in Corcoran Inc. are transferred to Investco at their new cost. Ray and Gloria take back common shares as consideration for the transfer.

By following these transactions, Ray freezes a considerable portion of the current value of Gizmo in the form of the preferred shares. They will not increase in value, since they have a specific retraction price. However, he and Gloria will still participate in the future appreciation of Gizmo through the common shares that they still hold.

Ray retains majority control of Gizmo through the new voting preferred shares and his ability to exercise control over his children's shares as trustee of the trust that holds those shares.

While a good portion of Ray and Gloria's future retirement income still depends on the continued success of Gizmo, Ray reduces the risk of cashing in his investment to some degree. The preferred shares carry specific dividend rights that must be honoured before dividends can be paid on the common shares. These dividends will flow through Corcoran Inc. to Investco, which is wholly owned by Ray and Gloria. Once in Investco, this income is beyond the reach of Gizmo and any of the other shareholders and creditors.

Another possibility that Ray is exploring with his tax and legal advisors is to have Corcoran Inc. redeem the preference shares soon after Ray has transferred them to Investco. The preference shares would be replaced by an interest-bearing debenture owing by Corcoran Inc., which would be secured by some of that company's assets. This could provide a measure of creditor protection. However, there could be a tax cost of converting the preference shares to a debenture if Revenue Canada were to take the position that this transaction was part of a "series of transactions" involving a subsequent arm's length sale of the shares of the company.

---

**Caution!** Estate freezing usually involves the use of complex reorganizations, not all of which are formally sanctioned by tax law. Although there are various tried and true techniques, there are also a number of exceptions to the rules that could cause adverse tax results in particular circumstances. Estate freezing is definitely not for the "do-it-yourselfer". Obtaining the advice of experienced tax and legal advisors is a must.

---

## RETIREMENT

Ray's pension plan from his previous employer is still intact, but will provide only a small amount of Ray's and Gloria's expected pension requirements. Ray has been contributing to an RRSP the past five years. Gloria also contributes to an RRSP, although it has been during only the last five years that she has begun to earn more than pocket money. Her annual RRSP contributions have beefed up her RRSP statement to the point where it no longer looks like a small bank account.

Gloria is also considering opening a small shop with a friend who makes pottery. This should generate additional income and provide more opportunities for Gloria to accumulate a larger pension investment fund.

However, Ray is not counting on these sources, plus government income, to fully fund their retirement. He expects that his investment in the business will have to provide a substantial part of their retirement income. The major question facing Ray is how to ensure that his investment is available in ten or fifteen years. After all, businesses don't always perform as expected. If Gizmo Inc. falls on hard times, Ray wants to be able to get his accumulated profits out of the company without too much erosion.

Being on the far side of his mid-forties, Ray agreed with his advisor that the time had come to consider setting up a designated registered pension plan (DRPP – see Chapter 9) for himself. Individual plans for Suzanne and members of the management team could also be established if desired. Projections supplied by Ray's advisor showed larger contributions could now be made to the DRPP than to his RRSP, and the difference would continue to grow until he retired. The funds in this plan and his RRSP ought to continue to be conservatively invested since Ray figured he was assuming enough risk having most of his accumulated wealth tied up in Gizmo.

The DRPP would afford other advantages, too. As noted earlier, DRPPs are creditor proof. As well, regulations allow any surplus, up to specific amounts, to be distributed to the member over a period of years if the member is retiring. The DRPP is flexible enough that, should Gizmo Inc. be sold, Ray's accumulated benefits could be transferred to another DRPP, perhaps one sponsored by Corcoran Inc. This would prevent amounts in the DRPP having to be transferred to a locked-in RRSP, if required by provincial legislation. In fact, Ray might even consider setting up the DRPP in Corcoran Inc., if sufficient salary could be paid to Ray from Corcoran Inc. to justify maximum contributions and benefits from the DRPP and the corporation could make use of the deductions resulting from the contributions to the plan.

Ray also planned to give Gloria any funds she needed to expand her business, particularly if she sets up a retail shop with her friend. Any income earned by Gloria will be taxed in her hands since the attribution rules don't apply if the recipient of the funds earns business income. Splitting income in this manner should reduce their combined tax bill somewhat during retirement.

## LEASECO IS A POSSIBILITY
Ray also considered looking into the possibility of transferring Gizmo's major asset, its manufacturing and research plant, to another company, Leaseco, which would then lease the facility back to Gizmo. Ray and Gloria would own Leaseco outright and participate in any profits and capital appreciation.

Ray looks on this action as an insurance policy should he not be able to accumulate sufficient retirement assets. It may also offer some protection should Gizmo fall on hard times and creditors come knocking. The land and building should be safe from most creditors and provide the family with a financial cushion.

## THE UNEXPECTED

Ray and Gloria have been happily married for 23 years. Divorce doesn't seem to be in the cards. But after five years of running his own business, Ray has said more than once, "You never know!" However, since Ray owns a majority of the shares of Gizmo, he figures that he is at least protected from outside interference in the company should he and Gloria split up, and assuming Gizmo remains intact.

However, he has no idea what a divorce would do to Gizmo. And there isn't a lot of planning to be undertaken to ensure that Gizmo survives in the event of a divorce, short of Ray and Gloria signing a marriage contract. And even this may provide only a small amount of protection.

Suzanne's future is a little easier to deal with, at least for the time being. Her shares are held in trust. Ray and Gloria are trustees of the trust and therefore have control over the shares, including voting rights, possible sale, and distribution of dividend income. Ray intends to retain control over the trust until he has some assurance that Suzanne's marriage to Adrian works out, if it even takes place. Similarly, Whit's shares are held in a trust that Ray controls.

### THE NATURE OF TRUSTS

Trusts are an important part of succession and estate planning. In its simplest form, a trust merely involves the holding of property by one person for the benefit of another person. In more technical terms, a trust is created when a "settlor" transfers property to a "trustee" who holds the property for the benefit of a "beneficiary". A trust may be either "testamentary" (that is, arising upon your death) or "inter vivos" (that is, arising during your lifetime).

Trusts are useful and flexible devices in that they allow you to transfer ownership of an asset to an intended heir, while you, or actually the trustees of the trust, are able to maintain control over the asset. A trust permits you to accomplish a number of your succession planning goals. Trusts may also be used for such varied purposes as funding a child's education, providing for handicapped children, or obtaining professional property management.

To achieve tax savings, you first must relinquish ownership of the assets held by the trust, although in some cases you may still control the management and operation of the trust itself. Secondly, one would normally want to avoid the attribution rules.

### TRUST EARNINGS

Income earned and left in a trust is taxed as if the trust were a separate individual taxpayer. An inter vivos trust is taxed at the top personal rate. However, if trust income is distributed to a beneficiary, it can be taxed either in the beneficiary's hands or in the trust, depending on what the trustees decide. Income that is left in the trust and reinvested can also be taxed in the hands of beneficiaries by means of the preferred beneficiary election (see below), assuming the attribution rules do not apply.

Certain forms of income earned in a trust retain their character when distributed to beneficiaries. For example, eligible Canadian taxable dividends received by a trust and distributed to a beneficiary are eligible for the dividend tax credit. Capital gains retain their identity and are eligible for the beneficiary's lifetime capital gains exemption, if they are so designated by the trust.

## PREFERRED BENEFICIARY

By making a preferred beneficiary election, income earned by the trust is taxed in the hands of the beneficiary, even though the income remains in the trust. A preferred beneficiary must be a Canadian resident and one of the following:

- the settlor of the trust, or his or her spouse or former spouse;
- a child, grandchild, or great-grandchild of the settlor, or
- the spouse (but not former spouse) of a child, grandchild, or great-grandchild of the settlor.

In addition, the settlor must have contributed more to the trust than any other contributor.

A trust is deemed to have disposed of all its capital property every 21 years for notional proceeds of sale equal to the fair market value of the property. This prevents the trust from deferring tax on accrued capital gains indefinitely. The main exception to the 21-year rule applies to certain spousal trusts that are deemed to dispose of their property on the death of the surviving spouse.

Major amendments to the 21-year deemed disposition rules have been proposed by the government. If enacted, the new rules will allow a trust to postpone the deemed disposition date until the death of the last "exempt beneficiary" of the trust. These will be defined to include the settlor's children, but not the grandchildren.

At the time of writing, the proposed changes have been released only in draft form. It is possible that changes to the rules will be made before they are passed into law.

## THE UNTHINKABLE

To date, Ray has made almost no plans that would take effect if he were to die tomorrow. He does have $500,000 of term insurance, with Gloria as the only beneficiary. And he knows that Gizmo Inc. is worth well over $1 million, which would hopefully see Gloria and the two children through any financial ups and downs, assuming Gizmo could be readily sold for cash. On the other hand, if Gizmo is sold, chances are slim that

Suzanne would get her chance to move up in the company's hierarchy and possibly take over some day.

Obviously, Ray has to make a decision. Is Gizmo to be sold if he gets hit by a bus tomorrow? Or does he put a plan in place to keep Gizmo in operation, try to ensure its continuing profitability, and keep Suzanne involved one way or another? Ray's existing pension investments, plus the insurance, plus Gizmo's current health all prompted him to opt for keeping the business up and running. This was not going to be easy, doing it "from the grave", but Ray figured he owed it to Suzanne. And one way or the other, Gloria would be more than adequately provided for.

Having decided in favour of Suzanne and Gizmo, he knew he had to protect Suzanne's ownership interest as she learned more about the business. This would involve ensuring that her future husband will not have an opportunity to gain control "too soon", ensuring that any minority shareholders who crop up are held at bay for a few years, and ensuring that Gloria and her possible future husband respect Ray's wishes.

## RAY'S WILL

One of the most troublesome aspects of Ray's succession plan was grappling with the terms of his will, which needed updating. Devising a plan to achieve all his goals would be a tall order in any professional advisor's books, especially considering Gloria's lack of interest in the business and Suzanne's inexperience.

Ray turned to two older and trusted friends. One had just recently retired; the other was only a couple of years away. Both had decades of hands-on business experience – one as a senior executive with a medium-sized business, the other as owner-manager of his own small business for more than 40 years. They liked what Ray had accomplished with Gizmo to date. Both agreed to oversee the business for a few years should Ray die unexpectedly, and they promised to give Suzanne a chance to take over. They also agreed to follow up on any succession program that Ray might put in place, bearing in mind external factors that could affect the health of Gizmo and the aspirations of Gloria and the two children.

## INSURANCE

Recognizing that the family's income needs had shot up dramatically over the last few years, Ray knew that he had to increase his life insurance. Ray figured higher amounts would give Suzanne sufficient funds to buy out Whit's shares of Gizmo and begin to gain control of the company if she chose to take her career in that direction. If the family decided to sell Gizmo, Ray considered requiring that they first had to offer the shares to the current management team. Key personnel would be encouraged to take out policies on Ray for just such an eventuality. In the meantime, Gloria and the two children would be adequately provided for through the insurance proceeds.

Ray carries a fairly healthy amount of disability insurance through the company. He doesn't feel the need to increase the insurance now that he has his management team in place and has developed enough confidence in them.

## RAY'S SUCCESSION PLAN

It has taken Ray several months and many sessions with his professional advisors to articulate his concerns, decide on priorities and set a variety of goals. One of the hardest parts was talking with family members and including them in much of the process. Ray has always made decisions himself and until the past year had run Gizmo entirely by himself. Now however, he has confidence in his management team and has been able to delegate much of the work and major decisions. Opening up the "lines of communication" at Gizmo actually helped Ray as he began to deal with his succession problems with the family.

By the time he was ready to begin putting the various steps in the plan into operation, he was confident that Gloria understood the basics of the program and agreed with what he had set up, and that Whit was happy that his ties with Gizmo would eventually be severed. He was most pleased with Suzanne's reaction. He discussed every step with her and incorporated a few ideas she had. It was only after these many family pow-wows that Ray was certain Suzanne was committed to the business and his trust and expectations were properly placed.

## WHAT DOES THE FUTURE HOLD?

Ray's comprehensive succession and estate program should hold up well if events unfold approximately as Ray has anticipated. About the time Ray wants to begin to bow out of Gizmo, Suzanne should be in a position to take over and control Gizmo. Whit will have received cash over a seven-year period equal to the fair market value of his shares in Gizmo.

Ray and Gloria should have more than enough to see them comfortably through any number of years of retirement. If Gizmo continues on its current path, Ray figures he and Gloria couldn't possibly spend just the retirement income generated by the business. But better safe than sorry. Their lifestyle could change dramatically. And Gizmo may run into some rough patches.

## AND IF EVENTS UNFOLD A LITTLE DIFFERENTLY?

But what might happen if the future takes a considerably different turn? For instance, what if:

- Suzanne marries Adrian, gets divorced, and Adrian makes a play for Gizmo?
- Suzanne loses interest in Gizmo and takes up bird-watching?
- Gizmo discovers it can't compete with two new entrants in the GIZMO field and the company goes belly-up?
- Ray and Gloria divorce. Gloria is determined to get every nickel she can immediately, even if it means the demise of Gizmo Inc.?
- Whit feels cheated out of his share of Gizmo, which proves to be worth several million dollars, and attempts to get his shares back?
- Ray's two trusted friends have heart attacks the day they are supposed to begin acting as advisors to Suzanne, Gloria and the business?

In a number of instances, it is likely that Gizmo may have to be sold. However, this depends on how tightly Ray's succession plans have been arranged and how quickly Suzanne learns the business and is put in a controlling position. We look at selling your business in the next chapter.

Trying to guess what might go wrong with your plans is just as important as trying to trace your path along a map of your uncertain future. Again, flexibility is key as you work out a plan for succession and retirement. Many decisions you make could be irrevocable and harm both you and your family, and probably your business too.

For example, estate freezes are effective because they have a permanence about them. It is never easy and it's always expensive trying to thaw out what you just finished freezing. Sometimes it's just impossible. If your children end up owning their shares directly, that is, there is no trust intervening, the only way you might have of getting them back is to buy them at an outrageous price.

If your children have finally taken control of the company and you have not taken the proper precautions, you may discover that your preferred shares or long-term debt is not as secure and lucrative as you planned. There is very little you can do to change things, other than jump back in and put the company back on its feet, or perhaps as a last resort, sue.

## EFFORT-WELL-REWARDED
You won't put together a successful succession plan overnight. Then again, you didn't put together a successful business overnight either. But the rewards you will reap from a well-thought-out succession plan are worth your efforts. The plan will see to your, and your family's, wants, and at the same time be flexible enough to adapt to changing circumstances. It bears repeating: if you've worked hard to build up your own "Gizmo", it's worthwhile putting the energy into ensuring that "Gizmo" provides for you far into the future.

# 13/Is It Time To Sell Your Business?

Not every owner-manager simply gives his or her business to the children and strolls off to a sun-filled retirement. In fact, a recent survey estimated that less than half of all small businesses are passed on to children who actually take over the operation of the enterprise. And in most cases, the transfer of the reins of power is accomplished as a sale, not as an outright gift.

If you are not selling the business to your children, then you will likely sell it to one of three parties: other shareholders, employees, or outsiders (that is, arm's length buyers with whom you may not be familiar).

. No matter to whom you sell, you want to get a fair price. You've spent years building up the value of the business, making sure it's a success. Now you're looking forward to the business providing for much of your retirement funding. And you might be looking at it to provide a tidy nest egg for your heirs.

Whether the buyer is your children or someone whom you have never set eyes on, you want to ensure that the value you've built up in the business is indeed available to you when you need it the most. At the same time, you undoubtedly want to minimize any costs related to the sale, including taxes, and expose yourself to as little risk as possible.

Defining your objectives before you get down to the details of actually selling your business should be relatively easy. If you have an up-dated succession plan in place, you already have the answers to the hard questions. Keying in on a method of selling the business that actually achieves all your objectives may be a taller order to fill.

## MAJOR ISSUES
There are a number of issues that must be addressed when setting out a plan to sell your business. Assuming that you have identified the potential buyer, the major issues include:
- Ensuring that the $400,000 special small business corporation capital gains exemption is used by all family members involved in the sale, that each family member's $100,000 general capital gains exemption, if available, is also used, and that all taxes associated with the sale are minimized.

- Ensuring that the proceeds from the sale are secure. In many instances, it will not be possible to simply receive a cheque for the proceeds. Amounts will likely be large, and the buyers may have to pay for the sale over time out of profits from the business. If the business or the new owners fall on difficult times, you want to ensure that you have sufficient "pounce power" to either get your money out of the company or guarantee the income stream.
- Ensuring that the sale price and terms of the sale are fair, while at the same time ensuring that you and your family are not exposed to any liability after the sale.

Later in the chapter, we'll look at some of the special problems and sales techniques that are appropriate for sales of a business to the four types of buyers we have identified. First, let's examine the three major aspects of any sale that you, the owner-manager, ought to be familiar with before you enter negotiations – valuation of the business, choosing an appropriate method of sale, and financing the sale.

## VALUATION
Valuing a business is anything but straightforward. Many owner-managers have little idea how to assign a value to their companies, even though they have built them from the ground up and have a good knowledge of their industries. And business valuation can be extremely complex. Most owner-managers are not doing themselves and their families any favours by setting a value on their businesses and using this as a sale price. Over- or under-valuing your business can lead to serious problems that perhaps can't be remedied.

---

**Caution!** Don't dismiss the idea of using a professional business valuator simply because of the cost that might be involved. These professionals are in the business of assigning fair values to the intricate, vibrant entity that is your business. You've heard the admonishment to the legal profession, "A lawyer representing himself has a fool for a client." Similarly, attempting to value your own business may mean that you're stepping well outside your area of expertise.

---

Valuing a business isn't simply a matter of assigning a value to a group of assets. The professional valuator will:
- Analyse financial figures from several years back and work with you to prepare forecasts for the near term.
- Assess assets for current value and need to replace. As well, the

layout of your premises, and any needed improvements, will be considered.
- Review your product line and what stage each product has reached in its life cycle. The dependence on a single product line will also be considered.
- Appraise your employees, particularly key management employees, and assess whether they will stay and how they will perform if the business is sold.
- Assess the management organization and how dependent the business is on the owner-manager.
- Evaluate the industry and the market to determine the future prospects of your business and the state of current and potential competition.
- Chart commitments and contingencies to see what effects these may have.

And of course the existence of prospective buyers will have an effect on the value of your business, as will the way the sale is structured.

## STRUCTURING THE SALE

There are dozens of different ways the sale of your business can be structured. We'll look at some of the common methods of arrangement for a sale. Please note that using one particular method, or a combination, may depend on the nature of the buyer and how the buyer would like the sale to be structured. We look further at the four classes of buyers later in the chapter.

### SALE OF SHARES

This is the most common way to sell a small business, particularly if it is a qualifying small business corporation (QSBC) and the owner-manager and other shareholders have not yet used their special $400,000 SBC capital gains exemptions. A sale of shares also has the advantage of being relatively straightforward, once a value has been placed on the business. Problems, or more correctly complications, most often arise when arranging financing of the sale.

### ASSET SALE

Selling the assets of the business rather than the shares is often attractive from the buyer's perspective, and also from the point of view of the owner-manager and his or her family if they have used up their capital gains exemptions. Such a sale often increases the depreciable base for the acquired assets, which the buyer may then depreciate for tax purposes. However, the remaining shell corporation may have to pay taxes resulting from capital gains and recaptured depreciation that has already been claimed.

The major problem with asset sales is assigning values to the particular assets being sold. Assuming a total price has been agreed upon, the vendor would generally prefer that more of the purchase price be allocated to non-depreciable capital property and goodwill than to inventory and significantly depreciated assets. The reason is straightforward. The tax liability on capital gains and the sale of eligible capital property (the technical term for goodwill and other intangibles) is less than the tax that might have to be paid on inventory profits. As for depreciable property, recaptured depreciation is taxed at full rates, while any gain realized on a sale is a capital gain. As well, no reserves (see financing below) are available on recaptured depreciation or goodwill gains.

The purchaser would prefer an allocation in approximately the opposite order, primarily because inventory and rapid write-off depreciable property provide early tax relief. Purchasers also prefer that more of the purchase price be allocated to depreciable assets with fast rates of write-off rather than to buildings, for instance, that can be depreciated at the rate of only 4 per cent a year.

In any purchase and sale agreement, deciding on an allocation formula is as important as determining a price. If the allocation of the aggregate purchase price to individual assets or groups of assets is unreasonable, Revenue Canada has the power to reallocate the amounts agreed on by vendor and purchaser in a more reasonable manner.

### CORPORATE SHARE REPURCHASE
Your company may consider borrowing money to repurchase some of your shares. The person buying the business by way of a purchase of your remaining shares then may acquire the company at a much lower cost. Although this may seem like a very straightforward approach, the potential tax consequences for the company, the purchaser and you are anything but straightforward. Among the key tax issues are whether the interest on the borrowed funds will be deductible to the company and whether the repurchase of the shares from you will be treated as a dividend or as a capital gain.

For interest to be tax-deductible, a number of criteria must be met. The most important test is that the borrowed money must be used by the company for the purpose of earning its income. Where the funds are used to repurchase shares, the tax authorities will consider this test to have been met only to the extent that the borrowed money is replacing funds already used in the business and represented by the shareholder's equity. Consequently, as long as the amount borrowed does not exceed the amount originally contributed by the shareholder for the shares being repurchased plus the retained earnings of the company reasonably attributable to those shares, the interest should be deductible.

The major advantage of this method, if structured and carried out properly, is that you will receive the bulk of the proceeds from the sale in the form of dividends, rather than capital gains. Depending on your province of residence, dividends could bear three or four percentage points less tax than taxed capital gains. This will work to your advantage if you have either already used up all your capital gains exemption or will do so on the sale of the remaining shares to the purchaser.

However, if you have not always held the shares, but purchased them from a previous shareholder, your cost will usually be greater than the amount for which the shares were originally issued. In these circumstances, a redemption by the company could result in your having to pay tax on a dividend much greater than the amount of the gain you actually realize.

If you held your preference shares in an investment or holding company, it could receive at least some of the dividends, including the deemed dividends arising on redemption, completely free of tax. If, and as long as, the preference shares represent more than 10 per cent of the voting shares and more than 10 per cent of the fair market value of all issued shares of the operating company, the dividends received by your investment company will not be subject to the 25 per cent special refundable tax imposed on portfolio dividends.

The calculation of safe income and its apportionment to different classes of shares is very complex. Your professional tax advisor can help you carefully plan for the redemption of your preference shares to ensure that the tax consequences are properly identified and that the plan is properly carried out to achieve the intended results.

### STAGGERED SHARE REDEMPTIONS

It may be possible to convert your common shares to preference shares. The buyer would then acquire common shares in your company, which would then redeem your preference shares according to a pre-arranged schedule. Your preference shares should bear an agreed-upon dividend rate so they will earn income until actually redeemed.

The major disadvantage to this method of sale is the risk that you may not receive the full proceeds from the sale because the business is unable to redeem the preference shares because it runs into financial difficulty. This risk could be lessened to some degree if you retain control of the business or safeguards are built into the schedule of redemption.

Nevertheless, this method does have its advantages. Depending on how you structure the redemption and preference shares, you might be able to continue to participate in the good fortunes of the company while you own the shares. Most importantly, staggering the receipt of the proceeds from the sale in a manner such as this means that you have more options of choosing a suitable buyer. For instance, this may be the only way family members, employees, or even other shareholders may be able to afford to acquire the company.

Another advantage to the vendor is being able to delay receipt of the purchase price for a number of years. If, for instance, shares are sold but the proceeds are due over a number of years, the resulting capital gain can be deferred only by means of claiming a reserve over five years (ten years if a farming business is sold). Using the preference share redemption method, there is no tax liability until the shares are actually redeemed.

---

**Caution!** Bear in mind that by delaying the receipt of funds, you are making an investment decision. You are assuming that the company will be run well enough to continue to be able to pay the dividends and redeem your shares at some future date. As well, you have become a minority shareholder with limited rights compared with a controlling shareholder's position.

---

## EARN-OUT

Under an earn-out arrangement, your ultimate profit from the sale of the business depends on the future performance of the enterprise. Rather than assigning a specific value neither the vendor nor the purchaser might be happy with, an earn-out essentially reconciles the optimism of the vendor with the healthy scepticism of the purchaser.

For example, the price of the business might be set as a guaranteed minimum equal to the net book value of the business assets. The balance of the purchase price would depend on the increased earnings of the business, or the cash flow of the business over time. With a reverse earn-out, a maximum sale price is set, and this is reduced if sales or profit levels do not live up to expectations.

Earn-outs also may be attractive if the vendor and purchaser cannot agree on a purchase price, but want to go ahead with the deal. The disagreement is resolved as the disputed portion of the price is or is not reflected in earnings over the next few years.

A number of conditions should be present in the earn-out agreement for it to be effective, including the following:

- There should be a clear, reasonable and detailed definition of the earnings upon which the earn-out payments are to be based. If the definition of earnings is not precise, there will almost certainly be a dispute over the calculation of the final price.
- The acquired business should be operated essentially as an autonomous division or subsidiary of the purchaser. If the purchased business is integrated with other business operations, it will be

extremely difficult, and maybe impossible, to calculate the earnings separately.
- The purchaser should be willing to involve the former owners in key decisions that will affect the profitability of the purchased business.
- The parties must have a reasonable expectation that the co-operative spirit necessary for an earn-out to be effective will be forthcoming.

Generally, Revenue Canada permits the cost recovery method to be used when reporting any gain or loss arising on a sale that involves an earn-out agreement. For example, let's assume that the cost base of the shares is $300,000 and $100,000 is paid immediately. The remainder of the purchase price is to be determined over the next five years based on an earnings formula. There is no minimum amount that must be paid.

At the time of sale, the down payment of $100,000 is immediately applied against the cost base, reducing it to $200,000. In the first year of the arrangement, $150,000 is paid under the earn-out agreement. Following the cost recovery method, the cost base of the shares is again reduced by this $150,000. Since the cost base of the shares is still positive ($50,000), there is no gain or loss yet. Next year, $100,000 is paid under the agreement. The cost base is wiped out and now there is a $50,000 gain, which is reported as a capital gain by the vendor. Any amounts paid under the earn-out agreement over the next three years will be reported as capital gains in the years the amounts are received.

A capital loss may be claimed only when it can be firmly established that the maximum amount to be paid does not exceed the vendor's cost base.

To qualify for this cost recovery treatment:
- the vendor and purchaser must be dealing at arm's length;
- the gain or loss must be a capital gain or loss;
- the earn-out feature relates to goodwill, the value of which cannot be agreed upon at the time of sale;
- the sale agreement does not extend beyond five years, and
- the vendor elects to follow the cost recovery method.

Amounts must be recognized as sale proceeds when they can be calculated with certainty. For example, if the earn-out agreement stipulates that a minimum amount is payable in each year, the aggregate of such amounts would have to be taken into account as proceeds in the year the shares are sold.

If a capital gain arises by applying the cost recovery method, but part of the proceeds that have already been taken into account in the calculation are not due until after the end of the year, a capital gains reserve can also be claimed to defer recognition of the gain.

## FINANCING THE SALE OF YOUR BUSINESS

When selling your business to an outsider with whom you deal at arm's length, financing for the purchase is usually the buyer's concern. As you'll recall from Chapter 1, Guy Lafontaine effectively sold a portion of his business when he brought in a "partner", a local software and hardware distributor. It was a straight cash deal for 15 per cent of the common shares and certain guarantees.

When Guy merged with the national distributor a couple of years later, the deal was also structured as a sale. Guy's partner was bought out for cash. Guy sold a portion of his shares also, leaving him with 25 per cent of the common shares in the original company. He received cash, plus shares in the purchasing company, plus a five-year contract that promised to be very lucrative.

Some businesses in some industries cannot, however, be sold as easily or as "cleanly". Often, the vendor will have to help in some manner with the financing and may have to help in other ways, such as committing to an employment contract, perhaps to act in an advisory role until the new owners are assured they can operate the business successfully.

Nevertheless, these situations crop up most frequently when selling to employees, children, and often to other shareholders if you have essentially been running the company and the other shareholders have participated only in minor roles. We'll discuss various financing techniques below as we look at sales to these three parties. Many of the ideas also apply to sales to outsiders if you participate in the financing.

## FINANCING A SALE TO OTHER SHAREHOLDERS

Agreeing on how the shares will be sold under a shareholders' buy-sell agreement is only the first step in the process. For each shareholder to be adequately protected, the other shareholders or the corporation must be able to obtain financing for the purchase if the transaction is to go forward. Most importantly, the financing must be adequate, appropriate and cost-effective to ensure a smooth transition during a change in ownership.

If the business has been extremely successful, the purchasing shareholder may have sufficient cash to acquire the shares. If not, conventional bank loans are the next obvious place to look for financing for virtually any sales transaction. However, in many situations, the purchaser is not able to borrow adequate amounts and often the cost of such a loan threatens to impair the operation of the business. However, there are other options.

### LIFE INSURANCE

In Chapter 12, we looked at various life insurance arrangements that might be adopted to fund buy-sell arrangements. Life insurance typically provides sufficient funding to buy out a deceased shareholder. However, if a shareholder decides to sell because of a dispute or disability, a life insurance policy will not help in financing the sale.

## MORTGAGES

If the business owns real estate, it may be possible for the corporation to obtain a mortgage and use the proceeds as part or all of the financing to buy out a shareholder's interest. The new owner then becomes responsible for the debt. In this situation, the sale would probably be structured as a corporate purchase or redemption of shares. Remember that the deductibility of interest on the mortgage will be an important consideration. This issue needs to be resolved before you go ahead.

## SALE-LEASEBACK

The corporation's real estate and other fixed assets could be sold to a finance company, with an agreement that they will be leased back to the business. Then the corporation could use the cash from the sale to buy out a shareholder's interest. The business may have an option to repurchase the assets when the lease expires.

Some sale-leaseback arrangements are no longer as attractive as they once were. New tax rules ensure that no more depreciation can be claimed by the lessor than if the asset were actually owned by the lessee. Leasing is discussed in more detail in Chapter 4.

## LONG-TERM BUY-BACK ARRANGEMENT

With this type of arrangement, the company owns small life insurance policies on each shareholder. When a shareholder dies, the company uses the insurance proceeds to redeem some shares. The company buys the remaining shares over several years using the company's retained earnings.

## FINANCING A SALE TO EMPLOYEES

Sometimes, employees are the most logical successors. You may want to reward key employees for long careers with the company, and these employees may also best understand the intricacies of the business. Some companies, particularly service companies, are only as good as their employees. And, there is always the risk that good employees will learn the business and then leave to start out on their own, especially if the business is about to be sold. This could seriously impair the value of the business. Part ownership may be one way to retain them.

## DEBT FINANCING

The major problem in selling to employees is that the sale is likely to be financed largely by debt. Often, employees don't have enough funds to pay the full purchase price and will not have the credit rating to obtain the full amount of financing on their own. It then becomes essential for the owner-manager to assist the employees in obtaining financing for the purchase.

Still, you may want to test the commitment of your employees to the reality of becoming an owner of the business by asking them to assume personally as much of the purchase financing as possible. You may also have to provide some financing personally to your employees to demonstrate to lenders that you have confidence in and are committed to the succession arrangement. However, be prepared to subordinate your security to that of other creditors. Your banker is the first one to approach. He or she is familiar with your business and may be willing to participate in financing an employee buy-out.

## ASSISTING EMPLOYEES' TAX PLANNING

You also may be able to help your employees structure their shareholdings so that they can service their debt on a tax-efficient basis. For example, the employees might establish a holding company. They would then contribute the amount required to purchase your shares to their holding company in exchange for common shares. The interest payable by the employees on money borrowed for this purpose should be deductible against their salary income for tax purposes.

As long as the shares purchased from you by the holding company represent more than 10 per cent of the voting shares and more than 10 per cent of the value of all the issued shares of your company, all dividends received by the holding company are tax-free. The holding company can then distribute the amount of such dividends to the employee-shareholders as a partial return of capital. Although such amounts received by the employees reduce the cost base of their shares in the holding company, no immediate tax is payable until such time as the full amount of their original investment has been repaid.

The advantages of this strategy are that the employees realize tax savings by deducting their interest expense against their salary income and are able to use the cash dividends received on their new investment to service their debt without paying current tax on the dividends.

## ASSET SPIN-OFF

If the value of the business is still beyond the reach of your employees, you might consider reducing the purchase price of the business by removing redundant assets, such as investments, and assets that can be leased back to the business, such as real estate and plant equipment.

## DEFERRED PAYMENT

Many owner-managers who plan to sell the business to their employees may have little choice but to take some of the purchase price now and the rest later. The major questions then become how much can you wait to receive, when do you need to receive it, what are the financial consequences of delaying receipt, and how assured are you of collecting in full?

You certainly don't want to jeopardize your retirement by being overly generous to the prospective owners of the business, so you might want to receive a sufficient amount to fund your retirement years properly at the time of sale. Getting this much out immediately may be the least you would expect from the employees who are making the purchase.

If you sell an asset, such as the shares of your company, and realize a capital gain, but do not receive the entire proceeds at the time of the sale, you can claim a reserve for proceeds not yet received, which acts to reduce the amount of capital gain that you must report for tax purposes. At least one-fifth of the gain must be recognized in the year of sale, two-fifths of the gain by the end of the year after the sale takes place, three-fifths by the end of the next year, and so on. You are permitted to claim a reserve only for four years – the remaining portion of the gain must be brought into income for tax purposes in the fifth year.

For example, let's assume that at some point in the future, Ray Corcoran sells his shares to his employees (his daughter Suzanne has lost interest in the business) for $1 million. His cost is $200,000, so he realizes a capital gain of $800,000. His employees come up with some funding, but $500,000 remains to be paid. They promise to pay $50,000 a year beginning next year. Thus, Ray will have received the entire proceeds at the end of the eleventh year.

This year for tax purposes, Ray must report $400,000 of the gain, and he will claim a reserve for $400,000. Since he has not yet received half the proceeds ($500,000/$1 million), his reserve is limited to one-half the capital gain or $400,000. Next year he reports $40,000 (one-twentieth of the gain since he received one-twentieth of the proceeds). He claims a reserve of $360,000 ($40,000 less than the previous year's reserve). At this point, he has reported 55 per cent of the total capital gain. In the following year, he again reports a capital gain of $40,000 and claims a $320,000 reserve, which is the maximum he can claim, since for tax purposes he must have recognized at least three-fifths or 60 per cent of the gain by the third year ($480,000).

In the fourth year, he receives another $50,000, but must report $160,000, since the maximum reserve he can claim is now down to $160,000 (he must have reported at least four-fifths of the gain by the end of the fourth year). In the fifth year, he can no longer claim a reserve and must report the final $160,000, even though he still receives only $50,000 on payment of the debt. No gains need be reported over the next six years as he receives the remaining $300,000 of the debt, since he has now reported the entire $800,000 gain.

Obviously, Ray will expect some compensation for being forced to pay tax on any gain when he has not yet received all the proceeds. This might take the form of higher interest on the debt.

Ray also may choose to structure the sale differently. Assuming that he has used his $500,000 total capital gains exemptions, he may be much better off having the corporation purchase some of his common shares and converting the rest to preference shares that then could be redeemed over the 11-year timetable. The rate of tax on the dividend that Ray will be deemed to have received will be lower than the rate of tax on the capital gain, and Ray will not be penalized for receiving the proceeds of sale over a period longer than five years (we discussed this corporate repurchase option earlier in this chapter).

---

**Caution!** By choosing to receive dividends over a period of years, Ray is making an investment decision. He is assuming that the company will remain healthy and he will have no trouble receiving his dividends each year and eventually redeeming his shares. There are risks involved in making such a decision, which should be factored into the sale price of the company.

---

### SECURITY

Since Ray has not received the full proceeds at the time of sale, he will most certainly want some form of security that ensures the unpaid proceeds will indeed be paid. There are a variety of ways that you can increase security:

- retain some control through the preference shares or through a management contract with the company;
- demand representation on the board of directors;
- require the buyer to pledge his or her shares as security for proceeds so that, if you don't receive full payment, you regain control of the company, which unfortunately may be the last thing you want if you have been retired for a few years;
- take back a charge on assets as security, or purchase and lease the business assets back to the company with an option to repurchase, or
- obtain life insurance on the purchasers.

Chances are that your continuing involvement in the business is the best security you can arrange, and it may be the most appreciated by the new owners. After all, you've been responsible for getting the business to the point where it is now attractive to your employees. They will likely be interested in keeping you around for as long as you still have that magic touch.

## EMPLOYEE STOCK OPTION PLANS

If your succession plan is developed well in advance of your retirement, employees may begin buying into the company over a number of years. This can be done through employee stock options that form part of their remuneration package. This is one of the techniques being used by Ray Corcoran in his Gizmo business. Stock option plans are discussed in more detail in Chapter 9.

## TAX INCENTIVES AND GOVERNMENT FINANCING

From time to time, the provincial and federal governments implement various tax incentives and financing programs to help employees and others wishing to invest in small businesses. Several provinces have venture capital programs in place and a couple offer partial or complete tax holidays for new small businesses for short periods of time (as Quebec does, for example). In this latter case, the sale may have to be structured so that the enterprise qualifies as a new corporation for purposes of the tax holiday. The Federal Business Development Bank has an Investment Banking Division that may provide some assistance.

## MEZZANINE FINANCING

This is one option that offers a mid-cost alternative to bank debt and venture capital when traditional financing is not available. The lender accepts greater risk in return for a higher rate of interest because loans are unsecured or subordinated to other debts (that is, the lender is the last in the line of creditors). Sources of mezzanine financing include institutional investors, private capital pools, banks and pooled institutional funds invested by specialty finance companies. Junk bonds, so popular in the halcyon leveraged-buyout days in the 1980s, were an extreme form of mezzanine financing.

## VENTURE CAPITAL

Venture capitalists may be approached if outside investors are required because the employees cannot come up with sufficient financing. This is usually considered an option of last resort because it is often the most expensive financing alternative. Venture capitalists normally require a substantial equity position and representation on the board of directors. Generally, the financing lasts for a short-term period of two or three years. As well, venture capitalists generally expect projected annual growth rates in the plus 30 per cent range.

# FINANCING A SALE TO A CHILD

Few owner-managers and their children are in a position to transact a cash sale for shares or assets when the time has come to bow out. On the other hand, few owner-managers pick one specific date on which such a sale must take place. The transition is generally gradual. Ray Corcoran's planning is typical. As Suzanne's skills, knowledge and desire gradually develop, Ray will involve her more and more in the business and in the ownership of the business. She is in no position to always pay cash for the shares she is steadily accumulating, but she will be some day. Ray planned that "some day" would coincide with the date he decided to retire.

As well, Ray, like so many owner-managers, discovered that only one of his children was interested in the business. He wanted to treat both fairly, but he foresaw problems if both children continued to participate in their minority ownership of Gizmo Inc. on an even footing. Therefore, he instituted a plan to begin buying out his disinterested son.

Ray's succession plan contains all the classic elements for passing on a business to a child:
- gradual transfer of ownership to eventual owner-manager;
- buy-out of other children;
- conversion of common shares to preference shares to secure gains already accrued in the company;
- realization of sufficient gains to use up his and his wife's capital gains exemptions;
- retention of control through common and preference shares;
- eventual sale of remaining common shares for debt and eventual redemption of preference shares, and
- implementation of measures to ensure the business would survive, his wife would be taken care of, and the children would inherit if he died prematurely.

Ray will actually be using several methods of sale and financing as Suzanne takes over the business, and he has planned carefully to use other techniques if necessary.

## SALE OF SHARES

A direct sale of shares to a child almost invariably means not receiving cash at the time of sale. Few children have the means to buy the shares outright or obtain adequate conventional financing, although this would be more likely if you were to guarantee loans and use assets of the business as security. However, this puts your future at some risk, which probably goes contrary to your succession planning.

Therefore, you'll likely have to assume some amount of debt on the sale. The nature of your business and current and expected conditions likely will dictate the terms of the debt. If the business is healthy, prospects are good, and you have no immediate cash needs, a non-interest-bearing note with definite but flexible repayment terms may be sufficient.

The major problem with this arrangement is the lack of security you retain over your invested capital. In most situations, owner-managers who take back notes for large amounts also retain control of the business, or take back sufficient security to ensure access to the business's assets if the child should have trouble meeting the payments on the note.

And as noted above, tax considerations of this type of sale cannot be ignored. You may not have the funds to meet the tax liability on a large capital gain if you are not to receive any funds from the child for a number of years. The reserve provisions only defer some tax for up to five years (ten years for sales of farm businesses). As well, it may be more desirable to receive the proceeds of sale in the form of a dividend rather than a capital gain since less tax will likely be paid and you should not run into any alternative minimum tax (AMT) problems.

### CORPORATE REPURCHASE

This method may be more attractive if your business has sufficient liquidity to purchase your shares. Your child will have to finance a much smaller amount when the remaining shares are purchased, you will receive dividends on the corporate repurchase, rather than capital gains, and you will have much less of your invested capital at risk.

Unfortunately, not every business is in a position to be able to repurchase a significant number of the owner-manager's shares. The corporation's funds could be tied up in expansion or modernization, much of the retained income could already have been paid out as dividends and be deferred in the owner-manager's holding company, and the business might be carrying a debt load that makes such a repurchase impossible.

This problem could be overcome by staggering the repurchase and the sale of common shares to the child over a number of years. Of course, the owner-manager would retain considerable control of the business over this period.

### REDEMPTION OF FREEZE SHARES

A sale by means of the staggered preference share redemption method is one of the most common ways to transfer a business to one's child, primarily because it dovetails nicely with the owner-manager's estate and succession planning, particularly any estate freezing program that has been undertaken.

Under the typical corporate freeze, the owner-manager converts his or her common shares to preference shares, and the child subscribes for new common shares. The child now participates in the future growth in the business, the owner-manager retains voting control of the business through the preference shares, and as well, the owner-manager continues to participate in the company's income through dividends on the preference shares.

Since the child owns all the common shares, no actual sale need take place for the child eventually to take over the company. The parent simply redeems the preference shares over a period of time, gradually getting his or her capital out of the company and surrendering control of the enterprise to the child.

Once again, dividends, not capital gains, are realized on redemption of the shares, and the redemption can be timed to suit your income needs. Of course, you should first have used up your capital gains exemptions before undertaking a share redemption program.

## ASSET SPIN-OFF

Removing business assets from the operating company is sometimes used as a method of distributing different corporate assets to children. One child controls the company and leases the business assets from another child. This method can also be used to help finance the purchase of the company by one child.

Note that such transactions should be carried out on a tax-deferred rollover basis. Otherwise, the sale must be made at fair market value, which likely will result in a tax cost.

As you'll recall from Chapter 12, Ray Corcoran was considering using this method to generate retirement income. He would, if necessary, transfer the real estate and perhaps the equipment owned by Gizmo Inc. to a separate corporation and lease these assets back to Gizmo. Eventually, his daughter Suzanne, or the company itself, would be in a position to buy that corporation from Ray. Until then, Gizmo itself would be worth less, stripped of its assets, making it easier for Suzanne to finance the purchase of her shares.

The advantage of this arrangement is the security afforded the owner-manager, since he or she still owns a significant piece of the company, even though the operation itself may have already been sold. The lease agreement also gives the owner-manager considerable control over the operating company, although certainly not as much compared with an owner-manager who retains preference shares in the operating company.

## CORPORATE PARTNERSHIP

This method allows the transfer of ownership after a period of time and provides the owner-manager with sufficient security in respect of the assets being sold to the child. The child forms a new corporation, which enters into a partnership agreement with your corporation. The profits from the business operated by the partnership are split according to a pre-determined ratio that may be altered as the child becomes more responsible in the business.

This allows the child to build up equity and credit worthiness in his or her own corporation well before you sell the business, while you retain control over the operation of the business. Eventually, if the agreement is so structured, the child would buy the parent's corporation when sufficient funding is available.

## KEEPING YOUR OPTIONS OPEN

There are dozens of different ways to structure the sale of your business while retaining sufficient control to protect your assets and assure that you do indeed generate the income you need to see you and your family through your retirement years.

Control can be exercised through retaining voting shares, keeping certain assets, or even an integral part of the business if that's possible, and entering into a shareholders' agreement. Several of the same methods can be used to generate retirement income. And as well, you might consider the payment of a significant retirement allowance before selling the company. All or a portion of the allowance can be rolled over into an RRSP and escape immediate taxation. And the value of the company will be reduced appropriately, which should ease the purchaser's financing burden.

Planning for the sale of your business shouldn't begin a few days before you decide to retire. It should be an inherent part of your succession plan and should be updated as your circumstances change. In most cases, a sale of a business demands a certain amount of long-range planning. Often, it will be necessary for you to continue your involvement with the business even though you have sold your interest in it and received all the proceeds. In other cases, you'll want to retain control over a period of time, often many years, to ensure you eventually receive the full purchase price, since you have participated directly in financing the purchase by the new owners.

In all cases, it is extremely important to retain as much flexibility as possible over the process. Your financial needs change as do your personal circumstances. And your business will also change over time. The method of sale that's suitable today may not work tomorrow, or may result in painful tax consequences.

## CONCLUSION

Putting as much effort into tax planning as you do into your business operations can be just as financially rewarding. It's not necessary that you understand all the ins and outs of hundreds of tax strategies; you merely have to be aware of situations where tax savings might be achieved. Then it's a simple matter of getting together with your professional advisor to design the proper technique that will attain your objectives.

# Appendix A

**FEDERAL CORPORATE INCOME TAX RATES AND SURTAX**
The 1986 federal budget introduced a schedule to reduce the corporate income tax rate to 43 per cent by July 1, 1989. Subsequently, new tax rate changes were announced as part of the federal Tax Reform. Meanwhile, the federal surtax was amended effective January 1, 1987. With all those changes, it should be noted that taxation years in progress when a change occurs in the federal tax rate, the federal surtax rate, or a provincial corporate tax rate or surtax require a proration of income for the periods before and after the effective date of each change. The following table summarizes the federal corporate tax rate changes from 1986 onward.

After deducting the 10 per cent abatement for provincial tax but excluding surtax, the federal tax rates for corporations are:

|  | Prior to July 1, 1987[1] | Rates are effective from July 1 of year indicated[1] | | | | |
|---|---|---|---|---|---|---|
|  |  | 1987 | 1988 | 1989 | 1990 | 1991 |
| Active Business Income |  |  |  |  |  |  |
| • Not Eligible for SBD |  |  |  |  |  |  |
| • General | 36% | 35% | 28% | 28% | 28% | 28% |
| • Manufacturing & Processing[2] | 30 | 28 | 26 | 25 | 24 | 23 |
| • Eligible for SBD |  |  |  |  |  |  |
| • General | 10 | 14 | 12 | 12 | 12 | 12 |
| • Manufacturing & Processing[2] | 10 | 8 | 12 | 12 | 12 | 12 |
| Other Income |  |  |  |  |  |  |
| • CCPCs[3] | 36 | 36 | 28 | 28 | 28 | 28 |
| • Other corporations | 36 | 35 | 28 | 28 | 28 | 28 |

Refundable portion of federal tax

|  | To Dec. 31, 1986 | 1987 | 1988 and after |
|---|---|---|---|
| Part I tax | 16 2/3% | 25% | 20% |
| Part IV tax | 25% | 33 1/3% | 25% |
| Refund rate | 1:4 | 1:3 | 1:4 |

## FEDERAL SURTAX

As with corporate rates, the corporate surtax has undergone changes in recent years.

- July 1, 1985, to December 31, 1986: 5 per cent federal surtax on federal tax after the 10 per cent abatement for provincial tax and after excluding the tax on income eligible for the small business deduction.
- January 1, 1987, to June 30, 1989: 3 per cent federal surtax on federal tax after deducting the federal abatement, the small business deduction, the M&P credit and the amount credited to the company's refundable dividend tax on hand account for the year, but before taking into account a number of other tax credits.
- After June 30, 1989: 3 per cent surtax is calculated after the federal abatement but before the small business deduction and M&P credit, without deducting the amount credited to refundable dividend tax on hand account for the year and before taking into account a number of other tax credits.

Notes:

1. All figures are net of the 10 per cent abatement for provincial tax. Federal surtax is not reflected in these rates.
2. The manufacturing and processing deduction is 5 per cent for income subject to the small business deduction and 6 per cent for other eligible income up until June 30, 1987. This rises to 6 per cent and 7 per cent for the period from July 1, 1987, to June 30, 1988. Beginning July 1, 1988, the deduction for income subject to the small business deduction is eliminated, while the general M&P deduction drops to 2 per cent, then increases by 1 per cent annually (on July 1 of each year) until it levels off at 5 per cent in 1991 (and the effective rate for corporations not eligible for the small business deduction levels off at 23 per cent).
3. The effective 36 per cent rate was intended to remain for investment income of CCPCs and net taxable capital gains of mutual fund and

investment corporations in the rules adopted just prior to Tax Reform. The rate decrease from 36 per cent to 28 per cent introduced under Tax Reform was effective January 1, 1988, for income of investment corporations (other than capital gains) and investment income of CCPCs to correspond with changes to the refundable tax rules effective on that date.

## 1991 PROVINCIAL CORPORATE INCOME TAX RATES[1]

| | Basic Rate | Small Business | Small Business M&P | M&P | Tax Holiday[2] |
|---|---|---|---|---|---|
| Alta.[3] | 15.0/15.5% | 6.0% | 6.0% | 15.0/15.5% | |
| B.C.[4] | 15.0 | 9.0 | 9.0 | 15.0 | |
| Man.[5] | 17.0 | 10.0 | 10.0 | 17.0 | yes |
| N.B.[6] | 17.0 | 9.0 | 9.0 | 17.0 | |
| Nfld.[7] | 17.0 | 10.0 | 10.0 | 17.0 | yes |
| N.W.T.[8] | 12.0 | 8.0/5.0 | 8.0/5.0 | 12.0 | |
| N.S.[9] | 16.0 | 10.0 | 10.0 | 16.0 | yes |
| Ont.[10] | 15.5 | 10.0 | 10.0 | 14.5 | yes |
| P.E.I. | 15.0 | 10.0 | 10.0 | 15.0 | |
| Que.[11] | 14.95/16.25 | 3.45/3.75 | 3.45/3.75 | 6.33/6.9 | yes |
| Sask.[12] | 15.0 | 10.0 | 10.0 | 15.0 | yes |
| Yukon | 10.0 | 5.0 | 2.5 | 2.5 | |

Notes:

1. Corporations with taxation years in progress when a tax rate change takes effect are required to prorate income to the periods before and after the change before applying the applicable rate.
2. Tax holidays generally apply to income subject to the federal small business deduction, which would otherwise qualify for the provincial small business deduction. See the notes for the individual provinces for relevant dates.
3. An M&P credit of 6 per cent or 5 per cent was in effect for the period from April 1, 1985, to March 31, 1990. The 6 per cent rate applied to income not eligible for the Alberta SBD, while the 5 per cent credit applied to income eligible for the provincial SBD, resulting in a zero per cent rate on eligible income. On April 1, 1987, the basic corporate tax rate rose from 11 per cent to 15 per cent. Effective April 1, 1990, the SBD fell from 10 per cent to 9 per cent. Effective April 1, 1991, the basic corporate rate rose to 15.5 per cent. The small business rate was not affected by this change.
4. On January 1, 1987, the basic corporate tax rate in British Columbia fell from 16 per cent to 15 per cent and on January 1, 1988, to 14 per cent. On January 1, 1991, it rose to 15 per cent. On July 1, 1987, the

small business rate rose from 8 per cent to 11 per cent, but, effective July 1, 1988, fell to the current 9 per cent.

5. Manitoba provides a tax holiday (small business tax reduction program) for CCPCs applicable for the first five years of any new business incorporated after August 8, 1988, and before the end of 1991. The rate reduction in the first year is 10 per cent (yielding an effective rate of zero per cent). The reduction then decreases by 2 per cent each year, so that, after the fifth year, the full 10 per cent provincial small business rate applies.

6. The basic corporate rate in New Brunswick increased from 15 per cent to 16 per cent, effective January 1, 1988.

7. The basic corporate tax rate in Newfoundland increased from 16 per cent to 17 per cent, effective January 1, 1989. A three-year tax holiday applies to qualifying small businesses incorporated in that province after April 2, 1987, and before April 3, 1991.

8. Effective January 1, 1990, the basic corporate tax rate in the Northwest Territories rose from 10 per cent to 12 per cent and at the same time, the rate on eligible small business income fell from 10 per cent to 8 per cent. The small business rate was again changed in the 1991 budget. It falls from 8 per cent to 5 per cent on July 1, 1991.

9. Nova Scotia's basic corporate tax rate increased from 15 per cent to 16 per cent effective January 1, 1990. The provincial tax holiday applies to the first two taxation years of an eligible business incorporated in Nova Scotia after April 18, 1986.

10. A three-year tax holiday applies to certain corporations incorporated in Ontario after May 13, 1982, but before April 21, 1988. Beginning in 1992, there will be a clawback of the Ontario small business deduction when taxable income exceeds $200,000. The 3.7 per cent surtax eliminates the small business deduction when taxable income reaches $497,297.

11. Quebec's corporate tax rates were scheduled to rise on January 1, 1992. However, in the 1991 budget, the increases were advanced to September 1, 1991. Furthermore, the corporate surtax (15 per cent up until September 1, 1991) is incorporated directly into the new rates. Prior to September, 1991, the basic corporate rate was 13 per cent. A 7.5 per cent Quebec rate reduction for active business income earned in Canada applied to all corporations, producing a provincial rate of 5.5 per cent on eligible income while the small business deduction produced a rate of 3 per cent (all before the surtax). The 7.25 per cent surtax was increased to 12 per cent on May 16, 1989, and to 15 per cent on April 27, 1990. The surtax is included in the pre-September 1 rates of 14.95 per cent, 3.45 per cent and 6.33 per cent. A three-year tax holiday is available to certain corporations incorporated in Quebec after May 1, 1986.

12. In Saskatchewan, the basic corporate tax rate fell from 17 per cent to 15 per cent effective January 1, 1989 and it is scheduled to rise to 16 per cent on January 1, 1992. Income eligible for both the federal SBD and M&P credit was taxed at zero per cent in 1988, but, beginning in 1989, the rate on such income rose to 10 per cent. A two-year provincial tax holiday applies to certain companies incorporated in Saskatchewan after March 26, 1986, and before April 1, 1992.

# APPENDIX B

## CAPITAL TAX RATES[1]

|  | Exemption ($ millions) | General Rate | Financial Institutions |
|---|---|---|---|
| Alta.[2] | – | | 2% |
| B.C.[3] | $500 | – | 2 |
| Man.[4] | 1 | 0.3% | 3 |
| N.B.[5] | 10 | – | 3 |
| Nfld.[6] | 0.5 | – | 3 |
| N.S.[7] | 0.5/2 | – | 3 |
| Ont.[8] | | 0.3 | 0.8/1 |
| P.E.I.[9] | 2 | – | 2.5/3 |
| Que.[10] | | 0.52/0.56 | 1.04/1.12 |
| Sask.[11] | 10 | 0.5 | 3 |
| Federal Financial Institutions[12] | $200 | – | 1.25% |
| Large Corporations[13] | 10 | 0.2 | |

Notes:

1. The rates shown are those currently in effect. Where a taxation year is in progress when a rate change occurs, the tax is generally prorated between the periods before and after the rate change takes effect.
2. The Alberta capital tax on financial institutions came into effect April 1, 1990.
3. B.C. eliminated its 0.2 per cent general capital tax, effective April 1, 1987. On April 1, 1987, the rate for financial institutions rose from 0.6 per cent to 2 per cent and at the same time, the rate for banks with paid–up capital under $5 million rose from 0.8 per cent to 2 per cent. B.C. corporate tax payable is deductible in computing liability for the continuing capital tax on financial institutions.
4. In Manitoba, the general rate went from 0.2 per cent to 0.3 per cent,

185

on April 1, 1987. For years ending after June 30, 1987, corporations with paid-up capital in excess of $10 million are subject to a 0.2 per cent surcharge on that excess. The rate for banks rose from 1.9 per cent to 3.0 per cent on June 30, 1986, and the rate for other financial institutions went from 0.6 per cent to 0.9 per cent on June 30, 1986, and to 3 per cent on July 1, 1987. In Manitoba, a special notch provision limits the tax payable where paid-up capital is less than $1,003,000.

5. New Brunswick introduced a capital tax on financial institutions for fiscal years ending after March 31, 1987. The initial rate of 2 per cent of paid-up capital rose to 3 per cent effective April 1, 1988.

6. The Newfoundland tax on financial institutions rose from 1.5 per cent to 2 per cent on April 2, 1987, and from 2 per cent to 3 per cent, effective April 1, 1990.

7. Nova Scotia capital tax was introduced for fiscal periods ending on or after June 30, 1986. The initial rate of 1.5 per cent rose to 3 per cent effective January 1, 1990.

8. On April 28, 1988, the capital tax rate for financial institutions rose from 0.6 per cent to 0.8 per cent and on April 29, 1991, it rose to 1 per cent. Prior to April 20, 1988, special rates (basically flat amounts) applied where paid-up capital was under $1.2 million. For taxation years after April 20, 1988, small corporations (those with total assets and gross revenue each under $1 million) are exempt from Ontario capital tax, while other corporations whose taxable capital is under $2.3 million are generally subject to flat rates.

9. In Prince Edward Island, a capital tax on financial institutions was introduced for fiscal periods ending after June 30, 1988. The initial rate of 1.5 per cent rose to 2.5 per cent effective April 1, 1990, and to 3 per cent effective April 10, 1991.

10. Prior to September 1, 1991, a 15 per cent surtax was applied to Quebec capital tax. Starting on that date, the surtax is incorporated into the rates. The rates shown for the period before September 1, 1991 include the surtax.

11. In Saskatchewan, the capital tax rate for financial institutions rose from 1.2 per cent to 3 per cent on January 1, 1987. The general rate is scheduled to rise from 0.5 per cent to 0.6 per cent on January 1, 1992.

12. In the 1990 federal budget, it was proposed that life insurance companies be subject to the financial institutions capital tax, effective February 20, 1990.

13. The government has proposed to increase the federal tax on large corporations from 0.175 per cent to 0.2 per cent, effective January 1, 1991.

# Appendix C

## 1991 MARGINAL RATES ON INVESTMENT CANADIAN DIVIDENDS[1]

| Taxable Income | Alta. | B.C. | Man. | N.B. | Nfld. | N.W.T. |
|---|---|---|---|---|---|---|
| $28,785 | 24.61% | 24.78% | 27.36% | 26.13% | 26.44% | 23.59% |
| 30,001 | 24.61 | 24.78 | 29.86 | 26.13 | 26.44 | 23.59 |
| 38,864 | 24.61 | 24.78 | 29.86 | 26.13 | 26.44 | 23.59 |
| 43,021 | 25.20 | 24.78 | 29.86 | 26.13 | 26.44 | 23.59 |
| 50,001 | 25.20 | 24.78 | 29.86 | 26.13 | 26.44 | 23.59 |
| 57,569 | 31.02 | 30.65 | 35.75 | 32.31 | 32.70 | 29.18 |
| 61,675 | 32.00 | 31.63 | 36.73 | 33.29 | 33.68 | 30.16 |
| 76,525 | 32.00 | 31.63 | 36.73 | 33.29 | 33.68 | 30.16 |
| 78,831 | 32.00 | 32.64 | 36.73 | 33.29 | 33.68 | 30.16 |
| 83,632 | 32.00 | 32.64 | 36.73 | 33.29 | 33.68 | 30.16 |
| 92,886 | 32.00 | 32.64 | 36.73 | 33.29 | 33.68 | 30.16 |
| 96,158 | 32.00 | 32.64 | 36.73 | 34.23 | 33.68 | 30.16 |

| Taxable Income | N.S. | Ont. | P.E.I. | Que. | Sask. | Yukon |
|---|---|---|---|---|---|---|
| $28,785 | 26.05% | 25.02% | 25.81% | 31.68% | 27.04% | 23.75% |
| 30,001 | 26.05 | 25.02 | 25.81 | 31.68 | 27.04 | 23.75 |
| 38,864 | 26.05 | 25.02 | 25.81 | 31.68 | 28.61 | 23.75 |
| 43,021 | 26.05 | 25.02 | 25.81 | 31.68 | 28.61 | 23.75 |
| 50,001 | 26.05 | 25.02 | 25.81 | 32.93 | 28.61 | 23.75 |
| 57,569 | 32.21 | 30.94 | 31.92 | 36.25 | 34.70 | 29.38 |
| 61,675 | 33.19 | 31.92 | 32.90 | 37.23 | 35.68 | 30.35 |
| 76,525 | 34.36 | 31.92 | 32.90 | 37.23 | 35.68 | 30.35 |
| 78,831 | 34.36 | 31.92 | 32.90 | 37.23 | 35.68 | 30.35 |
| 83,632 | 34.36 | 33.17 | 32.90 | 37.23 | 35.68 | 30.35 |
| 92,886 | 34.36 | 33.17 | 34.04 | 37.23 | 35.68 | 30.35 |
| 96,158 | 34.36 | 33.17 | 34.04 | 37.23 | 35.68 | 30.35 |

Note:

1. These tables show the marginal tax rates (combined federal and provincial) on dividends. Marginal rates are the rates that apply to

each additional dollar of dividend received and which is taxable within the particular tax bracket. The rates assume that taxable income before considering the marginal income was subject to tax at regular rates. To illustrate the application of marginal rates, if you are a resident of Ontario and your 1991 taxable income before dividends is $50,000, the combined rate of tax on each additional dollar of dividend received, until the next tax bracket is reached, is 25.02 per cent, taking into account the gross-up and credit.

# INDEX

# SOCIAL SECURITY
# AND
# PRIVATE PENSION PLANS:
Competitive or Complementary?

# Pension Research Council

Other Publications of the
PENSION RESEARCH COUNCIL


Concepts of Actuarial Soundness in Pension Plans—*Dorrance C. Bronson*
Social Aspects in Retirement—*Otto Pollak*
Positive Experiences in Retirement—*Otto Pollak*
Ensuring Medical Care for the Aged—*Mortimer Spiegelman*
Legal Protection of Private Pension Expectations—*Edwin W. Patterson*
Legal Status of Employee Benefit Rights under Private Pension Plans—
    *Benjamin Aaron*
Decision and Influence Processes in Private Pension Plans—*James E. McNulty, Jr.*
Fulfilling Pension Expectations—*Dan M. McGill*
Collectively Bargained Multi-Employer Pension Plans—*Joseph J. Melone*
Actuarial Aspects of Pension Security—*William F. Marples*
Status of Funding under Private Pension Plans—*Frank L. Griffin, Jr.* and
    *Charles L. Trowbridge*
Guaranty Fund for Private Pension Obligations—*Dan M. McGill*
Preservation of Pension Benefit Rights—*Dan M. McGill*
Retirement Systems for Public Employees—*Thomas P. Bleakney*
Employer Guarantee of Pension Benefits—*Dan M. McGill*
Reciprocity among Private Multiemployer Pension Plans—*Maurice E. McDonald*
Fundamentals of Private Pensions—*Dan M. McGill*
Pension Mathematics—*Howard E. Winklevoss*

# Social Security and Private Pension Plans:
## Competitive or Complementary?

A compilation of papers presented at the 1976
Symposium for Institutional Members of the
Pension Research Council of The Wharton
School, University of Pennsylvania

Planned and edited by

**DAN M. McGILL**
Chairman and Research Director
Pension Research Council
The Wharton School

Ralph H. Blanchard Memorial Endowment Series
VOLUME I

Published for the
**Pension Research Council**
The Wharton School
University of Pennsylvania

by

RICHARD D. IRWIN, INC.   Homewood, Illinois   60430
Irwin-Dorsey Limited   Georgetown, Ontario   L7G 4B3

ISBN 0-256-01968-1
Library of Congress Catalog Card No. 76–49315
*Printed in the United States of America*

## PENSION RESEARCH COUNCIL

v

Bert Seidman, *Director, Department of Social Security*, AFL–CIO, Washington, D.C.

Robert Tilove, *Senior Vice President*, Martin E. Segal Company, New York City

Charles L. Trowbridge, F.S.A., *Senior Vice President*, Bankers Life Company, Des Moines

L. Edwin Wang, *Executive Secretary*, Board of Pensions of Lutheran Church in America, Minneapolis

Howard E. Winklevoss, *Associate Professor of Insurance and Actuarial Science*, University of Pennsylvania, Philadelphia

Howard Young, F.S.A., *Special Consultant to the President*, United Automobile Workers, Detroit

## PURPOSE OF THE COUNCIL

The Pension Research Council was formed in 1952 in response to an urgent need for a better understanding of the private pension mechanism. It is composed of nationally recognized pension experts representing leadership in every phase of private pensions. It sponsors academic research into the problems and issues surrounding the private pension institution and publishes the findings in a series of books and monographs. The studies are conducted by mature scholars drawn from both the academic and business spheres.

# Foreword

FROM THE TIME that the Social Security Act was first being considered
in 1935, there has been concern in some quarters that the old-age insurance component of the program would unduly constrict the role of private
pension plans. That concern was felt so strongly by some businessmen
in 1935 that a serious effort was made to exclude from the impending
program employees already participating in a corporate pension plan and
those who in the future might come within the scope of such a plan, the
exclusion continuing so long as the employees remained in the plan. This
effort failed in the United States, but the concept of permitting employers
to "contract out" from the coverage of a social insurance program by
providing equivalent benefits under a private plan was later embraced by
some other countries, notably the United Kingdom and Japan. In the
United States, Canada, and other countries, the consequences of concurrent participation by employees in both public and private pension plans
have been mitigated somewhat by officially sanctioned integration procedures.

Over the years each expansion of coverage and liberalization of benefits
of the OASDI component of the United States Social Security program
has rekindled the fears of large segments of the business community that
the government program will ultimately envelop corporate employee benefit plans, substituting the straitjacket of a mandatory national program
for the flexibility of voluntary, custom-designed private programs. Within
the last few years, these fears have been intensified by legislative increases
in Social Security benefits that greatly exceeded the rise in the cost of
living during the period covered by the increases.

Moreover, in 1972 Congress made provision for automatic increases in benefits in the future in accordance with a formula that recognizes increases in both wages and prices. Under this provision, the percentage increase in benefits triggered by a rise in the CPI applies not only to benefits in current-payment status, but also to the percentage components of the multi-step formula that determines the ultimate benefits of active employees. This procedure was used by Congress in making ad hoc benefit adjustments from 1954 to 1972 and under the economic conditions then prevailing produced reasonably satisfactory results. However, under the economic conditions expected in the future this adjustment technique will lead to benefit levels that must be considered excessive by any rational standard and will impose an intolerable cost burden on employers, workers, and possibly the whole body of taxpayers (which of course consists largely of workers and employers) if general revenue financing is injected into the program, as some propose.

In the light of these circumstances, a number of research and public policy organizations have placed a study of the impact of Social Security high on their agenda. For several years, various members of the Pension Research Council have urged that the Council undertake a study of the interrelationship between Social Security and private pension plans. The same suggestion has been made by several institutional members.

To carry out a full-scale inquiry into the proper roles of Social Security and private pension plans would entail a tremendous investment of financial and intellectual resources. (One research organization has been trying to raise $500,000 for such a project and contemplates enlisting scholars from many intellectual disciplines.) The subject has far-reaching economic, political, and social ramifications.

As a first step toward assessing the dimension of a project that would attempt to delineate reasonable bounds for Social Security in the light of a changing economic, demographic, and cultural environment, the Pension Research Council commissioned a series of papers to be presented and debated at its 1976 symposium for institutional members. The papers covered a wide spectrum of topics designed to provide the conceptual framework for a meaningful discussion of the major issues.

The subject matter of the symposium ranged from the philosophical basis of the Social Security system to current issues. Attention was focused on the philosophical basis of the private pension movement; coordination of public and private plans; the contrasting economic impacts of a currently financed national old-age insurance program and funded private pension plans; and the conflicting concepts of balance between Social Security benefits and those provided by private pension plans.

Special attention was given to the fiscal basis of the Social Security system and the potential impact of its financial problems on the future role of the system. The basis for the discussion was a paper by A. Haeworth Robertson, Chief Actuary of the Social Security Administration. That paper as it appears in this volume, has been updated to reflect the data in the 1976 Report of the Board of Trustees of the Federal OASI and DI Trust Funds.

Mr. Robertson stated that the most important test of the financial soundness of the Social Security program is whether the future income (tax revenue and interest on the trust funds) of the program can reasonably be expected to equal future benefits and administrative expenses, taking into account both present and future participants in the program. This test is not satisfied at the present time.

Social Security expenditures are expected to exceed income from taxes every year in the future, under each of three different sets of demographic and economic assumptions. During the next six years, the excess of expenditures over tax income is estimated to average 0.61 percent of taxable payroll under optimistic assumptions, 1.16 percent under pessimistic assumptions, and 0.82 percent under intermediate assumptions. Until provision is made for increased tax revenues (or decreased expenditures), this excess of outgo over income must be met from the trust funds. The Disability Insurance Trust Fund can absorb the shortfall only until 1979, at which time its assets will be exhausted. The Old-Age and Survivors Insurance Trust Fund can absorb the deficit until 1981 under pessimistic assumptions and for a few more years under more optimistic assumptions.

During the 25-year period from 1976–2000, the excess of expenditures over payroll tax revenues is estimated to average 1.03 percent of taxable payroll under optimistic assumptions, 2.89 percent of taxable payroll under pessimistic assumptions, and 1.91 percent of taxable payroll under intermediate assumptions.

The financial projections for the next 75 years are much more frightening, but are based on more fragile demographic and economic assumptions. On the basis of intermediate assumptions and continuation of the presently scheduled OASDI payroll taxes, which will be 4.95 percent for employees for 1976–2010 and 5.95 percent thereafter, expenditures are estimated to exceed tax income by an average of 7.96 percent of taxable payroll over the period 1976–2050. Unless the benefit structure is changed or events prove to be more favorable than projected, by the year 2050 a combined employer–employee payroll tax rate of 29 percent will be needed to support current benefit payments. These data translate into an actuarial deficit—the present value of future expenditures through 2050 less present assets and the present value of future scheduled income through 2050—of $4.3 trillion. The unfunded accrued liability, considering only persons now aged 21 or over and assuming a revised tax schedule that will support future outgo, is $3.1 trillion.

These financial projections are cause for concern but not alarm. Approximately half of the actuarial deficit would be eliminated if the automatic-adjustment provisions of the program were to be amended in such a manner as to ensure reasonably stable replacement ratios (i.e., the ratio of the employee's primary benefit to his earnings at time of retirement) over the years. Congress is currently considering a number of approaches to ensure stable replacement ratios, and the necessary legislation will likely be enacted this year.

Other adjustments in the benefit structure may have to be made to reflect lengthening longevity, improved health in old age, increased participation of women in the labor force, the changing role of the family unit, the changing demographic mix of the population, and other broad social forces. A modification in the program that would produce great cost savings and would seem to be justified by a number of emerging forces would be a later normal retirement age, such as 67 or 68, although this change would not have to be put into effect until some three decades hence. The ultimate costs may turn out to be lower than projected because of a lessened rate of inflation, a reversal in fertility rates, greater labor force participation of both men and women and of persons aged 65 or over, and other favorable developments.

In the present political and economic climate, however, it is doubtful that the benefit structure of the Social Security program can be adjusted sufficiently to avoid a substantial increase in payroll taxes, at least in the short term. As payroll tax rates go up, there will be increasing pressure on Congress to provide supplemental support out of general revenue, a public policy question of substantial dimension.

This volume is a compilation of the papers presented at the symposium. Supplementary materials from public and private sources on some of the topics are included in the appendixes. The Council is indebted to the eight individuals, Messrs. Preston C. Bassett, J. Douglas Brown, Geoffrey N. Calvert, John K. Dyer, Jr., Paul H. Jackson, Robert J. Myers, A. Haeworth Robertson, and Bert Seidman, who prepared the discussion papers for the symposium. They have provided an intellectual foundation for an enlightened consideration of the respective roles of Social Security and private pension plans. Both of these institutions have a distinctive contribution to make to American society, and a wise blending of their strengths is a goal worthy of zealous pursuit.

The symposium, and the resulting volume of papers, was financed by the Ralph H. Blanchard Memorial Endowment of the Pension Research Council. Mr. Blanchard was one of the founders of the National Health and Welfare Retirement Association (NHWRA), an organization that provides pension and insurance facilities for the employees of social welfare agencies. Mr. Blanchard served as President of NHWRA for 14 years and at the time of his death in 1972 was Honorary President. The Memorial Endowment was established and is being funded by NHWRA to perpetuate the memory of Mr. Blanchard and to further the social goals to which he was so deeply committed. This is the first project of the Council financed by the Blanchard Memorial Endowment.

Philadelphia, Pa.                    DAN M. McGILL
*February 1977*

# Contents

chapter

# 1

# Philosophical Basis of the National Old Age Insurance Program

J. DOUGLAS BROWN*

## EVOLUTION OF THE PROGRAM

IN THE STUDY of cultural history, there is a recognized principle that ideas like seeds must await their appropriate time to take on a life of their own and flourish. Many concepts in science have remained in forgotten treatises until the evolution of science and technology created the need for their application in the development of electronics, aeronautics, biochemistry, or energy. The difference between an interesting but impractical idea and one that changes our way of life lies more often in the vacuum which the idea may fill than in the originality of the idea itself. This is the justification of fundamental research whether in science, social science, or the humanities. The contributions of highly abstruse mathematics and physics, for example, permeate modern technology.

Just 200 years ago, Adam Smith in his *Wealth of Nations* put forth a cluster of ideas which for better or for worse changed the political economy of England. His ideas flourished because the time was ripe for the elimination of ancient mercantilist restrictions on trade and for the encouragement of free enterprise. He justified free private enterprise and

* Dr. Brown, Emeritus Provost and Dean of the Faculty, Princeton University, was a member of the old-age security staff of the Cabinet Committee on Economic Security that developed the original Social Security Act. He was also chairman of the first Advisory Council on Social Security and a member of every subsequent Advisory Council except the last one.

1

vigorous competition by inventing a concept of economic harmonies. He solved the problem of reconciling good business with good conscience by creating the concept of an Unseen Hand which transformed the seeking of individual gain into a public good. He helped England become a wealthy nation, but he also helped to make political economy the "dismal science." Adam Smith did not understand that the conscience of a society could not be divorced from the consciences of its individual citizens. Labor became an impersonal factor in production and poverty an unfortunate but incidental by-product.

As a young and growing country, America was one of the last industrial nations to learn the serious shortcomings of Adam Smith's concept of laissez faire. In the rural areas from which many of our people came, labor was usually in short supply and an energetic, thrifty man could usually find some way to maintain his family. If in exceptional cases children were left destitute, there were orphan asylums. If old people had no one to take care of them, there were poor houses. In the cities, when industry was booming, all was well. When hard times came, there were bread lines and other local charities. Cities had fewer old people to worry about since it was the young and vigorous who flocked to the cities from the rural areas or from overseas. There was always the feeling that business was bound to pick up soon. It usually did.

The deep and long depression which began in 1929 undermined the confidence of the American people that our economy was a self-correcting mechanism which would soon right itself if left alone. Even in 1913, the Federal Reserve system was established to help the banks, but now industry, trade, and agriculture, as well as the banks, were in deep trouble. In the face of massive unemployment, laissez faire had lost its charm. As the depression continued, just as the receding tide makes visible the rocks which are covered when the tide is in, so the shortcomings of our urban, industrial economy in taking care of the old, the disabled, and the destitute became all too clear. Something had to be done by the *government* to take care of those whom the economic system discarded through no fault of their own.

## UNDERLYING CONCEPTS

### Right to Protection

In the United States, the development of a concept of a *right* to protection against distress caused by economic forces was slow in coming.

There was a persistent notion that those adversely affected were in some way tinged with blame. The use of the word "pauper" was a hangover from the Elizabethan poor law. Even in recent times, the struggle to eliminate the concept of blame in compensating employees for industrial accidents indicates our fondness for legal mechanisms as a substitute for public or social responsibility. Property rights were deeply embedded in the Anglo-Saxon tradition. In drafting the Declaration of Independence, Thomas Jefferson was far ahead of his time. But he was more a political philosopher inveighing against George III than a social economist concerned with the shortcomings of Adam Smith's thesis. Perhaps he can be excused, since he was a farmer from Virginia and not a prophet.

The idea that American citizens had a right to protection against distress caused by economic conditions beyond their control is a clear example of an idea whose time had come. University circles had discussed it in intellectual terms for years. But a great depression was needed to bring it into the consciousness of the American people because it satisfied a deep want. Needs-test relief, and the deep-set chagrin at loss of self-reliance, the overtones of blame, and the humiliation of prying investigation which came with it, might be a last resort, but it did not seem a just or fair remedy when a person would work hard if a job were available—unless he or she were too old to work.

The political spearhead of the change in American thinking on the *right* to protection, as against the acceptance of public charity, was the Townsend movement. The old people who had worked hard all their lives and had lost their farms and their savings had a clear-cut case. With millions of votes and effective propaganda, they had Congress scared. President Roosevelt had in June 1934, called for constructive measures in the prevention of distress due to unemployment, old age, and sickness, but he did not specify the details. The concept of an old-age insurance system that would provide benefits as a matter of *right* was the contribution of the small old-age security staff of the Cabinet Committee on Economic Security. The logic of the solution might have convinced Congress in time, but it was the pressure of the old people and the political genius of the President that put the concept into law. There were doubters in the staff of the Cabinet Committee and even in the White House, but a good idea whose time has come takes on a life of its own. The remarkable thing to me looking back to those strenuous days was how few people recognized the fundamental significance of the change in political philosophy inherent in our proposals. Congress and the President were concerned with a *condition* and not a *theory*.

A distinction should be made between the forces that led to unemployment insurance and those that resulted in old-age insurance. In the depth of the depression in the 1930s, there was fear that hardship might lead to violence. The war veterans had invaded Washington. There were sit-down strikes. It was the employer who laid off people and who took the blame in the mind of the worker. Those over 65, however, were too old to fight. They looked to the federal government to respect their *rights* as citizens and not to an employer to give them a job. The concept of a benefit as a matter of right was, therefore, more central in the development of federal old-age insurance than in the spotty beginnings of unemployment insurance. The history of the two systems over the last 40 years demonstrates the difference.

**Prevention Rather than Alleviation**

A second basic concept in the development of old-age insurance was to *prevent* poverty in old age rather than to *alleviate* it after it had occurred. Prevention required forward planning to be sure that funds would be available to pay benefits in the long years ahead as each age group became eligible. Rights without funds to meet them would be not only bad fiscal economics but also bad social policy. To relieve anxiety and to gain the full advantage of a shift from needs-test relief to a benefit based on an attained right would require a mechanism in which people could have confidence, not only in old age, but throughout their working lives. The Townsend plan, which promised $200 a month to every old person, was an awful example of a right assured on the basis of an impossible concept of financing. Contributory social insurance would provide a mechanism by which rights to protection could be assured *and* financed— not for the aged as an amorphous body of people, but to each individual who had by his own contribution developed an individual right.

**Individualization of Benefit Rights**

The *individualization* of *benefit rights* as a corollary of the prevention of poverty for the persons participating in the system might be considered a third basic concept. The emphasis upon the rights of the individual as opposed to the rights of a class was peculiarly appropriate to the American mores. In America, we do not assume that we belong to a class. We like to hold our own ticket, especially if we feel that we have paid for it. Further, the poverty to be prevented was itself related to the individual's customary way of life and the normal costs of sustaining that way of life under widely different circumstances. A benefit which would prevent poverty in a small town in Iowa would fall far short of doing so in New York City. Also a benefit for a skilled craftsman, to provide a sense of security, needed to be more than that of a farm laborer. The wide variation in customary standards and customary costs of living in the United States made individualization of benefit rights an essential requirement.

## Differential Contributions

To justify differentials in individual benefit rights it was almost axiomatic that there must be *differential contributions* to any American system of old-age insurance. Differential compensation for differential economic contribution is a basic concept in American thought. We might not go all the way with Adam Smith on the doctrine of economic harmonies, but the work ethic and a sense of self-reliance in a new country supported a reward for incentive. Since differential benefits could be considered a reward for incentive and not merely an adjustment to imputed need, it was logical to implement an American philosophy of economics in an American philosophy of social insurance. This marriage of *equity* and *adequacy* has not always run smoothly in the many later debates concerning which partner should have most influence.

## Compulsory Participation

A corollary concept to that of the prevention of poverty was that an old-age insurance system should be *compulsory*. In our early study of the old-age problem in the fall of 1934, those of us on the small old age security staff tried every possible device to avoid outright compulsion in gaining a widespread coverage for an old-age insurance system. We found that every consideration—financial, actuarial, administrative, and flexibility to change—made a voluntary system impractical. Most important of all, such a system would not provide the broad base of security upon which to build a system intended to lift millions of Americans out of the risk of dependency on relief in old age. All the evidence concerning the shifting age balance in the American population indicated that we were already late in planning for the next 50 years. In 1930, those 65 and over constituted 5.4 percent of our people. By 1980, it was estimated, they would constitute 11.3 percent. Further, the federal-state program of old-age *assistance* we were recommending, was, at best, a temporary makeshift which improved somewhat a patchwork of needs-test relief. It would only be a brief period of time before another Townsend plan would sweep it away, unless a constructive, broadly based system took over.

## National Scope

It also became clearly evident that an old-age insurance system should be *national* in every respect to attain our purpose. Again every alternative considered proved to have serious shortcomings. The mobility of the American population over the working span of life would make the long-run actuarial estimates required in planning a contributory old-age insurance system almost impossible on a state-by-state basis. While estimates of population growth, age distribution, and mortality could be made with some degree of accuracy for the country as a whole, estimates for a single state covering a span of many decades would be crude indeed. Varying standards of eligibility for benefits might leave many mobile workers inadequately protected. Varying contribution rates would create interstate differentials in the cost of doing business. Even more serious under old-age insurance would be the problems of financing state systems in a way that would protect workers over a lifetime spent in several states. Full reserves would involve serious actuarial, fiscal, and investment problems. A pay-as-you-go approach would be extremely risky as the responsibility and taxing power of states varied. The handling of interstate transfers of records and funds seemed to involve vast administrative complications unless the beneficiary was to receive as many checks each month as the number of states liable for his protection. Since there was an economy of scale in the administration of a vast record-keeping operation, costs would be lower in a national system. In sum, considerations of actuarial planning, sound financing, assurance of benefits, avoidance of arbitrary and unnecessary interstate differentials, and excessive administrative costs all militated strongly for a single national system under which benefits would be related to contributions wherever made and benefits paid wherever claimed.

## The Problem of Constitutionality

At this stage in the planning of a national old-age insurance system for the United States, the old-age security staff of the Cabinet Committee on Economic Security was contending not only with the ideas of Adam

Smith but, much more brashly, with the ideas of the framers of the Constitution of the United States as piously interpreted by learned justices, time out of mind. In drafting our report, we took the bull by the horns.

> In its consideration of the advantages of old-age insurance, the staff is fully aware of the limitations imposed upon the Federal Government by our Constitution which would affect the adoption of such a program. The staff is convinced, however, that it should first seek out the most constructive proposals for old-age security adapted to American economic and social conditions and then, and only then, test as far as possible whether such proposals can be made effective within our legal system. Since law is a living science, it is reasonable to assume that if a sound program of old age security can be projected, our system of constitutional law will evolve in time to support that program. In the meantime, adjustments may be necessary to mold such a program to existing legal precedents.

In our attempt to provide a legal basis for a national system, on the advice of four leading professors of constitutional law in the country, we invented a bifurcated device of contributions under the federal power of taxation and benefits under the federal power of appropriation which might get by the Supreme Court. Fortunately, the Supreme Court, with Justice Cardozo giving the opinion, supported the concept that law *is* a living science and that the welfare clause in the preamble of the Constitution meant what it said.

**Financing the System**

The idea that both workers and their employers should contribute to an old-age insurance system was far from original. It was customary in foreign plans. The worker was helping to protect himself. The employer who profited by the use of labor should help meet the true costs of labor services, not day by day, but over both the productive and retired periods of adult life. The employer set aside reserves for the depreciation of his machines, why not reserves for the superannuation of his employees? The further question concerning the ratio of the contributions of the worker and his employer never seemed to create any difficulty. In the absence of any tenable argument for a different ratio, that of equal shares was accepted and never altered. It was an example of "esthetic" logic. We tried out the idea on William Green, the president of the American

Federation of Labor. He agreed that labor should go along with equal sharing under old-age insurance "because everyone gets old." He insisted, however, that workers should not pay one cent for unemployment insurance since it was the employer who laid men off.

The concept of government contributions in the financing of an old-age insurance system was accepted from the first by the old-age security staff of the Committee on Economic Security. By establishing such a system, government as a whole, federal and state, would be increasingly relieved of the costs of old-age assistance. Further, government as such, had allowed a heavy "accrued liability" to develop which it, like an employer under a private pension plan, should meet over time. It was also reasonable that those elements in a social insurance plan which introduced a degree of social redistribution, such as reasonable minimum benefits or graduations in benefits favoring lower-paid workers, justified a contribution by the government. Such social redistribution should not be at the cost of the higher-paid workers within the system, but rather a cost to be spread over the nation as a whole which would derive a general benefit from the prevention of poverty. Without government contributions, the range of differential benefits related to differential contributions might be unduly narrowed and the concept of reflecting incentive impaired.

In recommending an old-age insurance program in 1934–35, the old-age security staff of the Committee on Economic Security was departing from several deeply held assumptions in the minds of most Americans. It proposed substituting *governmental intervention* to meet a growing social problem rather than relying upon the free play of economic forces. It proposed protection as a matter of *right* rather than of proven need. It called for the *prevention* of poverty rather than its alleviation after it had occurred. It proposed that rights to protection should be *individual* rights based on individual contributions and not a general right of a dependent class to receive an across-the-board dole. Rather than accepting the concept of need as the sole determinant of grants, it proposed *differential benefits* for differential contributions which would, in some degree, reflect *imputed* need. In proposing a *national, compulsory* system, the staff sought to controvert the most rigid precedent in our legal system, the separation of the functions of the federal and the state governments. This was brash enough, but as the idea of a national contributory old-age insurance scheme began to gain support, it was none of these novel ideas that proved the hardest to sell. It was rather that a national old-age insurance system could only be financed effectively on a *pay-as-you-go* basis with but a contingency rather than a "full" reserve.

**The Problem of Research Policy**

In the minds of most people, protection for one's old age required saving and savings became a reserve. If one paid premiums to an insurance company, the company should invest the money to be prepared to pay the annuity when due. A private pension plan without a funded reserve against accumulating liabilities was subject to grave suspicion. It was always the assumption of those approaching social insurance for the first time in those days that the old-age insurance program should build a vast funded reserve against the time when increasing millions would become eligible for benefits. The Secretary of the Treasury, Henry Morgenthau, stuck to this position even after the plan had gone to Congress.

It was the conviction of the staff that anything approaching a full reserve was unnecessary in a compulsory, national, social insurance system. A large reserve invested in government bonds would be no safer as a funded reserve than the taxing power of the same government to provide a return of principal and interest on those bonds. The compulsory contributions of employees and workers required under the system were, therefore, as taxes, as secure a resource for future benefit payments as government bonds. Further, reliance on future contributions had two great advantages: (1) it did not require the deflationary withdrawal of more funds than necessary from the free economy while the reserves were being accumulated and (2) it did not involve the many potential complications in investing vast funds which might even exceed the then outstanding debt of the government. The idea of investing old-age insurance funds in railroad bonds was not a happy one.

After 40 years, it is hard to understand how difficult it was for those accustomed to the financial arrangements of private enterprise to take the mental leap to thinking through the proper financial arrangements for a public enterprise by a sovereign government. It was far harder to make the leap when the public enterprise involved assurances of benefits years ahead such as under old-age insurance than similar assurances that government salaries, services, and facilities would be indefinitely maintained. One had to perceive that while old-age insurance was for the worker an accumulating individual credit to be cashed many years ahead, it meant for the *government* a carefully planned series of transfers, year by year, from taxes currently received to benefits currently due. A reserve was needed only to help balance the flow from taxes to benefits when conditions suddenly changed.

This concept of current-flow financing with a contingency reserve was far easier to develop in principle than to work out in terms of tax rates and benefit schedules. The actuaries in our staff ran many projections incorporating the best demographic and economic data available. A basic difficulty was a "funnel" problem. Even the lowest practical rate of contribution from those of working ages would, in the early years, provide far more than would be required to pay benefits. Even with a very gradual rise in contribution rates, the reserve would become many billions more than needed for contingency purposes. But years later as the number of beneficiaries increased, even this reserve would be insufficient to avoid the need for a sharper rise in the contribution rate than then seemed feasible. It was at this point that a government contribution would be necessary. Interestingly, we estimated that this would be about 1967.

## RECOMMENDATIONS OF FIRST ADVISORY COUNCIL

In the haste to have legislation ready for the opening of Congress in January 1935, the old-age security staff of the Committee on Economic Security did not have the time or the inventiveness to develop a satisfactory program of benefits which would be socially desirable as well as helpful in the avoidance of excessive reserves. The critical mission was to make sure that a national, compulsory, contributory system of old-age insurance was established by Congress and approved as constitutional by the Supreme Court. Since benefits were not due to begin until 1942, there would be time to work out a sound benefit schedule.

The Social Security Act became law in August 1935, and was declared constitutional in May 1937. In the same month the first Advisory Council on Social Security was appointed. At the suggestion of Gerard Swope, I was elected chairman of the council. After more than a year of intensive study, the 25 member council hammered out a benefit structure which provided, in addition to basic old-age benefits, those for the protection of wives, widows, and surviving children starting in 1940, not 1942. The old-age security staff of the committee had indicated in principle the advisability of such benefits, but the newly established Social Security Board had had the time and staff to make the studies required. The Advisory Council also approved, in principle, disability benefits, and established basic guidelines on coverage and financing.

Dealing with an established mechanism, the Advisory Council could focus its attention upon making it socially effective within a self-imposed caveat that the eventual annual cost of the benefits recommended should not exceed the eventual annual disbursements under the 1935 act. The goal was to bring forward in time the use of the mounting collections under the new payroll taxes in a way which met current social needs without, at the same time, incurring commitments for a higher level of *individual* benefits in future years. The council recognized the need and justification for government sharing of cost, but recognized, as had the staff of the committee, that the contributions of the government should be postponed until the changing balance of tax income and benefit disbursements required such contributions.

### Computation of Benefits on Basis of Average Earnings

The most significant concept introduced by the council for the first time was the use of *average* earnings, rather than *accumulated* earnings, in the determination of individual benefits. By this means, a covered worker approaching retirement with a minimum of time under the system could receive a benefit at a level related to his customary earnings. The 1935 act had used a formula based on total earnings over a lifetime which both delayed the payment of adequate benefits and accelerated the cost as the system matured.

### Aged Wife's Benefit

A second significant change proposed by the council was the introduction of a supplementary allowance of 50 percent of the husband's benefit for a wife age 65 or over, provided she was not eligible for a larger benefit in her own right. This also raised immediate benefit disbursements without introducing an accelerating factor over time. The inclusion of a widow's benefit at age 65 acted in the same way.

### Survivorship Benefits

While the use of average earnings in determining the primary benefit, the allowance for aged wives, and the benefit for aged widows were all means of enhancing protection in old age, the Advisory Council introduced a new concept of protection of the family unit during the normal working life of the covered worker. In the words of the council: "A dependent child of a currently insured individual upon the latter's death prior to age 65 should receive an orphan's benefit, and a widow of a currently insured individual, provided she has in her care one or more dependent children of the deceased husband, should receive a widow's benefit." It was the intent of the council that the benefits for survivors should be determined as monthly amounts related to the average earnings of the deceased worker and that the death benefit in the original law be strictly limited and payable on the death of *any* eligible individual. The substitution of survivors' benefits on an annuity basis for a lump-sum return of contributions was a significant step in shifting from a misapplied concept of equity to an appropriate concept of imputed need within a social insurance system. The death benefit was to become a small payment for funeral expenses.

In retrospect, the extension of the concept of social insurance from the narrower purpose of protecting against poverty in old age to the protection of the family unit against poverty caused by the death of the breadwinner at any time greatly broadened the public support of the "social security" system. The Advisory Council of 1937–38 fully realized that it was recommending a significant forward step. Consistent with its belief that the protection of the family unit was the proper goal of social insurance, it unanimously supported in principle the provision of benefits to an insured person who became permanently and totally disabled and to his dependents. It was divided on the question of the proper timing of the introduction of such benefits because of the additional costs and the administrative difficulties involved.

### Extension of Coverage

The Advisory Council of 1937–38 was firm in its conviction that the revised social security system should be extended as rapidly as possible to all gainfully employed workers. It called for the immediate coverage of employees of nonprofit religious, charitable, and educational institutions. The coverage of farm employees and domestic workers should begin as soon as administratively possible. Further studies should be made of the administrative, legal, and financial problems involved in the coverage of self-employed persons and governmental employees.

### Tripartite Financing

In its recommendations on the financing of the social security program, the council justified contributions by the government on the grounds that dependent old age had become a national problem and that the nation as a whole, and not just the beneficiaries, would gain both materially and socially by the program. It was stated that there were definite limits in the proper use of payroll taxes and that an analysis of the incidence of such taxes led to the conviction that they should be supplemented by general taxes. It recommended that the eventual cost of the system should be shared by means of approximately equal contributions by employers, employees, and the government.

### Maintenance of Contingency Fund

The council further recommended that there should be a reasonable contingency fund to insure the ready payment of benefits at all times and to avoid abrupt changes in tax and contribution rates. The taxes received, less the cost of collection, should, through permanent appropriation, be credited to an old-age insurance trust fund to be used exclusively for the payment of benefits and the administration of the program. On the difficult problem of the timing of changes in the rates of contribution by employers and employees and of contributions by the government, the council recommended further study and report on the basis of five years' experience under the revised program, with periodic studies thereafter.

## CONCLUDING REMARKS

When one reviews the recommendations of the Advisory Council of 1937–38, the great influence of the council on the future development of the American social security system becomes clear. The basic philosophy developed within the old-age security staff of the Committee on Economic Security in 1934–35 was confirmed, refined, and enlarged by a council representing the major interested groups in the country, ably assisted by the staff of the newly established Social Security Board. In the 38 years since the council submitted its report, the Old-Age, Survivors, and Disability Insurance (OASDI) program has, step by step, filled out in large measure the design envisaged by the council. Benefits and coverage have been greatly improved. Effective administrative and financial procedures have been developed. The concept of three-way sharing of costs by employers, workers, and the government is still to be accepted.  Perhaps, with the introduction of Medicare, for which the concept is even more appropriate than in the case of OASDI, the philosophy of the early planners of the system will become implemented. The Advisory Council reporting in 1971 so recommended. Ideas must await their proper time to take on a life of their own and flourish.

chapter

# 2

# Philosophical Basis of the Private Pension Movement

PAUL H. JACKSON*

PRIVATE PENSION PLANS in the United States preceded our social insurance program by some 60 years. The first well-known U.S. program was adopted by the American Express in 1875 providing a pension of 50 percent of final ten-year average pay to employees over 60 with 20 years of service who were permanently incapacitated for future performance of duties. It is clear from the benefit design that this program was not set up to retire inefficient workers, to attract new employees, to create a favorable working climate, or to utilize a tax advantage. The program was a clear-cut discharge of what management saw as an obligation to long-service employees who were unable to support themselves. Following on the heels of the American Express Plan, a number of plans were adopted by railroads, public utilities, and banks, most of which were noncontributory and provided for retirement benefits to be paid after 65 regardless of disability. In describing the Baltimore and Ohio Railroad Pension Plan established in 1880, the Carnegie Foundation's 13th Annual Report, New York 1918, stated:

> The primary object of this plan was to relieve the company and the employees from being called upon to make contributions in aid of employees distressed by sickness, accidental injury, old age, and death. Provision was

---

* Actuary, The Wyatt Company, Washington, D.C.

here made for aged employees who reached the age of 65 and had contributed regularly to the relief association in any amount. If the contributions were continued until the contributor reached the age of 65, the
contributor was entitled to receive an annual allowance for life of ten cents
on each dollar he paid in, and an addition of one-half cent on each dollar
for every year his contributions had continued. It will be noted that nothing
more was intended than to provide the employees with an opportunity to
protect themselves against poverty in old age; there was no consideration,
for example, of the problem of improving the efficiency of the service or
of promoting cooperation between the employers and employees. Further,
the amount of the pension was uncertain and held out but slight induce-
ments to the employees. It is not surprising, therefore, that in 1882 the
secretary of the relief association wrote in his report: "I regret to report
that the annuity feature has not prospered in the same ratio as that providing relief for disablements. The subject of annuities is a new one in this
country and the small countenance given the pension features of other
benevolent associations shows that our people have not yet realized the
importance and value of this form of protection against want in old age."
In fact, the pension feature attracted but one contributor between 1880
and 1889 when the charter of the relief association was repealed.

The first pension plan in a manufacturing establishment was established in 1882 by Alfred F. Dolge, a felt manufacturer. Under this plan
a disabled employee, after ten years of service was entitled to draw a
pension of one-half his last year's wages and after 25 years' service, a
pension of 100 percent pay. The Dolge firm went out of business in 1898.
The Carnegie Steel Company established a plan in 1900 and Standard
Oil in 1903 and by 1930, 420 plans in private industry had been established, of which 28 had been discontinued.

Most of the early U.S. pension plans were set up by fairly sizable
organizations. The formal pension plans were usually installed to replace
informal personnel practices which in turn can be traced back to a first
instance in which the employer made some provision for an individual
employee with long service who was unable to continue working and was
in financial need. After five or ten such individual situations had been
considered, some sort of pattern was established that served as a useful
rule of thumb in setting the amount of benefit so that the employer could
treat all employees in a fair and equitable manner and avoid the difficult
choice of deciding upon the proper amount on an individual case by case
basis. While this "pay them what they need" informal basis is sometimes
considered to be ancient history, as late as 1955 the Aetna Life Insurance
operated a program of this type for its 15,000 employees. Under the Aetna

program the retiring employees were awarded a pension that took into account their length of service, absence records, personal assets, and financial obligations; a benefit was determined that would "make things right."

During the early days of the pension movement, it was an accepted fact that a pension plan was a voluntary program adopted by an employer to discharge a moral obligation to his older, long-service employees. For example, a British actuary, in describing the problems with contributory plans, wrote in 1901:

> Funds intended to provide a retiring allowance for the members of a staff, are started by employers with the very best intentions, but it is doubtful whether they have ever proved altogether satisfactory. They have the tendency to breed a discontented spirit amongst the employees, and in some cases have proved more costly to the employers than if they had created their own Reserves and promised to give a guaranteed scale of superannuation for long and faithful service.
>
> . . . The principle that everyone should make a provision for his old age is one which we shall all approve. To encourage this principle, the employer says to his employees: "If you will all consent to contribute a percentage of your salaries to create a Fund for providing pensions in your old age, I will subscribe an equal amount each year"; or, "I will give you a sum down to start the Fund." Sometimes he adds: "and I will guarantee that the Fund shall be accumulated at a fixed rate of interest." In this way he feels that he has acted the part of a philanthropist in encouraging thrift; he thinks that his staff will be more contented and settled, and are not likely to leave him when they have a stake in the Fund; and he has allayed an uneasy conscience which half recognized an unpleasant responsibility to help, in his old age, a man who has given him a lifelong service. The employee's view of the arrangement is very different. To him the contribution is a hardship and an obnoxious tax; and, although he gave his consent to subscribe, it was an agreement made under moral compulsion. What benefit will it be to him? He will never live to 65! and if he does, he is not going to stick in that firm all his life. He does not see why he should be taxed for the benefit of the old members of the staff, who will be retiring soon. The governors might at least raise their salaries to enable them to pay the tax. And if the employer does take a generous view of the case and raise their salaries, the contribution to the Fund does not cease to be a tax. It is always a tax, and is always a very good excuse for asking for increase of salary. . . ."[1]

---

[1] William Henry Manly, "On the Valuation of Staff Pension Funds," *Journal of the Institute of Actuaries*, vol. 36, 1901, pp. 209–87.

Because of the close tie between service to an employer and the perceived magnitude of the employer's moral obligation to help out in old age, most private pension plans established by single employers provide benefits based on length of service and on compensation. The general trend in the type of compensation used in benefit formulas since 1900 has been from final average pay to career pay (1940), then back to final average pay (1975). The outlook for the future is perhaps for a shift back to career pay, but throughout this entire period, length of service has remained a primary variable in benefit determinations.

## DESIGN OF THE SOCIAL SECURITY PROGRAM

In describing the design of the social security system, in 1938 Reinhard A. Hohaus, one of the early experts, stated that it was assumed that "the benefit formula apparently ought to produce pensions so far as practicable, sufficient in amount to provide those entitled to them with the essentials of life." Also,

> Since . . . a wife is more likely than not to survive her husband in advanced ages, a relatively large volume of aged widows can presumably be expected. In the absence of a continuation of some of the income benefits their husbands were receiving while living, the widows of the pensioners (unless they are entitled to pensions on their own account as former employees or have other means of support) will have to resort to charity in one form or another and thus become a direct problem to society. Not only would a contributory old-age insurance plan so confined indirectly shift heavy burdens on to old-age assistance, but it would probably also precipitate a situation that could not long prevail unchallenged and unchanged for political and social reasons. As a result, it would appear only realistic to recognize that an extension of the present old-age benefits plan to include pensions to widows of annuitants is indicated sooner or later.[2]

Clearly in the initial design of the social security program, the principles employed in deciding on the proper benefit and tax formula did not center about any moral obligation or upon any earned right, but rather on the need for income. The system is thus grounded on the concept of social adequacy. Social adequacy, of course, concerns not only the size of the benefits but also the proportion of the population covered under

---

[2] Reinhard A. Hohaus, "Factors in Old Age Security," *The Record* of the American Institute of Actuaries, vol. 27, 1938, pp. 76–120.

a social insurance plan. The broader the proportion covered by a plan, the more it represents that national commonality of purpose which can support a rationalization of greater adequacy of benefit levels and less of a direct tie-in of benefits to taxes paid. While social security does have moderate benefit differentials based on contributory years of service and level of wages, by and large the benefits are weighted heavily in favor of the lower paid or short service workers. The minimums, disability benefits, family benefits, and survivor's benefits further enhance the adequacy of the benefits at a loss in each instance of some of the personal equity that might otherwise have been expected in the relationship between taxes paid in and benefits to be received.

## OBJECTIVES UNDERLYING PRIVATE PENSION PLANS

Following the adoption of the social security program, some rethinking of pension objectives by the sponsors of private pension plans was obviously required. First off, private pension programs had become a supplement to a basic national program and the private employers' provisions had been moved back to a second line of defense. On the other hand, a basic social security benefit universally available made it easier to develop a reasonable total benefit for a retiring worker. In any case, a hindsight review of the situation by plan sponsors led to the development of a list of rationalizations as to just why a firm with a pension plan should continue the plan even though social security was going to provide a good basic income for the long service worker. The most commonly cited objectives were:

1.  Discharge a moral obligation by the employer.
2.  Permit the retirement of inefficient workers while retaining older skilled workers who are still efficient.
3.  Attract capable, well-trained, new employees.
4.  Maintain a favorable working climate.
5.  Develop a good corporate image.
6.  Develop a more effective working relationship with a union by putting long-term problems on the bargaining table.
7.  Reduce the employee's total dependence on government to a more manageable level.
8.  Utilize a tax advantage.

The first six of these reasons relate to the employer/employee relationship. From the very beginning, there has been a direct tie between eligibility for a pension and its amount and the length of an employee's service for the employer. Benefit formulas based only on service or on career pay can be considered to be based, in rough measure, on the employer's moral obligation to provide for the worker in his or her old age. The substitution of final average pay may inject some needs-based considerations into the formula or may merely be considered to be a rough adjustment of the underlying obligation to take into account inflation. Disability and survivor benefits again have dual aspects of perceived employee need and adjustment in the perceived employer obligation. Early retirement supplements, on the other hand, are clearly grounded on the employer's interest in maintaining an efficient staff, although an overly generous level of benefit (perhaps the result of collective bargaining) may actually be counterproductive by encouraging the retirement of efficient and experienced workers who are in good health and able to find work elsewhere. Taken as a whole, however, the typical private pension benefit formula can not be said to be an accurate measure of employee need; there is simply too heavy a dependence on past service and pay history.

The reduction of the employee's reliance on government is an ancient reason rarely mentioned anymore. Apparently, the basic principle no longer arouses a "give me liberty or give me death" spirit in the average citizen today. Anyway, with the injection of the Department of Labor into various procedures and suits on behalf of the employee, it is doubtful if it is still valid.

The tax advantage has been emphasized in recent years as a major reason for the rapid growth in private pensions. In reality, for the employer sponsoring a pension plan, the tax advantage in prefunding as opposed to paying pensions out-of-pocket (no longer permitted but clearly tax-neutral) is that the funds deposited on behalf of a given employee earn compound interest at the full rate of yield on plan assets until they are paid out in benefits when they reduce a business expense deduction and are thus indirectly taxed at the 50 percent rate. Without the special treatment, the funds would compound at only 50 percent of the yield rate until date they are paid out in benefits and then would be fully deductible to the employer. This advantage at a 6 percent interest rate and 50 percent tax rate over a 20-year funding period saves the employer about 14 percent of the annual cost of benefits. Over a 30-year period the saving is 28 percent. On the other hand, at a 4 percent interest rate, the 20-year period tax savings is only 7 percent and the 30-year savings only 14 percent. Clearly, the question of sponsorship of a private pension plan or its level of benefits does not depend in any major degree on the current tax advantage. Indeed, for the top executive the deferral of earned income subject to a 50 percent personal income tax rate into the period after retirement means that it may be taxed then at a 70 percent rate.

While the advantage of deferring income was obvious when personal income tax rates went up to 92 percent and capital gains tax was limited to 25 percent, the advantage is clearly less when personal income tax rates are limited to 50 percent and capital gains to 35 percent. Then, too, the accepted principles that income levels will be lower and taxes lower after retirement has not really worked out too well in practice, at least over the last 40 years. At best the tax laws and regulations are complex and unreliable, and it is unlikely that a private employer would base any long-term benefit decision on current tax differentials.

As viewed from our bicentennial year with the advantage of 40 years of 20–20 hindsight, most experts would agree that objectives six, seven, and eight can be deleted from the list. Further, objectives four and five follow from an acceptance and faithful discharge of the employer's moral obligation. The 1976 objectives of a private pension plan, as viewed by the knowledgeable plan sponsor, can thus probably be reduced to:

Discharge a moral obligation.

Permit retirement of inefficient workers.

Attract new employees.

These are pretty basic objectives and will probably stand up under a considerable degree of governmental overregulation. The giant-sized tax bonanzas cited by pension reformers are more imagined than real and they have now been buried under a welter of regulations, reporting requirements, excise taxes, and employer liability.

## PRINCIPLES USED TO SET BENEFIT LEVELS

A number of principles have been set forth and used in the process of deciding on appropriate levels of benefits under a pension plan. Some of the most commonly cited principles are:

1. A pension is a gratuity. If a pension is essentially a gift from an appreciative employer to a loyal employee, then any pension amount can be justified, however modest or arbitrary.
2. A pension is a moral obligation and socially responsible behavior on the part of the employer requires that some provision be made for employees after they are unable to work. This theory supports certain

needs-related benefits such as widows' pensions and disability benefits.

3. Pension benefits are deferred compensation. A pension plan is a method whereby a part of the compensation for services rendered can be deferred. Since the tax advantages are usually apparent to highly compensated executives, their influence on benefit design may result in a higher degree of deferment than the lower paid employees might voluntarily choose. Note, however, that many unions have negotiated pension plans at a percentage of payroll cost far in excess of the cost of most salaried plans.

4. Pension cost is similar to the depreciation charges for the other resources used by an employer. Thus, a pension is the end result of good cost accounting for the deterioration of the personnel assets of a company. This theory supports a career average or service-related benefit formula.

5. A pension is a form of incentive pay. A pension provides extra compensation to encourage employees to have long and unbroken service. Essentially this is a reward for steadiness and reliability that is over and above the regular compensation for current services rendered.

6. A pension plan is a necessary expedient. An employer has to have a pension plan or nobody will work for him. By this theory benefits should be set at the lowest level that is sufficient to permit the hiring of employees who are fully qualified to perform the necessary tasks.

In my judgment no single one of the above principles can be adopted exclusively without serious distortion in the resulting conclusions. Each of them expresses a particular aspect of the pension promise and a valid analysis of pension benefits must include all of them. While the idea that a pension is a gratuity may seem unacceptable by today's standards, it is merely a shorthand way of saying that an employer is not required by law to establish a pension plan and the undertaking is so beset with restrictions and forms, legal obligations, and potential penalty, that by sponsoring a pension plan and agreeing to take all of this on, an employer has indeed gone the extra mile for the workers. Sponsoring a pension plan today is a gracious and a generous act, indeed perhaps even a bit self-sacrificial.

## ERISA

The framework within which private pension plans operate has been changed considerably by the passage of the Pension Reform Act of 1974.

The Employee Retirement Income Security Act (ERISA) imposes a cold legal framework of employee rights and employer obligations on the employee/employer relationship. The employer who sponsors a pension plan is answerable in a court of law for a great many actions and decisions in the whole pension area. There is heavy emphasis under ERISA on the desirability of having an employee institute legal suit in order to change the benefit provisions in a plan to a more acceptable set of provisions or of obtaining redress for what he or she believes to be unfair treatment. By imposing plan termination insurance on certain plan sponsors (those who have adopted defined benefit plans as opposed to profit sharing, thrift, or target benefit plans), ERISA changes the relative advantages and disadvantages of the various programs. Under the defined benefit plan the Pension Benefit Guaranty Corporation (PBGC) can terminate the program and collect up to 30 percent of the employer's net worth, whereas this threat is nonexistent under a defined contribution plan. Also under ERISA, it may well be illegal to pay a pension to a retiring worker who needs income without also promising a pro rata benefit to all of the active workers and arranging for full actuarial funding of that promise. Thus ERISA appears to have pinched off one of the fundamental sources of new pension plans, namely the provision of out-of-pocket payments after the retirement of a single needy individual, followed by the establishment of a precedent of granting similar benefits to other individuals who subsequently retire and, finally, the emergence of a benefit formula and eligibility provisions in a formal plan and the setting up of a fund. All of this must now be accomplished in one grand and final act.

ERISA has also imposed a considerable complexity on the benefits to be provided under private pension plans. The standard form of benefit must be on a 50 percent joint and survivor basis even though the benefit is expressed in terms of a single life annuity without refund or survivorship features. The many plans providing early retirement rights must also offer a preretirement spouse's option which, unless paid for fully by the plan sponsor, reduces the defined benefit, as initially computed by the benefit formula, in an extremely complicated manner. Under programs providing for offsets of social security from the gross pensions developed by the benefit formula, IRS rules now prohibit a decrease in benefit on the occasion of an increase in the level of social security benefits so that a series of additional calculations purporting to show what the individual would have received if he had retired one month, two months, and so forth, earlier than he actually did, may be necessary in order to establish the minimum benefit required by the act. Employee contributions must be carried forward at a 5 percent interest rate and when the employee terminates, forfeiture of the total pension upon withdrawal of contributions is not permitted but still another calculation must be made to determine the minimum employer-bought pension by converting the returned contributions into an equivalent pension benefit and deducting that value from the total accrued pension. In all of these cases a "defined" benefit has been made so complex that it may well be almost as vague as the explanation of the amount of monthly pension that can be expected from a profit sharing or thrift plan. Certainly, any lack of definition of the benefit delivery under a target benefit plan is minimal when contrasted with so arcane a "defined" pension benefit.

Even the administration of private pension plans has been seriously handicapped by cumbersome regulations requiring the use of two different kinds of "hours of service," three different 12-month computation periods, and breaks in service that must start either before employment ceases (not more than 500 hours of service before, however) or be deferred well after termination of employment to the end of some computation period. Employers tend to react negatively to an arrangement which, if adopted, requires them to count as an "hour of service" an hour for which an employee neither performed service nor received any pay. Administrative "overkill" in the development of the implementing regulations by the Department of Labor and the IRS has left those employers who are now sponsoring private pension plans in a state of shock. Few indeed are likely to tell their fellow businessmen, "Come on in. The water's fine."

The requirements of ERISA and its implementing regulations do not fall uniformly on all employers as, for example, basic wage and hour regulations do. Only the employer who provides a pension for his employees is affected. Only the sponsors of defined benefit pension plans are forced into the PBGC requirements for premium paying, reporting on "significant" events, and the risking of 30 percent of net worth. Only the plan which offers early retirement benefits gets stuck with the preretirement spouse's option. Only the plan providing immediate disability income is forced to offer a costly and awkward deferred survivor option. Indeed, it might well be said that under ERISA no generous act goes unpunished.

The substantial impact of ERISA must, of course, result in a total reassessment of the purpose and value of private pension plans. In this process the employer who already has a program will no doubt reach different conclusions than the one who has not yet adopted a plan. In any case, plan sponsors can now see quite clearly that in the future there will be an increasing amount of federal regulation on all aspects of their business, a substantial burden in added paperwork to provide the required reports to Treasury, Labor, and PBGC, and substantial cost in developing descriptive material in simple terms to communicate the details of the plans to all employees, whether or not they are covered by the plan. As a practical matter, however, the employer who already has a plan has no convenient way of backing out on it without encountering serious legal problems, providing advance notice to his employees and forfeiting a part of the business. Further, pension plans have always been voluntary under-takings and presumably have been adopted because they are good for the employees and, for that reason alone, most existing pension plans would be maintained. One predictable result, however, is that while many em-ployers will retain their pension program, the benefit formulas will be frozen in their tracks and the degree of benefit improvement that oc-curred in the 20-year period preceding the passage of ERISA will come to an end. Another predictable result is that fewer new plans will be undertaken on a purely voluntary basis—the commitment is simply too all-pervasive.

## SOCIAL SECURITY

In the United States up through the 1960s, the social security program was considered to constitute a basic floor of protection. To the extent that social security can be limited to a basic subsistence level, there will be room and need for private pension plans. Over the years, however, all social insurance programs have had a tendency to expand. In some coun-tries (Italy, Spain, Portugal, and some of the Latin American countries are examples), the governmental social insurance program is expected to provide all of the benefit needed by almost everyone. In other countries, such as France and the Scandinavian countries, the governmental social security system provides only modest benefits, but there are mandatory, regulated, quasigovernmental systems that meet nearly all of the remain-ing needs so that voluntary supplementary private pensions are not needed. In a few countries (e.g., Germany, Switzerland, the Netherlands, and Belgium), the governmental benefits have been deliberately limited to a level such that there will still exist a need for private supplementation. In the United States this decision has not been consciously finalized, and the debate continues as to whether we would be better off providing all benefits through social security or holding back on an unlimited expansion of social security so as to permit the development of a strong private pension movement.

The one major limitation on benefit improvements under social insurance programs is that of cost. Apart from the purely economic factors, demography has become quite important. A projection of current benefit trends suggests a substantial reduction in the work force as a portion of the total population and a significant increase in ratio of retired to working members of the population. Thus, after the turn of the century, it is expected that there will be fewer active workers whose social security taxes must pay benefits for a far greater retired population. Even with no change in benefit and under fairly favorable economic assumptions, the present 10 percent of payroll cost is expected to rise to 20 percent or so over the next 50 years. Part of this is due to the overindexing of primary benefit levels for cost of living increases as a result of the 1972 changes in our social security program. If there is an increase in the cost of living, there will be a direct increase in the benefit percentage and an indirect increase in the taxable wage base which in turn increases the dollar benefit further. A "decoupling" of the benefit formula could correct for this aberration. A major cause for the sharp rise in required tax rate, however, may be attributable to demographic factors. The ratio of the number retired to the number working, whose taxes must support the former's benefits, is expected to increase sharply in the early part of the next century.

In the long run, in order for our social security system to continue in existence, it will obviously be necessary to "decouple" the program from the double-indexing for cost of living. Even so, however, cost of living adjustments on the benefits in course of payment would continue and the delivery of benefits will continue to run on the order of 30 percent or 35 percent of final pay at the maximum tax base level for the worker alone retiring at or after age 65. This combination will still result in substantial increases in social security taxes which, of course, will affect the ability of every American employer to compete in the world markets. In any case, it has become obvious that some control on total pension benefit is going to be necessary in the long run and for this reason, many larger employers are considering adoption of a "cap" on private plan benefits which would limit the sum of the private pension plus social security to 85 percent or 100 percent of final pay.

The projection of a rise in future social security benefit delivery also suggests that the matter of the integration of private pension plan benefits with social security benefits could be most important. Integration does help solve the problem of total benefit delivery. Unfortunately, Congress views integration as a private taking-away of a governmentally established benefit. The congressional debate necessary to increase social security benefits involves a weighing of the value of the benefits added, on the one hand, against the necessary increase in social security tax to support them on the other. When this balance has been struck by Congress, it can be assumed that the added benefits are worthwhile in comparison to the added tax. This comparison, however, is obviously distorted when the added social security benefits are merely the cause of a concomitant reduction in private pension benefit with the net income to the individual retiree remaining constant. Currently, a congressional task force is studying the matter of integration and it is entirely possible that the historic forms of direct integration may be made illegal by future legislation.

## GENERAL TRENDS

In addition to ERISA and social security, a number of other developments can be expected to affect private pension programs. The increasing activity of the Equal Employment Opportunity Commission (EEOC) aimed at eliminating discrimination on the basis of sex or age must, of necessity, result in further changes being forced on private pension plans. One possible change is to force the use of unisex factors for any benefit determination such as early retirement, election of joint and survivor option, and so forth. Another possible change is an increase in the age 65 mandatory retirement age which is now accepted as a standard throughout the country in private plans. An increase in this age to 68 or 70 could take some of the demographic heat off of the social security system while at the same time permitting employees to continue to accrue private pension benefits until their total retirement income would be adequate. Any added cost arising out of an increase in the retirement age is likely to show up in the form of decreased efficiency and a general lowering of productivity.

In American society the various efforts to correct past inequities have served, in part, to weaken the direct link between work performed and income received. Indeed, the proliferation of welfare payments, unemployment compensation, and the other special benefits all serve to emphasize the need for income as opposed to the direct relationship between the current income or benefit and some period of work actually performed in the past. This greater emphasis on need and on a correction of past wrongs, real or imagined, when coupled with the emphasis on legal enforcement of employee rights under ERISA means that the sponsor of a private pension plan may have many more problems than the employer who simply sets aside certain sums of money for his workers in a series of individual bank accounts.

Inflation is another factor which has its primary impact on defined benefit pension plans, since the flat benefit or career average pension promise will sooner or later be deemed inadequate in terms of current purchasing power. Thus, the sponsor of a defined benefit pension plan in a period of inflation can expect considerable pressure from his employees for improvements in pension benefits to provide more realistic current benefits, whereas with a defined contribution plan, such as a thrift or profit sharing plan, the pressures are minimal. There is really very little that one can do about an inadequate bank balance except wish that it were larger.

Now that Congress has passed ERISA, the process of biennial review shortly before major elections can be expected as a matter of course. After all, Congress can improve the benefits for thousands of participants under private pension plans by the mere passage of a law without having to worry about raising any tax revenue to provide those benefits. Here again, the impact is felt only by the sponsor of the defined pension plan. When all of this is coupled with the contingent employer liability of up to 30 percent of his net worth and the right of the PBGC to terminate a plan or to take it over, the end result must be a shift away from defined benefit plans to defined contribution plans. Indeed, as noted, some of the ERISA-introduced complexities mean that the employer who has a defined benefit plan cannot even tell the covered employees what the benefit is going to be so that he may well be better off defining the amount of his current contribution. This sort of trend would appear fully consistent with the general thrust of ERISA which is to have the employer promise less but make sure there is full delivery on whatever is promised.

The employer who sponsors a private pension plan must also rationalize the continuation of a benefit program that jeopardizes 30 percent of his or her net worth. To the extent that the employer sponsors a pension plan that is designed to operate with little management control on benefits such as a final pay plan with cost of living indexing on pensions, the firm is exposing the stockholder's investment in the business to a serious risk of loss that can be avoided or minimized. Thus, fewer plans will adopt cost of living indexing, since the process of providing ad hoc increases from time to time when they can be afforded seems much more business-

like. Final pay plans may be shifted to a career average basis for future
benefit accruals. Rarely have these plans shown employees a projected
benefit that incorporates future pay increases. A higher benefit percentage
can be used on a career pay basis. Career benefits that are demolished
by inflation can be restored on an ad hoc basis by updating the pay base
for past service benefits to a final three or five-year average. Further, if
social security gets out of hand, the updates can be foregone, if necessary,
to maintain reasonable total benefits. Employer reluctance to take on
open-end pension promises may make the renegotiation of labor agreements far more difficult in the near term future. On the other hand, if
the major unions cannot negotiate a satisfactory level of private pension
benefits, they may direct the pressures from their membership toward
Congress in an effort to increase social security instead.

## CONCLUSION

The 1972 social security amendments have increased the role to be
played by social security in retirement income and decreased the need
for private pension supplementation. ERISA penalizes the employer with
a defined benefit pension plan to such an extent that private supplementation in the long run is likely to diminish considerably. The likely increase
in future social security taxes to support even the present level of benefits
will seriously diminish the employer's ability to provide benefit supplementation, at least in those industries which face competition from
foreign imports. Finally, the increasing emphasis on the enforcement of
an employee's legal right and the imposition of legal obligations on employers sharply diminish the degree of the moral obligation which an
employer might otherwise recognize and accept to look after a long service
employee who is unable to continue work. There will be fewer private
pension plans and they will provide relatively smaller benefits. But they
will be protected by the PBGC, the Department of Labor, and the IRS
from everything except inflation. And that's where the moral obligation
will have to come in.

chapter

# 3

# Coordination of Private and Public Pension Plans: An International Summary

JOHN K. DYER, JR., F.S.A.*

IN MOST of the industrial countries of Europe and North America, some development of private, employer-sponsored pension plans preceded, often by many years, the introduction of social security pensions. Indeed, in many cases it was the very existence of such private plans, tending to be quite restrictive in their coverage, which stimulated the development of the government-sponsored, mandatory old-age benefits, paid as a matter of right, which we commonly know as Social Security pensions.

Probably the ideal social security pension system is one that provides a uniform basic pension for all employees, whether in the private or public sector, and regardless of industry, occupation, or earnings level. I know of no such ideal system in existence today, although the Canadian basic old-age pension is a close approach, and the British system as it has evolved from Lord Beveridge's proposals of over 30 years ago, also comes close to the ideal.

The pension provisions of the United States social security system, some distance from the ideal, seem to be headed *toward* rather than *away* from it. Many of the earlier exclusions, made primarily for administrative

---

* Editor, International Benefits Information Service, Beach Haven, New Jersey, and Member of the Pension Research Council.

reasons, have been eliminated. Perhaps we shall see in the not too distant future the inclusion of federal government employees, and even state and local government employees on a mandatory basis, once they recognize that Social Security offers at least a partial answer to the financial difficulties many of them are having with their existing plans.

In other countries specific occupational and industrial groups have typically been excluded from the general social security system. In most cases groups so excluded are covered under special government-administered programs, presumed to be designed so as better to meet their special employment conditions. Our Railroad Retirement System was an illustration of this type of situation, but the recent amendments have now brought railroad employees effectively under the general social security system.

In some countries this fragmentation of social security into a main system and a series of satellite systems for particular industrial and professional groups seems to have become a fixed pattern, with little hope of eventual consolidation. The special systems are often the result of collective bargaining on an industry basis, and in any event the possession of a special social security system tends to become a "status symbol" for the groups so singled out. You will recall that it took a close approach to bankruptcy to bring the railroad employees in the United States into the common fold.

I have mentioned these things about the structure of social security systems since they could be viewed as one approach to the problem of coordinating public and private pensions—the satellite systems are in effect the contracting out of certain employee groups from the main system, in the presence of the real or presumed existence of special conditions or needs. Moreover, in approaching the problem of coordinating public and private pensions, the existence of satellite systems adds an extra dimension to the problem.

However, I shall not pursue this aspect further, but turn now to the problem as it confronts most employers in the private sector, especially the multinational employers—how best to provide for the coexistence of a private occupational pension plan with a mandatory social security system that provides the same employees with pensions as a matter of right.

Briefly, there are two basic alternatives that are generally available:

1.  To provide under the social security law for "contracting out," that is for permitting individual employers to opt for the exclusion or

partial exclusion of his employees from the normally mandatory social security system, subject of course to his providing appropriate replacement benefits through a private arrangement.

2. To structure the private plan so that its benefits are "integrated" with those of the social security system, that is, so that the two sources combined produce benefits that are adequate but not excessive at all earnings levels.

Combinations of the two alternatives are found. In fact where "contracting out" has been permitted it seldom applies to the full social security benefit, so there still remains the problem of integrating the private plan benefits with the residual benefits of the social security system.

**CONTRACTING OUT**

First, I should like to review some of the experiences with "contracting out," not because this is the best or the most prevalent approach, but because the experiences with it are not widely known, and do provide an important part of the background against which the "integration" approach has evolved as the most popular.

I start with a few notes on the "nonhistory" of contracting out in the United States. In 1935, when the social security system of the United States was in the process of being legislated, there were not many employers who really believed that the adoption of such a system could be avoided. There was, however, an important and vocal group of employers, encouraged and assisted by insurance companies that were just developing the field of insured pensions, who urged that employers with pension plans for their employees should be permitted to continue these plans unimpaired, and have their employees exempted from social security. These fought long and hard for a contracting out amendment, but lost. The effort was never revived, although there was an equally unsuccessful attempt to eliminate the social security law as unconstitutional.

Turning now to some more positive experiences, so far as I have been able to discover only four countries have made a serious attempt to use contracting out as a method of coordinating private and public pension plans. These countries are Belgium, Japan, New Zealand, and the United Kingdom.

*Belgium* may have been the first, but here the experiment was so limited in scope as to be of minor significance. For some years up to 1968, employees covered under the staff social security system of Belgium were permitted to opt that a part of their own social security contributions for retirement and widows' pensions be diverted to a private insurance company for the purchase of similar benefits, enhanced by the inclusion of cash options and other special features.

In 1968 the various Belgium Social Security funds were merged, and a new benefit formula, essentially the one in use today, was introduced for all employees. The individual contracting out feature was eliminated, but the insured benefits secured by the previously diverted employee contributions were preserved for the benefit of those who had them, without any corresponding offset in the new social security benefit formula. Thus the employees who had elected the option were granted a "free ride" to the extent that they received double benefits for the contributions they had diverted to insurance, resulting in a significantly higher total pension, especially for those who were nearing retirement age.

In *Japan*, the problem of coordinating private retirement benefits with social security is of fairly recent origin, and even now has not loomed very large. Japanese employers have provided retirement benefits for a long time. However, the traditional and still prevailing form of such benefits is a lump sum based upon the employee's final earnings level and his length of service. The service usually includes the employee's entire working lifetime, due to the Japanese tradition of lifetime employment. These lump sum retirement benefits have always been looked upon as deferred wages, so when social security pensions were first introduced in 1959 the possibility of coordinating them with the lump sum retirement benefits was apparently not even considered.

In 1962 the Japanese tax law was amended, extending to employer-sponsored annuity plans tax exemptions and deductions quite similar to those provided in the United States. The objective was to give employers encouragement to provide retiring employees with pensions, in lieu of or in addition to the traditional lump sum retirement benefits. Many employers did set up annuity plans, but the annuities provided were, and still are to a large extent, term certain rather than life annuities, and usually include a lump sum option which is almost always elected.

The tax incentive having proved less than satisfactorily effective in stimulating the growth of true pension plans in Japan, the next step, in 1966, was to amend the social security law to permit a measure of contracting out. This was limited in a number of ways:

1.  It applied to the wage-related part of the two-tier Japanese social security benefit formula.

2.  It required that replacement benefits be at least one-third higher in value than the social security benefits they replaced.
3.  The option was available only for employers or employer groups with 1,000 or more employees.
4.  Employee and union consent were required.
5.  The reduction in employee and employer contributions from contracting out was only about one third.
6.  Lump sum commutation of the replacement benefits could not be permitted.
7.  In case of termination of the plan providing the replacement benefits, the actuarial value of accrued benefits must be turned over to the social security reserve fund.

Not surprisingly, contracting out has not proved very popular, although it has been reported that as many as 900 qualifying plans, with 5 million covered employees, are in effect.

The viability of the Japanese contracting out procedure has been impaired by the fact that since 1973 social security benefits have been indexed to the Consumer Price Index. Contracting out, however, is limited to the nonindexed part of the benefit replaced, the increases due to indexing remaining with the social security system. Benefits increased over 40 percent from 1973 to 1975 as a result of the indexing. It is not difficult to visualize the contracted out benefits becoming so insignificant in relation to the whole that there remains little justification for continuing the option. In the absence of a complete overhaul of the Japanese social security system, the need for which is widely recognized quite apart from the question of coordination with private benefits, there are indications that contracting out has a very limited future in Japan.

Contracting out in *New Zealand* has had a very brief history—less than a year—and is now in limbo. In August 1974 the Labour Party-dominated New Zealand Parliament enacted the New Zealand Superannuation Scheme, a compulsory contributory national plan of the money purchase type. This plan became partially effective in April 1975, the beginning of what was to have been a five-year phase-in period. Contracting out was permitted, under conditions that never had a chance to become fully clarified.

In the November 1975 national election the Opposition National Party took over the government of New Zealand. They had made a promise, during the election campaign, to liquidate the New Zealand Superannuation Scheme and to replace it with something much better. One of the first acts of the new government was to discontinue the mandatory contributions, which was done in mid-December. They are now in the process of returning the contributions made, both employee and employer contributions being paid over to the employees, without interest but free of income tax.

During the election campaign the National Party released considerable publicity regarding the plan they would, if elected, substitute for the Labour Government scheme. Contracting out was not among the details mentioned, but it was stated that private schemes were to be treated as a "second tier," and were promised "generous tax concessions." There is nothing I can add at this point, but I rather suspect that contracting out is dead in New Zealand.

Coming finally to the *United Kingdom*, we find that one experiment with contracting out has come to an end, and another is in the process of implementation. From 1946, when Lord Beveridge's national pension program was installed, to 1961, the British system strictly followed the Beveridge pattern of uniform weekly benefits supported by uniform employee and employer contributions, each increased from time to time to keep pace with the rising cost of living.

In 1961 the so-called "graduated scheme" was introduced. This called for matching earnings-related contributions from employees and their employers, and provided fully vested pension benefit accruals directly related to the aggregate amount of the contributions. An employer could contract out his employees by establishing equivalent replacement benefits, under specified conditions, through a private scheme. The contracting out privilege applied initially to the full graduated scheme contributions and benefits, but as increases in contribution rates and the level of earnings to which they applied were introduced from time to time, the increases were not subject to contracting out. Contracting out was permitted only with respect to the original level of contributions, so the scheme developed to an increasing degree as a partially contracted out arrangement.

The financial terms for contracting out were fairly attractive to employers, even with the low rates of interest prevailing 15 years ago. Many employers, including a large proportion of those in the public sector, opted for a private scheme. As interest rates rose, making contracting out even more attractive to employers, additional employers contracted out. By 1975, when the scheme was terminated, perhaps as many as 50 percent of employees under private schemes had been contracted out.

Discontinuance of the graduated scheme in 1975, with accrued benefits "frozen," was a feature of the Conservative Government's new "Strategy for Pensions," which was to create a full partnership between government and employers in providing employee pensions. This program had a form of contracting out under which the emphasis was focused on the provision of private plan benefits, with a government "reserve scheme" available only for those employees whose employers made no pension provision for them. This somewhat idealistic program was supposed to have become effective in April 1975.

The Labour Government which took over after the February 1974 national elections promptly decided to follow the Conservatives' plan to discontinue the graduated scheme, but to throw out all the rest. In due course the new government came up with its program, which has now been enacted and which is scheduled to take effect in April 1978. It also has a "contracting out" feature, with terms considerably less favorable than those of the 1961 scheme.

So at present British employers and their advisors are struggling with the question of whether or not to contract out of the earnings-related second tier of the Labour Party scheme. There are many complicated issues, not the least of which is a requirement that replacement benefits must be fully indexed, as are the social security benefits they replace, except that at retirement age the national plan will take over the guarantee and payment of subsequent cost of living increases.

It may be that the British are almost alone today in their continuing belief that contracting out is a feasible and desirable concept. Whether or not this faith will sustain them through the many difficulties that lie ahead, both before and after 1978, should be one of the more interesting chapters in the history of public and private pensions.

Looking back through this brief history of contracting out as a device for coordinating public and private pensions, one is struck with the omnipresence of politics as a factor at all stages—adoption, development, and ultimate demise.

### Integration

Turning now to the other alternative in coordinating public and private pensions, integration, we find that the political factor is far less important. The reason is fairly obvious—provisions for contracting out generally require specific legislation, in the form of amendments to the social security laws, while integration is inherently the problem of the employer. He must, of course, satisfy the bureaucrats who must approve his program and verify his tax deductions. Thus the choice, from one viewpoint, depends on whether employers get along better with legislators or bureaucrats.

I happen to belong to that generation of actuaries who started practice in the private pension field during the period when the original social security legislation in the United States was being developed, revised, and implemented. Once the possibility of contracting out had been eliminated, as I have described before, the constitutionality of the legislation affirmed, and the 1939 amendments which created the present benefit structure enacted, the major problem of the employer with a pre-existing pension plan became the coordination of that plan with a social security system that had become a reality.

**United States**

The Revenue Act of 1942 was the first national legislation in the United States to impose detailed control over private pension plans. The primary objective of this legislation was to limit the use of such plans as shelters against the high wartime tax rates, both corporate and individual. The principal provision designed to implement this objective was that which prohibited a tax-qualified plan from "discriminating" in favor of highly compensated employees.

Regulations under the new law did not appear until over a year after its enactment. When the regulations did appear it was found, to the shocked surprise of many employers and their advisors, that the Internal Revenue had interpreted the nondiscrimination provision to limit any and all benefits that might be provided with respect to earnings in excess of those covered by social security (then $3,000 per year). Efforts to defeat this interpretation were unsuccessful. The formula limitation for integration is still with us, becoming more complicated with each successive change in social security, and with each fresh effort on the part of the tax administrators to refine the formula and its application.

Some details of the first 25 years of integration regulations in the United States are contained in Appendix A, which is a paper I prepared in 1968 for the American Enterprise Institute. This paper was prepared primarily to present the arguments against a major reduction (from 37.5 percent to 24 percent) in the integration limit, proposed by the Internal Revenue Service in 1966 on the basis of a stricter interpretation of the concept. A secondary objective of the paper was to show how impractical and unrealistic the whole subject had become. Widespread objection to the IRS proposal resulted in a long delay in its adoption, and after substantial increases in social security benefits adopted in 1967 made the proposal even more difficult to justify, it was finally dropped. The 37.5 percent limitation was retained, and this still constitutes the basic limitation on the extent to which benefits on earnings above the social security limit may exceed those superimposed upon social security in the covered earnings zone. However, the technical details surrounding the adjustment of the basic limit for different types of benefit formula, different compensation bases, death benefits, employee contributions, and other variations continue to complicate the picture. The interpretation and application of the integration regulations has assumed the proportions of a special field of expertise within the Internal Revenue Service and the pension consulting profession.

There has always been a tendency for the integration regulations to lag at least one step behind developments that would normally affect them. Thus, the effect of automatic cost of living indexing of social security benefits, introduced some four years ago, has yet to be recognized in the integration regulations. Looking ahead, a new formula for the calculation of social security pensions is now before Congress, with an excellent chance of passing, and thereby again rendering the regulations obsolete. Discounting the unlikely possibility that the Internal Revenue will finally decide upon a simpler and more practical view of integration, it appears that this aspect of pension plan design and administration will continue to be one of the most complicated and frustrating problems faced by those in the pension field in the United States.

Very early in this process it was recognized that there were two major variations of the integration principle. One was to adopt or continue a benefit formula defining the full objective benefit, deducting from it all or a part of the social security benefit. This may be called the "subtractive" approach, although those who prepared plan documents went to great lengths in attempting to avoid the impression that something had been taken away. These efforts often failed, with the result that the so-called "social security offset" under this type of plan had a tendency to erode, especially under union pressure, and in some cases eventually to disappear. Where this has happened the loss in terms of redundant benefits is generally permanent; there is no turning back and reintegrating the plan on some other basis.

The other variation on the integration theme, and the one that is probably the most widely used, not only in the United States but in other countries, is to design the private plan benefit formula so that it complements the social security formula. An almost universal characteristic of social security benefit formulas is that they relate to earnings up to some specified level (which of course tends to change), with earnings above that level ignored. Thus the integration formula is generally made up of a certain percentage applied to earnings up to the social security "ceiling," and a higher percentage of earnings above the ceiling. This of course is pretty elementary to all pension practitioners. A subvariation of this type of formula, found in some European countries where the social security benefit is a flat amount, unrelated to earnings or service, consists in omitting entirely from the private plan benefit formula, and from the contribution base as well, all earnings up to a specified level. The level is determined as that point where the flat social security benefit alone produces a satisfactory benefit in relation to earnings. In Holland this is known as the "franchise" method of integration.

Both of the major variations of integration are found in pension plans in the United States. In the late 30s and early 40s, when employers and their advisors were still uncertain as to the future of social security, the subtractive method was adopted for many of the older plans, sometimes as an interim arrangement pending the development of an entirely new and different pension program. Some employers who started with a subtractive integration, then went to a new plan based on career pay with employee contributions, have completed the full circle and are now back to where they started, with a final pay noncontributory plan.

### Europe

Most European countries with a significant development of private occupational pensions have met the integration problem in much the same way that it has been met in the United States. Both variations of the integration approach have been used, but in no country has the application of integration principles been surrounded with anything like the volume of technicalities and formulas that employers in the United States have had to cope with over the past thirty years.

In *Belgium, Germany,* the *Netherlands,* and *Switzerland,* where private occupational pensions have developed along lines quite similar to those with which we are familiar in the United States, both the subtractive and the split formula methods of integration are used. There is probably some increase in the popularity of the subtractive method, since in all of these countries social security pensions are indexed to the cost of living, generally by formula, and subtractive integration seems to be simpler and more satisfactory under these conditions.

The *Republic of Ireland* until very recently had a social security system which excluded from compulsory participation all employees earning above a specified level—a feature which was found in Germany and some other countries some years ago. This led to a practice of limiting participation in private occupational plans to those who were not covered by social security, and the practice of so limiting coverage still persists to some extent in Ireland.

In *France* there is a basic social security system, plus a unique series of complementary pension systems superimposed. For the very high paid employees there is often a third layer of pension coverage. This is a most interesting structure, but much too complicated to discuss here. Suffice it to say that the whole complex is integrated on the basis of salary slices (tranches), although some overlapping has recently crept in through collective bargaining.

*Sweden* has a flat rate basic pension, plus an earnings-related complementary tier of social security, plus a third tier of privately financed pensions created by industrywide collective bargaining. This may be the most perfectly integrated system to be found, but only because the individual employer has no choice but to go along with the standard pattern. Only at the top levels of salary can the employer make his own deal with his executives.

## MANDATORY PRIVATE PENSIONS

As mentioned before, the *Netherlands* and *Switzerland* belong to that group of countries where national and private pensions are coordinated by integration, in much the same way as in the United States. However, in both of these countries it has been decided as a matter of national policy—confirmed by referendum in Switzerland more than three years ago—that, rather than continue expanding social security, every employer should be required by law to maintain an occupational pension plan, privately financed and administered but meeting prescribed minimum standards. The development of these "second pillar" programs has been stalled in both countries by immediate and serious economic problems. In Switzerland, enabling legislation has finally reached the Parliament and will probably be enacted in 1976, with the program starting a five-year phasing-in period on January 1, 1978. The time table in the Netherlands is not yet clear.

The Swiss and Dutch proposals, it should be emphasized, are not to be confused with the "two-tier with contracting-out" programs in effect in Japan and being implemented in the United Kingdom. The Swiss and

Dutch plans do not include any government-administered alternative; they simply call for a second tier private plan as a statutory requirement upon every employer. It might be noted that such a program has been in effect in Finland for over ten years, although on a basis which does not provide much guidance for the larger industrialized countries.

## CONCLUSION

In considering this collage of public and private pensions, and their diverse efforts to coexist, one is greatly tempted to look for some common denominator—perhaps a direction in which all of the elements are heading toward some ultimate goal. The pursuit of this line of inquiry, however, quickly involves far greater questions of economic and political evolution, areas in which no actuary would venture. Thus any conclusions that might be derived from the picture as I have drawn it must necessarily be narrow and highly equivocal.

If in any country there is a significant movement in the relative positions of public and private pensions, it will inevitably be in the direction of giving public pensions a larger role. If the cold war between public and private pensions is ever to come to an end, public pensions will be the winner; the rules of the game are so written. Thus, in most of South America the public pension movement developed like any other South American revolution—it was over before most people knew it had started. Private pensions never had a chance.

I am not wholly pessimistic, however, as to the future of private pensions in North America, or even in Europe. Perhaps 25 years ago an eminent authority on international benefits predicted that private pensions in Europe had no better than a ten- or fifteen-year life expectancy, so far as rank and file employees were concerned. Today we see that they have virtually disappeared in Italy, and probably must be considered a lost cause in Spain, but they still seem to be alive and in reasonably good health in most of Northern Europe. So I am not about to be a prophet of doom for the private pension movement in my generation.

chapter

# 4

# Fiscal Basis of the OASDI Program, Including Long-Range Cost Projections

A. HAEWORTH ROBERTSON*

THE FINANCIAL CONDITION of the social security program is very much in the news these days. It is a healthy sign that various viewpoints are being put forth regarding the role of the social security program and the method by which it is financed. However, sometimes the debate tends to be confused because of the misunderstanding of various concepts and the words used to describe them. The purpose of this paper is to present a few facts, figures, and explanations which may be helpful to the reader in understanding the debate over the social security program and its financing. The paper is limited to the Old-Age, Survivors, and Disability Insurance (OASDI) portion of the social security program, excluding Medicare, and presumes the reader has a basic knowledge of this program.

## NATURE OF THE TRUST FUNDS

The federal Old-Age and Survivors Insurance Trust Fund was established on January 1, 1940, as a separate account in the United States Treasury to hold the amounts accumulated under the Old-Age and Survivors Insurance (OASI) program. All the financial operations which relate

---

* Chief Actuary, U.S. Social Security Administration, Baltimore, Maryland.

to the OASI system are handled through this fund. The social security amendments of 1956, which became law August 1, 1956, provided for the creation of the Federal Disability Insurance Trust Fund—a fund entirely separate from the OASI trust fund—through which are handled all financial operations in connection with the Disability Insurance (DI) system.[1] These two trust funds are held by the Board of Trustees under the authority of Section 201(c) of the Social Security Act. The board is comprised of three members who serve in an ex officio capacity. The members of the board are the Secretary of the Treasury, the Secretary of Labor, and the Secretary of Health, Education, and Welfare. The Secretary of the Treasury is designated by law as the Managing Trustee. The Commissioner of Social Security is Secretary of the Board.

The Board of Trustees reports to the Congress once each year, in compliance with Section 201(c)(2) of the Social Security Act. These annual reports contain considerable information on the financial operation of the OASDI program, including historical information on the income and outgo of the trust funds for prior years, a detailed statement as to how the assets of the trust funds are currently invested, detailed estimates of the income and outgo during the next 5 years, and less-detailed estimates of the income and outgo during the next 75 years. Reference should be made to these annual reports for more complete information on the financial operation of the OASDI program.

The major sources of receipts of the OASI and DI trust funds are (1) amounts appropriated to each of them on the basis of contributions paid by workers and their employers, and by individuals with self-employment income, in work covered by the social security program and (2) amounts deposited in each of them representing contributions paid by workers employed by state and local governments and by such employers with respect to work covered by the program. All employees, and their employers, in employment covered by the program are required to pay contributions with respect to the wages of individual workers (cash tips, covered as wages beginning in 1966 under the 1965 amendments, are an exception to this; employees pay contributions with respect to cash tips, but employers do not). All covered self-employed persons are required to pay contributions with respect to their self-employment income. In general, an individual's contributions are computed on annual wages or self-employment income, or both wages and self-employment income combined, up to a specified maximum annual amount, with the contributions being determined first on the wages and then on any self-employment income

---

[1] A limited amount of disability benefits is payable from the OASI program.

necessary to make up the annual maximum amount. In this paper, "contributions" payable by both workers and employers are sometimes referred to as "taxes."

The contribution rates applicable to taxable earnings in each of the calendar years 1937 and later, and the allocation of the rates to finance expenditures from each of the two trust funds, are shown in Table 1. For 1977 and later, the contribution rates shown are the rates scheduled in the provisions of present law. The maximum amount of annual earnings taxable in each year, 1937–76, is also shown in Table 1. Beginning with 1975, the maximum amount of earnings taxable in each year is determined in the preceding year under the automatic increase provisions in

**TABLE 1**
**Contribution Rates and Maximum Taxable Amount of Annual Earnings**

| Calendar Years | Maximum Taxable Amount of Annual Earnings | Contribution Rates (percent of taxable earnings) | | | | | |
|---|---|---|---|---|---|---|---|
| | | Employees and Employers Each | | | Self-employed | | |
| | | OASDI | OASI | DI | OASDI | OASI | DI |
| Past experience | | | | | | | |
| 1937–1949 ........ | $ 3,000 | 1.000 | 1.000 | — | — | — | — |
| 1950.............. | 3,000 | 1.500 | 1.500 | — | — | — | — |
| 1951–1953 ........ | 3,600 | 1.500 | 1.500 | — | 2.2500 | 2.2500 | — |
| 1954.............. | 3,600 | 2.000 | 2.000 | — | 3.0000 | 3.0000 | — |
| 1955–1956 ........ | 4,200 | 2.000 | 2.000 | | 0.0000 | 0.0000 | — |
| 1957–1958 ........ | 4,200 | 2.250 | 2.000 | 0.250 | 3.3750 | 3.0000 | 0.3750 |
| 1959.............. | 4,800 | 2.500 | 2.250 | .250 | 3.7500 | 3.3750 | .3750 |
| 1960–1961 ........ | 4,800 | 3.000 | 2.750 | .250 | 4.5000 | 4.1250 | .3750 |
| 1962.............. | 4,800 | 3.125 | 2.875 | .250 | 4.7000 | 4.3250 | .3750 |
| 1963–1965 ........ | 4,800 | 3.625 | 3.375 | .250 | 5.4000 | 5.0250 | .3750 |
| 1966.............. | 6,600 | 3.850 | 3.500 | .350 | 5.8000 | 5.2750 | .5250 |
| 1967.............. | 6,600 | 3.900 | 3.550 | .350 | 5.9000 | 5.3750 | .5250 |
| 1968.............. | 7,800 | 3.800 | 3.325 | .475 | 5.8000 | 5.0875 | .7125 |
| 1969.............. | 7,800 | 4.200 | 3.725 | .475 | 6.3000 | 5.5875 | .7125 |
| 1970.............. | 7,800 | 4.200 | 3.650 | .550 | 6.3000 | 5.4750 | .8250 |
| 1971.............. | 7,800 | 4.600 | 4.050 | .550 | 6.9000 | 6.0750 | .8250 |
| 1972.............. | 9,000 | 4.600 | 4.050 | .550 | 6.9000 | 6.0750 | .8250 |
| 1973.............. | 10,800 | 4.850 | 4.300 | .550 | 7.0000 | 6.2050 | .7950 |
| 1974.............. | 13,200 | 4.950 | 4.375 | .575 | 7.0000 | 6.1850 | .8150 |
| 1975.............. | 14,100 | 4.950 | 4.375 | .575 | 7.0000 | 6.1850 | .8150 |
| 1976.............. | 15,300 | 4.950 | 4.375 | .575 | 7.0000 | 6.1850 | .8150 |
| Changes scheduled in present law | | | | | | | |
| 1977............. | Subject | 4.950 | 4.375 | .575 | 7.0000 | 6.1850 | .8150 |
| 1978–1980 ....... | to auto- | 4.950 | 4.350 | .600 | 7.0000 | 6.1500 | .8500 |
| 1981–1985 ....... | matic | 4.950 | 4.300 | .650 | 7.0000 | 6.0800 | .9200 |
| 1986–2010 ....... | increase | 4.950 | 4.250 | .700 | 7.0000 | 6.0100 | .9900 |
| 2011 and........ later | | 5.950 | 5.100 | .850 | 7.0000 | 6.0000 | 1.0000 |

Section 230 of the Social Security Act, unless modified by intervening congressional action. Except for amounts received by the Secretary of the Treasury under state agreements (to effectuate coverage under the program for state and local government employees) and deposited directly in the trust funds, all contributions are collected by the Internal Revenue Service and deposited in the general fund of the treasury as internal revenue collections; then, on an estimated basis, the contributions received are immediately and automatically appropriated to the trust funds. Periodic adjustments are subsequently made to the extent that the estimates are found to differ from the amounts of contributions actually payable on the basis of reported earnings.

That portion of each trust fund which, in the judgment of the Managing Trustee, is not required to meet current expenditures for benefits and administration is invested, on a daily basis, in interest-bearing obligations of the U.S. Government (including special public-debt obligations utilized only by the trust funds), in obligations guaranteed as to both principal and interest by the United States, or in certain federally sponsored agency obligations that are designated in the laws authorizing their issuance as lawful investments for fiduciary and trust funds under the control and authority of the United States or any officer of the United States. The trust funds earned interest of $2.8 billion during the fiscal year 1975, equivalent to an effective annual rate of 6.5 percent on the total assets of the trust funds.

Expenditures for benefit payments and administrative expenses under the OASDI program are paid out of the trust funds. All expenses incurred by the Department of Health, Education, and Welfare and by the Treasury Department in carrying out the provisions of Title II of the Social Security Act and of the Internal Revenue Code relating to the collection of contributions are charged to the trust funds. The Secretary of Health, Education, and Welfare certifies benefit payments to the Managing Trustee, who makes the payment from the respective trust funds in accordance therewith. Administrative expenses for fiscal year 1975 amounted to 1.5 percent of benefit payments from the OASI trust fund, 3.3 percent of benefit payments from the DI trust fund, and 1.8 percent from the combined OASDI trust funds.

## FINANCING BASIS: SELF-SUPPORTING AND CURRENT-COST CONCEPTS

Throughout its history the OASDI program has been self-supporting and since the 1950s has been operated on what may be termed a current-cost financing basis. It is self-supporting in that the only source of funds to pay benefits and administrative expenses is the social security taxes collected from workers and their employers covered under the program (and the interest earned on the invested balances of the trust funds).[2] Under the current-cost method of financing, the amount of taxes collected each year is intended to be approximately equal to the benefits and administrative expenses paid during the year plus a small additional amount to maintain the trust funds at an appropriate contingency reserve level. The purpose of the trust fund under current-cost financing is to reflect all financial transactions and to absorb temporary differences between income and expenditures. Thus, whatever normal ratio of trust fund assets to expenditures is established, it can be expected that the fund will vary somewhat from that level from time to time as it absorbs those fluctuations. The following table illustrates for selected years the size of the combined OASDI trust funds in dollars and as a percentage of expenditures during the following year:

| (1) | (2) | (3) |
| --- | --- | --- |
| | OASDI Trust Fund Assets, at the Beginning of the Year | |
| Calendar Year | Dollar Amount (in millions of dollars) | Percentage of Expenditures during Such Year |
| 1960 | $21,966 | 186% |
| 1965 | 21,172 | 110 |
| 1970 | 34,182 | 103 |
| 1971 | 38,068 | 99 |
| 1972 | 40,434 | 93 |
| 1973 | 42,775 | 80 |
| 1974 | 44,414 | 73 |
| 1975 | 45,886 | 66 |
| 1976 | 44,342 | 57* |

* Estimated.

Since the inception of the OASDI program, past payroll taxes together with interest on the trust funds have been adequate to provide all past

---

[2] In addition to social security taxes and interest earnings, the trust funds receive annual reimbursements from the general fund of the Treasury for certain costs that are not financed by payroll taxes. In fiscal year 1975, such reimbursements amounted to $499 million, or about three fourths of 1 percent of the $66.7 billion in total income to the Old-Age, Survivors, and Disability Insurance trust funds.

benefits and administrative expenses. More specifically, with respect to the period from 1937 through calendar year 1975, cumulative income to the trust funds amounted to $586 billion and cumulative disbursements amounted to $542 billion. The balance of $44 billion was in the trust funds at the end of the calendar year 1975. Based upon current projections,[3] it is estimated that, during the calendar years 1976–1981, income to the trust funds will total $581 billion and disbursements will be $616 billion. This is a projected decrease in the trust funds of $35 billion during the period 1976–1981, which would reduce the trust funds to about $9 billion by the end of calendar year 1981. For purposes of illustration, the preceding figures are for the Old-Age and Survivors and Disability Insurance trust funds, combined, although these are independent trust funds and must be considered separately. These figures illustrate that under current financing procedures the assets of the trust funds play a relatively minor role; it is the ongoing collection of social security taxes which is the most important factor in providing benefits under the program.

## LONG-RANGE COST ESTIMATES: ACTUARIAL DEFICIT OR ACTUARIAL SURPLUS

The Congress, in setting future tax rates for the OASDI program, has normally followed the principle that estimated future income to the trust funds (including interest earnings on invested assets) should be equal to estimated future disbursements, taking into account both present and future participants in the program.

When estimated future disbursements and estimated future income over the 75-year valuation period (used since 1965) are not in balance, an "actuarial deficit" or an "actuarial surplus" exists—depending upon whether disbursements are greater than income, or vice versa. The OASDI program has been in close actuarial balance throughout most of the program's existence. When there was an imblance, i.e., an actuarial deficit or actuarial surplus, the Congress has acted in due course to revise either taxes, benefits, or both so as to bring the program into close actuarial balance over the 75-year valuation period. Therefore, it is essen-

---

[3] In the 1976 Annual Reports of the Board of Trustees of the Social Security trust funds, cost estimates were prepared on the basis of three alternative sets of economic and demographic assumptions. Alternative I could be characterized as an optimistic set of assumptions; alternative III as a pessimistic set of assumptions; and alternative II as an intermediate set of assumptions which produces expenditures (measured as a percentage of taxable payroll) approximately midway between those produced by the alternative I and III assumptions. In this report, all quoted projections are based upon the alternative II, or "intermediate," set of assumptions.

tial to the sound financial operation of the OASDI program that periodic estimates be made of the future income and outgo to ensure that they are still in balance, and, if not, to provide information to enable appropriate action to be taken to restore the balance.

Actual future income from social security taxes, and actual future expenditures for benefit payments and administrative expenses, will depend upon a large number of factors, including the following:

1.  Size and composition of the active working population, which depend in turn upon fertility rates, mortality rates, migration rates, labor force participation and unemployment rates, disability rates, and retirement-age patterns.
2.  Size and composition of the population which is receiving benefits and the level of benefits, and the level of earnings of the active working population, which depend in turn on the previously mentioned factors, as well as upon wage patterns, the Consumer Price Index, marriage rates, and others.

It is obviously impossible to know what the future holds with respect to these demographic and economic factors which will determine the actual income and expenditures under the OASDI program during the next 75-year period. The best that can be done is to make assumptions as to the future behavior of these demographic and economic factors, and to make long-range estimates based upon such assumptions which will indicate the trend and general range in future income and outgo. Such estimates, and their underlying assumptions, if revised periodically in the light of developing trends, provide information which is essential for making informed policy decisions.

In reviewing long-range estimates based upon demographic and economic conditions postulated to exist in the middle of the next century, it would be well to keep in mind the following: Although the underlying assumptions for these long-range estimates may appear to be reasonable, based upon current understanding, in some cases the assumptions produce results so different from the current situation that attention should be directed toward the overall implications of these assumptions and not just toward their effect on the single issue of financing the OASDI program. For example, since the selection of particular demographic assumptions implies a certain future composition of the U.S. population, it is important to recognize that, if the population composition should change in accordance with these assumptions, it is likely to result in substantial changes in many of the nation's social and economic arrangements. Although it is beyond the scope of this paper, it would be desirable to extend to the year 2050 the analysis of possible effects throughout the society of the postulated changes in the population, in order to view the long-range financing questions from a broader perspective.

## LONG-RANGE COST ESTIMATES UNDER PRESENT LAW

To facilitate the presentation of long-range cost estimates, in this paper expenditures are expressed as a percentage of taxable payroll. The expenditures consist of outgo from the trust funds, and include benefit payments; administrative expenses; interchanges between the Old-Age, Survivors, and Disability Insurance trust funds and the railroad retirement trust fund (including the reflection of net income from that fund); and payments for vocational rehabilitation services for disability beneficiaries. The payroll consists of the total earnings which are subject to social security taxes after adjustment to reflect the lower contribution rates on self-employed income, tips, and multiple-employer "excess wages"; this adjustment is made so as to facilitate both the calculation of contributions (which is thereby the product of the tax rate and the payroll) and the comparison of expenditure percentages with tax rates.

Table 2 displays the projected expenditures, together with the scheduled taxes and the resulting excess of expenditures over tax income, under the OASDI program during the next 75 years. These figures were derived from the 1976 Annual Report of the Board of Trustees of the federal Old-Age and Survivors Insurance and Disability Insurance trust funds, and reference should be made to that report for complete details of the projected future expenditures under the OASDI program, and the assumptions and methodology used in determining them.

As indicated in column (2) of Table 2, the expenditures are expected to rise slowly during the remainder of this century. After the turn of the century, the expenditures are expected to rise more rapidly until reaching a level of almost 29 percent of taxable payroll in the year 2050. The excess of projected expenditures over tax income, shown in column (4), is relatively low during the remainder of this century, but rises rapidly thereafter. The average excess of expenditures over taxes for the 75-year period is 7.96 percent of taxable payroll—the figure usually quoted as the actuarial deficit.

This large actuarial deficit is not something which has already occurred; rather it is something which is expected to materialize in the future. Why did the 1976 Trustees Report forecast an actuarial deficit of 7.96 percent

**TABLE 2**
**Estimated Expenditures of Old-Age, Survivors and Disability Insurance System as
a Percentage of Taxable Payroll for Selected Years, 1976–2050 (based upon intermediate set of assumptions, 1976 Trustees Report**

| (1) Calendar Year | (2) Expenditures | (3) Tax Rate in Law | (4) Excess of Expenditures over Taxes | (5) Portion of Excess in Column (4) Attributable to Increase in Replace-ment Ratios* |
|---|---|---|---|---|
| 1976 | 10.78 | 9.90 | .88 | — |
| 1985 | 11.16 | 9.90 | 1.26 | .04 |
| 1990 | 12.06 | 9.90 | 2.16 | .21 |
| 1995 | 12.89 | 9.90 | 2.99 | .45 |
| 2000 | 13.41 | 9.90 | 3.51 | .85 |
| 2005 | 14.33 | 9.90 | 4.43 | 1.49 |
| 2010 | 15.99 | 9.90 | 6.09 | 2.30 |
| 2015 | 18.40 | 11.90 | 6.50 | 3.31 |
| 2020 | 21.29 | 11.90 | 9.39 | 4.45 |
| 2025 | 24.09 | 11.90 | 12.19 | 5.62 |
| 2030 | 26.03 | 11.90 | 14.13 | 6.64 |
| 2035 | 27.04 | 11.90 | 15.14 | 7.45 |
| 2040 | 27.45 | 11.90 | 15.55 | 8.10 |
| 2045 | 27.92 | 11.90 | 16.02 | 8.72 |
| 2050 | 28.59 | 11.90 | 16.69 | 9.34 |
| 25-year averages: | | | | |
| 1976–2000 | 11.81 | 9.90 | 1.91 | .23 |
| 2001–2025 | 17.95 | 11.10 | 6.85 | 3.04 |
| 2026–2050 | 27.04 | 11.90 | 15.14 | 7.74 |
| 75-year average: | | | | |
| 1976–2050 | 18.93 | 10.97 | 7.96 | 3.68 |

* Please refer to the text, particularly pages 50–51 for an explanation of the figures in this column.

of taxable payroll when just four years earlier in 1972 it was not anticipated that there would be any actuarial deficit?

The relatively small deficit which began in 1975 and is expected to continue during each of the next 25 years is primarily a result of these factors:

1. Unprecedented and unanticipated inflation in recent years and ap-proximately corresponding increases in benefits (benefit increases of 11 percent in 1974, 8 percent in 1975, and 6.4 percent in 1976), and an expectation that inflation will continue at higher levels than was formerly anticipated.

2.  Unexpectedly high rates of unemployment beginning in 1974 result-
    ing in less than anticipated tax income.
3.  Higher than expected disability insurance expenditures in recent
    years and an expectation that future disability costs will be higher
    than formerly anticipated.

With respect to the deficit expected after the turn of the century, this
is primarily a question of our now having a different view of the future
than we had a few years ago. Beginning with the projections made in
1974, our expectation about the fertility rate in the future has changed.
We now expect the fertility rate to be lower in the future than we had
formerly assumed. This will eventually result in a much larger number
of OASDI beneficiaries in relation to the active tax-paying population.
The number of beneficiaries per hundred active workers is now expected
to increase by about 65 percent by the year 2035. Since the social security
program is financed on a current-cost basis, collecting only enough in taxes
to pay benefits currently due, it follows that expenditures will rise by about
65 percent solely as a result of the population changes now anticipated.

This demographic area is not the only one in which our outlook has
changed. Beginning with the projections made in 1975, we have assumed
higher rates of inflation and wage changes than we had formerly assumed.
Because of the complex and arbitrary way in which future benefits are
related to future changes in wages and the Consumer Price Index, under
the particular assumptions made regarding such changes the benefits
projected to materialize under present law reach unreasonably high levels
(when the initial benefit which is payable is considered in relation to the
wages being replaced) for persons who first become entitled to benefits
in the next century. The estimated future costs which result from a
projection of these high benefit levels may be somewhat unrealistic and
should be interpreted with caution and in light of the virtual certainty
that legislative changes will be made to prevent these projected benefit
levels from materializing.

To illustrate the degree to which these apparently unintended increases
in future benefits contribute to the actuarial deficit shown in Table 2,
column (5) has been included. Column (5) indicates the portion of the
actuarial deficit shown in column (4) which is attributable to an increase,
above the levels prevailing at the beginning of 1978, in the replacement
ratio (the ratio of the initial benefit payable at retirement to the individual's preretirement earnings). Approximately one-half of the 75-year
average actuarial deficit is attributable to rising replacement ratios. The

resolution of this problem of rising replacement ratios is one of the most important tasks which must be faced during the coming months by those concerned with the social security program.

## SOCIAL SECURITY'S TRILLION DOLLAR "ACTUARIAL DEFICITS" AND "ACCRUED LIABILITIES"

As indicated in the previous section, the Board of Trustees, in their 1976 annual report to the Congress on the financial status of the OASDI program, reported the average annual amount by which expenditures were expected to exceed tax income over the next 75-year period was 7.96 percent of taxable payroll. This represents a sizable actuarial deficit since the average amount of taxes expected to be collected each year during the next 75 years according to current law is 10.97 percent of taxable payroll. As was noted previously, this actuarial deficit should be interpreted with caution since it is attributable, in part, to a projection of benefit levels which will not materialize if appropriate legislation is enacted.

Another way to express this actuarial deficit is as a single-sum amount, determined by computing the excess of expenditures over income in each of the next 75 years and discounting these amounts at interest to the present time. As of mid-1976 this single-sum amount was $4.3 trillion. This computation, as well as the following computations in this section of the paper, were determined as of mid-1976 based upon the intermediate set of assumptions[4] set forth in the 1976 OASDI trustees report and an annual interest rate of 6.6 percent.[5]

As further illustration of the meaning of the actuarial deficit the following examples may be of value. If the actuarial deficit determined in 1976 is to be eliminated by the payment of additional taxes it could be achieved, at least in theory, in one of two ways: A single-sum amount of $4.3 trillion could be placed in the trust fund immediately, and the resulting trust fund together with interest thereon, supplemented by the currently scheduled social security taxes, would be sufficient to pay all benefits which will fall due during the next 75 years. At the end of this period, the trust fund would have returned to a relatively low level as at present.

As an alternative to this obviously impossible solution, additional taxes

---

[4] See footnote 3.

[5] For the purpose of these calculations an interest rate of 6.6 percent has been assumed. This is a "real rate of interest" of 2.5 percent, compounded with an assumed 4.0 percent annual increase in the Consumer Price Index.

could be collected over the next 75 years. The average additional taxes would have to be the equivalent of 7.96 percent of taxable payroll (compared to the average scheduled taxes of 10.97 percent). Assuming it is desired that the trust fund be maintained at a relatively low level to serve as a contingency fund—as it has in recent years—the additional taxes would not be constant throughout the next 75 years but would increase as benefit payments increase. In this event, the average additional taxes (over and above the taxes already scheduled) would be about 1.9 percent of taxable payroll until the turn of the century, 6.9 percent during the first quarter of the next century, and 15.1 percent thereafter.

Obviously this actuarial deficit must be eliminated. The financing goal for the social security program has always been and should continue to be that, based upon the best information available, anticipated future expenditures will equal anticipated future income. As indicated earlier, the appropriate revision of the automatic adjustment provisions which result in erratic and unpredictable replacement ratios (the ratio of benefits to preretirement earnings) is an important step in eliminating about one half of this actuarial deficit. For example, the actuarial deficit would be reduced from $4.3 trillion to $2.2 trillion if replacement ratios are stabilized at current levels. In terms of a percentage of taxable payroll the actuarial deficit would be reduced from 7.96 percent to 4.28 percent. As soon as they can be devised, steps should be taken to eliminate completely the projected actuarial deficit over the entire 75-year period.

Once this has been achieved and the program is back in actuarial balance with anticipated future income being equal to anticipated future expenditures, there is still the question of the "unfunded accrued liability." This is a completely separate issue from the "actuarial deficit." The existence of, and the amount of, the "unfunded accrued liability" has no relationship whatsoever to the "actuarial deficit."

The "accrued liability" can be defined as the present value of benefits which have been earned or accrued as of a given date but which will not actually be paid until a later date. For example, in mid-1976 there were 32.5 million persons receiving social security benefits of about $75 billion per year. All conditions have been met for these benefits to be payable in the future and these benefits may be considered to have been fully earned or accrued. The present value of these future benefits is about $700 billion; that is, a fund of $700 billion invested at interest[6] would be just enough to pay all the future benefits to these persons, and the fund would

---

[6] See footnote 5.

be exhausted at the time the last benefit payment fell due. Accordingly, the "accrued liability" for benefits payable to these 32.5 million persons may be said to be $700 billion.

It is more difficult to define the accrued liability for the more than 100 million persons who have participated in the social security program at some time in the past and who are potential recipients of benefits at some time in the future. Because of their prior participation these persons may be considered to have earned or accrued a certain portion of the benefits which will be paid to them at some time in the future, although it should be emphasized that these benefits are not vested from a legal point of view. There is a variety of methods which can be used to calculate the amount of benefits and the value thereof which should be assigned to this prior service. These calculations have not been performed with respect to the social security program in recent years; however, if they were, it is likely they would indicate an accrued liability of about $2,400 billion.[7] When this is added to the accrued liability of $700 billion for those persons already receiving benefits, the result would be a total accrued liability of some $3,100 billion. Since the trust fund had assets of about $45 billion in mid-1976, the *unfunded* accrued liability" could be considered to be about $3,055 billion, or $3.1 trillion. It should be emphasized here that it is only a coincidence that this "unfunded accrued liability" is of the same general magnitude as the "actuarial deficit" of $4.3 trillion. If the actuarial deficit were zero, the "unfunded accrued liability" would still be $3.1 trillion. The unfunded accrued liability may be viewed as the amount by which benefits, which have been paid or promised with respect to prior years of participation in the system, have exceeded the amount of taxes paid during such prior years by employees and their employers.

If the social security program were a private system, under normal circumstances it would be considered desirable to begin to collect more

---

[7] A convenient method of estimating this accrued liability is to compare (a) the present value of future benefits and administrative expenses for persons age 21 and over under present law, and (b) the present value of future taxes for persons age 21 and over based upon a tax schedule under which there would be no 75-year actuarial deficit (i.e., under which future tax income, including present trust fund assets, would be equal to future benefits and administrative expenses, taking into account both present and future participants in the program). The excess of (a) over (b) (i.e., the amount by which future outlays for persons age 21 and over exceed future taxes paid by such persons) can reasonably be used as one measure of the accrued liability. The accrued liability under present law computed in this manner is $3,700 billion (including the accrued liability of $700 billion for persons already receiving benefits). If this same computation were made based not upon present law, but upon a revised law under which replacement ratios would remain approximately constant rather than rise, the total accrued liability would be $3,100 billion. This latter figure is considered by the author to be more appropriate to illustrate the magnitude of the accrued liablity and was used in the text.

income than is necessary for current benefit payments, and to accumulate a substantial fund and begin to transform this *"unfunded* accrued liability"* into a *"funded* accrued liability."* Reasons for doing this would include the following:

1.   Security of benefits. The existence of a large fund would give the employees some assurance that in case the system should terminate and no future income to the system were available, the benefits which had accrued to date could in fact be paid—at least to the extent the accumulated fund was adequate. (The Employee Retirement Income Security Act of 1974 requires that most private pension plans accumulate a fund in order to give employees this added security that their benefits will ultimately be paid.)

2.   Reduction of future contributions. If a fund is accumulated the amount of investment earnings on the trust fund can be used to pay a portion of the future benefits, thus permitting a reduction in the amount of future contributions otherwise required to finance the benefits.

3.   Allocation of costs to the period during which they are incurred. Even though benefits may not be paid until some future date, the cost of those benefits can be considered to have been incurred gradually over an employee's working lifetime as he earns the benefits.

Although these are valid reasons for funding the accrued liability associated with a private pension system, they are less valid for national compulsory social insurance—such as the social security program—covering substantially the entire population. With respect to security of benefits: It is usually assumed that the social security program will continue indefinitely into the future and that the taxing power of the government is adequate assurance that the benefits will be provided. With respect to the reduction of future contributions: Since social security trust funds are invested in government securities, the interest on which is paid from general revenues, it could be argued that the accumulation of a fund will result in lower future social security taxes but higher general taxes. In other words the total future cost will be about the same but it will be distributed differently among the population. With respect to the appropriate allocation of costs to the period during which they are incurred: An argument can be made (under a national social insurance system as well as under a private pension system) for recognizing that a liability is accruing during a person's active working lifetime even though the benefits, and the costs thereof, may not be paid until a later date. The recognition of this liability may or may not take the form of accumulating a fund which is related to a somewhat arbitrarily determined "accrued liability."

There is an argument being made in some quarters these days for funding the accrued liability under the social security program for a reason which does not apply to an individual private pension system and which goes something like this: Since a large part of a person's retirement needs are met by the social security program, his private saving for retirement needs is reduced; this results in the nation's capital accumulation needs being partially unmet; and to offset this reduced saving by the individual, the social security program should collect higher taxes and fund part or all of its accrued liability; the assets of the trust fund would be invested in government securities, thus reducing the amount of government securities held privately and freeing up more private saving for use in developing the economy. The elaboration of this argument, including a statement of its pros and cons, will not be discussed in this paper; however, it should be noted that this argument for funding is a controversial one and it is difficult for various experts to reach agreement on the extent, if any, to which the social security program has resulted in a reduction in private saving.

This section on "actuarial deficits" and "accrued liabilities" can be summarized as follows: The most important test of financial soundness for the social security program is whether the future income (taxes and interest on the trust funds) can reasonably be expected to equal future benefits and administrative expenses. This condition does not exist for the present social security (OASDI) program and there is a substantial "actuarial deficit" of 7.96 percent of taxable payroll, equivalent to $4.3 trillion which must be eliminated. About one half of this actuarial deficit can be eliminated by the stabilization of benefits at their current levels in relation to preretirement earnings. However, this is entirely separate from the question of the "unfunded accrued liability" of some $3.1 trillion and whether or not there are valid reasons to change it into a "funded accrued liability" by collecting more in social security taxes now and less in social security taxes (and more in general revenues) later.

## CONCLUSION

There is much more to be said about the financial aspects of the social security program. Unfortunately the space available does not permit further elaboration of the subject. This paper is not intended to resolve any questions, but merely to offer some explanations in order to facilitate future discussions about certain financial aspects of the social security program.

The social security program is so large and well established, and such an important and integral part of our national socioeconomic structure, that its momentum will not be halted. The only question is in what direction and by how much will the social security program grow: Will it grow in an uncontrolled and irrational manner, or in a logical way so that it will best match the economic needs of the beneficiaries and the financial ability of the taxpayers? The answer to this question will depend in large part upon the extent of the dialogue among an informed citizenry.

chapter

# 5

# Contrasting Economic Impact of OASDI and Private Pension Plans

GEOFFREY N. CALVERT*

*The dragon Keynes rode out to slay was the formidable Puritan ethic which has always applauded savings, condemned spending, and considered the accumulation of riches as the occasion for stewardship. No doubt the ethic had its uses when capital was scarce, and saving vital to economic expansion. . . . Elsewhere Keynes himself had eloquently sketched the benefits of high saving in a period like 1870–1914. During a war saving became virtuous indeed. But in advanced economies afflicted with persistent tendencies toward economic sluggishness and high unemployment, thrift impeded economic growth. Not the least of Keynes' successes was the weakening of the identification between virtue and thrift.*

From *The Age of Keynes*
by Robert Lekachman

## THE PROPENSITY TO SAVE

IT WAS IN THE AGE of Keynes that the U.S. social security system was designed and established. This was a period of economic breakdown, of heavy unemployment throughout the world, and widespread poverty. It

---

* Founder of the Consulting Actuarial Division, Alexander & Alexander, Inc. (Retired), Sidney, British Columbia, Canada.

was Keynes who had identified the gap between excessive savings and inadequate new capital investment as one of the keys to the phenomenon of economic depressions, and hence to the tragic economic malaise of the time. To stimulate consumption, spending, not savings, was perceived to be the great need of the day. Public works, with their multiplier effects on the economy, accomplished through deficit financing and similar measures to achieve full employment, gained economic respectability. Welfare systems financed on a nonfunded basis through concurrent "transfer payments" fitted nicely into this pattern.

Forty years later, in his testimony before the House Ways and Means Committee on May 15, 1975, Dr. Martin Feldstein, professor of economics at Harvard University, put it in these words:

> When the current social security program was designed, the nation was at the bottom of the great depression. The length of the depression and the failure of financial institutions had wiped out the lifetime savings of a great many families. More than 20 percent of the labor force was unemployed. The new Keynesian economics stressed that the depression would persist as long as the full-employment rate of savings remained greater than the rate of investment. The fear that an excessive savings rate would cause a permanent depression remained a firm conviction of many leading economists into the 1940s.
>
> The early fear of excessive saving has now changed to a serious concern about a capital shortage in the years ahead.

What has caused this reversal? Why has the former concern as to excessive savings in relation to capital needs now given place to a concern as to inadequate sources of new capital? There are many causes. The abrupt realization that the vast, capital-intensive energy industries will have to be radically transformed as quickly as possible to depend less on oil, is one. The need to rebuild cities, suburbs, and transportation systems on a basis less wasteful of energy is another. The housing of the surge in families formed by the post-war boom in births, and the creation of record numbers of new jobs for them, are others. Figures for the new capital needs for each job range from $20,000 to $70,000, and many millions of new jobs must be provided. Large sectors of industry are obsolete and must be modernized and reequipped. America is now lagging seriously behind other leading industrial nations in its rate of capital formation. Environmental improvements such as pollution control or the improvement of the safety of nuclear power plants are voracious devourers of capital. On a world scale, burgeoning population growth has placed critical pressure on food supplies. To increase these, and to help many third-world countries become more self-sufficient, not only in food but in other ways also, new capital is needed on a scale that beggars the imagination. Though some of this capital is available at the moment from OPEC countries, this will prove inadequate and temporary as the world population doubles in the next few decades.

It is in this context of a prospective shortage of capital that we have to look at the contrasting economic impact of the private pension plans, the state and local government plans and the Old-Age, Survivors, and Disability Insurance (OASDI) system in America. The wheel has gone full circle. The surging power of population growth, the denial and depletion of resources, and the rising expectations of the third world have brought the practices of excessive consumption sharply into question and gone far to restore the virtue of savings and frugality.

But it may be too late for us to expect much response from the individual. Forty years ago the individual objective of savings was to provide for a rainy day, for a hoped-for eventual retirement, for burial and estate needs, and, as means of accomplishing these objectives, for the accumulation of a portfolio of insurance and investments of one kind and another. From these individual savings the economy obtained much of the new capital it required. There was mutual benefit.

The individual has little reason to do much of this kind of saving any more. Most of it is done for him through group insurance, through pension and other fringe benefit plans, and through the social security system. He looks at the taxes and contributions he pays to these systems as a substitute for the savings he would otherwise have to make, and to some extent he is right. These collective plans generally do a more systematic and efficient job of providing security to the worker and his family than he could do on his own. He no longer has the same need to accumulate his own nest egg, nor in many cases does he have the ability. Though pay levels have risen over the years, social security taxes for example have risen far more than proportionately. What was a $30 maximum annual "contribution" in the years 1937–49 had become $120 in 1959, $374 in 1969, and $895 in 1976. It increased by 374 percent in the last ten years, and more than doubled in the past five years alone, leaving most other economic indicators far behind, and squeezing out the ability of the individual to save for himself. No tax credit is given for these compulsory contributions.

Meantime millions of employees are being provided annually with individualized printouts, prepared by computer, showing the total of their prospective harvest of benefits from each source, both private and government, in the event of their death, disability, or retirement, while employers vie with one another, in attracting and holding staff, as to the amount of security they offer along with the wage or salary level.

None of this is the stuff that leads the employee to increase his individual rate of savings. On the contrary, he is shown on his annual statement the amount that both he and the employer are setting aside each year, or the annual dollar value of his own personal fringe benefit package, and from this information he gathers a very real sensation that he is indeed saving for a rainy day and building a nest-egg for his retirement, death, and estate needs. In many and perhaps most cases, the accumulating value of his expectations under these various pension and security plans exceeds the value of all his equity in everything else he owns, including his house, automobile, and all his personal property. For example, the present value of a pension of 60 percent of pay to a worker about to retire would be about six or seven times his annual earnings. If the total of his private and social security (primary plus spouse) benefit equals or exceeds his full-time earnings while employed, as is often the case now, then this present value (including allowance for medical and other benefits) could easily exceed twelve times annual gross earnings. At younger ages these values would be less, but would be substantial and would be building steadily. In the aggregate the total value of all this "benefit plan wealth" would be several times the gross national product.

Looked at in this way, these various benefit plans have accomplished a far more uniform and widespread distribution of wealth than is generally believed to exist. What substance lies behind this view of wealth and its distribution we shall examine later. But the point to notice here is that the impression and expectation of all this wealth exists in the minds of the work force, and the urge to save money is correspondingly reduced.

In his 1975 [testimony] "Strengthening Social Security" referred to earlier, and in other papers, Feldstein estimates broadly that the social security system alone has reduced total private savings (individual plus corporate) by about 35 percent, and that the nation's capital stock would have been some 55 percent higher, and the gross national product and wage rates 14 percent higher if this "asset substitution" had not occurred. Robert Myers, in his paper, "The Role of Actuaries and Economists in Cost Analysis and Financing Aspects of Social Security," presented to the Society of Actuaries in April 1976, takes issue with this conclusion, stating:

> If we had not had the payroll taxes at all, because we did not have an
> OASDI system, there would almost certainly have been almost equally

large expenditures for a public assistance program that would have filled the social needs actually met by OASDI. Taxes (which some would have labeled as "economically undesirable" because they did not build up the nation's capital stock) would have been required to finance such expenditures, and these taxes would not have been much less than the OASDI ones actually were. So, we are back at about the same point under either set of circumstances, and the capital stock of the nation would not have been greatly affected either way.

If Feldstein is right, the social security system has had the effect of greatly debilitating the economy, slowing down the improvement in productivity, lowering the gross national product, and with it wage levels and living standards. All of this is too important to dismiss lightly. If Myers is right, none or very little of this is true, and we are about where we would have been with or without the social security system. What are we to conclude?

It seems to this writer that the realities would be somewhat different from those described by either of the above eminent authorities.

1.   In making up employee statements, no employer to my knowledge ever shows the amount or value of welfare payments that the employee might receive if he or she is needy enough to qualify for them.

2.   With no OASDI program, the impression of "entitlement" or "insurance," so widely disseminated in social security literature, would not exist. Government benefits would be more likely to be means tested, as is normal for welfare benefits, and many employees would avoid the indignities of claiming them.

3.   Private pension plans, which are normally funded, would not have had to reduce their benefits to make way for the (nonfunded) social security benefits. Hence their benefits, costs, and funding levels would be substantially higher.

4.   Even with this assist from the private plans, and the increased contribution to capital formation implied in it, the benefit expectations of the work force would in total be considerably less than those which have in fact developed under the combination of social security plus integrated or supplementary private plans, since these private plans would still not provide universal coverage or full portability or spouse benefits or tax freedom or indexing. Rather than face the indignities of welfare benefits or the limitations, uncertainties or absence of private pensions, or both, many individuals would thus have good reason to exert every effort to establish their own savings arrangements. Employers would no doubt also respond to this need with a greater emphasis on thrift, savings, profit-sharing, stock purchase, and similar group plans supplementing their pension plans. All of these responses to the situation that would exist

in the absence of OASDI would contribute handily to the process of capital formation.

5. Even with all of this effort, there would undoubtedly be many cases of benefit forfeiture through job changes, improvidence and loss of savings, and outright failure to make suitable provision for misfortune or old age, so that the welfare system would have to carry a greater burden than at present.

To sum up, it would seem that Feldstein had a very good point to make, but by assuming that social security taxes would, in their absence, probably be replaced in full by other and more effective forms of saving, he carried his argument too far. Myers, while justifiably challenging his conclusion, would seem to have not anticipated the practical realities and responses of the private employee benefit world.

Perhaps a good parallel exists in the medical field into which it is proposed that the government now extend a vast bureaucracy which would cover all workers. The fact that this has not so far been done does not mean that no alternative exists except in some other form of government-administered medical services. The private sector through its group medical plans, its Blue Cross and Blue Shield organizations, and private individuals have combined their efforts and resources with those of publicly supported agencies so that in total a very wide availability of medical services exists, only a part of which receives support from the taxpayer.

The point is important, since in the pension field there is the additional and quite fundamental distinction between the social security system and the private plans, namely that the former is a nonfunded system and the latter funded. Not only does the social security system make no contribution at all to the process of capital formation, but on the contrary, as we have seen, it tends to discourage individuals from saving, hence assisting capital formation. In the aggregate, the result would seem to be quite basic.

How different are the private pension plans in this respect?

1. They are actuarially funded. Minimum funding standards have in fact been set by the government. While removing incentive from the individual to save, they do indeed substitute another form of saving just as real and effective from the viewpoint of the economy.

2. They are very often and increasingly noncontributory, thus leaving more of his apparent earnings in the hands of the employee and available for saving if he so chooses.

3. They are less portable. It is one of the criticisms of private pensions that they can be lost as a result of termination of employment before

vesting. To that extent, the individual can rely less on receiving his pension, and has more reason to save up for the eventuality of reaching retirement age without his pension or some part of it.

4. They are seldom indexed. Again a point of some criticism, this aspect of private plans at least has the virtue of encouraging the individual to take steps to protect himself and his family against inflation, such as through home ownership.

5. They are not tax-free. Except for any portion arising from the contributions of the individual employee, they are generally subject to regular income taxes, and are therefore less effective, dollar for dollar, than social security pensions in providing purchasing power in retirement. Whether or not this is an equitable relationship is not the point here. In the present context, they are less inclined to nurture in the mind of the retired worker the concept that he is being looked after, and in the mind of the active worker that he need not save for he, too, in his turn will be looked after.

Conspicuously different from the corporate pension plans in the private sector are many of the state and local government plans which have not been brought under the coverage of the ERISA legislation, even though in much greater need of this discipline, and which are known in many cases to have cavernous deficiencies in their pension funds.

Articles have appeared highlighting the financial crisis in many cities, due often in large part to the upward surge of their pension costs and unfunded liabilities. This is only the tip of the iceberg. First to grant indexed pensions, costly early retirement on full pension, and similar burdensome concessions, though seldom up to standard as to their vesting provisions, these governmental plans are often the last to bring their funding up to normal standards, relying instead on their power to tax future generations, unreliable as this may turn out to be. For example, in a survey of 122 police pension plans completed by the author in 1971, it was found that 56 were operating on a completely nonfunded basis even though in nearly all cases the police officers themselves had made contributions. Of the remaining plans, 13 were less than one quarter funded, and 26 were less than one half funded in relation to benefits accrued on the basis of current (but not projected) pay levels, though nearly all provided benefits based on final earnings. Where funds existed, the investment policies followed were often open to great improvement. The disaster of New York City's financial problems is not the only, but merely the most widely publicized, example of tragic mismanagement of state and local government pension plans. In a mood of helplessness before the weight of these unfunded and all-too-often unrecognized pension liabilities, the New York City budget director was exclaiming in 1971, "This pension cost is an enormous, invariable piece of granite which is insensitive to priorities and policy!" Four years later came the collapse. How many other states and cities could make the same exclamation today, with inflation having carried their often indexed and final-pay-based pension liabilities up out of sight during those same four years? Here, obviously, is an area in which the public interest requires most urgently that actuarial studies be made so that sound benefit and funding policies can be put in hand before more states and cities are bankrupted, or the next generation saddled with intolerable burdens.

These local authorities have the option of entering the social security system or of leaving it. While most have entered, there are disturbing signs from areas as widely separated as New York, Sacramento, and Alaska and from several hundred other points between, of moves to quit the system, often under budgetary pressure, but sometimes to secure the advantages of a funded plan with its lower long-term costs (and to take advantage of windfall benefits already accrued and vested).

Where does all of this leave the propensity of the employee to save? In the state and local authority field the picture is very mixed. With wages at high levels and job tenure generally more secure than in the private field, though not wholly reliable, with more liberal pensions (sometimes unrealistically liberal) often marred by an absence of vesting, with frequently abysmal funding and investment practices buttressed by a possibly dubious or misguided reliance on the willingness or ability of future taxpayers to pick up the tab, and with a variable and perhaps unreliable outlook as to participation in the social security system, the contribution to capital formation through savings to be expected from employees covered by these plans, and from the funding of these plans themselves (pending a needed cleaning up), would probably on the whole be less than in the private sector. With proper funding and investment, it could become about the same or perhaps even more.

## PENSION FUNDS, CAPITAL MARKETS, AND THE PROCESS OF CAPITAL FORMATION

With the spotlight now on the need of the U.S. economy for new capital in the coming decades, there is great interest in the role of private pension plans in filling this need, and questions have also come up as to the wisdom or otherwise of funding or perhaps partly funding the social security system both in recognition of this need for new capital, and also in anticipation of the need to provide for the demographic bulge of new pensioners in the early part of the next century. Survivors of the high birth rates in the decade following World War II, these swollen cohorts of the population will be entering pension age in the decade commencing about the year 2010, and would force social security payroll taxes up by about 50 percent in an otherwise unchanged nonfunded system. Should they not help to provide for their pension costs while they are still working, thus easing what would seem otherwise to be a real problem of intergenerational inequity, and a danger of an outright refusal on the part of the next generation to meet these costs? With more capital and hence higher productivity, these burdens would be less.

The term "capital formation" is, like the gross national product, the cost of living, and the total money supply, a term often loosely used without a very clear concept of what it implies. Does the borrowing of money through bond issues to meet the current payroll or pay war pensions comprise capital formation? Or merely debt formation? Does the building of an aircraft carrier or a private residence (neither of which is used for the production of goods or services, though each of which has an economic function) comprise capital formation? Does the issue of bonds by a local authority to its own pension fund, thus relieving present taxpayers and enabling them to consume more now so that future taxpayers will consume less later, comprise capital formation? But what if the capital so raised is used to build a needed bridge or airport?

In the sense here used, capital formation implies the creating of both tangible and intangible assets including such items as research information, educational values, exploration and development costs as well as industrial plant and equipment, and social capital such as hospitals, water supply and transportation systems, inventory, and all such items as can be expected to have future or continued economic value, or to replace or maintain in useful condition items previously created.

Working in the context of the Canadian economy, for example, the writer has recently been looking at these figures for the year 1975 as furnished by Dr. Douglas D. Peters, Chief Economist of the Toronto Dominion Bank:

|  | (*$ billion*) |
|---|---|
| Housing | $ 7.2 |
| Social capital | 6.6 |
| Business capital investment: | |
|     For energy sources | 6.2 |
|     For other industrial capital | 17.1 |
| Total capital spending | $37.1 |

In the decade 1976–1985, this total need for capital spending is projected to grow to:

$ 52.1 billion by 1978
80.7 billion by 1982
116.5 billion by 1985

For the decade as a whole, a total need for $735 billions is foreseen, of which $155 billions would be for energy sources alone, $310 billions for other business purposes, $150 billions for housing and $120 billions for social capital.

Where is this capital to come from? In the year 1974, of a total of $35.8 billions, $15.2 billions was furnished from capital consumption (depreciation) allowances, leaving $20.6 billions to come from foreign sources, bank loans ($2 billions), retained earnings ($10 billions) and other forms of domestic savings. In 1975 and 1976, Canada, which already has a problem of excessive foreign ownership of its industrial capital, still finds it necessary to import capital at the rate of $4–5 billions annually. To what extent can the growth of private pension funds be looked to for help in this situation?

In pursuing this question, the writer recently requested Dr. John A. G. Grant, Chief Economist of Wood Gundy Ltd., to perform certain research into the role of private pension funds in providing the capital needed by industry. Among the various findings resulting from this highly significant work, it emerged that:

| Industrial corporations might reasonably be expected to raise capital through new issues as follows: | ($ billion) | |
| --- | --- | --- |
| | 1976–80 | 1981–85 |
| Through new bond issues | 9.0 | 11.6 |
| Through new stock issues | 11.3 | 14.5 |
| Total | 20.3 | 26.1 |

At the same time, barring any sudden change in the situation:

| Private pension fund increases can be expected to furnish new capital for investment as follows: | | |
| --- | --- | --- |
| Nongovernment bond purchases | 4.1 | 6.6 |
| Stock purchases | 8.9 | 14.1 |
| Total | 13.0 | 20.7 |

The vital role of the private pension funds in the raising and channeling of new capital into areas where it can best be used by industry stands out in sharp relief in these figures. Between 70 and 80 percent of all the new capital needed by industry in Canada, and raised through new bond and stock issues, is expected to be furnished by these private pension funds. It is generally at the point when new issues of bonds and stocks are made that the most important phases of new capital formation are taking place. According to Dr. John A. G. Grant:

> A decision by Canadians to substitute present for future consumption (which is the underlying implication of a switch from prefunding to pay-as-you-go deferred income plans) would either require a return to heavy reliance on foreign equity capital with its undesirable implications for control of our resources, or would force a sharp slowdown in the rate of our economic growth. . . . Even the power to pay the deferred incomes on a pay-as-you-go basis would be less.

While the work outlined above has been done in the context of the Canadian economy, there is every reason to think that a somewhat similar result would emerge from a parallel study done in the context of the U.S. economy, and that correspondingly, any tendency to overexpand the nonfunded social security system would tend to debilitate the economy by damaging the capital formation process. An alternative approach, and the associated political and other problems related to the possibility of a partial funding of that system, would seem to deserve more attention than they are getting.

In his testimony before the Senate Finance Committee on May 7, 1975, Treasury Secretary William E. Simon made these comments about the needs for new capital formation in the United States:

> For many years our advantageous ratio of capital to labor has been acknowledged as the basis of the remarkable rise of the U.S. economy.
>
> . . . other nations during recent years have allocated a substantially larger share of resources to new capital formation.
>
> The reduced pace of capital investment in the U.S. economy has also been emphasized by Professor Paul W. McCracken, former Chairman of the Council of Economic Advisors.
>
> . . . he estimates that commitments in the United States during the 1970s are 22 percent below the level reported in the 1956 to 1965 decade.
>
> We are a consumption-oriented society, and this pattern has been developing for several decades.
>
> As a result, despite our high per capita incomes, the accumulations of

high gross savings flows required for capital investment are lower in the United States than elsewhere.

Experience has demonstrated that inflation and unemployment problems have been created in part by capacity shortages. Many of our current difficulties are the direct result of the energy and raw materials strains that developed in early 1974. . . . The continuous deterioration of our international trade balance during the 1960s . . . was also at least partly the result of the loss of competitiveness of U.S. products. . . .

The private sector continues to be the best means of increasing capital investment in the United States. . . .

We must avoid legislation and regulation that is punitive of profits honestly earned. The result could only be that capital formation would be inhibited, and the real purchasing power of wage earners would rise more slowly.

We must always be alert to the fact that profits translate into jobs, higher wages, and an increased standard of living for all of our people.

We must also be concerned about the capacity of our capital markets to provide adequate financing.

Though Secretary Simon did not specifically point to the role of the private pension funds in providing this new capital, the connection is clear enough.

Equally plain should be the role of the expanding social security system, with its nonfunded "transfer payment" system of financing, in America's transition from a capital-oriented to a consumption-oriented economy.

## OWNERSHIP AND CONTROL OF PRIVATE ENTERPRISE

In the year 1966 we pointed out that pension funds had become the largest buyers of common stocks, accounting for 10 percent of all transactions, and were already holding $50 billion or 7 percent of the value of all stocks listed on the New York Stock Exchange.[1]

At that time private pension funds had total reserves of $90 billion. The equity portion of their portfolios had increased from 32 percent in 1960 to 42 percent in 1965, or on a market value basis from 43 percent to 55 percent. In only five years the value of stocks held had increased by 150 percent and had grown faster than the new supply of stocks. The total value of all listed stocks at the end of 1965 was $780 billion.

Projections made at that time indicated that by 1980 private pension

---

[1] Geoffrey N. Calvert, *Land and Real Estate as a Field of Investment for Pension Funds* (New York: Alexander & Alexander, 1966).

funds would have total reserves of $225 billion, and that state and local government funds would amount to $120 billion, making a total of $345 billion in all. By the end of 1973 the private pension funds had in fact grown to $193 billion (well ahead of the projection) and the state and local funds to $82 billion (not ahead of the projection), for a total of $275 billion in all and growing at about 11 percent annually.

Notwithstanding the poor stock markets and high bond yields of recent years, pension funds have continued to be heavy buyers of common stocks which represent the actual ownership of private industry. "Through their pension funds, employees of American business own today at least 25 percent of the equity capital of American business. The pension funds of the self-employed, of public employees and of school and college teachers own at least another 10 percent, giving the workers of America ownership of more than one-third of the equity capital of American business," stated Peter Drucker recently in his landmark article "Pension Fund Socialism" published in *The Public Interest*, Number 42, 1976. Drucker goes on to predict that by 1985 at the latest these pension funds will own at least 50 percent of the equity capital of American business, and waxing to his theme, he adds:

> But what is even more important . . . . the large employee pension funds . . . own a controlling interest in practically every one of the "command positions" in the economy. These include the 1,000 largest industrial corporations . . . and the 50 largest companies in each of the nonindustrial groups—that is in banking, insurance, retail, communications and transportation.

It is unfortunate that Drucker attributes the whole swing of pension funds into equity forms of investment to the strong impulse which was given by Charles Wilson when the General Motors plan was launched in 1950. He writes:

> . . . the GM plan had an unprecedented impact. Within one year after its inception, 8,000 new plans were written—four times as many as had been set up in the hundred years before. And the one innovation of the GM plan was adopted by every single one of the new plans and has since been written into most of the older company plans as well. The GM plan was to be an "investment trust"—that is, it was to invest in the capital market, including equities. Practically all earlier plans had been "annuity" plans, to be invested in standard life-insurance investments, such as mortgages and other fixed-interest-bearing instruments. Wilson reached this design in part because he genuinely wanted to create employee ownership of American business. But he also argued that, to be financially sound, pension

assets had to be invested in American industry as a whole rather than in the company for which the employee works.

There was far more history than this to the sweeping movement of pension funds into the purchase of equities. Since this is now regarded as a turning point in the development of our form of society, it may be as well to get some of this on the record. A good place to start would be a technical paper presented to the Institute of Actuaries in London in 1929, by E. H. Lever, a past president of the institute. In this paper, Lever traced the relative investment performance of bonds and equities during the period 1912–28. The equities handily outperformed the bonds. In the year 1937, while the present author was in correspondence with him about this subject, Lever brought his researches forward through the depression years to 1936, and showed that during those deeply troubled times the equities lost some ground but regained it within the same eight-year period, so that over the long period they were still well ahead of the bonds.

In 1942 pension fund contributions in the United States were given exemption from corporate income tax, laying the ground for a vast surge in private pension plans, and in 1946 the Employment Act had accorded top priority as an objective of government policy to the principle, accepted throughout the world, of full employment, more cautiously described in America as a "high and stable level of employment." Lord Keynes, who had been the great champion of the whole idea of full employment, had also warned all who would listen that its price would be creeping long-term inflation, which to a pension fund, with its very long time-horizons, spelled serious problems. In 1949 the present author had published in the *New York Journal of Commerce* the results of a study into the relationship between the investment yield of a pension fund and the long-term costs of the plan, and had first pointed out the enormous leverage exerted by the investment yield as a factor in cutting pension costs. "Each 0.5 percent by which the yield is raised will cut 12 percent from the cost of the plan" became a widely quoted though only partly accurate thumb rule, and throughout the pension field all concerned searched diligently for ways to improve the investment yield.

Now it happened that at that same time (1949) the Dow Jones averages had sunk to levels such as 220. Blue chip price earnings ratios were below 10, and the cash yield available from dividends on common stocks was a full 6 percent, while bond yields were typically 2.6 percent. We were at the very base of the long bull market.

With equity investments thus in a position to provide substantially higher cash yields than bonds, and a hedge against inflation as an added bonus, one did not need any excess of social altruism to see which way pension fund investments should be directed. The plain economics and the arithmetic of the situation were compelling.

In that same period, insurance companies were prevented by their state regulations from placing more than 1 percent of their assets into equity investments, but the alternative of the trusteed plan had long since been developed, and trustees were not restricted from investing in equities. Even so, it took something of a battle of persuasion to convince many of the larger trustee banks in New York to begin using equity investments in the pension funds of their clients. It was John A. Blanchard, a senior and respected officer in charge of pension fund investments at the Old Colony Trust Company in Boston, who first joined the present author in coming out publicly in favor of using equities in pension funds, though after the idea had gained wide acceptance there were those in New York who claimed to have always held this view. The City of Dallas, in establishing its new pension plan designed by the present author in 1948, used equity investments from the outset, and there were others, out of New York, who also used this approach with great success.

By the time GM with all its weight and prestige entered the field in 1950, splitting its pension fund among several large New York trustee banks with the instructions that 35 percent of the assets were to be invested in equities, the battle had largely been won. Among other things, we had developed the idea of split-funding (combining an insured fund for fixed-yield investments with a trust fund for equities). Mathieson Chemical (later merged with Olin) was the very first and American Airlines was among the first off the mark with this system. It took several more years before the insurance industry obtained legislation permitting it to escape from the shackles of its investment restrictions and to set up the "segregated fund" mechanism which at last gave access to equity investments on the scale needed by pension funds. In 1950, in addition to the numerous trusteed plans that already existed, there were 11,270 fully insured pension plans with virtually no equity investments. By 1974 there were more than 206,000 insured pension plans, and the insurance companies had long since become large buyers of equities, competing in the market place with the trusteed plans.

What does this sweep into equity investments portend for the American economy and society? First, it should be recognized that a pension fund, in acquiring equity investments, is acting in effect as an agent for the employees covered by the plan. Contributions paid into the pension fund by the employer are paid irrevocably. By the time they arrive in the pension fund, they are no longer part of the assets of the employer. It is here that we run into conceptual paradoxes.

Every carefully drawn text or trust agreement governing the operations of a pension plan includes somewhere within it a provision which says that no plan member has any claim to any of the assets which comprise the fund. The trustee is merely holding the assets in trust, and does not own them. The employer has paid his contributions irrevocably and does not own the pension fund assets. Who then can wield the power that goes with the ownership of equity investments?

The point would be less important if the pension funds held only a small part of the equity capital of American industry, as they did when Paul Harbrecht first pointed out these problems in his 1959 book *Pension Funds and Economic Power*. But already they hold a third and soon will have a clear majority. What once seemed a bit academic is now a major issue. To whom is management responsible?

It is clear that the employer who sponsored the plan and pays its costs cannot vote the stock. The individual employees covered by the plan have no title to it, and little beyond a vague awareness of its presence in the investment portfolio of the pension fund. They had no voice in buying it, and will have no voice in deciding when to sell it. It is the investment manager who makes these decisions.

What if something goes wrong with the management or fortunes of a company whose stock is held by the pension fund? Do the pension funds, as responsible owners, move in and take over or change the management of the company? Not at all. The stock is merely an investment and if the company is going sour, its stock is cleared out of the portfolio. In any case there is not just one pension fund, but many hundreds or thousands which, in the aggregate and diffusely are in this position of paralysed command.

Obviously, something very big is drifting off the track. Changes are needed. As pension funds grow rapidly into a position of overwhelming economic ascendancy through majority ownership of American business capital, they will have to develop a new form of organization in order to use their new found power and live up to the onerous responsibilities that go hand in hand with ownership. Drucker suggests that a new form of management must be created, representing the beneficiaries of pension plans and having a clear relationship to them.

The asset managers must also be truly independent and free from any suspicion of conflict of interest. They must serve the beneficiaries and no one else.

I agree with him. The fact that no one pension fund is likely to own more than a very small fraction of the stock of any one company may pose something of a problem in giving effect to this concept, but this can be overcome.

There seems to be another vacuum. There is no present form of organization through which pension funds can communicate with each other for the purpose of discussing their emerging responsibilities as the majority owners of American industry.

Nor do the pension funds satisfactorily fill the key role of providing the seed money which is vital in the early stages of new enterprises. When xerography, for example, was little more than a gleam in the lone inventor's eye, no pension fund trustee constrained by the prudent man rule could gamble on its success. There are too many failures. Though certain of the largest trustee banks maintain pools of the stock of small, high-risk companies, and invest a small percentage of the assets of each pension fund in these pools, thus effectively spreading the risk, this practice is not universal, and the more usual substitution of prudent man thinking for entrepreneurial thinking contains a real threat of economic ossification. "Today, capital market decisions are effectively shifting from people who are supposed to invest in the future to people who have to . . . invest in the past," states Drucker.

It was on June 24, 1872, that Karl Marx and Fredrick Engels declared in their angrily written Manifesto of the Communist Party:

> The proletarian is without property . . . . The proletarians cannot become masters of the productive forces of society. . . . They have nothing of their own to secure and to fortify.

and from this they went straight on to urge all proletarians:

> Their mission is to destroy all previous securities for, and insurances of, individual property.

Today, the wheel has gone full circle. The proletarians, the work force of America, through their private pension funds, are moving swiftly toward a position of ownership and ultimate control of "the productive forces of society." Though the form of their ownership is indirect, and they have not yet learned how to use their emerging control, the form of people's capitalism that is now unfolding leaves nothing for the Communists to strive for. The diversification of pension fund assets into equities will have effectively eliminated what was regarded only 20 years ago as an ugly threat to the American economy and way of life.

## CONCEPTS OF PENSION AND SOCIAL SECURITY WEALTH

We have seen that the private pension funds had marketable assets in their custody in 1973 amounting to $275 billion, and that they are advancing steadily each year and will in time not only own but must also learn to control vast segments of the economy in a decentralized form of people's capitalism. The individual expectation of benefit, with all its limitations and uncertainties, is thus on the whole backed by solid assets and is further strengthened by the provisions of the recently established Pension Benefit Guaranty Corporation, though these do not yet extend to the state and local government field. Further, as the worker advances in seniority, it is normal for his claim on fund assets to advance in priority, so that when he has retired the provision of his pension, along with that of others similarly retired, constitutes a first charge on the *entire* assets of the pension fund. It is true that the value of all accrued pensions is often greater than the assets currently held in the pension fund, and that the unfunded liabilities under corporate pension plans are often a subject of concern, and that under state and local government plans they should often be a subject of even greater concern. But these are in general in process of amortization, and on the whole, as the worker looks forward to his retirement, and later enjoys his pension, he has no reason to feel that there is anything illusory about the "wealth" represented by his pension. It is backed by real assets, and it has helped significantly to create those assets which are a very large part of the aggregate wealth of America.

Now let us consider the other part of the pension wealth of the individual, namely that part which is to come through the social security system. In this case there are no assets. True, there is a cushion fund containing less than a single year of benefit payout, or less than 2 percent of the value of the benefits accrued. But what of the other 98 percent? This must be collected in the future from taxes yet to be paid. The social security "wealth" of the individual, amounting to some $3.1 trillion in all, is thus based on an expectation, not on tangible assets but on the "taxing power of the government."

Since the demographic and other realities of the present and future indicate that the maintenance of the present pattern of benefits will require the collection of social security taxes at levels well above the present tax rates, there is a question of taxpayer resistance involved.

It has sometimes been said that the public has no resistance when it comes to social security tax increases, since taxpayers think that if they pay more they will get more. Since in the present circumstances this is not true, and since there are disturbing signs of various local government groups opting out of the social security system, the writer took the opportunity at the occasion of a meeting of the Western Pension Conference in San Francisco on March 25, 1976, to test this matter by asking the audience to vote as to which they felt would be preferred: (a) gradually rising levels of taxes to maintain the present relative benefit levels intact, or (b) gradually declining relative benefit levels so that present tax levels could be retained without increase. The audience voted overwhelmingly in favor of (b).

Though not conclusive, this straw in the wind does clearly indicate that an informed public may have a great deal to say about this whole matter, and that the $3.1 trillion of notional "social security wealth" which has been assumed to exist may not be as real an illusion as one is accustomed to think. Even as an expectation it may have to shrink when the next generation is faced with its cost.

If it comes to a choice as to which form of benefit wealth can do the most good for the American economy, granted the pitfalls and problems of each and that each is necessary in its place, does it not seem that the private plan wealth has the edge? If the social security plan were funded to some greater extent and could overcome the political temptations that this implies and pitfalls inherent in an overconcentration of power, would this reverse the advantage? In the context of the economic needs of the future, this question cannot be brushed aside.

## INDEXING OF PENSIONS AND OTHER INCOMES

It has become orthodox in these times to think that all pensions should be adjusted at least in accordance with changes in the CPI, so that their purchasing power will be preserved in inflationary times. Many kinds of government pensions are so indexed, including those provided under the social security system, though advance funding adequate for this purpose is rarely if ever provided. Though better funded, private pensions are almost never indexed, and there are some who are inclined to question whether private employers are not failing in their social obligations to their former employees by not following the example of their various governments in this regard.

All of this is quite a reversal from the atmosphere that existed in 1954 when the present author first introduced the idea of soundly designed cost-of-living pensions in the September–October issue of the *Harvard Business Review* and designed the pioneering plan based on this principle for National Airlines with the collaboration of First National City Bank as trustee. In that era, and despite the safeguards designed into it, the whole idea met little but silent scepticism. It was an idea whose time had not come. Today, with all safeguards swept aside, vast commitments to indexed pensions are freely made with scant regard for their long-term effects on future taxpayers or on the economy. After all, why should pensioners suffer from an inflation? They have no defense. We owe it to them.

It is probably a good rule that when universal or near-universal acceptance is accorded to an idea, it is time to reexamine the idea itself, to challenge and test its fundamentals, and to see if it is still as valid as when first promoted. In this spirit I have for some time been quietly reevaluating the whole concept of cost-of-living pensions, and would like to take this opportunity to state my conclusions.

In the context of the 1950s inflation was not the rampaging menace that it has since become. In researching the history of the CPI as far back as records would go, which means long before the beginning of the present century, we could find only two very brief periods when sharp discontinuities and double digit inflation occurred. One followed soon after the end of World War I and the other when controls were released after World War II. Over the long period since the beginning of the present century we could fit a 2¼ percent compound growth curve to the CPI fairly well, and in the period from 1950 to 1965 its growth rate averaged only 1.9 percent annually.

In this period there was no oil shortage or quadrupling of prices imposed from abroad, and very little awareness of an impending problem of availability of raw materials, pollution or other environmental limits. President Eisenhower had made the pronouncement that birth control was not the business of governments. Rachel Carson had not published *Silent Spring*, there was no Club of Rome and no concern about the limits to growth or population pressures. America had the problem of storing its bursting grain reserves, and land was being taken out of production with government assistance. Mankind did not seem to be at any particular turning point. Looking back, these seemed to be halcyon days of innocence and naïveté when the extrapolation of long-observed trends could be done with a reasonable feeling of confidence. In promoting the idea of cost-of-living pensions, we could at that time see no reason to think that these might one day place their recipients, along with others receiving indexed incomes, in an unfairly advantageous position. Today it seems to me that this is indeed the prospect, and that we have to rethink the whole idea of indexing pensions, civil service, and other incomes.

To the extent that an inflation is imposed on a nation from abroad (as has recently been done by the OPEC nations), is it fair to exempt one segment of the people so that these can carry on as though nothing at all had happened, while the remainder must bear two burdens, namely the direct burden resulting from the externally imposed inflation and *also* the added tax or similar costs of providing the higher pensions and incomes of the protected segment? Similarly, to the extent that inflation is caused by higher costs arising from the drying up of resources, the battle against pollution or other environmental factors, or the defence of the nation, this reflects a burden that should in fairness be shared by all and not shifted off any one segment.

In a period of unlimited resources, rapidly increasing productivity, and steady increases in "real" standards of living, this problem of distortion through indexing was not significant. But as population pressures mount throughout the world, pointing to an era of higher food prices, and America grows more and more dependent on imported raw materials and oil, and mounting costs of substitute forms of energy have to be faced with all their repercussions throughout the economy, there are fundamental changes occurring with consequences that should be faced and borne by all. To exempt a privileged section from their effects is to create a transfer of wealth to them which was not intended.

What then should be the future of indexing? I am not suggesting that pensioners should be exposed to those forms of inflation that result from excessive labor demands, the inflating of the money supply, or similar internal causes which are not imposed on the nation or necessary to its survival. It seems to me that we must begin to consider a form of adjusting pensions and other incomes that recognizes something less than the full extent of the changes in the CPI. A new form of index that does not exist now would seem to be required for this purpose.

chapter

# 6

# Concepts of Balance between Social Security (OASDI) and Private Pension Benefits

BERT SEIDMAN*

OUR NATION has developed a variety of programs to maintain income in old age for those who are no longer able to work. This framework of programs has to be judged in terms of the combined impact on the problems related to retirement. The effectiveness of a public retirement system such as social security (Old-Age, Survivors, and Disability Insurance, or OASDI) cannot be judged separately from private pension programs. But a national retirement program and a private pension system are not identical in philosophy or purposes.

Neither are they identical in their coverage. They are not now and they are unlikely to be for a long time to come, if ever. So the concept of balance does not just involve the degree to which reliance is placed on OASDI and private pension benefits for the entire population. This would be all that would have to be considered in countries which have built on top of their basic social security structure additional universal wage-related benefits, public or private. But in the United States, while virtually everyone is covered by OASDI (or in the case of many public employees, by other public programs), only a fraction of the population, although a growing one, is covered by supplementary private pensions.

* Director, Department of Social Security, AFL–CIO, Washington, D.C., and Member of the Pension Research Council.

## COVERAGE OF SOCIAL SECURITY (OASDI) AND PRIVATE PENSIONS

Americans have come to take social security for granted to such an extent that we sometimes forget how pervasive it is in our lives. Social security is the nation's basic program for retirement protection and group insurance. There is almost no American family which is not touched by social security in one way or another.

Last year 100 million Americans paid social security taxes and 31 million received benefits every month. More than nine of every ten people 65 or older are eligible to receive social security benefits, and this percentage is still increasing. Today about 95 percent of those reaching age 65 receive benefits.

Of course, social security is not just a retirement system. Ninety-five percent of all families are protected by the survivor provisions if the family breadwinner dies and 90 percent if he or she becomes disabled. Thus, it is not just old people who are "on social security." Monthly social security payments go to some 5 million children and 2.5 million disabled beneficiaries and their spouses.

In contrast with OASDI, coverage of private pension plans is still quite limited. Approximately half of full-time employees in private jobs are covered by private pension plans but only one-third of present retirees have supplemental pensions. Moreover, the coverage is by no means even over the labor force. Coverage is proportionately higher for men than for women and for whites than for blacks and other racial minorities. It is also broader in large firms than in small ones and for higher wage workers than for those at lower wage levels.

Thus there is a large proportion of the population—especially among women, blacks, the low-paid, and workers in small firms—for whom social security [for some supplemented by Supplementary Security Income (SSI)] is by far the major, if not the sole, source of retirement income. While in time, some people in these categories will begin to be covered by private pension plans, social security and SSI will continue to be their dominant sources of income for many years to come.

## OBJECTIVES OF OASDI AND PRIVATE PENSIONS

While both OASDI and private pensions provide retirement income, they have different characteristics which are quite important in determining the degree of protection they afford.

Under social security there is virtually complete portability of covered service and pension rights. Earnings with different employers are combined and full credit is given for these earnings in computing the individual's retirement benefits. Unlike private pension arrangements, there is minimum incentive to change jobs or remain in one because of losing or gaining pension rights.

Other attractive features include a broad array of benefits—survivors and disability benefits as well as health benefits for disabled beneficiaries and those over 65. In contrast with private pension arrangements, social security includes elements of social adequacy. The benefit formula is weighted in favor of the lower wage and shorter duration workers. This makes possible more adequate benefits for those currently retiring or disabled individuals who have not had the opportunity to work many years in covered employment.

As a social insurance program financed through earmarked payroll taxes, social security can more easily adjust benefits to reflect the increased cost of living and the rising incomes of the rest of the population. In fact, recent legislation has made automatic provision for this. Benefits are periodically increased automatically to reflect increases in the Consumer Price Index. Following such an automatic benefit increase, the social security wage base, on which maximum benefits are computed, is also automatically increased according to the rise in average wages covered under the social security program.

The new pension reform law, the Employment Retirement Income Security Act of 1974 (ERISA), has forced us to take a new look at private pension plans in the United States. If there are two words which can be used to characterize them, they are "diverse" and "complex." Social security is not a simple program but it is infinitely simpler in structure, more uniform, and easier to understand and explain than private pension plans.

It is important to consider why it is that unions have negotiated private pension plans. They did so essentially because they found that the retirement income paid by social security was grossly inadequate to meet the needs of their members. If they could have obtained what they considered to be adequate social security benefits, they would not have turned to private pension plans. They resorted to them not because they considered them superior to the social security program as a program but because unable to get the Congress to improve social security benefits sufficiently, they saw no other way of providing a decent income for their retired members.

Clearly now there is no turning back. There is no possibility that the private pension plans will be eliminated and replaced by an expanded social security. But the necessity to turn to private pension plans to supplement inadequate social security payments has not been an unmixed blessing. Private pension plans have no doubt enhanced general economic security for some retiring workers, but their impact on both workers and employers has been very uneven. While it is true that the financing of the social security system is somewhat regressive, taken as a whole, the financing of private pension plans is far more regressive.

Economywide spreading of the risk makes the social security system both stronger and more equitable than private pension plans. Resources for financing social security come out of our entire economy. In strong contrast, each firm (or in the case of multiemployer plans, group of firms) whether big or small, strong or weak, prosperous or failing, must finance its own pension plan.

Even more important, however, is the marked difference in the benefit structure. The financially weaker enterprises, which tend to pay the lowest wages, can finance only very low payments if they can finance any pensions at all. So the workers who are paid the lowest wages while they are working also receive the smallest pensions after they stop working—smallest not just in absolute terms but even relative to their preretirement income.

In proportion to preretirement income, social security, unlike private pension plans, pays higher benefits to those with lower earnings records. If we look at private pension plans as if they too were a system, the reverse is true. Workers in lower wage brackets can look forward to no supplementary pensions at all or if they are covered, to pensions which are lower in relation to their preretirement earnings than those of higher paid workers.

Other differences ought not to be ignored. There has never been a breath of scandal about the social security program. Its administrative costs are extremely low and, by and large, its administrative procedures are efficient and provide good service to those who come under the program. Administration of private pension plans varies greatly. No doubt there are many plans which are very efficiently administered and entirely in the interests of their participants and beneficiaries. But the reason it was found necessary to include the provisions on fiduciary responsibility, reporting, and disclosure in ERISA is that this was not true of all plans. Thus the inadequacies in social security which led to resort to supplementary pension plans have involved trade-offs which are by no means all positive.

There are still other significant differences between private pension plans and social security. Private pension plans, unlike social security, tend to deal selectively with the specific retirement problems of the work force of an individual employer.

The pension benefit is usually related to the individual's length of service with a particular employer or in an industry in the case of multiemployer plans. Generally, as with the social security benefit, the pension amount is related to a worker's wages but frequently greater weight is given for earnings above the social security wage base. In contrast to social security, private pension plans tend to place greater emphasis on more adequate benefits for the average and above-average wage earners and for long-term workers rather than for low-wage employees or for workers with a short-term attachment to an employer.

Some of the discussion of the appropriate relative roles of private pension plans and social security tends to focus on anticipation of increased costs for social security because of certain assumptions as to future demographic and economic trends. Based on these expectations, it is argued that there can be no further improvement in social security or even that the program must be deliberalized in the future.

This is not the appropriate occasion to contest the validity of these pessimistic assumptions. It is appropriate to point out, however, that if these assumptions are valid, they will affect private pension plans at least as much as social security. Therefore, they provide no basis for arguing for a shift toward a larger relative role for private pension plans.

## INFLUENCE OF SOCIAL SECURITY ON PRIVATE PENSION PLANS

The social security system has had, and will continue to have, great influence in shaping the provisions of private pension plans. Many private pensions have been improved in recent years to provide more liberal benefit formulas, earlier retirement ages, earlier vesting, and disability and survivor protection. These trends have raised a number of questions about the appropriate combination of public and private pension programs where similar protection is provided to the same group of workers. As a result, though few pension plans today directly coordinate benefits with social security benefits, most pension decisions take these benefits into account in setting or negotiating benefit levels.

The pension agreements that resulted from the union push for pensions in the major manufacturing industries in the 1950s were generally tied to social security benefits. The union pattern setters in the collective bargaining area—steel, aluminum, rubber, auto—all utilized this approach. But all have shown a similar pattern of development of revising, lowering, and eventually eliminating the social security offset. Today, the typical collectively bargained pension plan provides benefits which are over and above any social security benefits received.

Many collectively bargained plans do coordinate early retirement benefits with social security payments. The private pension provides an early retirement benefit amount. When the employee is eligible for social security benefits, the total amount remains the same except that the social security payment represents a portion of the total and the employer portion is correspondingly reduced. There are, of course, many variations in this approach and the total amount is often increased when the worker is eligible for social security benefits—although not by the full amount of the social security payment.

## EARLY RETIREMENT

Early retirement has become a major and growing factor in both the social security system and private pension plans. In fact, it can no longer be said that age 65, the so-called "normal retirement age" in both social security and most private pension plans, is really the normal retirement age of most retirees.

Many people think that age 65 is the customary age for retirement and retirement prior to that age is "early retirement" because it is considered a departure from what is typical.

This is a myth. The fact is that in 1961, the first year social security began to pay actuarially reduced benefits to men between the ages of 62 and 65, more men retired on reduced than on regular benefits. The proportion of "early" retirees is now more than 60 percent.

But there is another myth. That myth is that most workers who retire before they are 65 voluntarily quit working because they prefer receiving social security and other pension benefits to continuing at their jobs. The fact is that for most early retirees, retirement is involuntary.

A social security study published in 1971 indicated the reasons workers retire are, in order of importance: health, desire to retire, loss of job, and compulsory retirement.

Poor health was by far the major reason. Of the workers who retire before age 65, 54 percent indicated poor health as the reason for retirement. Poor health was defined to include all identifiable physical problems or inability to keep up with the pace of work. At age 65, the percentage of workers who left their jobs primarily because of health dropped to less than one fourth—clearly reflecting the key role played by health as a factor in inducing retirement before that age. The social security research centered on men rather than all social security retirees because the retirement patterns of married women are influenced by factors not common to the retirement patterns of most retirees.

The second largest category was those who indicated they retired early because they wanted to—but only 17 percent of the total were in this category. Their responses ranged from mildly negative attitudes toward work to a positive anticipation of retirement.

There was a strong correlation between retirees who wanted to retire and higher levels of retirement income. Of those with retirement income of less than $1,000 per year, only 15 percent wanted to retire. But 75 percent of those with retirement benefits exceeding $5,000 wanted to retire. Obviously, a second pension in addition to social security benefits was a major factor in determining a worker's willingness to retire early. For example, in the group aged 62, workers with a second pension were 2.5 times more likely to want to retire than those with only a social security benefit. A large proportion of union members are undoubtedly represented among those with a second pension. Clearly, many more workers would retire if assured of adequate retirement income. Improved social security benefits and the growth of private pensions seem certain to increase the size of this group.

About 13 percent of early retirees indicated termination of jobs or layoffs as the reason for retiring. Most of this group were obviously unsuccessful at securing other employment and would have preferred to continue working since only about 10 percent of the total said they would probably have retired even if they could have kept their jobs.

Compulsory retirement was a major factor in causing early retirement in the sense that it forced workers to retire earlier than they wished but not in forcing people to retire before age 65. Fifty-two percent of the workers aged 65 and over receiving unreduced benefits listed compulsory retirement as the reason for retirement. That contrasts with an overall average of only 4 percent of the 60–64 age group. As expected, compulsory retirement appeared to be closely related to coverage by private pensions. Of the men compulsorily retired, about 80 percent were either receiving or expecting to receive pensions in addition to social security benefits.

The early retirement decision is rarely based on one factor but usually involves a number of reasons. For example, workers in failing health may wish to retire for health reasons but the lack of adequate retirement income may leave them little alternative but to continue working as long as they can. But if their retirement income situation changes through pension improvements, collective bargaining, or social security, they will choose to retire—with the decision based on an interrelationship of health and income.

A trend toward more early retirement is developing in the private pension area. A Bureau of Labor Statistics report, based on a study of early retirement provisions of private pension plans in 1971, found that a significant number of individuals are electing to retire under these provisions and forecasts an acceleration of this trend as a result of recent collective bargaining settlements such as those in the rubber, auto, and farm equipment industries. The report pointed out that more than 90 percent of the 21 million workers covered by private pension plans in 1971 were in plans with early retirement provisions.

A good example of the pace setters among collectively bargained pensions is the contract between the United Rubber Workers and the Firestone Tire and Rubber Company. This plan provides for a normal retirement age of 62 after ten years of service. Early retirement is permitted at age 55 with ten years of service and no actuarial reduction if the employee has worked for the employer for 30 years. For those who retire early with less service, there is an actuarial reduction for each month under age 62. However, a supplemental benefit ranging from $77.50 to $145, based on age, service, and date of retirement, is payable until age 62 when the employee is eligible for social security.

## THE FUTURE OF PRIVATE PENSION PLANS AND SOCIAL SECURITY

When originally passed, social security was conceived as a minimum floor of income. It was assumed that savings, investments, and pensions would fill the gap not covered by social security benefits. Indeed, this "floor of protection" concept is at the heart of the views of the other speaker in this symposium.

It is hard to see how this idea had any validity at all when the social security system was first getting under way some 40 years ago. There were few workers then who could count on private pensions or other forms of private income to meet even their minimal needs. This is no longer true today. Some workers who are covered by good private pension plans are in that fortunate position, but they are a distinct minority though their numbers should increase in future years.

The fact is that only a minority of beneficiaries will be covered by private pensions in the foreseeable future and the amounts they receive will be small. If the American people really mean to provide our retiree population with an adequate income, it will have to be largely through an improved social security system.

Now, in the past, the labor movement generally felt that the most important steps to improve the social security system were to effect across-the-board increases in benefits plus even more sizable boosts in the minimum benefit. Overall benefit increases may be needed again at some time in the future, but this is not where we place our priority today. Nor, now that the SSI program has been established, do we favor an increase in the minimum benefit. Instead, we would like to see the SSI floor raised immediately to at least the poverty level and, in time, to the BLS lower level budget amount.

We would support specific social security improvements aimed at raising the incomes of those who are most disadvantaged under the present system and those least likely to have appreciable supplementary income from private pensions—and generally these tend to be the same individuals.

Because, as I have said, so many workers are involuntarily retiring before age 65 because of ill health, job displacement, or a combination of the two, the pressure will become more intense to reduce the "normal" age of retirement under social security from 65 and to provide unreduced benefits at an earlier age. One solution to the problem would be to reduce the age of eligibility for full benefits to age 62 or 60 (some have even suggested 55) but the economic and social costs would be considerable. The high cost of such a drastic change makes it virtually certain that such provisions would come at the expense of other urgently needed improvements. This approach would probably induce expansion of compulsory retirement at earlier ages than the traditional 65. Forced retirement is still overwhelmingly applied now at age 65.

Our nation is experiencing a growing retiree population and a declining birth rate which could mean a proportionately smaller labor force supporting an increasing retiree population. If on top of these demographic trends we were also to encourage an even more rapid increase in early retirement, we could face a situation of less production and a lower standard of living. Instead, the nation must strive to achieve and maintain full employment opportunities for everyone, including the elderly who can still work—even if on shorter schedules—and want to do so.

But, it is neither just nor possible for the social security system to ignore the causes or the results of early retirement. The only alternative to an across-the-board reduction in the age of eligibility for benefits is to make the system more flexible.

There are a number of things that could be done to improve the economic condition of forced early retirees.

As I have previously indicated, poor health is the single most prevalent reason for early retirement. A majority of early retirees attribute their decision to retire to poor health. In terms of the requirements of the job market, these people are effectively disabled, but they are not eligible for social security disability benefits.

The present definition of disability for social security disability benefits is very stringent, requiring that workers be unable to participate in any substantial gainful activity. This is particularly hard on older workers who frequently suffer from chronic ailments, are unable to work in their usual occupations, or cannot secure other employment because of age and ill health. They are unable to meet the definition of disability only because, theoretically, if someone would hire them they might be able to work in some kind of job, however unrelated to their previous occupation. To correct this injustice, the definition of *disability* should be changed to allow older workers to receive benefits if their impairment bars them from their regular occupation.

In addition to changing the definition of disability for older workers to conform more realistically with their severely constrained job opportunities, disabled widows should be eligible for full benefits at any age. Their problem is somewhat like that of older disabled workers. They can receive benefits at age 50, ranging from 50 to 71.5 percent of the deceased spouse's primary insurance amount. This leaves them with a pitifully low stipend at a time when nearly all of them have no real possibility of obtaining employment. There is no reason why disabled widows should be expected to live on social security benefits that are much smaller than those of aged widows, especially since the aged widows' benefits are by no means munificent.

As I have already stated, the majority of social security beneficiaries now come on the rolls before age 65 after involuntary retirement. Many of them retire at age 62 with a full actuarial reduction of 20 percent. Those who have been sick or jobless during the years before they reach the minimum social security eligibility age often are faced with the double blow to the living standards they can maintain during their later years of a primary benefit reduced because of a number of years of low wages or none at all cut still further by the actuarial reduction for early retirement.

Because millions of sick and jobless older workers have had to eke out their lives first with no retirement benefits at all and then from age 62 on severely reduced benefits, pressure has developed for dropping the retirement age under social security to 60 and even 55 and for payment of full benefits at the lower age of eligibility.

However desirable this might be to meet genuine needs of some of the elderly now severely disadvantaged by the system, it is not desirable that this be done because it would be extremely costly and, as I have already stated, it would unnecessarily encourage early retirement. But short of such drastic steps, other measures could be taken to improve the condition of forced early retirees.

One would be to permit early retirement under social security at less than full actuarial reduction. It has been suggested, for example, that retirement could be permitted at age 60 but with the full actuarial reduction reduced by one-third, one-half, or even three-quarters. The costs of this change would range from an additional 0.5 to 1.35 percent of payroll. In 1974, this would have added $3 to $5 billion to social security payments.

Another change should be considered which would particularly benefit workers with a long-term attachment to the labor force who lose their jobs in late middle age and are unable to obtain new employment. They soon run out of whatever unemployment insurance they are entitled to, are too young to receive social security benefits, are generally ineligible for welfare, and are thus stranded without any source of income. To deal with this problem, the law should be changed to permit workers who are unemployed for two full years after age 55 to be entitled to social security benefits on the same basis as if they had reached the minimum age of eligibility for retirement benefits. Somewhat similar arrangements for dovetailing unemployment insurance and retirement benefits have been adopted in a number of European countries.

I should like to repeat that in making these suggesions, I am singling out measures which would be most likely to benefit workers who now retire early at very low social security benefits and with either low or much more likely, no private pension eligibility.

There are a number of other ways of meeting the problems of those now retiring whose social security payments are at very low and even subpoverty levels.

One is to improve the minimum benefit—not for everyone but for long-service workers. There is a minimum benefit guarantee amounting to $8.50 multiplied by a worker's years of social security coverage over ten years up to a maximum of 30 years. For the 30-year worker, this special minimum benefit would amount to $170 a month and for a couple $255.

The trouble with this benefit is that it is frozen and even at the highest amount, it provides only a subpoverty level of living today and it will become less and less adequate as time goes on. I would suggest, therefore, that this benefit should be improved to provide a more adequate benefit for people who have worked all their lives at low earnings. There is no reason why people who have been deprived during their working lives should have the choice on retirement of a subpoverty social security benefit or submitting to a degrading means test. Society owes them more than that for the contribution they have made during their working lives.

As a first step, the minimum benefit for long-service workers should be unfrozen; that is, it should be adjusted to changes in living costs in the same manner as basic social security benefits. In addition, consideration might be given to raising the minimum benefit for 30-year workers to at least the poverty level and then adjusted periodically as are other benefits.

Another helpful change would be to modify the manner in which the present benefit formula is computed. Benefits are now based largely on earnings long before retirement and fail to reflect a worker's earnings and standard of living prior to retirement. The Social Security Act allows dropping out of only five years of low or no earnings in computing the average wage on which benefits are based. This helps produce a low benefit bias which is greatly aggravated for those older workers who are victims of plant shut-downs, technological unemployment or ill health and must include years of low or zero earnings in computing their benefits. Basing benefits on the high five or ten years of earnings in the manner of many private pension plans would provide higher benefits and would make workers less vulnerable when forced into early retirement. Increasing the number of dropout years in the benefit computation would be a good first step.

## FINANCING SOCIAL SECURITY IMPROVEMENTS

The AFL–CIO has always maintained that it is irresponsible to advocate social security improvements without also recognizing that additional financing will be necessary. The particular changes I have suggested do not involve an across-the-board benefit increase. They are intended to improve upon the *social* insurance mission of social security by increasing the protection of those who are now among the most disadvantaged under the system. But these improvements will have a cost which must somehow be met.

Let me digress for a moment to say that if these same objectives were somehow to be met by private pension plans—and I do not see how this could be accomplished—additional financing would still be necessary. But in this case, the financing in each case would be restricted to the employers, employees, or both groups directly involved in the plan. As I have already indicated, this is the least efficient and most regressive way of financing retirement protection for those who now get the least protection, in terms of ability to meet their needs, from both social security and private pension plans. Thus, even if this were, in practical terms, an alternative way of providing decent retirement incomes for these low-paid workers, it would certainly not be the desirable method of attacking the problem from either the economic or social standpoint. Thus the problem of assuring decent retirement incomes to low-income workers can only be dealt with effectively through welfare or through social security.

As long as the receipt of welfare in this country involves the stigma that is, however unjustly, generally attached to it, there is no reason why workers who have kept off welfare all of their working years should be forced onto it in the declining years of their lives. The question then becomes: What is the most appropriate means of social security financing?

I would argue strongly against any further increase in the payroll tax beyond what is already legislated. As long as there is a maximum taxable wage base—and I do not recommend its complete elimination—the social security tax on workers will continue to be regressive. Any further increase in the payroll tax would place a still heavier financial burden on low and middle income wage earners. We in the AFL–CIO have become more and more concerned about the increasingly heavy burden of the payroll tax. We would vigorously oppose enactment of any further increase in it.

Instead, we would urge reliance on two other sources of financing, both of which involve returning to principles which were accepted in the early years of social security but since then seem to have been lost sight of. I refer to increasing the earnings base and contributions from general revenues.

When first enacted, the social security program covered the full earnings of 97 percent of covered workers. It would take a wage base in excess of $28,000 to cover the same proportion today. The wage base should be raised to this amount in a series of steps in the next few years. The higher wage base will mean higher benefits for those affected since these higher amounts will increase their average wage on which benefits are based. The new maximum should then continue to be adjusted automatically as wages rise as is provided for in present law.

In addition, the employer should pay social security taxes on his entire payroll. The wage base is necessary to determine the employee contribution and the average wage on which benefits are based but it plays no role in the employer's tax. An employer's responsibility for the welfare of his employees should be based on his total payroll not just a portion of each worker's earnings. Employees must pay federal income tax on their contributions to social security but employers deduct their tax as a business expense. These factors should be taken into account and the employer share appropriately increased.

In addition to the changes in the earnings base I have suggested, additional funds, if needed, should be raised from general revenues. This source of financing should be used to the extent necessary for the benefit improvements I have recommended plus any additional improvements that may be considered necessary in the future. To the extent that additional funds for such purposes are needed, there should be a gradually increasing contribution to the social security trust funds from general revenues until it covers one third of the program's cost. A first step in this direction would be to restore to the Social Security Act the provision for general revenue, sponsored by Senator Arthur Vandenberg, that existed from 1944 to 1950. That provision stated:

> There is also authorized to be appropriated to the Trust Fund such additional sums as may be required to finance the benefits and payments provided for in this Title.

General revenues are a source which most other countries tap. Many European countries, in addition to payments from employers and employees, assign general revenues to the social insurance system. In fact, some, notably Sweden and Great Britain, utilize general tax sources to finance a major portion of their social insurance costs. Among the nations of the world, governmental participation in sharing social insurance costs is the general rule and sole reliance on payroll taxes, as in the United States, is the exception. Yet none of these countries feel that partial financing from general revenues is inconsistent with social security principles.

But what is less well known is that a general revenue contribution to social security has long been contemplated in the United States. The 1934 Committee on Economic Security, the group which drafted the original Social Security Act, predicted the system would need general revenue financing by 1965. Almost every Social Security Advisory Council since then has recommended some general revenue financing.

The reasons for infusion of general revenue are well known. There is no reason why only workers and employers should pay the higher cost which was involved for the benefits of those who entered into the system during its early phase in relation to the taxes they paid. Neither should the entire burden of the social aspect of the program—an aspect which I have urged should be strengthened—fall on the shoulders of those two groups. These are social costs which through the general tax system should be borne by society as a whole.

Actually, it is no longer a question whether the social security system should use general revenue financing; it already does to a limited degree. The only question is whether it should be extended.

At the time of its enactment, Medicare covered 3 million older people not otherwise entitled to social security benefits. This cost is paid from general treasury funds. The special benefits to persons age 72 and over who are ineligible for regular social security benefits is also largely paid from general revenues. The cost of the government's share of Part B of Medicare (physicians' services) is paid from general revenues. In short, the Congress already has made general revenue financing available for certain aspects of social security and it should now be gradually increased until it covers one-third of the total cost of the program.

## CONCLUSION

A number of conclusions seem to evolve from these observations. The nation will continue to rely on the social security program as the basic instrument for providing adequate income to the retired population. Though private pensions will continue to expand and improve, it is likely that for the foreseeable future only a minority of retirees will have private pensions in addition to social security benefits. Private pensions will, of course, remain a major factor in the overall retirement picture but their main function will continue to be supplementation of social security benefits.

While there is no urgent present need for a general increase in social security benefits, certain specific improvements are needed to improve conditions for the most disadvantaged. These improvements should include changes in the benefit formula to better relate benefits to earnings at time of retirement as well as more flexible provisions to enable the social security program to better deal with the problems of involuntary early retirement.

The financing of the program will be caught between the pressures for improvement and the burden that increases in the payroll tax represent for low- and middle-income families. The result should be an end to the virtual total reliance on a uniform payroll tax to finance the program with a shift to partial general revenue financing. The conflict over financing will intensify the debate over some old issues—what standard of living is the retiree population entitled to, and where to set program limits in regard to the gap to be filled by private pensions, savings, and other income.

Through improving social security and expanding coverage and raising benefits under private pensions, organized labor will press to eliminate the age-old link between retirement and lowered living standards.

chapter

# 7

## Concepts of Balance between OASDI and Private Pension Benefits: A Partnership or, Instead, the Lion's Share for OASDI?

ROBERT J. MYERS, F.S.A., M.A.A.A.*

THERE IS probably universal agreement that a reasonable and desirable goal in the economic security field is that, in all cases when the risk of old-age retirement, disability retirement, or death of the breadwinner eventuates, the persons affected should have sufficient continuing income so as to maintain approximately their previous standard of living. Where the differences of opinion occur are as to whether such income should come solely from governmental sources, solely from the private sector, or from a combination of both.

### THE SEVERAL PHILOSOPHIES OF SOCIAL SECURITY

Relatively few people these days hold the view that all economic security with regard to these long-term risks should be provided solely through the private sector. This situation is probably the result of the recognition by those who might philosophically hold this view that the political presence of the social security system—Old-Age, Survivors, and

---

* Professor of Actuarial Science, Temple University, Philadelphia, and member of the Pension Research Council.

Disability Insurance (OASDI)— is here to stay. One of the axiomatic characteristics of social security programs is the virtual impossibility of deliberalizing them, let alone abolishing them. This is both a great strength and a great danger. Accordingly, the nation should be very slow and deliberate about expanding a social security program.

Thus, for all practical purposes, only two philosophies on this subject are of significance. The first one, which I denote as the expansionist belief, holds that the vast majority of the population should have their full economic security needs against the long-range risks met through the governmental program of OASDI, and that the small remainder of the population should have the substantial floor of OASDI on which to build such additional benefit protection as they may need or desire. To put it another way, this expansionist approach would assign the lion's share of the economic security field to OASDI and leave only the crumbs to the private sector. Actually, one might point out that Aesop, in his fable, referred to the lion's share as being the totality, and such a result in the economic security field is not entirely an impossibility, or perhaps even undesirable insofar as the expansionist philosophy at its extreme is concerned.

The other philosophy I denote as the moderate belief, because it favors a division of the economic security needs of the nation between the public and private sectors, although not necessarily in exactly equal proportions, but certainly not on the basis of the lion's share and the remainder. The supporters of the moderate philosophy believe that this approach can be achieved if OASDI provides benefits on a floor-of-protection basis, so that then ample opportunity for building on it by the private sector is possible.

## FLOOR OF PROTECTION CONCEPT

As is always the case when one deals with words, there are problems in defining what a floor of protection is. Some would have it so high that there would be little room for supplementation of OASDI by the private sector—or, in other words, the expansionist goal would be achieved without directly saying so or admitting it. Still others might set the floor so low that OASDI would not be doing an effective job, and then a high proportion of the beneficiaries would have to turn to public assistance under the Supplemental Security Income (SSI) program for necessary income for their support.

Although a precise determination of exactly where the floor of protection should occur cannot be made, general guidelines can be given to establish its approximate level. A good criterion is that the proportion of OASDI beneficiaries getting public-assistance supplementation is relatively low—say, about 10 percent.

We might examine briefly whether OASDI is now at a floor-of-protection level. My conclusion would be that, on the whole, this is the case. The proportion of beneficiaries also receiving SSI is close to 10 percent. If anything, in the last few years we have moved somewhat above the floor-of-protection level, or at least we are in the upper areas of what that concept connotes.

This conclusion, in my view, is based on the fact that the increases in the general OASDI benefit level and in the maximum taxable earnings base which were legislated in the first Nixon Administration, 1969–72, were significantly in excess of what should have been done to keep the program up to date with changing economic conditions. During that period, benefits were increased by 23 percent more than was justified by changes in prices, while the earnings base was raised about 20 percent more than was justified by changes in wages.

Legislative changes since 1972 have not similarly expanded the OASDI system, and in fact some of the overexpansion of the benefit level was remedied by small underadjustments in both 1974 and 1975 for the changes in prices that actually occurred (about 7 percent combined). As a result, the net effect might be said to be that the general benefit level was expanded in real terms since 1968 by about 15 percent, while the present earnings base of $15,300 would instead be only $12,300 if it had only kept pace with the general wage level.

In passing, it may be noted that, if the overexpansion of the benefit level in 1969–72 had not occurred, we would not now be having the short-term cash-flow financial problems of the OASDI trust funds which we now have. In fact, if the benefit increase had been 10 percent in the 1972 amendments, rather than 20 percent, the trust-fund balances would be rising over the next few years, rather than falling toward the point of exhaustion.

## ARGUMENTS FOR THE EXPANSIONIST APPROACH

Accepting the goal that available income after the risk of old-age retirement, disability retirement, or death takes place should approximate that before then, one could take the simplistic view that the expansionist approach is the best solution because, by definition, it would do the job completely and efficiently.

This goal could be accomplished through a greatly expanded OASDI program—such as a 50 percent higher benefit level, on the average, and a maximum taxable earnings base currently of about $30,000, so that the replacement ratio (primary benefit relative to final pay, just before the risk insured against occurred) would average about 65 percent of gross earnings and would be about 50 percent for those at the highest covered earnings levels for retirement at age 65 or older.

The expansionists would thus argue that, by their approach, everybody would have the needed income, and the problem would be completely solved. The benefit protection, they would assert, would be provided not only comprehensively, but also with a minimum of administrative expense and effort through the time-tested single system of OASDI, rather than through a myriad of different plans giving only patchwork protection and having many gaps and cracks. One might note, however, that the great administrative performance of the social security system that was so evident when it was only paying cash social-insurance benefits has considerably deteriorated in the past decade, after the advent of Medicare in 1966 and SSI in 1974.

The impossibility of any real, effective partnership between the public sector and the private sector in providing full, adequate protection against the risks of old-age retirement, disability retirement, and death of the breadwinner, as the expansionists see it, is that private pension plans do not, and probably cannot ever, do a complete job of covering all workers. Moreover, it is asserted that the private plans will have excessively high administrative costs, which will leave smaller amounts available for benefit purposes.

Furthermore, the expansionists point out that the benefits under private pension plans generally do not keep pace with changes in economic conditions and thus are not adequate over the long run. Specifically, even though private pensions may be based on final average earnings and be adequate initially, they are generally fixed in terms of dollars, and thus deteriorate over the years as inflationary trends in prices take their toll.

The same situation is even more serious in the case of vested deferred pensions which are not payable until many years in the future. This problem is quite well exemplified by the different results occurring for two persons with the same earnings history over their working lifetimes who are covered by final-pay pension plans with identical provisions, where one person works his entire career with one firm, while the other works for several different firms. Even though the latter has full vesting for each of his service periods, his aggregation of pensions will be less than the single pension of the former—with a significantly large difference if there is serious inflation. The reason for the difference is two-fold. Under static general economic conditions, the rising salary scale by age that generally is present will produce lower final salaries for computation purposes for each of the several pensions for the multi-job individual (except for that from the final employer) than will be the case for the final salary for the single-job person. Further, inflationary general economic conditions will exacerbate the foregoing situation.

Still another problem pointed out by the expansionists in connection with private pension plans currently is the inadequacy of the survivor benefit protection. Even though the retired worker may have adequate income during his lifetime, the widow will often have a sharp reduction in available income, because only OASDI will be available. The same situation may also be true as to widows of workers dying before retirement, especially as to the widow at age 60 or over with no eligible children. As it so happens, OASDI alone provides quite adequate protection for widowed mothers with children, much more so than for the aged survivor cases.

Some of the problem of inadequate protection for widows has been alleviated by the Employee Retirement Income Security Act (ERISA) of 1974. One provision of that legislation requires the retiring married employee to be paid his pension in the form of a joint-and-survivor pension benefitting his widow. This filling-in of the gap in protection in private pension plans can be obviated unilaterally by the employee by his rejection of this option in favor of a single-life pension—and without his wife having knowledge of such action and agreeing to it. Another provision requires that an employee be permitted to make an election that would have the effect of providing joint-and-survivor annuity benefits to his spouse if he dies after becoming eligible for early retirement but before actual retirement. The employee may not elect the coverage since it would reduce his eventual pension, unless the employer absorbed the cost of the protection.

## DIFFICULTIES IN ACHIEVING THE EXPANSIONIST GOAL

The expansionists see the solution of the problem of providing economic security for all persons as being quite simple on the benefits side of the coin. The difficulties, however, occur with regard to that essential element, how to find the money to finance the expanded outgo.

As a broad, general matter, the expansionists assert that there is really no problem, since, to a considerable extent, the money is being provided anyhow for the support of the economically dependent segment of the population. Thus, they assert, the financing needed is merely a matter of routing the funds through different channels—that is, almost entirely through the government—than is currently being done.

But the situation is not as simple as all that. Significant effects, both tangible and intangible, can occur through a different channeling of the funds for financing economic security. Our economic and social developments have a certain parallelism with the workings in the physical sciences. For example, in the field of chemistry, quite different results can occur when a number of substances are combined, depending upon the order and manner in which this is done, even though in each instance the same quantity of each is used. Or, as a more familiar example, a skilled cook by combining the ingredients for a cake in just the right order can turn out a masterpiece, whereas a novice taking the same raw materials would produce an inedible mess.

In any event, however, the expansionists do have the problem of proposing where the vast sums necessary to finance their recommendations will specifically come from, even if "only a transfer of funds" is involved. Until now, OASDI financing has been entirely through payroll taxes (and the interest earnings on balances accumulated from such taxes) insofar as the permanent ongoing portion of the program is concerned. If this tax basis has worked out so well in the past, why not continue it in a consistent manner and raise the necessary revenues for an expanded program in this manner?

The difficulty, apparently insurmountable, facing the expansionists in this respect is the great public reaction against higher and higher payroll taxes. It is no small matter to workers to have such large sums deducted from their pay for OASDI purposes as is now the case, up to a maximum of $757.35 in 1976 and $816.75 in 1977 (plus $137.70 and $148.50, respectively, for the Hospital Insurance portion of Medicare). And the employer too has the same tax burden, which some economists assert as really actually also being borne by the worker in the final analysis.

This reaction of covered workers against higher payroll taxes is clearly illustrated currently—or at least politicians believe that it is present—by the congressional refusal to alleviate the short-term financial woes of only the present program, let alone an expansion of it. President Ford has proposed an increase of 0.3 percent in both the employer and employee tax rates, to be effective in 1977 (and thus in addition to the increase in tax income to OASDI resulting from the rise in the maximum taxable earnings base from the present $15,300 to $16,500 resulting from the automatic-adjustment provisions).

In my opinion, this increased financing proposed by President Ford, although a substantial step in the right direction and although accompanied by a small reduction in cost under certain recommendations as to benefit provisions, is not sufficient. I believe that an increase of 0.5 percent on each party is needed, disregarding any benefit deliberalizations.

Perhaps the current uproar about increasing payroll tax rates is much more political than real. Certainly, at several times in the past, Congress has legislated small increases in the OASDI tax rates in election years to provide the necessary financing, albeit that such rises became effective at the beginning of the next calendar year—i.e., *after* the election had taken place. In fact, if this type of rationale were carried out to its logical end, there would never be a good time to legislate OASDI tax increases. Such legislation in an "off" year would become effective *in* an election year, and certainly that would never do either!

Nonetheless, even though I believe that actually the general public would not react unfavorably to a small increase in the OASDI tax rate to remedy the financial difficulty of the existing system, it would seem to be a different situation if a large increase in the rate were proposed so as to finance greatly expanded benefits. And the expansionists well recognize this too!

As a result, the expansionists pin their hopes for the attainment of their goal on the euphemistic concept of what they call a government contribution, which I prefer to denote as a government subsidy. Simply put, this source of financing would merely be derived from undesignated, nonearmarked general funds of the government derived from general revenues. This approach pleases the expansionists because they do not feel that they need go any further and explain where the General Treasury will get the money. That is somebody else's problem, they believe!

But even more important, the expansionists believe that, in the government-subsidy basis of financing OASDI expansion, they have the ideal approach to selling their aims to the general public. Many persons believe that money coming out of the General Treasury is not really paid by anybody—or, at most, by somebody other than themselves. They feel that "the government" is really a separate entity, with its own separately derived financial resources. Anybody who is at all sophisticated and knowledgeable in economics knows full well that "the government is us." The only "outside party" from whom we as a nation can get financial help for our social security system would be another country, and as yet no oil-rich land has proposed doing this for us in any area, let alone social security!

Some expansionists, although not all, will argue that the OASDI taxes are regressive and weigh more heavily on the low-income and middle-income workers than on those with earnings higher than the maximum taxable base ($15,300 in 1976 and $16,500 for 1977). Digressing a moment, one might wonder how far those who are opposed to regressivity of any tax, and conversely in favor of progressivity of all taxes, would go. After all, the extreme of progressivity would be achieved if taxes were such as to level out completely all incomes.

The viewpoint as to tax regressivity is readily countered when the entire picture of both OASDI taxes and benefits is looked at. As I see it, if the OASDI taxes are an undue burden on the low-paid, so too are their other expenses. The remedy then lies in providing them with more income, rather than subsidizing certain of their expenditures. Such providing of additional income for the poor can be accomplished through either direct grants or reduced income taxes (including even negative ones). Moreover, it should be pointed out that, even if we look only at taxes, the test of regressivity versus progressivity should be made for the aggregate of all taxes, not each one separately.

Other expansionists may well argue that, although the OASDI system taken as a whole is not really regressive, any additional financing needed should now be obtained from progressive taxes. It is asserted that general-revenues taxes are, on the average, progressive. On the surface, looking at personal income tax rates, this would certainly seem to be so. But is it really?

What seems to be completely overlooked by those who merely glance at the general tax structure and declare it to be progressive is the shifting of taxes that occurs after a tax has been enacted.

Fiscal economists indulge in great intellectual exercise in attempting to measure the actual incidence of taxes back to people. It is important to note that only people, and not organizations, pay taxes in the end. I am convinced, however, that there are so many intangibles necessarily involved that it is impossible to ever accurately determine the true incidence of taxes. Such impossibility ranks with the similar situations of medieval theologians trying to determine how many angels can sit on the head of a pin or of mathematicians attempting to prove that, in Euclidian geometry, an angle can be precisely trisected.

Any attempts to estimate the incidence of taxes are founded on many arbitrary assumptions, and so the results are of questionable value—even though they may be computed by elegant electronic computer techniques. Moreover, some of the results of such economic studies—little faith as I have in them—show some surprising results, namely, that the incidence of taxation measured relatively varies only slightly by income class. For example, Roger A. Herriot and Herman P. Miller in a paper entitled "The Taxes We Pay" (*The Conference Board Record,* May 1971) derived the result that, in 1968, for all income classes between $4,000 and $50,000, taxes represented about 31 percent of income. Only for the highest income groups, over $50,000, was this percentage significantly higher (45 percent). For the two lowest income groups, under $2,000 and $2,000–4,000, there was a problem of analysis because of the different ways of treating transfer payments; under one approach, the overall tax rates were 50 percent and 35 percent, respectively, while under another approach, they were 26 percent and 25 percent, respectively.

Accordingly, considering the unmeasurable shifting of taxes that occurs, especially when a new tax is instituted, I am of the belief that, over the long run, the incidence of taxation for any new general-revenues taxes raised to provide a government subsidy to OASDI will not be too greatly different from that of the payroll taxes. Thus, financing OASDI partially by a government subsidy essentially has the effect, possibly even the purpose, of hiding the cost aspects of the program from the general public. One might even characterize such approach as being deceptive, dishonest, and demagogic.

A great danger involved if there is a government subsidy to OASDI is that the necessary funds may not be obtained by directly and immediately increasing general taxes. Instead, the "easy" way out of merely using the printing presses to turn out money, and thus add to the national debt, might be followed. The obvious consequence of such imprudent fiscal management would be more inflation.

Another approach that the expansionists advocate for financing OASDI, either for alleviating its current short-range financial problems or for liberalizing benefits, is to increase the maximum taxable earnings base more than would result under the automatic-adjustment provisions. Those provisions merely keep the base up to date with rises in the general level of earnings, so that the same proportion of payroll in covered employment is taxable for OASDI purposes (about 86 percent under the present provisions). It has been argued that the base should be increased to as much as $24,000 in 1977, although possibly attaining this relative level by gradual steps over a few years in the future.

Increasing the earnings base is not really an effective financing device over the long run. It seems expedient, however, because relatively large amounts of additional revenue are produced in the short run. But, at the same time, large future benefit liabilities result, and so the apparent financing gain is partially offset. Moreover, the law of diminishing returns enters in, and the maximum possible gain from raising the earnings base—by eliminating it completely—is only sufficient, on a long-run basis, to provide a one-time benefit increase of about 10 percent.

The real reason for proposals to raise the earnings base beyond what the automatic-adjustment provisions will do that underlies the thinking of those who fully understand the OASDI program is to increase the scope of the benefit structure, a fundamental aim of the expansionist philosophy. With a much higher base for benefit purposes, it would be argued that a floor of protection (at least) must be provided at this income level, and of course a much higher relative benefit level at the incomes below. This would mean a further shift of the economic security responsibilities from private pension plans and other private-sector savings activities to governmental plans.

Still another reason for obtaining additional financing for OASDI through raising the earnings base is the purely political, even demagogic, one that fewer people are then affected than under a straightforward increasing of the tax rates. Naturally, nobody enjoys paying more taxes, and raising the base affects only about 15 percent of the covered workers, not 100 percent. And the expansionists attempt to mollify the 15 percent by informing them that they will thereby get more benefits—the "political" approach of the best of all worlds for everybody! Actually, some higher-paid workers (the oldest ones, like the author, for example) will get additional benefits worth far more actuarially than their additional taxes, but the majority will fare less well.

We have now examined the expansionist goal of providing substantially all economic security in the retirement area through OASDI, leaving only little responsibility for private pension plans and other private-sector activities. We have also discussed how this goal could be financed and the difficulties and dangers of such methods. Let us now turn to the more positive matter of what is the moderate philosophy, its advantages, and how it can be achieved.

## ARGUMENTS FOR THE MODERATE APPROACH

The moderates have no disagreement with the expansionists as to the desirability of the general goal that people in retirement should have, not merely income on a floor-of-protection level, but also sufficient above that to provide a level of living comparable to that of their preretirement days. The basic difference of opinion is as to the best way for all concerned to achieve this result.

The moderates believe that, on the whole, it is better for the supplementation of the floor of protection to come through the private sector. There are a number of reasons why this is so.

First, from the standpoint of the individual, I believe that people generally have more pride and satisfaction in things that they do for themselves than in things provided by others, whether the government or a private charitable organization. Certainly, this is so for OASDI as compared with public assistance or relief. And I think that it is even more so for economic-security provisions through the private sector, whether on a group basis through an employer-sponsored or collectively bargained pension plan or on a completely individual basis. Many would rather have somewhat less income and feel that they had provided it for themselves than somewhat more given to them by others no matter how benevolent they are.

Although I believe there is more individual self-satisfaction in economic-security provisions through the private sector, I am not by any means arguing that this approach should supplant the social insurance approach of OASDI. The latter is most certainly essential to furnish the foundation on which to build the entire economic security structure. Further, in any event, there should be an adequate public assistance program (such as the Supplemental Security Income program) to serve as a second line of economic-security defense after private efforts when added to OASDI are not sufficient.

It is, of course, true that OASDI benefits—especially those currently being paid—are not completely "provided" or "purchased" by the beneficiary and his former employer, even though many believe so. Nonetheless, this is at least partially the case, and such a feeling should desirably be fostered among the public, although of course not overemphasized. This is a further reason for not injecting a government subsidy into the OASDI system.

Second, from the standpoint of the nation, I am convinced that the general economic productivity of the country will be better sustained and improved if people feel that they have some responsibility for their own future economic security, rather than it all coming from the government. Under these circumstances, people will have more initiative and will work harder. As a result, a larger economic pie will be available for division than if people rest on their oars in the "safe" belief that the government will take complete care of them.

Once again, I am not arguing for the other extreme, no governmental provision of a social-insurance foundation. Under such circumstances, people would have to do everything for themselves through the private sector, and then, if failing or only partially succeeding, would have to fall back on public assistance (and have little or nothing from their own efforts).

Finally, and once again from the standpoint of the nation, the virtual elimination of all forms of long-term private savings that would result if the expansionist goals were achieved would produce dire results on our economy. Most economists believe that our country needs an enormous amount of capital funds to increase our productive capacity. These would not be nearly as available through the private sector if the expansionist philosophy were to prevail.

With such a vacuum occurring, the government would have to step in and make loans, possibly by merely printing the money, thus adding to the national debt and creating additional inflation. This would naturally lead to supervision, regulation, and controls and would be a significant step toward governmental ownership and socialism.

Still other arguments in favor of the moderate approach were given in the previous section that dealt with the difficulties and disadvantages of the expansionist approach.

### SUCCESSFUL ACHIEVEMENT OF MODERATE APPROACH

Even if we can agree that, desirably, the moderate philosophy on OASDI is the best and proper result, still remaining is the problem of how it can successfully be achieved. This will not be easy, and moreover it will involve a continuing battle to hold the line against the expansionist philosophy. On the other hand, due to the "ratcheting" theory that social benefits can rarely be deliberalized, if the expansionist goal were ever realized, the war would be over.

The best that moderates can do—and they must do it—is to wage a continuing campaign to hold the same *relative* position. Note that I say "relative," not "absolute," because the moderate philosophy recognizes that the OASDI system, both as to benefit structure and financing provisions, cannot be static in the face of dynamic economic conditions, but rather must keep up to date.

The solution to achieving and maintaining the moderate approach is quite simple, although to accomplish it will require much effort to educate the general public as to its desirability, even necessity. First, the OASDI system must be prevented from expanding further. Second, the economic-security provisions under the private sector must be strengthened and expanded.

The benefit level under OASDI remained relatively level in real terms (i.e., relative to prices) during the 1950s and through 1968. In 1969–72, however, because of political competition between the legislative and executive branches of the government, the real benefit level was expanded by about 23 percent.

Ad hoc legislation in 1974 increased the benefit level by 11 percent, and the automatic-adjustment provisions produced an 8 percent increase in 1975. Inadvertently, these actions resulted in a partial correction of the previous overexpansion. These increases, when measurement of the "necessary" change to reflect the rise in prices is made in a consistent manner, were "insufficient" by about 7 percent. As a result, the real increase in the OASDI benefit level since 1968 has been in the order of 14 percent (i.e., 1.23 times .93, minus 1.00).

Another way of analyzing the relative benefit level under OASDI is to examine the so-called replacement ratios over the past experience. These ratios are derived by comparing the initial Primary Insurance Amount (the benefit payable for retirement at age 65, not considering any supplementary benefits for dependents) with the "final" gross earnings up to the maximum earnings base (assuming an earnings record of a relatively stable trend over the years).

The replacement ratio for workers with maximum creditable earnings in all years since 1951 was generally about 29–31 percent for attainments of age 65 in 1953–76, and, with the exception of only one year, were never above 33 percent. For workers with median earnings, this ratio was about 41–43 percent; for those with low earnings (at about the level of the federal minimum wage), it was about 60–65 percent. In the future, assuming that decoupling through indexing by wages will take place (as it rationally should), these ratios will be stabilized, possibly at slightly higher levels. This will be especially so for the maximum-earnings case, for which—depending upon the specific decoupling formula used—the ratio may be about 34–35 percent. And it should be noted that this higher ratio applies to a somewhat overexpanded maximum earnings base (relatively), to be discussed next. Thus, there is clear evidence of the overexpansion of the system that has occurred since 1968.

The maximum taxable earnings base too has been overexpanded in the last few years. Its level in 1972 ($9,000) was about the same as had prevailed since 1950. Such base covered about 78 percent of the total payroll of all covered workers (this proportion was about 80 percent in the period 1951–71 for the first years when the base was increased by various ad hoc legislation). Expressing the situation in another way, in 1972, about 75 percent of all covered persons had all their earnings covered for benefit and tax purposes. But for 1973 and 1974, the base was increased far higher than called for by the changes in the general level of earnings—to $10,800 and $13,200 respectively.

Following 1974, the base has been increased only to the extent of the changes in the general earnings level (to $14,100 for 1975 and $15,300 for 1976); this resulted from the operation of the automatic-adjustment provisions. As a result, for 1974–76, the base has been such as to cover about 86 percent of the total payroll in covered employment and, expressed differently, by coincidence the same 86 percent results for the proportion of all covered workers who have all their earnings credited for benefit purposes and taxed.

Accordingly, the strategy of those who espouse the moderate philosophy should be to maintain at most the *relative* status quo as to the benefit level (as measured by replacement ratios) and the size of the maximum earnings base and to provide any additional financing that may be needed *solely* through increases in the tax rates. Of course, in order to accomplish these results, the general public (especially Congress) must be educated and informed about the merits and advantages of the moderate approach and, conversely, about the serious, often hidden or obscure, dangers and disadvantages of the expansionist approach.

Specifically, any increases in benefit levels beyond those provided by the automatic-adjustment provisions must be avoided. Digressing a moment, the presumption all along in this paper is that these provisions as they relate to benefit computation procedures for persons initially going on the rolls will be "decoupled" by a wage indexing method (as recommended in general by the 1974–75 Advisory Council on Social Security and more specifically by the author in testimony before the Subcommittee on Social Security of the House Ways and Means Committee, "Hearings on Financing the Social Security System," May 7 to June 19, 1975, p. 400 and 569, and "Hearings on Decoupling the Social Security Benefits Structure," June 18 and July 23 and 26, 1976, p. 129).

For reasons discussed previously, it is extremely important that the benefit formula* should have a very low percentage applicable to the highest band of average indexed earnings considered, so that the replacement ratio for the maximum-earnings persons will not be too greatly in excess of the traditional 29–31 percent level that prevailed in the past. Certainly, this should be done so as to maintain the social-adequacy basis of the program and, at the same time, to leave more opportunities for the private sector to provide economic security for the higher-paid category.

Further, the maximum taxable earnings base should not be increased any more than the automatic-adjustment provisions will do. Some people might like to roll back all the overexpansions in the benefit level and the earnings base that have occurred since 1968. However, this seems both politically difficult and socially undesirable and inequitable as "taking something away that had been promised." But it might be feasible and desirable to have some moderate reduction in eventual benefit levels (such as 10%), so as to alleviate some of the long-range financing problem.

Particularly important is to prevent the injection of any government subsidy into the OASDI system on a general or permanent basis. It seems likely that even a small subsidy or a temporary, limited general subsidy would inevitably lead to larger, permanent ongoing ones. In this connection, the expansionists might argue that government subsidies are already present in the social security program, so what is new about this and why not have more?

Such quoted subsidies are with respect to (1) the special payments made to the closed group of persons who, in the vast majority of the cases, attained age 72 before 1968 and did not meet the insured status requirements, (2) certain military service wage credits, and (3) the matching of the enrollee premiums under the Supplementary Medical Insurance portion of the Medicare system. In my view, these are not valid precedents for a permanent, long-run government subsidy to a payroll-tax-supported program such as OASDI (or Hospital Insurance). The first category is a limited, temporary one which is being rapidly phased out. The second category is essentially the government paying as the employer. The third category differs from OASDI in being a voluntary system of enrollee participation, with the actuarial, administrative, and underwriting necessity of a second party participating in the financing.

In conclusion, the nation should bear in mind the warning attributed to the British historian, Alexander Tytler, shortly after our nation was founded:

> A democracy cannot exist as a permanent form of government. It can only exist until the voters discover they can vote themselves largess out of

the public treasury. From that moment on, the majority always votes for the candidate promising the most benefits from the public treasury—with the result that democracy collapses over a loose fiscal policy, always to be followed by a dictatorship.

Let us hope that our nation can escape this dangerous temptation to use the apparently painless way of financing such expenditures as OASDI indirectly through "largess out of the public treasury."

chapter

# 8

# Current Issues

PRESTON C. BASSETT, F.S.A.*

## INTRODUCTION

MANY OF THE CURRENT ISSUES regarding social security have already been covered in considerable depth by preceding participants. For this reason, the comments on current issues discussed below will be partially repetitive. However, some current issues have not been touched upon at all. Thus, this paper will attempt to touch on most of the current issues for social security, but will not treat any in great depth.

The issues covered in this paper are:

1. Who should be covered by social security?
2. How large should the pensions provided by social security be?
3. When should pensions begin?
4. What types of benefits should be provided?
5. How should benefits be adjusted for inflation or changes in the standard of living?
6. How should social security benefits be financed?
7. In what form should the benefits be provided?

## COVERAGE

From time to time, Congress has amended the Social Security Act to bring more and more workers under its umbrella. Almost all nongovern-

---

* Vice President and Actuary, Towers, Perrin, Forster & Crosby, and a member of the Pension Research Council.

ment workers now are covered by the act. The largest noncovered group are employees participating in U.S. Civil Service retirement programs. Some groups are allowed to decide whether or not they wish to be covered. These include members of the ministry and employees in other nonprofit organizations. The largest block of workers in this category, however, are state and municipal employees. The principal reason for giving state and municipal workers the right to choose whether to be covered is the constitutional question regarding the legality of a federal payroll tax on states and municipalities. Even if municipal employees agree to participate in social security, they can later elect to terminate coverage. However, the effective date of discontinuing participation must be two years after the election and at least seven years after the initial election to participate.

This brings us to one of the current issues. Should workers, including government employees, be required to participate in social security? The primary purpose of social security is to assure that retired people have at least a floor of protection in their old age. Since government workers are already covered by pension plans—in many cases, very generous pension plans—there is no need to provide the protection of social security. One reason social security is compulsory for private sector employees is that, if given the choice, many people would opt out, only to become wards of the government in their old age because they do not have adequate income. But that argument does not apply to government workers.

In addition, many government plans, unlike nongovernment plans, require significant employee contributions. Therefore, there are obvious objections to requiring employees to contribute to social security also. Add to that the fact that some states make it illegal to reduce current benefits provided by government plans even if they are replaced by social security benefits. To add social security on top of current municipal benefits, therefore, would result in extremely generous retirement plans for government workers. Even without social security, benefits for municipal employees frequently are considerably more liberal than those available in private industry for similar positions.

On the other hand, many government employees manage to acquire a sufficient number of calendar quarters of social security coverage through employment in private industry to become eligible for at least minimum social security benefits. Thus, a government worker may not only receive benefits from a federal, state, or municipal plan, but may also get social security benefits at a low cost. Therefore, the argument goes, government workers should be brought under social security during their entire working careers and pay taxes as everyone else does.

Presently, many municipalities find the burden of social security taxes on both the municipality and employees so great that they believe that opting out of social security is the best course. Historically, however, social security benefits have exceeded participants' contributions. So these municipal employees will be exchanging a short-term advantage for a long-term disadvantage. It appears that in many cases the decision to opt out has been made before adequate consideration was given to all factors. This issue requires careful study before one can give an answer to whether or not government employees should be required to participate in social security.[1]

What about those groups of employees whose participation is now compulsory? Should they be given a choice to opt out? The answer is probably, "no." Participants who opt out might later find themselves without adequate retirement income and thus forced to apply for welfare's benefits. It is better that they pay for social security during their working years.

As John K. Dyer noted, another approach is used in Great Britain and has been tried in a few other countries. Under this approach, an employer and his employees can decide to opt out of the government social security program provided they establish their own equally generous program. The benefits are then provided through the private pension system. This approach has not been entirely satisfactory. Problems have arisen when government benefits have been increased retroactively, particularly if an employee has moved from one employer to another during his working career.

A variation that might be considered is for social security to provide a very low basic floor and to require all employers to provide additional benefits from the private pension system. In other words, employers would have to provide a minimum pension just as they now pay a minimum wage. This minimum pension would be a supplement to social security so that the two combined would provide a minimum standard of living after retirement. This would keep the government part of the program at a low level and provide for further participation by the private pension system. This approach would relieve the pressure to increase social security benefits further and would permit the private pension sector to carry a greater share.

---

[1] For a more detailed analysis of this issue, see Appendix D.

In summary, on the issue of who should be covered by social security, the most significant question is whether or not government employees, civil service employees, and state and municipal employees should be required to participate in the federal social security program.[2]

## LEVEL OF BENEFITS

At the present time, social security benefits have both minimum and maximum monthly amounts. In between, the benefits depend on employee's covered earnings. Determining the benefit level based on the employee's covered earnings over past years would not have been a satisfactory method had Congress not made periodic adjustments to avoid potential inequities. Unfortunately, in the eyes of many, the 1972 amendments to the Social Security Act, which were designed to correct the problem, only created more and worse problems. Thus, we find that benefits may get completely out of line under certain future economic conditions. The benefits between some practical minimum and maximum should bear a relationship to the employee's pay at the time of retirement. Most experts agree that to base the benefits on the employee's earnings during the total period of employment (except for a five-year dropout), as the present act provides is unsatisfactory.[3] Benefits should be related to the employee's pay during the last year or few years prior to retirement or to an indexed average pay over a longer period.

Also, it is generally accepted that the replacement ratio—the ratio of the social security benefit after retirement to the pay immediately before retirement—should be higher for low paid employees and lower for high paid employees. This is known as the balance between individual equity and social adequacy. Individual equity would require that each employee's benefit be specifically related to his own contributions to the social security fund. However, this would produce benefits that were completely inadequate for some participants and perhaps overly generous for others. From a social point of view, it is important that all participants receive at least a minimum benefit, that lower paid people receive a higher proportion of their pay than those higher paid. To some extent, particularly at the higher levels, some recognition should also be given to the

---

[2] For a more detailed discussion of this issue, see Appendix B and Hearings of the Subcommittee on Social Security of House Ways and Means Committee, 94th Congress, 2d Session, April 26, 1976.

[3] Unless the basis for computing average monthly earnings is changed, benefits will eventually reflect average earnings over a 35-year period—from age 22 to age 62, with a dropout of the 5 years of lowest earnings.

fact that social security benefits are not taxable income. The change in tax status should be indirectly recognized in setting the replacement ratios.

Even if we accept the above principles, many touchy questions arise. For example: Should the replacement ratios vary by marital status? Currently, spouses' benefits are 50 percent of primary benefits. Is this the right ratio? The relationship between benefits for single persons and benefits for married couples, when compared to taxes paid, is causing considerable concern.

In addition, what adjustments, if any, should be made in replacement ratios for either early or delayed retirements? Pensions beginning before the stated retirement age now are reduced on an approximate actuarial equivalent basis. On the other hand, if an employee delays retirement, the increase in benefits is almost insignificant. Should we encourage employees to work beyond the stated retirement age by increasing the benefits for delayed retirements?

Should social security benefits be decreased for outside earnings? Or, should they be decreased for any type of outside income? At the present time, social security benefits are decreased for outside *earnings* but not for other outside *income.*

I believe that, in order to encourage and maintain the private pension system, social security benefits should be maintained at a level that provides a floor of protection only. Currently, for the low paid worker, the primary insurance amount is about 60 to 65 percent of final pay. This reduces to about 30 to 35 percent for the employee with maximum covered earnings. With these replacement ratios, there is room for the private pensions to build onto this basic floor. Private pensions should be encouraged and should be used to supplement social security pensions.

One problem resulting from this basic premise is that not everyone is covered by the private pension system. For many workers, their own savings and social security are the sole sources of retirement income. One solution to this problem was suggested above—employers be required to provide at least a minimun pension to all employees.

Under the provisions of ERISA, it is now possible for individuals not covered by a private pension plan to establish Individual Retirement Accounts (IRAs) on a favorable tax basis. These IRAs should help the problem of missing coverage. The government should further encourage private savings so that a reasonable supplement can be provided to the social security benefit floor. One way would be to increase the low limits now applicable to IRAs.

The present benefit computation method under social security is unsatisfactory. It does not maintain the current replacement ratios under different economic conditions. This problem has been discussed by several previous speakers.[4] I will not repeat the problem and the proposed solutions. Suffice it to say that the current method should be amended promptly.

## NORMAL RETIREMENT AGE

At the present time, benefits are generally available for covered workers at age 65. Benefits are available at earlier retirement ages with a discount (6⅔ percent per year) and at older retirement ages with a slight increase (1 percent per year). For practical purposes, however, social security retirement age is fixed at 65.

It appears to me that there is a fundamental policy decision to be made: At what age do we want to encourage employees to retire—65, earlier than 65, or later than 65? If we want to encourage earlier retirement, then the current reductions should be decreased as was proposed by Bert Seidman. On the other hand, if our policy is to encourage employees to work beyond age 65, effective social security benefit increases should be granted for delayed retirement. The current increase of 1 percent per year is only a token adjustment.

Dr. J. Douglas Brown confirmed that age 65 for retirement was determined somewhat arbitrarily back in 1935.[5] Since that time, there have been significant changes—the life span has lengthened, the health of older people has improved, and jobs themselves have become less demanding. These factors indicate that it would be quite logical to extend the retirement age from 65 to 66 or some higher age. Politically, it is difficult to increase the retirement age for those who are within a few years of retirement. Thus, if the retirement age is to be increased, it must be done at some future date and the year 2000 has been suggested. The Social Security Act could be amended, for example, to provide that the retirement age would be 66 rather than 65 for anyone retiring after the year 2000.

If it is desirable to move the retirement age to an age higher than 65, two courses of action could be followed. The first would be to provide for greater benefits on delayed retirement, which would encourage em-

---

[4] See Appendix B, pp. 139–40.

[5] This point was made by Dr. Brown during the discussion that followed his formal remarks.

ployees to elect to work longer. Or the act could be amended to provide that the normal retirement age be increased to 66 or some other age. Politically, the former is probably more possible and could become effective at an earlier date.

Of significance is the fact that if the retirement age should be increased to say, age 66 starting in the year 2000 without an actuarial increase in benefits, there would be substantial cost savings that would alleviate somewhat the anticipated financial crisis.

In considering when to begin benefits, we might want to review the effect of reducing benefits because of outside earned income and providing benefits at age 72 no matter what the outside income. These two conditions have been debated extensively in the past but need not necessarily be considered sacred for all times.

Another fundamental question: Should the commencement of government-provided benefits be based upon need? In other words, should we discard the present social security system of providing benefits for all participants, regardless of need? Would we be better off with a simple welfare program?

At this time, this is a theoretical question because promises have been made to those who have been paying taxes and it would be politically impossible and probably morally wrong to deny these participants their social security benefits. Employees feel they have earned these benefits as a right and expect to be paid. If a welfare-type program is to be considered, it must be considered only as a goal for the long range. Steps in this direction would be reducing social security benefits prior to age 72 by outside earnings and financing social security through general revenue.

## TYPES OF BENEFITS

Currently, under the Social Security Act, many benefits in addition to pensions are provided to participants and their dependents. Old age pensions are still the primary benefit of the Social Security Act. Benefits are payable both to the retired employee and spouse. This raises the first question under this section (which was mentioned earlier): How much should be paid to a married couple compared to a single person and how much should be paid to a surviving spouse? Another related question: When should payments commence to a surviving spouse if the participant dies at an early age? Before age 65, should payments be limited to dependent spouses and, if so, how is dependent defined? Alternatively, should payments be made only to surviving spouses with dependents, such as dependent children?

Should differences in death benefits according to sex be changed? Should fathers and divorced men be treated the same as mothers and divorced women? The courts have ruled in favor of equal treatment of fathers and mothers. Should benefits for husbands and widowers be provided without a support test? The whole area of differences in benefits upon sex needs critical review. All these questions have been addressed under the current act, but are the answers satisfactory?[6]

Other death benefits can be provided by a social security system. Should there be a temporary payment or lifetime annuities to, for example, dependent parents or dependent children? Are there other relativees who should be considered? Also, should a lump-sum benefit be paid upon the death of any beneficiary? This would be justified on the grounds that some terminal expenses always must be met.

Disability benefits are coming under criticism because the number of people qualifying for these benefits has increased substantially. Evidence indicates that different jurisdictions operate under quite different definitions. One very real problem in the disability program is an effective definition of who is and who is not disabled.

In addition to determining whether a person is disabled, there are other conditions for receiving benefits. These conditions include the participant's age and the years of coverage under the social security program. Again, what is the proper level of benefits to be paid? How often and how should a person requalify or continue to be qualified for disability payments? All these questions have been answered under the current provisions of the Social Security Act. However, the most serious problem today is the lack of uniformity in the administration of this program.

## ADJUSTMENT OF BENEFITS FOR INFLATION OR CHANGES IN THE STANDARD OF LIVING

This topic has been discussed in the previous papers and has been covered by various other groups studying the current social security provisions. The 1975 Report of the Advisory Council on Social Security went into the subject in great length. So did the Panel on Social Security Financing that reported to the Committee on Finance of the U.S. Senate.

---

[6] See Appendix C for a detailed analysis of the treatment of men and women under social security with respect to sex and marital status.

The 1975 report of the Board of Trustees also highlighted the problem.

There is no question that the current formula overreacts to changes in the rate of inflation and wage increases. Certainly one way to alleviate this problem is to adopt one of the decoupling formulas recommended by the various interested parties.

Prior to 1972, the solution for adjusting benefits for inflation had been periodic amendments to the act by Congress. This system would have worked quite satisfactorily had Congress not overreacted frequently. Under the present arrangement, benefits of retired employees and other employees are adjusted in proportion to changes in the cost-of-living index. Many people question whether this is proper or the best basis. For example, should the postretirement changes be based on changes in the standard of living? This could be measured by the change in average wages. Then there is the question: Is the cost-of-living index the proper index to be applied to retired people? The index is based on a market basket of goods that may not be a proper market basket for retired persons. If a special cost-of-living index for retired persons is developed, would this lead to a demand for separate cost-of-living indices for other groups—for example, particular economic groups or those who live in particular locations? How frequently and in what amount should changes be made? This is an administrative problem, but a practical one, nevertheless, from the participant's point of view.

## FINANCING OF BENEFITS

A. Haeworth Robertson reviewed this problem earlier and it has been discussed at some length by other participants. Currently, an equal tax rate is paid by both employees and employers and the tax rate is applied to earnings up to a stated amount called the earnings base. Under the act, the base is automatically adjusted, usually each year, for changes in the average wages. Also, the act schedules certain increases in the tax rate to occur at specified times in the future.

This procedure for automatic adjustment of benefits and the taxable wage base was developed after a study showed that expected income would meet expected outgo over the long run under a reasonable set of economic factors. However, recent history indicates that the economic factors may no longer be reasonable, creating problems with this system. A different set of economic factors may develop in the future and, under these, the expected outgo will exceed the expected income. The current fund could well be exhausted by 1980 or 1981. This would indicate that some changes must be made in the financing of the social security system within the next few years.

A limited number of basic alternatives exist for correcting the expected deficit. These are:

1. Increasing employer and employee tax equally. This continues the present system and has been recommended by various advisory groups as well as by the Administration.
2. Increase the employer's tax only.
3. Increase the tax base.
4. Increase the tax base for the employer only (for example, tax all earnings).
5. Make up the deficit from general revenue.
6. Make a specific contribution to social security from general revenue.
7. Use a new tax for this purpose.
8. Increase the retirement age.
9. Reduce the benefits.
10. Some combination of two or more of the above.

All these solutions have been given serious consideration within the past few months. The Advisory Panel to the Senate Finance Committee recommended increasing the employee and employer tax and amending the act so future benefits could be decreased by decoupling.

The Advisory Council indirectly recommended using general revenue, as well as decreasing future benefits by decoupling, to solve both short- and long-term problems. However, there was a dissenting opinion, particularly on the use of general revenue. The staff of the House Ways and Means Committee studied several different alternatives and combinations of increasing employee and employer tax rates and of increasing the tax base.

Senator Russell B. Long would like to find a new tax to cover the social security deficit. Otto Eckstein, a former member of the Council of Economic Advisors and a Harvard University professor, recommended a one-shot transfer of $5 billion from general revenue to make up the short-term deficit.

It is unlikely that this session of Congress will consider the financing problem seriously. Because there are still some funds left, consideration of the matter can be postponed for a year or two. However, the problem will have to be faced and we should be prepared to advance our recommendations.

Another question: What is the proper tax for the self-employed? At one time it was one and a half times the employee rate, but now it is a flat 7 percent. The current employee rate is 4.95 percent for old-age, survivors, and disability benefits.

While on the topic of financing, we can always raise the interesting question of whether advance funding of social security should be required as it is for private pension plans. Perhaps full funding should not be required, but some intermediate course should be adopted.

## FORM OF BENEFITS PROVIDED

We have come to assume that social security benefits should be paid in cash. The question of whether this is the best form has hardly ever been raised. There are alternatives to cash and many of them are in effect in other areas, some even under the Social Security Act. For example, instead of providing cash, services might be provided directly. We might subsidize housing for the elderly. The government could build retirement communities in which retired persons would receive all their necessities rather than cash benefits. Medical benefits could be provided on a service basis rather than paid in cash. Other examples are food stamps, which could be available to the elderly. In many areas, reduced rates are given to elderly people for medicines, transportation, and the like.

## CONCLUDING OBSERVATIONS

This paper has raised many, many questions and given very few answers. The present Social Security Act answered many of these questions at least to this point. And so the government probably will not address many of the questions unless someone is specifically interested in advancing a different point of view. On the other hand, some issues must be faced in the near future and Congress will need guidance. I would like to run through the more important issues and give you my personal observations.

The first question we raised was: Who should be covered by social security? The primary issue is whether or not employees covered by the U.S. Civil Service retirement program and other government employees should be required to participate in social security. I fail to see that a strong case has been developed for including these employees under social security. A subsidiary issue is whether state and municipal employees should be given the option of coming under social security protection. Because inequities can develop, my personal observation is that government employees, like the civil service employees, should not participate in social security. Alternatively, if they can be brought into the social security program on a basis that will not provide them with excessively large total benefits or provision can be made to reduce the benefits provided by the state or municipality, then I believe they should be allowed into the program, but then they should not be permitted to opt out at a later date.

The second question was: How large should the pensions provided by social security be? My opinion is that the present replacement ratios should not be allowed to increase. I could support a modest decrease. The Social Security Act should be amended to maintain the present replacement ratios regardless of future economic conditions. These benefits should provide a floor of protection that could be supplemented by the private pension system. I see many advantages in a program that would require all employers to provide a compulsory minimum pension just as they do a minimum wage. Where private pensions are not provided to individuals, the government should encourage individual savings through such methods as Individual Retirement Accounts. If benefits are provided through the private pension system rather than through social security and such benefits are funded there will be increased savings. This could solve some of the problems raised earlier by Geoffrey N. Calvert.

The third question raised was: When should pensions commence? I believe that pensions should commence normally at an older age than 65 and steps should be taken that are politically possible to achieve this. Thus, I would favor increasing the retirement age at some distant date, such as the year 2000, and in the interim, granting reasonable increases in social security benefits to employees who delay their retirement.

The next question was: What types of benefits should be provided? The current provisions of the Social Security Act seem to cover the necessary areas. I have no major changes to recommend.

The next was: How should pensions be adjusted for inflation or changes in the standard of living? I strongly favor a decoupling so that the benefits payable under social security are a function of the employee's final pay (averaged over a few years) thus automatically taking care of the standard of living prior to retirement. In the postretirement area, I believe the current formula of adjusting benefits for changes in the cost of living is satisfactory. Anything in this area has to be considered on an overall basis and in the broadest aspects. Cost of living differs for retired employees and for active employees; it also differs by the area as well as other factors. I do not believe that any further refinements are necessary.

How should social security benefits be financed? I strongly support the present system of an equal tax on employees and employers based on the same earnings base. To overcome the short-term deficit, I recommend that the tax rate be increased by .5 percent on both the employee and the employer.

The final question was: What should be the form of the benefits provided? Although some interesting questions were raised, I am of the opinion that cash benefits are the most satisfactory.

Finally, once again, may I urge you, no matter what your convictions, to express them to Congress so that intelligent decisions can be made in this most important area.

appendix
# A

# Concept of Pension-Social Security Integration*

JOHN K. DYER, JR.

THE CONCEPT of "integration of private pension plans with Social Security" first appeared in Internal Revenue Regulations 103,[1] and the related Mimeograph 5539,[2] promulgated by the Commissioner of Internal Revenue in July, 1943, pursuant to Section 165(a) of the Internal Revenue Code as amended by the Revenue Act of 1942.

The 1942 revenue act first introduced the requirement that a private pension plan must not "discriminate in favor of employees who are officers, shareholders, persons whose principal duties consist in supervising the work of other employees, or highly compensated employees"[3]—in order to be funded with "tax deferment"—tax free accumulation of reserves, immediate tax deduction of employer contributions, and no current taxability to employees of such contributions. This requirement

---

* This material appeared in a monograph entitled *The Integration of Private Pension Plans with Social Security* prepared by Mr. Dyer for the American Enterprise Institute for Public Policy Research and published in 1968. The monograph was intended to provide a historical perspective and theoretical framework for evaluation of pending IRS proposals for modification of the basic integration rules.

This material is reproduced with the permission of the author and the American Enterprise Institute.

[1] T.D. 5278, approved July 8, 1943 (C.B. 1943, 478).

[2] C.B. 1943, 499.

[3] Sections 165(a)(3)(b) and 165(a)(4) of the Internal Revenue Code, as amended by the Revenue Act of 1942.

was qualified by the stipulation that a plan should not be found discriminatory "merely because it excludes employees the whole of whose remuneration constitutes 'wages' (under social security or railroad retirement)," nor "merely because the contributions or benefits based upon that part of an employee's remuneration which is excluded (from wages covered by social security or railroad retirement) differ from the contributions or benefits based on employee's remuneration not so excluded."[4] The integration requirement, not explicitly required by the Code, reflected the Commissioner's solution to the problem of how to give quantitative expression to the "nondiscrimination" requirement and its limitations, and thereby to give employers a meaningful guideline to the design of pension plans supplementing social security, and to give local revenue agents a uniform and systematic basis on which to process and approve such plans.

While there were numerous objections raised in 1943 when the concept of integration was introduced, and there have been further objections and consideration of alternatives since that time, the concept has nevertheless survived down to the present. The specific formula for integration, while modified in some detail with each change in social security, has remained essentially unchanged since 1950.

The present importance of the integration question is an indirect result of the Social Security Act Amendments of 1965. In September, 1966, over a year after the social security amendments were enacted, the Internal Revenue Service released "Announcement 66–58."[5] asking interested parties for "background information for its use in developing the formula for integrating pension, annuity, profit-sharing, and stock bonus plans with the old-age and survivors insurance benefits provided under the Social Security Act as amended in 1965."

Included in the Announcement was an "illustrative" integration formula which, if adopted, would materially reduce the integration limits, and require the amendment of many existing plans. Over 2,500 letters were received by the Commissioner of Internal Revenue in reply to the Announcement, the great bulk of them opposing any change as drastic as that indicated by the illustration.

Private pensions are by their very nature long-range plans. Thus, it is essential that the ground rules under which they are designed and revised be subject to a high degree of long-range stability. Without such stability, the sense of security that these plans are intended to give employees is

---

[4] Section 165(a)(5) of the Internal Revenue Code, as amended by the Revenue Act of 1942.
[5] I.R.B. 1966–38, 87.

impaired, the financial planning of employers is disrupted, and the problems of the Internal Revenue Service in approving them are complicated. Whether this necessary stability in the administration of a nondiscrimination requirement can ever be achieved under the present Code provisions was one of the serious questions brought into focus by Announcement 66–58.

In a public statement made in May, 1967, Assistant Secretary of the Treasury Stanley S. Surrey summarized the problem as "one to devise the mechanics of integration in a way which avoids discrimination yet does not involve private plans in a constant process of change and difficult adjustments." He also stated that "any final results respecting this integration matter must, of necessity, await congressional action on the pending Social Security measure."[6] These statements, considered in the light of the fact that integration rules relating to the 1965 Social Security Amendments were still unsettled and involved in a heated controversy, underline the difficulties involved in continuing to apply the integration concept on a precise mathematical basis in the face of an ever-changing social security system.

## HISTORICAL OUTLINE

Any present consideration of the "nondiscrimination" requirement for funded pension plans, and the "integration" approach to the implementation of that requirement, must take cognizance of the legislative history of the requirement, the economic climate in which that legislation was enacted, and the evolution of its administration over the intervening twenty-five years. The significant highlights of this history are summarized below.

The idea that private pension plans should be required to be "nondiscriminatory" was first publicly advocated by Mr. Randolph Paul, Tax Advisor to the Secretary of the Treasury, in testimony before the House Ways and Means Committee on March 3, 1942.[7] He referred to the "tax avoidance potentialities of pension trusts," and stated that "the use of these trusts as a tax saving device for key officers and employees has been stimulated by increasing rates of tax." The specific nondiscrimination requirement that he proposed was essentially that which was incorporated

---

[6] The social security amendments of 1967 became law by approval by the President on January 2, 1968.

[7] Statement of Randolph Paul, Hearings of the House Committee on Ways and Means, 77th Congress, 2d Session, March, 1942, vol. 1, p. 87.

in the subsequently drafted House bill, and which appeared in the Revenue Act of 1942 as finally enacted.[8]

There was little opposition to the proposed nondiscrimination requirement, either in the preliminary hearings following Mr. Paul's statement, or in the hearings held later in 1942 on the House and Senate bills. This may have been in part because industry and insurance representatives saw a much more serious threat in certain other Treasury proposals, such as that for maximum pensions, compulsory vesting, and a 5 percent-of-payroll limitation on employer contributions, and focused their opposition on these.

Mr. Henry Beers, testifying on behalf of the insurance industry in the Senate hearings on the 1942 House bill, suggested that the Code should specifically provide that a plan would not be disqualified as discriminatory "merely because" it excluded employees earning under the Social Security wage limit, or "merely because" it provided larger benefits on earnings over that limit.[9] He pointed out the desirability of making it perfectly clear that plans supplementing social security would not be disqualified for that reason. The wording he suggested was included, without material change, in the bill as enacted. The Senate Report on the final bill reiterated this intent, and supported it with an illustration of a plan supplementing social security which would qualify as nondiscriminatory.[10]

Nearly a year elapsed between the enactment of the 1942 Revenue Act and the appearance of regulations on the pension sections. During that period, many pension plans were established, due both to the wartime pressure for "wage substitutes," and doubtless also to the fact that the final adoption of many plans had been held up during the more than six months that the Act had been in process. Many—perhaps most—of these plans were designed to supplement social security, and Section 165(a) was almost universally interpreted by employers and their advisors to permit the exclusion of employees earning under $3,000 (the then social security wage limit), and to permit the provision, for employees earning over $3,000, of any benefits which were nondiscriminatory within the covered group.

In July of 1943, the Regulations requiring "integration," and Mimeograph 5539 describing the formula whereby this principle would be imple-

---

[8] See footnote 3, p. 123.

[9] Statement of Henry Beers, Hearings of the Senate Committee on Finance on H.R. 7378, 77th Congress, 2d Session, July, 1942, vol. 1, p. 483.

[10] Senate Committee on Finance, Report No. 1631, 77th Congress, 2d Session, October 2, 1942.

mented, were published.[11] There were many protests from employers who had established plans that did not anticipate such a requirement. A number of members of Congress also protested, indicating that the requirement went beyond the intent of Congress. A subcommittee of the Senate Finance Committee held hearings on the subject, and a joint resolution "outlawing" integration was prepared. However, for reasons that are not clear on the record, this joint resolution was never reported out. The opposition gradually died down, and the integration requirement remained in the Regulations. In due course, the many plans not meeting the integration requirement were modified to conform with it.

The first postwar amendments to the Social Security Act were enacted in 1950, and in the following year the tax Regulations were revised and a new integration guide, Mimeograph 6641 was issued.[12] These established a new integration limit, in effect saying that the portion of social security benefits not financed by employee contributions was equivalent to a life income of 37.5 percent of earnings, at the maximum social security earnings level, and hence that a corresponding 37.5 percent private plan benefit on earnings above that level would be deemed nondiscriminatory. Detailed rules as to the modification of the 37.5 percent rule to take account of death benefits, employee contributions, and other factors, were also described in Mimeograph 6641.

Mimeograph 6641 still remains in effect today, in all of its essential respects. Minor modifications were introduced following the Social Security Act Amendments of 1952, 1954, and 1958, but the basic limitation of 37.5 percent (applied to the current social security wage base) has remained unmodified, except for the limited application of "interim guides"[13] first announced in December, 1966, since 1950.[14] Consequently, the impression was created in many minds that this percentage had been established as a permanent feature of the Internal Revenue administration of the pension plan sections enacted in 1942.

---

[11] See footnotes 1 and 2.

[12] C.B. 1951–1, 41.

[13] The "interim guides" issued by the Internal Revenue Service first appeared as T.I.R. 876, on Dec. 23, 1966, and were subsequently restated in early 1967 as Rev. Rul. 67–10. This ruling provided that a plan which satisfies the "present" integration requirements (i.e., those based on the 1958 social security amendments) would continue to qualify until amended regulations were issued. It further provided, however, that a plan integrated at an earnings level above the 1958 level of $4,800 could qualify only if the 1958 integration limit were related to such higher earnings level.

[14] Revenue Ruling 13 (C.B. 1953–1, 294); Revenue Ruling 56–692 (C.B. 1956–2, 287); Revenue Ruling 61–75 (C.B. 1961–1, 140).

The table included at page 132 summarizes the changing levels of social security benefits from 1939 to the present, and the corresponding changes in the integration limit prescribed for private pension plans. Actions reflected in this appended summarization clearly indicate, in the opinion of the writer, that the Treasury policy, at least from 1950 until the issuance in 1966 of Announcement 66–58, was to maintain a constant integration limit (37.5 percent) by adjusting as necessary the value imputed to employee contributions to social security.

An important fact brought out by the summary table is that the substantial reduction in the basic integration limit illustrated in Announcement 66–58, from 37.5 percent to 24 percent, resulted almost entirely from the use in the Announcement of a new concept as to the determination of the "attribution ratio"—the assumed average percentage of an employee's social security contributions to the value of his social security benefits. Heretofore, the "attribution ratio" has been based upon "employees retiring in the near future"; this was explained in Mimeograph 6641, explicitly confirmed in Revenue Ruling 13, and reconfirmed by implication in Revenue Ruling 61–75 (1961) by the statement that the integration basis provided in the 1960 Regulations is "analogous to that . . . of Memeograph 6641." The 50 percent "attribution ratio" used in Announcement 66–58 was, on the other hand, based upon the projected contributions and benefits of an employee retiring in the year 1990, the assumed year of retirement of "the average employee now in the work force."

## THE 1954 LEGISLATIVE PROPOSALS

The one serious attempt that has been made since 1943 to replace the integration concept with a different approach to the prevention of discrimination in private pension plans was in 1954. In that year, following intensive studies made by the Treasury Department with the advice and assistance of outside experts, an entirely new concept was developed. This was incorporated in H.R. 8300, the 1954 bill to revise and recodify the revenue laws. The bill called for the replacement of the 1942 "nondiscrimination" provisions with a new section prescribing a series of "objective tests" that could be applied with little or no administrative interpretation.[15]

---

[15] House Committee on Ways and Means, Report No. 1337, 83d Congress, 2d Session, March 9, 1954, pp. A165 to A168.

Under the 1954 proposals, a pension plan would have been disqualified as "discriminatory in favor of key employees or stockholders" only if more than 30 percent of the plan contributions were for the benefit of stockholders (employees holding, either directly or under certain attribution rules, 10 percent or more of the voting power of all classes of stock of the employer or of its parent), or if more than 10 percent of the plan participants were "key employees" (defined as the highest paid 10 percent, up to a limit of 100 employees). However, a plan would not be considered discriminatory, in the case of an employer having not more than 20 regular employees, if 50 percent or more of such employees were covered or, in the case of an employer having more than 20 regular employees, if 10 or more such employees or 25 percent or more of such employees, whichever were greater, were covered. Subject to these rules, a plan could have been limited, under the proposal, to any described category of employees, such as regular salaried employees, regular hourly-paid employees, employees who had been employed for a minimum period not exceeding 5 years, or employees whose annual compensation exceeded a specified amount not exceeding $4,000.[16]

The test of nondiscrimination in benefits, proposed by the 1954 bill was that the contributions or benefits under the plan must not bear a higher ratio to compensation for any covered employee than for any other covered employee whose compensation is lower. In the application of the rule, however, the first $4,000 of compensation could have been disregarded. The House Report on the bill pointed out that under these rules it would not be necessary to integrate the plan with social security or railroad retirement benefits. For profit sharing plans, a special rule would have required the allocation of at least 75 percent of a year's contribution on a uniform basis, with the remaining 25 percent or less allocable on a more flexible basis.

The Senate Finance Committee rejected these provisions, restoring in substance the provisions introduced in 1942. The Committee Report stated:

> The House bill made a major departure in the qualification requirements for pension, profit sharing, and stock bonus plans. The aim was to replace the Commissioner's discretion under present law with clear rules that would permit any employer to determine whether or not a plan was qualified and to do so in a way that would qualify all reasonable plans without opening the door to discriminatory plans. These broad objectives have

---

[16] Ibid.

received general approval. However, the mechanical rules in the House bill
have raised many problems in many different types of plans. In view of
the difficulty of developing adequate mechanical tests to meet these problems your committee's bill retains the framework of the present treatment
of pension, profit sharing and stock bonus plans pending further study.[17]

There is no record of any subsequent action on the part of Congress
to implement the promise of "further study."

                              *  *  *  *  *

## KEY FACTS AND OBSERVATIONS

The following seem to the author of this section to be the significant
facts and observations that may be recapitulated from the foregoing
analysis of the development of "integration" to the present time, and the
1967 Social Security Amendments:

1. The nondiscrimination requirement introduced in 1942 had as its
   sole announced objective the prevention of pension plans being used
   as devices for mitigating top bracket taxes on the incomes of high
   paid employees. While informal comments were made by Treasury
   officials as to the social desirability of broadening private pension
   coverage through the enforcement of nondiscrimination requirements, these "social objectives" were generally accepted as by-
   products rather than objectives of the legislation.
2. "Integration" was not and is not a requirement of the law, nor was
   this concept foreshadowed in any of the legislative history of the 1942
   Revenue Act. It was simply a concept developed by the Treasury to
   facilitate administration of the nondiscrimination requirement.
3. It appears to be recognized by most students of the subject that
   "discrimination" is not a mathematically measurable state; that there
   is a considerable range between what is clearly discriminatory and
   what is clearly nondiscriminatory. The spread between the 37.5 percent integration limit in effect for the past 17 years, and the 24
   percent limit suggested in Announcement 66–58, illustrates the wide
   range of possible mathematical interpretations that might be placed
   upon the nondiscrimination requirement.
4. The 150 percent of primary benefit that from the beginning has been
   the starting point in developing integration limits has not been seri-

---

[17] Senate Committee on Finance, Report No. 1622, 83rd Congress, 2nd Session, June 18, 1954,
pp. 53 and 54.

ously questioned, although many arguments have been advanced as to its accuracy. It can be justified on a number of grounds, perhaps the simplest being that this is the benefit actually payable to a married couple under social security when both the pensioner and his wife are over age 65, and that it would be impracticable for a private pension plan to provide different benefits depending upon whether an employee is married or single, or if married, whether his wife is over or under age 65.

The adjustment in integration limit based upon employees' social security contributions deemed to be applied against the "purchase" of their own benefits (see summary table, column 5) has been questioned on several grounds. It has been pointed out that:

1. The Code seems to permit plans that supplement social security or railroad retirement *benefits*, without regard to whether they are financed through employee or employer contributions or both.
2. The original integration rules (Mimeograph 5539) did not include any mention of such an adjustment.
3. The social security system is financed on essentially a pay-as-you-go basis; employee and employer contributions are used as received to pay the benefits of current beneficiaries. The benefits of these present contributors will be paid out of the contributions of future contributors; hence the continuation of the system hinges upon the ability and willingness of the future contributors to make the contributions now contemplated. Thus any concept based upon the idea that employees contribute towards their own future benefits is inconsistent with the realities of social security financing.
4. Even if employee social security contributions could reasonably be presumed to create future benefit rights by some process analogous to "purchase," the attribution of any uniform proportion of such benefits to employee contributions is open to serious question. The equitable application of such a presumption would require variations in the "attribution ratio" according to year of retirement, family status, sex, prior receipt of benefits and many other factors—clearly an impracticable refinement.
5. Should there be introduced into the social security financing structure a direct contribution out of general tax revenues, as has been proposed in some recent social security amendment bills, the determination of an appropriate "attribution ratio" would take on new complications.

**SUMMARY TABLE**
**Evolution of the Internal Revenue Formula for Integration**

| (1) Social Security Amendments | (2) Integration Ruling | (3) Maximum Primary Benefit as percent of Maximum Wage | (4) 150 percent of (3) | (5) Percent of Social Security Benefits Attributed to Employee Contributions | (6) Integration Limit |
|---|---|---|---|---|---|
| 1939 ...... | Mim. 5539 (July 1943) | $\dfrac{40(1+.01n)}{250}$ $= 16\%(1+01n)$ ($n =$ years under S.S.) | 24%+0.24% per year after 1937 | None | 25% + ¼% times years after 1941 |
| 1950 ...... | Mim. 6641 (1951) | $\dfrac{80}{300} = 26\ 2/3\%$ | 40.0% | 6.25% | 37.5% |
| 1952 ...... | R.R. 13 (1953) | $\dfrac{85}{300} = 28\ 1/3$ | 42.5 | 12.50 | 37.5 |
| 1954 ...... | R.R. 56–692 (1956) | $\dfrac{108.50}{350} = 31.0$ | 46.5 | 20.00 | 37.5 |
| 1958 ...... | R.R. 61–75 (1961) | $\dfrac{126.80}{400} = 31.7$ | 47.55 | 22.00 | 37.5 |

The effect of applying Mimeograph 6641 as amended through 1961, and the present regulations, under the social security amendments of 1965 and 1967 is shown below.

| | | | | | |
|---|---|---|---|---|---|
| 1965 ...... | Mim. 6641 and Amend. | $\dfrac{168}{550} = 30.5\%$ | 45.75% | 22.0% | 35.7% |
| 1967 ...... | Mim. 6641 and Amend. | $\dfrac{218}{650} = 33.5$ | 50.25 | 22.0 | 39.2 |

For comparison, the formula used as an illustration in Announcement 66–58, as applied to the Social Security Act as amended in 1965 is shown below.

Announcement 66–58

$$A^* \qquad \dfrac{132.70}{385} = 34.5\%$$

$$B\dagger \qquad \dfrac{168.00}{550} = 30.5\%$$

Av. 32.5%    48.75%    50%    24%

* Based on average maximum monthly wage from 1/1/51 to 12/31/66 (with 5-year drop-out).
† Based on average maximum monthly wage of $550.

6.  Every social security amendment increasing future benefits has also granted increases in benefits to those already receiving them. It may be taken as a practical certainty that this will apply to future amendments as well. Therefore, even if a reasonable and equitable determination could be made of an individual's proportionate contribution to his own social security benefits, such determination is almost certain to be invalidated by social security amendments enacted after his retirement.

appendix

# B

# Report by the Actuarial and Economic Consultants to the 1974 Social Security Advisory Council Subcommittee on Financing

OUR REVIEW of the financing of the social security program was confined to a few key issues, because of the short period that was available.[1] This report summarizes our conclusions regarding those issues which we consider most important; as noted below, it is supplemented by a separate report on "decoupling."

## 1. Method of Financing

The OASDI program is a national program requiring compulsory participation by the vast majority of employees, and presumably will continue to operate during all years in the future. These unique characteristics are the bases for our support of the conclusion that the current-cost method of financing the program provides sufficient assurance that funds will be available to pay benefits as they become due.

Under the current-cost method of financing, the amount of taxes to be collected each year is intended to be approximately equal to the benefits paid during that year.[2] The projected pattern of benefits which will be payable, under present law, results in the need for an increasing

---

[1] In particular, we did very little analysis of the disability and medicare aspects of the program.

[2] There are also other factors—expenses, interest on investments, and the desired increase in the trust funds—which have relatively minor effect.

tax rate over the next 75 years. An increase in the tax rate is already legislated for the year 2011. In fact estimates which we consider reasonable indicate that the tax rates will have to be higher than those now specified in the law.

The purpose of the trust fund under current-cost financing is to reflect all financial transactions and to absorb temporary fluctuations in the relative level of income and expenditures. Thus, whatever "normal" (or target) level is established for the fund, it is to be expected that the fund will vary from that level as it absorbs those fluctuations. There is no definitive basis for establishing such a normal level,[3] and the present level (approximately 70 percent of one year's outgo) is within the range of reasonable values. It is projected that the trust fund will decrease, in relation to outgo, over the next several years. Nevertheless, the trust fund should be adequate to fulfill its function, and any action to increase its level (relative to outgo) can be implemented over an extended period of time.

The requirements for future increases in the tax rate, and the relatively small size of the trust fund, do not conflict with the conclusion that the current-cost method of financing is actuarially sound for this social insurance program. Accumulation of a substantially larger trust fund, by raising taxes now, would not increase the actuarial adequacy of the program; however (as noted in Section 4 below) the economic and social consequences of alternative tax schedules, and resulting trust fund levels, are not fully understood and should be investigated further.

There has been a substantial number of articles in the public press which reflect the erroneous conclusion that the financing of the program is inadequate because there are not large (e.g., on the order of $2 trillion) reserve funds. That conclusion is based on lack of recognition of the unique characteristics of this program; instead, the attempt is made to apply standards that are appropriate for an insurance company, private pension plan, or other arrangement that cannot anticipate indefinite continuation of its operations. In that type of operation, the liabilities that have accrued should, as an ultimate goal, be offset by investments; thus there is reliance on future income, and repayment of principal, that is expected from those investments. It should be particularly noted that U.S. Government Bonds, and hence reliance upon the future taxing power of the government, are generally considered the most secure form of invest-

---

[3] However, one of the consultants strongly believes that it should equal one year's benefits plus administrative expenses.

ment with respect to assurance of timely payment of interest and principal.

Financing of the social security program relies directly upon the future
taxing power of the United States. The substitution of U.S. Government
Bonds (or any other investment) would create a formal contractual obligation to provide that future income, but there is no reason to believe that
under the current procedure, based on congressional intent, there is any
less assurance that funds will be available to pay future benefits.

## 2.  Variability of Benefits and Costs

Under current law, benefits that will be provided to future retirees are
related, in a complicated way, to increases in the Consumer Price Index
(CPI) and to earnings. Thus two important relations are quite sensitive
to the rate of change in the CPI, as well as to the rate of change in
earnings levels. These relationships are:

a.   An individual payee's "replacement ratio," which is his initial benefit
     level divided by his immediately preceding earnings level.
b.   The aggregate benefit payments for any year as compared with that
     year's taxable payroll; this is the approximate tax rate appropriate for
     that year under the current-cost method of financing.

We have submitted a separate report describing a proposal to "decouple" initial benefit determinations from changes that have occurred in
the CPI.[4] Such initial benefit determinations would depend only on
changes that have occurred in earnings levels.

The primary result of this decoupling is to make the system much less
sensitive to changes in economic conditions. For all practical purposes,
replacement ratios would become independent of the level of changes in
earnings or CPI, and the tax rate appropriate for each year would be less
affected by changes in earnings or CPI than under present law. A secondary result is that, using the assumptions of the 1974 Trustees Report, there
is a decrease in the estimated long-range deficits (as indicated in Section
3, below).

## 3.  Assumptions and Estimates

We gave extensive consideration to the conclusion, in the 1974 Trustees Report for the OASDI program, that there is an "actuarial deficit";

---

[4] CPI changes would continue to affect the adjustments of benefits after they have commenced.

that is, that future benefits will require more funds than will be produced by the tax schedule in the law.

Of course, when projections are made for 75 years into the future, and involve political, social, and economic forces—as well as natural forces such as mortality and fertility—it is not unlikely that actual experience may depart significantly from the assumed results. Nevertheless, we find the trustees' conclusion is a reasonable indicator of future experience, subject to the following comments:

a.  The actuarial deficit will be significantly affected by future changes in the CPI, as well as by the difference between those changes and changes in earnings levels. It is very difficult to predict these effects, and our concurrence with the Trustees' assumptions[5] is not unanimous. As noted in Section 2 above, we recommend that the program be "decoupled" in order to be less sensitive to those effects.

b.  Future fertility rates will have substantial effect on the program, and there is no reliable basis for predicting them. While a return to the replacement rate of 2.1 for total fertility seems reasonable (the present rate is less than that), two consultants expressed doubts about such an increase. In any event, there is a need to closely monitor fertility trends.

c.  While it seems reasonably certain that future benefits will require more financing than will be produced by the tax schedule in present law,[6] it is important to recognize the yearly pattern of this "actuarial deficit." The situation is not adequately indicated by a single figure, such as the 2.98 percent "average" deficit for OASDI, even though the latter is a convenient description of the results. For example, data shown below at 15-year intervals provide significant additional information. In addition to showing the expected actuarial deficits for OASDI under current law, as estimated in the 1974 Trustees Report, there is also shown below an indication of the deficit if the program is decoupled as we suggest.[7]

While these figures do not clearly indicate all the annual variations estimated to occur over the next 75 years, they do give a much more useful

---

[5] The long-range assumptions are: 3 percent annual increase in CPI and 5 percent annual increase in earnings, so that the annual difference between CPI and earnings changes equals 2 percent.

[6] This is likely to be true, even if the decoupling proposal referred to above is adopted.

[7] Decoupling can be achieved in various ways, and the precise form selected will determine the costs, but the figures give an indication of the probable result. One consultant believes that the deficit could be even further reduced by a satisfactory, but somewhat more complex, alternative decoupling formula.

**Estimated Deficit, as Percentage of Taxable Payroll**

| Year | Current Law | Decoupled |
|------|-------------|-----------|
| 1985 | 0.54% | 0.7% |
| 2000 | 1.41 | 1.5 |
| 2015 | 2.24 | 1.4 |
| 2030 | 5.70 | 3.9 |
| 2045 | 5.96 | 3.6 |
| Average | 2.98 | 2.1 |

indication of future results than is provided by the average annual deficit. Note that the 1974 Trustees Report shows current-cost estimates at five-year intervals (e.g., Table 22), but does not explicitly compare them with the tax rates in the law. Thus the incidence of future deficits (or surpluses) is not evident. It would be helpful if such a comparison were explicitly set forth in future trustee reports.

Based on the figures shown for the decoupled program, a deficit will occur within the next few years, but it does not exceed 1 percent of payroll until almost 1995; projections over this short-term period are fairly reliable. The longer-term projections show substantially higher deficits (about 3.5 percent of payroll), but are also less reliable; actual deficits could be significantly more or less.

### 4. Wider Implications

The most significant aspect of the social security cost projections is that they require an estimate to be made of certain conditions which will exist in the middle of the next century. Assumptions which we consider to be reasonable produce results so different from the current situation that attention should be directed toward the overall implications of those results, rather than toward their effect on the single issue of OASDI financing.

One of these assumptions is the future composition of the U.S. population. Aside from the difficulties inherent in projecting birth rates, it is probably more important to recognize that, if the population composition changes in accordance with these estimates, there are likely to be substantial effects on many of our social and economic arrangements. The 1972 Report of the Commission on Population Growth and the American Future dealt with many of these issues, but it limited its study to the period up to the year 2000; during that period OASDI financing is in fairly good balance. In order to put the issue of OASDI financing (and thus—of necessity—the issue of benefit levels, eligibility requirements, and so on) in proper perspective, it would be desirable to extend to the year 2050 the analysis of possible effects throughout our society of anticipated population changes.

Similarly, future changes in earnings rates and CPI can have substantial effects on OASDI (although, as noted, these would cause less problems if the program is decoupled). If (as some authorities have suggested) the annual increase in "real" earnings rates is less than the assumed 2 percent, the program, as defined by present law, would get substantially out of balance. However, it is likely that such a change in growth of real earnings (and presumably of productivity) would have substantial ramifications throughout our economic and social structure.

In any event, the OASDI program has become a major source of financing retirement, and it has effects on private pensions and individual savings. The implications of this on the nation's capital stock and the entire economy need further study and consideration.

Therefore, in the broader perspective of probable future developments, study should be given to questions such as: Will projected OASDI benefit payments become unduly burdensome on our economy? Will payrolls continue to be an acceptable basis for allocating the required taxes? Will the current-cost method of financing continue to be consistent with other economic and social goals?

## DECOUPLING OF OASDI SYSTEM

Your consultants suggest to the subcommittee, and hence to the entire Advisory Council, that the council recommend the gradual phasing out of the "coupled" OASDI system now established by law, and the phasing in of a "decoupled" system, the outlines of which are the subject of this memo.

### Rationale

We recognize that the rationale behind this suggestion is not immediately apparent. We do not claim that a decoupled system is per se superior to a coupled one. The case for the decoupled approach has been made in discussions we have had with the subcommittee, but will be summarized here.

The goal of the decoupling suggestion is to improve the stability of the OASDI system under conditions of price and wage inflation.

The current system has provisions by which benefits in course of payment are adjusted to reflect increases in prices, as measured by the Consumer Price Index. The decoupling proposal would not change this feature.

Under the present system, potential benefits for those still at work are "coupled" with benefits for those already beneficiaries, and hence also reflect consumer price increases. Since the benefits of the OASDI system are wage-related, potential benefits also reflect increases in wages, but only in part. Certain technicalities prevent the full recognition of wage increases.

The difficulty that decoupling is intended to cure is that potential benefits do not increase directly with average wages (as one would expect in a wage-related system), but instead increase in a complicated way, mixing consumer price increases with a portion (something less than half) of wage increases. This mixed rate will be always greater than the CPI increase, but it may be *either* greater or less than the average wage increase. The important replacement ratio (the percentage that the old-age, survivor, or disability income bears to the worker's wages just prior to becoming a beneficiary) is therefore unstable. It rises when the gain in real wages is small, falls when it is large. This instability not only thwarts good pension design, but makes future cost estimates depend heavily upon price and wage increase rates, over which the system can exercise no effective control.

A decoupled system can be designed to correct this instability, without negative effect on other aspects of the system. Potential benefits for those still working would fully reflect increase in average wages, but would be made independent of CPI changes. Replacement ratios, wherever they may be set initially, are therefore preserved, since potential benefits and wages increase together.

## Cost Effects

If the gain in real wages happens to follow the 2 percent assumption chosen by the Social Security Administration for long range cost estimate purposes, then replacement ratios will tend to rise—not so much in the near future, but after 20 years or so. Increasing replacement ratios are responsible for a part of the deficit shown in the most recent trustees report. The adoption of a decoupling proposal would therefore be helpful in reducing the deficit.

It is important to realize, however, that a decoupling proposal is *not necessarily* a cost-reducing one. If gains in real wages were to average 3 percent annually, replacement ratios under the coupled system would slowly fall. Under these circumstances a decoupled system would prevent replacement ratio deterioration, and hence be more costly than the present coupled system.

Your consultants recommend the decoupled system because of its ·improved stability under forces of inflation, not because it appears to reduce the actuarial deficit. The fact that decoupling would improve the actuarial balance (under assumptions which the consultants find reasonable) also commends it to us—but we would recommend it even if we thought that the effect would be in the opposite direction.

### The Average Indexed Monthly Wage

As a first step toward achieving our objectives, we suggest that benefits be based on an "average indexed monthly wage" (AIMW).

We propose no change in the averaging periods, in the rules about dropout years, or any other feature of the Average Monthly Wage (AMW) calculation, except that an indexing system will be applied to change the AMW to an AIMW (average indexed monthly wage).

The wage record of any past year is indexed by multiplying it by the ratio that average wages of the most recent calendar year bear to the average wages of the year being indexed. For this purpose, average wages for a calendar year are determined by the same method as is currently used for adjustment of the taxable earnings base and the exempt amounts under the retirement test.

In effect each year's wage record is being adjusted to current wage levels. Under conditions of continuously rising wage levels, the AIMW will always be higher than the AMW, with the difference depending upon how recent the record is. When the averaging period is long (as it is in retirement situations) the AIMW will be substantially greater than the AMW—but for short and recent wage records (as in young-age death or disability situations) the AIMW will only be slightly larger than the presently defined AMW.

The AIMW maintains for all past years the relative earnings of a worker in relation to the average earnings of all workers. The AMW does not do so, because it depends heavily on how many of the most recent years, and how few of much earlier years, are included in the average. The consultants therefore consider the AIMW superior to the AMW in achieving equity between generations of workers.

**The Primary Insurance Amount**

We suggest that the primary insurance amount (PIA) on which all OASDI benefits are based be calculated by a simple two-term formula of the following form:

$$\text{PIA} = \$A + B\% \text{ of AIMW}$$

The $A would rise as average wages rise (in accordance with the same average wage index as used in calculation of the AIMW, which is also the index used under present law in adjusting the taxable earnings base). The B% would remain level, but the AIMW would change each year with the average wage index. The PIA itself would therefore go up as fast as wages, and replacement ratios could be expected to remain constant over time.

The setting of the $A and B% would determine replacement ratios under the new system. Unless there are good reasons to set replacement ratios either higher or lower than they are today, A and B would be set to reproduce, as closely as possible, the PIAs of those becoming beneficiaries in year $y$ under the coupled system, where $y$ is the effective year of change to the decoupled system. The fit can be quite close for all levels of income, though obviously few beneficiaries will be fit exactly, many having slightly greater benefits in year $y$ than formerly, but some having smaller new-formula benefits. The new-formula benefits are likely to be the smaller when the AMW and the AIMW are close together, as when workers die or become disabled at the younger ages.

The illustration at the end of this appendix is intended to demonstrate that PIAs for those becoming beneficiaries in 1975 under the old system can be fit rather closely by the procedure suggested. For this illustration $A = \$85$ and $B = 28\%$. If the change were delayed to 1976 or later some modification of the value of A and/or B would be needed to produce a satisfactory fit.

**The Phasing-in Process**

The consultants have no intention of reducing benefits when the new formula produces a lower result than the old one. It is clearly important that the new beneficiary of year $y$ actually receive the greater of the new-formula PIA and the old-system PIA. For those becoming beneficiaries after year $y$ the same comparison is to be made, and the greater benefit granted; with the understanding, however, that the old-system benefit table will not be updated for CPI changes after year $y$. As time goes on, the new-formula result (dynamic with average wages) will be greater than the PIA from the old system (static at the year $y$ level) for a larger and larger percentage of the new beneficiaries, and the old system will be slowly phased out. The young-age death and disability cases will likely be the last to be payable on the new formula.

**The Transition Problem at Retirement**

There is an important technical advantage in the present coupled system in that problems of consistency between potential and actual benefits are neatly avoided. The PIA is essentially independent of the worker's choice as to when he retires, and the worker who retires in any month gets the same benefit as the otherwise similar worker who retires one month later.

Under the decoupled system potential benefits are increasing with average wages, while benefits after retirement are increasing with the CPI. Details of the timing of the CPI increases, of the timing of increases in the $A, and of the exact time period to which wage records are indexed must all be worked out to avoid inequities and to minimize incentives either to hasten or to postpone retirement.

The consultants are developing a set of procedures to best solve this technical problem. They have considered this matter in sufficient depth to conclude that a satisfactory solution exists. Recommendations as to the details will be furnished when needed.

**Side Effects**

Although decoupling is proposed to improve the stability of the re-placement ratios, and hence to avoid their drift either upward or down-ward as prices and wages change in relation to each other, the proposal will have effects on certain other internal relationships. The consultants consider these effects as improving the general level of equity between various members of the system; but others might have different views. The most important of these side effects are the following:

1. The present system provides higher replacement ratios in young-age death and disability situations than for workers who work to retire-ment, or who die or become disabled later in their careers. This feature of the present law was not intended, and has been the target

of considerable criticism, particularly since the young worker has contributed to the system for such a short period of time.

The wage indexing feature of the new system makes unimportant the differences in how recent the wage record may be; and in effect equalizes the replacement ratios between young and old. The young-age advantage persists for quite some period of time since it phases out very slowly; but it will eventually disappear.[8]

2.  The present system treats very differently the worker covered under the system for only a portion of his career, depending on whether the covered years were at the young adult ages or at ages close to retirement. The worker retiring today with ten years of covered service ending 30 years ago has a much smaller AMW, and hence a smaller PIA, than the otherwise similar worker who was in covered employment in the ten years just ended.

The wage indexing feature of the new system removes these differences, by bringing benefits for early-career workers (quite often women who worked prior to marriage) up to the level of short-service-in-late-career workers.

3.  It is our understanding that the council has voted to recommend that the $93.80 minimum PIA not be increased, even though other benefits go up with the CPI. Such an effect would take place automatically under this proposal, as soon as the new system became effective, because the old-system benefit table (which carries the minimum PIA) would then become static. It should be pointed out, however, that the $A in the proposed PIA formula becomes a new form of a minimum PIA, gradually replacing the old. Moreover, the $A is indexed to average wages, and will rise over time. Windfall benefits for those with very short covered service can not be eliminated by the decoupling procedure, unless the $A is somehow reduced for short covered service. The lengthening of the required quarters of coverage for the fully insured status will be of some help in this regard.

### Simplification

The replacement of the AMW by the AIMW perhaps leads to some element of complication in an already extremely complicated system. That the wage indexing principle is already employed in the adjustment

---

[8] Two of the consultants suggest that there are arguments for higher replacement ratios in death or disability situations, and recommend that such ratios be determined separately, rather than using the formula applicable to old-age benefits.

of the taxable earnings base (and the exempt amounts under the retirement test) makes the public understanding easier.

The replacement of the extremely complicated formula underlying the benefit table used in the current system by the very simple two-term PIA formula proposed is an important step toward ease of explanation. The important replacement ratio, for example, is $B + A/AIMW$, essentially independent of everything except where the worker has been, relative to others, in the wage distribution.

## Conclusion

The consultants recommend the decoupled approach here outlined without reservation. We recognize that this proposal is not completely worked out in all detail, and that its structure is somewhat foreign to that of the extremely complicated system we live with today. We trust that the council can look beyond the form and to the substance of these proposals. We believe it will find them sound.

**Illustration of fit—1975 as year when new system is first effective (for persons with earnings history of same steepness as average wage\*)**

Male Worker Retiring at Age 65 in 1975†

| Final (1974) | Old System | | Proposed Formula | |
|---|---|---|---|---|
| Pay | AMW | PIA | AIMW | PIA‡ |
| $200 | $127 | $139 | $200 | $141 |
| 400 | 254 | 196 | 400 | 197 |
| 600 | 381 | 251 | 600 | 253 |
| 800 | 508 | 303 | 800 | 309 |
| 1,100§ | 542 | 316 | 837 | 319 |

Worker Born in 1939—Dying or Becoming Disabled in 1975"

| | | | | |
|---|---|---|---|---|
| $200 | $153 | $151 | $200 | $141 |
| 400 | 306 | 218 | 400 | 197 |
| 600 | 459 | 282 | 600 | 253 |
| 800 | 612 | 349 | 800 | 309 |
| 1,100§ | 685 | 376 | 883 | 332 |

\* Where earnings history is steeper than average wages, PIA under the old system is more likely to be the larger. Where earnings history is flatter than average wages, proposed formula is more likely to produce greater PIA.

† For females reaching age 65 in 1975, the old system produces slightly higher results than males, because of shorter averaging period. The proposed formula treats males and females alike, because wage indexing makes the difference in averaging period unimportant. The averaging period is pulled together, in either system, for age 65 retirements in 1978 or later.

‡ PIA formula $85 + 28% of AIMW. A slightly modified formula would be required if first effective date of new system was to be 1976 or later.

§ Maximum taxable earnings case. AMW, AIMW, and PIA all reflect history of taxable earnings base—rather than earnings history of worker.

" Lower result under the proposed formula is less noticeable for those born before 1939—more so for those born later.

**ACTUARIAL AND ECONOMIC CONSULTANTS TO THE 1974 SOCIAL SECURITY ADVISORY COUNCIL**

**Phillip Cagan**—Professor of Economics, Columbia University; and Senior Staff Member, National Bureau of Economic Research.

**Martin Feldstein**—Professor of Economics, Harvard University.

**Robert J. Myers**—Professor of Actuarial Science, Temple University; former Chief Actuary, Social Security Administration.

**Charles E. Trowbridge**—Senior Vice President and Chief Actuary, The Bankers Life; former Chief Actuary, Social Security Administration.

**Howard Young**—Consulting Actuary; Special Consultant to the President, International Union, UAW.

appendix
# C

# Report of the Subcommittee on the Treatment of Men and Women under Social Security (with Respect to Sex and Marital Status), 1974 Advisory Council on Social Security

## INTRODUCTION

The Subcommittee on the Treatment of Men and Women under social security (with respect to sex and marital status) was appointed by the chairman of the Advisory Council on Social Security, W. Allen Wallis, during the council's first meeting, on May 3, 1974, to consider differences in social security benefits and costs that are related to sex and marital status.

The members of the subcommittee are Edward J. Cleary, Secretary-Treasurer, Building and Construction Trades Council of Greater New York, AFL-CIO; John J. Scanlon, Executive Vice President and Chief Financial Officer (Retired), American Telephone and Telegraph Company; and Rita Ricardo Campbell, Senior Fellow, Hoover Institution, Stanford University, subcommittee chairman. During its deliberations the subcommittee had the benefit of the capable assistance of Mr. Scanlon's associate, Therese F. Pick, Personnel Director-Employee Benefits, American Telephone and Telegraph Company.

The first meeting of the subcommittee was held in Baltimore on May 24. Subsequent meetings were held in Washington, D.C., on June 30, in Chicago on August 4, and in Washington on September 21, November 3, and December 7 and 8, 1974, and January 18, 1975. All subcommittee meetings were open to the public and notices of the meetings were published in the *Federal Register.*

The subcommittee appreciates the competent and efficient technical advice and assistance it received from the staff of the Social Security Administration in carrying out its work. James E. Crum of the Social Security Administration's Office of Program Evaluation and Planning served as executive secretary of the subcommittee.

## SCOPE OF STUDY

During its deliberations the subcommittee considered the following matters:

1. Social security provisions of the law that are different for men and women, including:
    a. Different dependency requirements for spouses' and surviving spouses' benefits for men and women;
    b. Provisions for a secondary benefit for categories of women (aged divorced wife or aged or disabled divorced widow, and mother with entitled child in her care) and not for the comparable categories of men.
    c. Differences in computation of benefit eligibility and benefit amounts based on a man's earnings, as compared with a woman's, for those men who reached age 62 (or died after reaching age 62) during 1954–74. (There are no differences for workers reaching age 62 after 1974.)
2. Inequities in benefits as related to taxes paid that exist between single workers and married workers.
3. Inequities in benefits as related to taxes paid by married women who work and married women who do not work and/or have not worked in covered employment.
4. The treatment under social security of married persons who do not work outside the home, and the pros and cons of permitting them to receive benefits on the basis of "imputed income" for work done in and around the home for which they are not paid wages.
5. The different effects of social security provisions that are the same for working men and working women who are permanently attached to the labor force but, because of the nature of the traditional jobs

held by women and/or the typical life cycle of work among women, affect women differently than men—for example, the special minimum benefit.

It was early agreed that the complex issues to be considered by the subcommittee in respect to treatment of men and women, married and single, under social security are intertwined and interdependent. It was also recognized that any package of recommendations might prove costly. The subcommittee, therefore, agreed that all decisions reached during the course of its deliberations would be tentative decisions until finally approved for submission to the council. Thus tentative decisions reached during the course of the subcommittee's deliberations were subject to continuing review and revision throughout its deliberations.

## Socioeconomic Changes

The subcommittee discussed in considerable depth the socioeconomic changes that have taken place since the enactment of the original Social Security Act, in 1935, which provided only a primary benefit upon retirement for a worker based on cumulative earnings and, for survivors, a lump-sum benefit less any benefits received by the worker. In 1939, the act was amended to add secondary benefits for dependents—wives, widows, and children—of workers. The 1939 amendments changed the system from one of taxes and benefits each on an individual worker basis to one with taxes on an individual basis and benefits on a family basis and assumed in general that married women as well as children were dependent on the male head of the household.

Among the socioeconomic changes discussed and documented were the following:

A trend away from early marriages started some 15 years ago, and a concomitant, almost continuous decline in birth rates from 23.7 births per 1,000 population in 1960, to 18.2 in 1970 and to only 14.8 for the 12 months ending September 1974.[1] Although birth rates per 1,000 population were also low in 1930, 21.3, and in 1940, 19.4, they were still higher than currently. Moreover, since then today's newer methods of birth control, changes in social values, and recent great improvement in the infant mortality rate (at 17.1 per 1,000 live births for January–June

---

[1] U.S. Department of Health, Education, and Welfare, Public Health Service; 1960: *Vital Statistics of the United States 1960*, vol. 1-sect. 1, p. 1–1; 1970 and 1974: *Monthly Vital Statistics Report*, vol. 19, no. 13, p. 1, and vol. 23, no. 9, p. 1.

1974, as compared to 26.0 per 1,000 in 1960, for example), all point to a probable continuation of a relatively low level of number of births.

Data from the annual survey of the work experience of the population 16 years old and older conducted in March 1974 by the Bureau of the Census for the Bureau of Labor Statistics show that in 1973, 54 percent of all women had worked at some time during the year, over two-thirds of them at full-time jobs. Among the regular part-time women workers, a group which has been increasing steadily over the past few years, 6 million worked 40 or more weeks during 1973 while 7 million worked less than this amount.[2] Today in all industrialized societies, the greater the percentage of women working, the lower the birth rate.

Smaller families have reduced the demands on women or on other family members to perform domestic duties within the home. In addition, especially in the United States, the increasing level and use of technology in the home—automatic washing machines and dryers, self-defrosting refrigerators, permanent-press clothing, readily available partially pre-pared foods, and their purchase as the family income rises when more than one person in the family works—have also greatly reduced the domestic workload of married women, with or without children. Con-comitantly, the service sector of the economy has greatly expanded, offer-ing the types of jobs which women have traditionally filled. Labor force data, which pick up fewer occasional or intermittent workers, show that while in 1920, 23 percent of all women 14 years and over were in the labor force, and only 25 percent in 1940, just a few years after the passage of the Act and one year after its important 1939 amendments, the propor-tion has increased to 34 percent of women 16 years and over in 1950, 38 percent in 1960, 43 percent in 1970, and 45 percent in 1973.[3]

Since the initiation of the Social Security Act, there has been a revolu-tion in the structure of the family. Married couples with only the husband working no longer comprise the majority of families. In March 1974 there were 36.4 million husband and wife families in which the husband was age 25 to 64. Of these 36.4 million families, 18.5 million, or 51 percent, were families in which both the busband and the wife worked in 1973.[4] There also has been a great increase in numbers of nonmarried individuals who are the heads of families, including women (divorced, separated,

---

[2] U.S. Department of Labor, Bureau of Labor Statistics, *Summary, Special Labor Force Report,* "Work Experience of the Population in 1973," September 1974, p. 3.

[3] 1920 through 1970, *Economic Report of the President,* January 1973, Table 21, p. 91; 1973, U.S. Department of Labor, Bureau of Labor Statistics, *Special Labor Force Report 163,* 1974, p. A–6.

[4] U.S. Department of Commerce, Bureau of the Census, *Current Population Reports,* series P–60, no. 97, computed from the table on p. 155.

deserted, or widowed) who often are in the lowest-paying occupations.

In March 1973, 15.4 million women were heads of households; 23 percent of all the households in the United States were headed by women. Of these women, 4.3 million had children under 18 years of age and 2.8 million had relatives other than husband or child living with them ("husband" if present would be the "head of household" in census data) and 8.2 million women lived alone.[5]

Another indication of the changing family structure is the increasing divorce rate; by 1970, 10 percent of all males and 12 percent of all females over 14 years of age had been divorced at least once. Increasingly, one-parent family units occur for a reason other than the death of the husband or wife.

Although the subcommittee has not ventured to estimate the anticipated future trends of these socioeconomic changes, it recognizes that the social security system was not designed to handle such drastic family restructuring. A major concept on which the system as amended through the years is based is that it is in society's interest to replace earnings lost by retirement, disability, or death.

About 83 percent of wives who became entitled to a primary benefit in the last half of 1969 based on their own earnings and whose husbands were age 65 or over or were receiving retirement benefits did not receive any supplemental benefit. This percentage is expected to increase. By 1970, 68 percent of women 45–49 years of age already had enough quarters of covered work to be insured for their own primary benefit.[6] Labor force data indicate that this percentage is also increasing. At the end of 1974, about 2.6 million aged wives of retired workers on the benefit rolls—about 58 percent of all such wives on the benefit rolls—were receiving only a secondary benefit. It is expected that this percentage will decline gradually over the next 45 years or so, to between 30 and 35 percent in 2020 and thereafter, as the current beneficiaries become widows or die and a larger percentage of newly entitled wives qualify for their own primary benefit.

That an increasing proportion of aged wives of retired workers receives either a primary benefit or a primary plus some part of a secondary benefit indicates the effect of women's increasing participation in the labor force on the social security system. Currently about 1.9 million aged wives of

[5] U.S. Department of Commerce, Bureau of the Census, *Current Population Reports*, series P–20, no. 258, p. 86.

[6] U.S. Department of Health, Education, and Welfare, Social Security Administration, Office of Research and Statistics, *Preliminary Findings from the Survey of New Beneficiaries*, Report No. 9, "Women Newly Entitled to Retired-Worker Benefits," by Virginia Reno, April 1973, pp. 4–5.

retired workers on the benefit rolls—about 42 percent of all such wives now on the rolls—are getting primary benefits based on their own earnings.

As noted, the OASDI tax is on an individual's earnings and in the case of a married worker the benefits to replace earnings may include an additional amount on the basis of presumed need of other members of the family. The present provisions for spouse's and surviving spouse's benefits for a nonworking spouse mean that two-earner families may be treated disadvantageously as compared with one-earner families, although two-earner families are in the majority and have geared their style of living to the earnings of two people.

If the earnings of one of the two earners in a family are not high enough to result in a benefit equal to 50 percent of the other earner's benefit, the family will get no more in benefits than they would have gotten had the lower paid of the two not worked and paid social security taxes. Similarly, when the higher paid worker dies, the surviving spouse may get no more in benefits than he or she would have gotten without having worked and paid taxes.

The concept of replacement of earnings of both family workers should be considered as compared to that of the current law, which in some cases (1) provides no more in benefits to two-worker (husband and wife) families than the amount of benefits based only on the earnings of the higher paid family worker plus secondary benefits based on this worker's earnings, and (2) permits the anomaly that a one-earner family may receive greater social security benefits (primary and secondary) than a two-earner family of equal size earning the same amount and paying the same OASDI taxes. It is the two-worker, husband and wife, family with relatively lower wages who fall within this inequitable category. For example, assume that a husband has average annual earnings under social security of $4,000, and his wife has average annual earnings under social security of $4,000, and they both reach age 65 and retire in early 1975. The monthly retirement benefit payable to the man is $228.50, and the monthly benefit payable to his wife is $228.50, for a total monthly retirement benefit for this couple of $457.00. If only one worker in a family had earned the sum of the above couple's earnings, and had average annual earnings of $8,000, the monthly primary benefit payable to that worker upon retirement at age 65 in 1975 would be $316.30, and one-half of that primary for the nonworking spouse would be $158.15, rounded to $158.20 under the social security law, totaling $474.50 a month for this couple. Thus, the benefits for the one-worker family would amount to $210.00 more for a year than the benefits for the two-worker family.

For another example, assume that in each year since the social security program began a husband earned 60 percent of the maximum taxable base in effect in the year, and his wife 40 percent of the base, and they both reach age 65 and retire in early 1975. The monthly retirement benefit payable to the man is $226.50, and the monthly benefit payable to his wife is $179.60, for a total monthly retirement benefit for this couple of $406.10. If over the same period of time only one worker in a family had earned the sum of the above couple's earnings or the maximum taxable base in effect in each year, the monthly primary benefit payable to that worker upon retirement at age 65 in 1975 would be $316.30, and one-half of that primary for the nonworking spouse would be $158.15, rounded to $158.20 under the social security law, totaling $474.50 a month for this couple. Thus, the benefits for the one-worker family would amount to $820.80 more for a year than the benefits for the two-worker family.

Some increasing participation of women in the labor force was anticipated in part of the arguments used to support provision of secondary benefits in 1939. The Committee on Ways and Means of the House of Representatives, and the Committee on Finance of the Senate, stated in their reports on the 1939 amendments:

> Because more wives, in the long run, will build up wage credits on their own account, as a result of their own employment, these supplementary allowances will add but little to the ultimate cost of the system.[7]

These predictions were made many years before additional amendments were passed which liberalized secondary benefits as, for example, by providing the surviving aged widow with 100 percent of her husband's primary benefit. The secondary benefits being paid at the end of 1974 to the 2.6 million retired workers' aged wives who were getting only a secondary benefit were being paid at an annual rate of about $3.2 billion, and to the 3.8 million aged or disabled widows getting only a secondary benefit at an annual rate of about $8.0 billion.

### Other Recent Changes

The subcommittee also reviewed recent legislation which might affect its recommendations, as for example the income tax law revision of 1969, which, over a wide range of income brackets, gives a working man and

---

[7] U.S. Congress, House of Representatives, Committee on Ways and Means, *Social Security Act Amendments of 1939*, 76th Congress, 1st Session, 1939, House Report No. 728 to accompany H.R. 6635, p. 11; and U.S. Congress, Senate, Committee on Finance, *Social Security Act Amendments of 1939*, 76th Congress, 1st Session, 1939, Senate Report No. 734 to accompany H.R. 6635, p. 11.

woman who earn similar amounts an economic incentive to remain single
or become divorced even though they might otherwise marry or remain
married.[8]

In addition, the subcommittee also took into consideration the new
program of supplemental security income, which began in January 1974
and sets a minimum floor of income, financed from general revenues, for
needy aged, blind, and disabled people, of $140 monthly for an individual
and $210 monthly for husband and wife, increased to $146 and $219,
respectively, as of July 1974.

### Recent Court Cases and the Proposed Equal Rights Amendment to the Constitution

The subcommittee reviewed several court cases where discrimination
by sex under the Social Security Act is an issue and additionally an 8-to-1
Supreme Court decision which held in violation of the due process clause
of the Fifth Amendment a federal statute which provided, solely for
administrative convenience, that spouses of male members of the uni-
formed services are dependents for purposes of obtaining increased quarters allowances and medical and dental benefits but that spouses of female
members are not dependents unless they are in fact dependent for over
one-half of their support. [*Frontiero* v. *Richardson,* 411 U.S. 677 (1973)].
Only four members of the Court agreed that different treatment by sex
was "inherently suspect." Three of the other four justices who voted, on
other grounds, that the law was discriminatory, indicated that they did
not want to "preempt by judicial action a mjaor political decision" pending before the states—that is, the proposed Equal Rights Amendment.
The Court found that classification and different treatment *"solely* for
the purpose of achieving administrative convenience . . . involves . . .
arbitrary legislative choice forbidden by the" Constitution. The Supreme
Court noted that "there is substantial evidence that, if put to the test,
many of the wives of male members would fail to qualify for benefits,"
and further that "The Constitution recognizes higher values than speed
and efficiency."

District court cases were also discussed which are concerned with the
differences in the social security law with respect to secondary benefits
for males as compared with females based on their spouse's primary

---

[8] See George Cooper, "Working Wives and the Tax Law," in *Rutgers Law Review,* Fall 1970,
pp. 67ff.

benefit under OASDI. On example is the U.S. District Court of New Jersey's Order of January 28, 1974 (Civil Action No. 268–73) in favor of Stephen Wiesenfeld [367 F. Supp. 981 (1973)], which held that section 202(g) of the Social Security Act unconstitutionally discriminates between men and women in that it provides mother's benefits for certain widows and surviving divorced mothers of deceased male wage earners, but does not provide "father's" benefits for similarly situated men. (The plaintiff's motion for the matter to proceed as a class action was denied.) The decision was appealed to the Supreme Court, June 18, 1974, and the Court has agreed to hear the case.

A recent Florida Supreme Court decision (273 So.2d 72; argued February 25, 26, 1974), which has been upheld by the Supreme Court, April 24, 1974, declares constitutional a Florida law which denies a widower an annual $500 property tax exemption which is available to widows in Florida. The court said the challenged state tax law was "reasonably designed to further the state policy of cushioning the financial impact of spousal loss upon the sex for whom that loss imposes a disproportionately heavy burden." [Kahn v. Shevin, 94 S.Ct. 1734, p. 1735 (1974).] Two justices dissented, stating in part that "While doubtless some widowers are in financial need, no one suggests that such need results from sex discrimination as in the case of widows." (At pp. 1739–1740.) They noted that the state could narrow the class of widow beneficiaries to those widows actually in need and exclude those of "substantial economic means" and suggested that the State of Florida redraft the statute. Additionally, one justice in a separate dissent, elaborated further, "It seems to me that the state in this case is merely conferring an economic benefit in the form of a tax exemption and has not adequately explained why women should be treated differently than men." (At p. 1740.)

In another area of concern re discrimination by sex under social security a 2-to-1 majority opinion of April 19, 1974, by the U.S. District Court, Northern District of Illinois, Eastern Division, dismissed the complaint of the plaintiff, Michael V. Polelle, that social security [42 U.S. Code Sec. 415(b) (3)] discriminates by sex in favor of females as compared to males by its use of additional months up to 36 months or three years as part of the divisor in computation of average monthly earnings for males, but not for females, thus generally providing on identical earnings records lower benefits for a male than a female the same age. The government successfully defended this distinction, which was phased out and does not exist for men who reach age 62 on or after January 1, 1975, on grounds, much simplified, as follows: that actual average earnings of females are so much lower than those of males that the different computation was partially to offset this differential, which is alleged to be at least in part because of sex discrimination prior to the Equal Pay Act and other federal legislation and related, affirmative action programs. This case has not been appealed. As mentioned above, this difference in computation of benefits phased out under existing law as of January 1, 1975, when the method of computing benefits for workers who reach age 62 on or after that date became the same regardless of sex.

The subcommittee has found that the courts are currently being asked in a number of cases to rule on whether various social security provisions of the law that are different for men and women are constitutional under the due process clause of the Fifth Amendment. The Supreme Court has not as yet ruled on the constitutionality of any provision of the social security law that is different for men and women. One case ( *Wiesenfeld* v. *Secretary of Health, Education, and Welfare*) involving this question is currently before the Supreme Court.

Some of the recent Supreme Court decisions in sex discrimination cases *not* involving social security may give an indication of how the court might react when it discusses whether those social security provisions of the law that are different for men and women are constitutional under the due process clause of the Fifth Amendment. However, the issues involved in the nonsocial security cases are complex, and the factual situations and statutes under consideration in them differ in certain important respects from the social security provisions which are the subject of pending litigation. Accordingly, it is impossible to predict with certainty the outcome of the current social security litigation.

If the Supreme Court should find that one of the social security provisions of the law that are different for men and women is unconstitutional under the due process clause of the Fifth Amendment, the constitutionality of the other provisions that are different would be seriously questioned unless the legislative justification for the differing treatment in the remaining provisions is distinguishable from the justification or basis for the provision found to be unconstitutional. Under the due process clause, not *all* discrimination, but only that which is "invidious," has been held to be unconstitutional by the courts. Discrimination would be "invidious" if the statute compelling such treatment did not meet the appropriate constitutional test, that is, the "rational basis" test (whether the legislative classification bears a rational relationship to a legitimate government interest) or the "compelling interest" test (whether there is a countervailing compelling government interest against a finding that a provision is unconstitutional). Such tests look to the legislative justification for the discriminatory treatment in order to determine whether the treatment is constitutional. Thus, in the present state of the law, it is not possible to conclude that every statute which treats one sex more advantageously than the other is unconstitutional.

The fact that 34 states have ratified the proposed Equal Rights Amendment to the Constitution, which, if adopted, would provide that "Equality of rights under the law shall not be denied or abridged by the United States or by any state on account of sex," and only four additional states (six if rescinding of ratification is constitutional) have to ratify the proposed amendment in order to make it the law of the land, has been of paramount interest. If the proposed amendment is ratified by the required number (38) of states, it would on its effective date become the preeminent constitutional authority for sex discrimination issues, and prior Supreme Court opinions based on the due process clause of the Fifth Amendment would almost certainly be reconsidered by the court in its deliberations on cases subsequently before it in light of the Equal Rights Amendment. Adoption of the proposed Equal Rights Amendment would raise serious doubts as to the constitutionality of any provision in the Social Security Act which is different for men and women.

## FINDINGS AND RECOMMENDATIONS

As a result of its deliberations the subcommittee has reached the following conclusions.

### Recommendations Concerning the Social Security Provisions of the Law That Are Different for Men and Women

The subcommittee recommends that, in general, the social security provisions of the law that are different for men and women be made the same for both in the future.

The subcommittee considered various alternative approaches to make the major provisions of the law that are different for men and women the same for both. The subcommittee found that each approach has both advantages and disadvantages and that the selection of one approach over the others involves weighing the advantages and disadvantages of each approach against the others and making a value judgment as to which is the best approach. The subcommittee believes that this decision is one the council as a whole should make. Accordingly, after initially endorsing the first of the options discussed below, the subcommittee upon reconsideration decided to present to the council, without recommendation, the following three options for its consideration.

1.  Eliminate the one-half support requirement in present law for men for entitlement to husband's and widower's benefits. (There is no such requirement in the law for women for entitlement to wife's and widow's benefits.) Provide spouses' (wife's and husband's) and surviving spouses' (widow's and widower's) secondary benefits under social security under the same implied test of dependency in present law for entitlement to secondary benefits by wives—that is, on the basis of "presumed need." If the spouse (or surviving spouse) is not eligible for a primary social security benefit as a worker, or is eligible for one that does not equal or exceed the secondary benefit, the spouse would be "presumed dependent" and eligible for a secondary benefit. The amount of the secondary benefit would be equal to the difference between it and the primary benefit (if any). A person precluded by his or her primary social security benefit from becoming entitled to a spouse's or surviving spouse's benefit under present law would continue to be ineligible for such a benefit.

    Provide benefits for a father who has in his care a child (entitled to child's insurance benefits) of his retired or disabled wife or deceased wife or former wife, and for an aged divorced husband of a worker entitled to old-age or disability insurance benefits, or an aged or disabled divorced widower of a deceased insured worker, on the same basis as benefits are provided for women in like circumstances.

    A major advantage to this approach is that it would be the least complex and easiest to administer. A major disadvantage is that many of the men who would get dependent's or dependent survivor's benefits under this approach that they cannot get under present law would be men who had worked in noncovered employment, such as federal civilian employment and certain state and local employment, and who were not financially dependent on their wives. Another major disadvantage is that this is the most expensive approach. It would increase the long-range cost of the social security cash benefits program by an estimated 0.11 percent of taxable payroll. Immediate universal coverage and, until fully effective, an offset for secondary beneficiaries who work in noncovered employment would help to overcome these disadvantages.

2.  Retain the one-half-support requirement in the present law for men for entitlement to husband's and widower's benefits, and make mandatory the same one-half-support requirement for women, including divorced women, for entitlement to wife's, widow's, or mother's benefits in the future.

    Provide benefits for fathers and for divorced men on the same basis as for women in like circumstances, including on the basis of meeting a one-half-support requirement.

    The major advantages to this approach are that dependent's and dependent survivor's benefits would not be provided for nondependent men, or women, and the long-range cost of the social security cash benefits program would be decreased—not increased—by an estimated 0.17 percent of taxable payroll. However, this approach would increase the administrative complexity of the social security program. Dependent men and women would still be able to get a dependent's or dependent survivor's benefit, but dependent women would have to prove their dependency on the husband in order to get the same benefits they would get under present law without proving dependency.

3.  Gradually phase out all secondary benefits except dependent children's benefits, or, alternatively, phase out all spouses' secondary retirement benefits keeping survivors' benefits. One way to do this might be to reduce gradually over time for new entitlements the proportion of the worker's primary benefit that is provided for dependents. For example, after six years the present 50-percent wife's or husband's benefit might drop to 40 percent, then to 30 percent after another six years, to 20 percent six years later, and so forth, until the secondary retirement benefits are completely eliminated.

    If it were to be recommended now that only spouses' (age 62 or older) secondary benefits should be phased out, at some future time other councils who might have more time to study the broader proposal and its interrelations with the demographic impact of lower birth rates and increasing labor force participation rates of women might recommend that other secondary benefits (except children's) could be reduced in a similar fashion.

    A gradual phasing out of secondary benefits would avoid disadvantaging those coming on the benefit rolls in the next several years who would not have much opportunity to provide a replacement for a benefit they may have been anticipating and planning their retirement around. For those becoming entitled to benefits later, the decrease in the benefits would be greater as the period of time available to them to replace the benefits lengthened.

This approach would eliminate most of the existing differences in treatment of singles and marrieds, for which this subcommittee found no acceptable alternative, and would also eliminate the differences in treatment of the married woman who works and the married woman who does not work.

The approach would also decrease the cost of the social security cash benefits program. The amount of the decrease would depend on how gradual the phaseout was and the length of time over which it was accomplished and whether surviving spouses' benefits were retained or not. The estimated long-range saving from phasing out spouses' (age 62 and over) secondary benefits as described above is 0.39 percent of taxable payroll.

### Recommendation Concerning the Computation of Benefit Eligibility and Benefit Amounts, Which Is Different for Men and Women Born Prior to 1913, but Is the Same for Those Born in 1913 or Later

The Subcommittee does not recommend any change in the computation of benefit eligibility and benefit amounts retroactively or retrospectively with respect to benefits based on the earnings of workers who reach age 62 before January 1, 1975, and whose benefit may reflect a difference by sex in the computation of the benefit. To do so would be very costly, estimated on a retrospective basis at about $1.8 billion a year for the next several years and still as much as about $1.5 billion a year some 10 years from now. (The law is the same for workers reaching age 62 after 1974.)

### Recommendations Concerning Social Security Provisions of the Law That Are the Same for Men and Women

1.  The retirement benefits that are payable under present law to a married working couple can under some circumstances amount to less than the benefits that are payable to a married couple with the same total earnings where only one member of the couple worked.

    In view of this difference under the system with respect to the replacement of individual earnings vis-a-vis family earnings, the subcommittee recommends that a married working couple coming on the benefit rolls in the future with each member of the couple having at least 40 quarters of coverage in the 20 years before entitlement to benefits should have the option of receiving retirement benefits based on the combined earnings of the couple. While the couple's earnings in each year would be combined, no more than the amount of the prevailing tax and benefit base in the year—the maximum amount of a worker's annual earnings that is counted in figuring social security benefits and is subject to social security taxes—could be counted in figuring benefits. Thus the proposal would benefit lower income families, that is, those in which neither worker earns as much as the prevailing tax and benefit base in a year.

Each member of the couple would get a retirement benefit based on a primary insurance amount that was equal to 75 percent of the primary insurance amount resulting from the monthly average of the combined earnings. Together the couple would get benefits based on an amount that was equal to 150 percent of the primary insurance amount resulting from the monthly average of the combined earnings, the same percent that a married couple with the same total earnings in each year would get where only one member of the couple worked.

Each member of a couple would have to have at least 40 quarters of coverage under the social security program in the 20 years before entitlement in order for the couple to elect to receive benefits based on their combined earnings, and both members of the couple would have to elect to receive benefits on this basis or neither of them could. Benefits based on combined earnings would not be payable after a divorce.

A widow or widower who is eligible for a widow's or widower's benefit could get a benefit based on the couple's combined earnings if the couple were receiving benefits based on their combined earnings when one member of the couple died, or if the deceased had 40 quarters of coverage and the survivor had 40 quarters of coverage in the 20 years before entitlement to benefits or the death of the spouse.

All other benefits based on either worker's earnings would be computed on the basis of the worker's individual earnings, as under present law.

2.  To improve the protection afforded under social security to regular but low-paid workers, the majority of whom are women, the subcommittee recommends that the dollar requirement for a year of coverage after 1950 for purposes of computing the special minimum benefit

be reduced from the present one-fourth to one-sixth of the prevailing contribution and benefit base.

## General Recommendation Concerning All Social Security Provisions of the Law

In general, words that do not denote gender should be used in the law wherever it is practical to do so, provided no change in the intended meaning of the law would result. For example, where possible it would be preferable for the law to refer to "spouse" instead of to "wife" or "husband", and to "surviving spouse" instead of to "widow" or "widower", and so on. The subcommittee understands that there is a general principle of statutory construction that calls for interpreting words in a provision of law which denote the male sex as meaning either the male or the female sex unless there is something else in the law or in the legislative history of the provision which precludes such an interpretation, and agrees that this should be the case where it is not practical to use words that do not denote gender.

## Other Major Findings

1. The social security law should not be changed to provide social security earnings credits to homemakers for work done in the home for which no earnings are received, nor to permit people to pay social security taxes with respect to such or similar work in or around the home in order to obtain credits. Such a change in the law would be unwise, impractical, and very costly.

   There is of course an economic value, however difficult to assess, to the work that women—and men—do in and around their homes, and an economic loss when such work ceases. However, no wages are paid for such work, so there is no loss of earned income that occurs when the work stops, as there is when a wage earner retires, becomes disabled, or dies.

   Social security is an earnings-replacement program. Its function is to replace, in part, earnings from work that are cut off by retirement in old age, disability, or death. It would be contrary to the earnings-replacement nature of the social security program to provide for the payment of social security benefits in cases where no loss of earnings occurs, and the subcommittee believes that it would be undesirable to change the nature and function of the social security program by providing for the payment of benefits under it in such cases.

Another consideration with respect to paying social security taxes to obtain earnings credits for work in and around the home is that those most able to pay such tax are nonworking wives of high-earning men. All workers, part-time, full-time, single, or married, could logically feel that this option should be open to them in accordance to the degree that they do work in and around the home. To impute earnings for certain homemaker services without imputing earnings for all types of such services—for example, gardening, housepainting, and so on—would raise serious questions of equity.

2.  The social security law should not be changed to provide a married worker some or all of a secondary benefit in addition to his or her primary benefit in all cases. Such a change in the law would create further inequities, and the increase in social security contributions that would be required to pay for the additional benefits would apply not only to married people but also to single people, who would derive no additional protection from it.

appendix

# D

# Should State and Local Governments Desert the Social Security Ship?*

ROBERT J. MYERS, F.S.A., M.A.A.A.†

## SOLVENCY OF THE SOCIAL SECURITY SYSTEM

THE CRY of crisis about the Social Security system continues to be heard throughout the land. In the past few years, great concern has been expressed about the financial problems of the program. These are indeed serious, but not at all to the extent of rightly proclaiming bankruptcy. Now, widespread publicity is given to the withdrawal from Social Security of a number of state and local governments. Is this a case of a run on the bank by those with inside information and ability to act quickly, or is it mistaken or uninformed action by only a small minority?

First, let us lay to rest the charge that Social Security (Old-Age, Survivors, and Disability Insurance) is bankrupt in the usual sense of the word. This would imply that it will shortly have to suspend payments to its 32½ million beneficiaries. OASDI does have financial problems, but these are readily solvable by a combination of actions, and the beneficiaries need have no worries about getting their checks.

* This material originally appeared in the 2d Quarter 1976 *Quarterly Newsletter,* a publication of Edward H. Friend & Company, Consulting Actuaries and Employee Benefit Consultants, Washington, D.C., and is reprinted here with permission.

† Professor of Actuarial Science, Temple University, Consultant to Edward H. Friend & Company.

## ADDITIONAL FINANCING AND "DECOUPLING"

A small amount of additional financing is necessary over the short range. At least half of the long-range problem can be solved by correcting a technical deficiency in the law with regard to benefit computation for those retiring in the future. A short-run increase in both the employer and employee tax of as little as one-half percent is essential, and this should not cause any financial hardship on the part of covered persons. Similar action has been taken quite a number of times in the past. Unfortunately, such action has not been taken yet this election year. A similar, further increase will be needed in the early 1980s.

Another problem, applicable only over the long range, is that the present method of computing benefits initially is technically faulty under likely future economic conditions. It will probably result in benefits which will, for individuals attaining age 65 in the long-run future, be excessively large (even more than take-home pay eventually) and thus, if the procedure is not changed, far higher tax rates would be required than now scheduled. The technical change referred to as "decoupling" or "uncoupling" is needed.

## "OPTING OUT"—THE NEW CRISIS

The new crisis being "discovered" by some in the public press is that a number of state and local governments are pulling out of Social Security insofar as their own employees are concerned. In fact, to read some accounts, large numbers of government workers have been so affected. Actually, the number of exits before this year have been relatively few, involving only about 45,000 employees who have actually been withdrawn, and another 53,000 for whom application to do so has been made. In the latter case, the governments can change their minds during the 2-year notice period and not withdraw.

What has drawn attention to this matter has been the recent announcement of New York City with its thousands of employees that it may withdraw after the termination of the 2-year advance notice period. Alaska, with its 13,000 employees, had similarly given notice, but it may well not implement its option after completion of the study that it is making. With these two exceptions, those that have actually opted out or have served notice consist of relatively small political units, mostly in California, Louisiana, and Texas.

## "OPTING OUT"—RULES OF THE GAME

What are the rules of the game in regard to state and local governments opting out of Social Security for their own employees? The law provides that, after electing coverage, such a political unit must remain in for at least 5 years, and then give advance notice of 2 years before the withdrawal becomes effective. Private employers, other than non-profit charitable, educational, and religious organizations, have no such voluntary coverage features. Such non-profit organizations have a similar option, except that they must remain in for 8 years and then have a 2-year advance notice.

Once that withdrawal has occurred, the entity cannot re-enter Social Security. It may be noted that undue manipulation of the withdrawal provision can be done. The notice can be revoked just before the end of the 2-year period, and then a new notice can be filed shortly afterward. As a result the option can be kept continuously alive.

This special treatment has been given to state and local governments solely on constitutional grounds—namely, that the federal government cannot tax such governments without their permission. It would, however, have been possible constitutionally for the employees of state and local governments to have been taxed compulsorily for Social Security, just as they are for federal income tax. The lenient withdrawal privilege was probably granted to state and local governments in the belief that it would rarely be used—and then only for emergencies—rather than so that they could take financial advantage of the Social Security system.

It is interesting to note that state and local employees who were under an existing retirement system had to vote favorably when Social Security coverage was obtained. However, only the employing entity makes the decisions about withdrawing.

Similarly, special treatment has been given to the particular non-profit organizations because of their traditional tax-exempt status. And it was thought that the withdrawal option would rarely be used—and then not to take advantage of the Social Security system.

### Legislative History of "Opting Out"

I have researched the legislative history of the optional coverage of state and local government employees and of non-profit employees with regard to the reasons given for allowing termination of coverage. Unfortunately, I can find no mention of this matter. Such action was allowable in all versions of the legislation as it was developed when the coverage was to be on an elective basis, and nothing was said in any supporting discussion, such as the committee reports, in explanation of the rationale for these provisions.

It is interesting to note that the 1950 Amendments as passed by the House of Representatives compulsorily covered *all* non-profit employees insofar as the employee tax was concerned, but permitted the employer to opt out. In that case, the employee received credit toward benefits of only 50 percent of the wages on which he paid contributions. If coverage was elected by the employer and later terminated (after at least 5 years of coverage and a 2-year advance notice), it could not again be elected.

The Senate version of the 1950 Amendments provided for complete compulsory coverage of non-profit employees other than those of religious organizations. The latter had the option, on an *irrevocable* basis, of complete coverage, with both employer and employee taxes being applicable. The conference agreement, however, dropped both the partial compulsory basis of both bills and the irrevocable features of the Senate bill and instead provided for the elective coverage presently in the law.

## IS SOCIAL SECURITY A "POOR BUY?"

Some state and local governments have withdrawn from Social Security because they believed it to be a poor buy. Although there are some instances where a political entity could provide far better benefit protection for its employees elsewhere by utilizing the money spent for Social Security contributions, these are the exceptions rather than the rule. Such a situation could occur for a group with a very young age distribution, especially if it was composed largely of married women, who would generally expect to draw Social Security benefits from their husband's earnings record in any event.

Many of the assertions about Social Security being a bad buy for a particular group are based on perfunctory or erroneous analyses. A number of elements operating in different directions are present in such comparisons, because no private plan will be anywhere near identical with the Social Security provisions.

Only a qualified actuary, making a very detailed study, could make proper analysis. And actually, these analyses are often attempted by unqualified laymen. For example, in one particular plan, it was asserted that a big improvement would be made in changing from a benefit of 55 percent of final salary plus Social Security to 80 percent of salary. Probably for most people, certainly those in the lower and middle salary levels, 55 percent plus Social Security would be well in excess of 80 percent.

A major error committed by those who recommend that state and local governments withdraw from Social Security is the failure to take into account a number of the special features of Social Security, such as the disability and survivor benefits. Also often ignored is the very significant effect of the provisions for automatic-adjustment of benefits with rising prices. Pension costs in a private plan that provides fixed or level annuities over the years after retirement are shown to be relatively low these days, as compared with what they would be under more stable economic conditions, because of the high investment returns of 8 or 9 percent that can readily be obtained. However, such interest rates are at that level because of inflationary conditions. Under these circumstances, Social Security benefits will not be level, uniform amounts over the future, but rather will rise steadily.

Accordingly, for comparability purposes, any private arrangements being considered in replacement of Social Security should be priced out on the basis of pensions increasing automatically at a rate of 5 or 6 percent a year, rather than on the basis of level amounts. If this is done, the pension costs under the private plan being considered in lieu of Social Security will be much higher. Or, conversely, the amount of pension that can be bought for the equivalent of the Social Security taxes will be much less and thus will compare less favorably with Social Security than would otherwise have been thought.

For example, the cost of a pension for a male aged 65 which increases at the rate of 5 percent per year (at the end of each year) is about 43 percent higher than the cost of a level pension. Conversely, a given sum will purchase only about $70 of monthly pension on the 5 percent increasing basis, as against $100 per month on the level basis.

## "WINDFALL" MANIPULATION—REAL OR APPARENT?

Under certain circumstances, a state or local government can unfairly and unethically manipulate its Social Security coverage so as to take advantage of the Social Security system. It might do this, for example, by staying in Social Security for exactly 10 years, so that the vast majority of its employees will be permanently fully insured for all retirement and survivor benefits and also for the Hospital Insurance benefits under Medicare.

Let us now look at several illustrative examples of how individuals fare when they are not covered by Social Security for all their potential working careers. Or, in other words, let us see what windfalls or, alternatively what losses, develop when an entity withdraws from Social Security. Such comparisons are fraught with dangers and difficulties because a very considerable difference can occur depending upon the assumptions made. For example, the interest rate selected can make a vast difference; the use of a high interest rate will make Social Security look like a bad buy, and vice versa.

The following calculations have been made under rather simplified assumptions, but ones which are believed to be reasonable, fair, and consistent. The situation is examined as of age 65, and no account is taken of past disability and survivor benefits protection, nor is account taken of the fact that, in many cases, death of an insured worker will produce only a very small lump-sum death payment (either when there is no eligible surviving dependent or when such spouse has Social Security benefits based on own earnings record).

### Comparative Situation 1

The first case is a man who attains age 65 in early 1976 and who was first covered in 1951, when he had a salary of $3,000, which increased at a rate of 5% per year (becoming $9,675 for 1975). We shall consider his combined employer-employee Social Security contributions accumulated at 6% interest. Further, we will take two cases—first, where he is covered the entire period, 1951–75; second, where he is covered for only the first 10 years, 1951–60. In the latter case, the contributions saved, accumulated at interest, amounted to $14,277 as of the beginning of 1976. The benefit payable to the retired worker alone (based on the benefit rates applicable for June 1976) is $361 per month for the full-coverage case and $181 per month for the partial-coverage case (or, by coincidence, exactly half as much). In both cases, there is the same qualification for Hospital Insurance benefits under Medicare.

The accumulated "excess contributions" for the partial-coverage case would "purchase" on an actuarial basis only $117 per month, so that withdrawal from coverage would have been a losing proposition in this case, since the Social Security benefit was $180 per month lower. (The "purchase" factor is based on population life tables and a 3% interest rate, so as to allow for the effect of the automatic-adjustment-of-benefits feature of Social Security.) If the individual had an eligible spouse, the "excess" Social Security benefit for full coverage would have been larger, and the "purchaseable benefit for excess contributions" would have been smaller, so that the "loss" for withdrawing from Social Security coverage would have been even more.

### Comparative Situation 2

But what about those now in the system at the younger ages or entering in the future? Here, the question of proper assumptions is much more difficult. Involved are future trends of wages and prices. Even more important, is the fact that the Social Security system is not now properly constituted as to benefit-computation procedures, as discussed previously. Also, even if that situation is remedied (as it must be), the financing now scheduled is not sufficient.

Accordingly, in order to produce rational results, we must assume *static* economic conditions in the future, since this is the only way that the present benefit formula makes sense. Also, we shall assume that the average combined employer-employee tax rate for the future for Social Security (including Hospital Insurance under Medicare) will be 16%. Let us take the case of a man now aged 25 with a salary of $10,000 per year (remaining level at this amount in the future). Again, let us take two cases—one where there is full coverage, from age 25 to age 65, and the other where coverage is terminated after 10 years.

The accumulated "excess contributions" as of age 65 (using a 3% interest rate, because of the assumption of static economic conditions) would amount to $77,262. In turn, this would "purchase" a single-life annuity of $632 per month. The benefit payable to the retired worker alone at age 65 would be $474 per month for the full-coverage case, as against $216 per month for the partial-coverage case—again, the latter receives about 50% as large a benefit, even though he has had only about 25% of the coverage. In this instance, it would be "profitable" for the individual to withdraw, because the "purchaseable benefit" ($632 per month) is well in excess of the reduction in benefits because of partial coverage ($258 per month).

In the above example, if the individual had an eligible spouse, the situation would not be advantageous for withdrawal from coverage, but only to a small extent. The "purchaseable benefit" from the "excess contributions" for the husband and wife combined is $353 per month, or somewhat lower than the reduction in benefits of $387 per month because of partial coverage. It should be noted that the married-couple case is *not* typical for the long-run cases, because in the future most wives will qualify for Social Security benefits on their own earnings records and thus will not receive full benefits (or any benefits) from their husbands' earnings records.

Under such circumstances, for many (but by no means, all) employees, the money "saved" with respect to future Social Security taxes will buy more benefits than the decrease in Social Security benefits resulting from the terminated coverage. But, at the same time, many other employees will be hurt by the termination—such as short-service workers, who will thereby have a gap in their Social Security coverage and will have acquired no benefits from the governmental plan.

## Comparative Situation 3

Also, it is not generally realized that employees who are very near retirement age when termination occurs will have a reduction in their Social Security benefits which will be far greater in actuarial value than the taxes that would have been applicable. For example, consider a male employee who was aged 60 when the coverage terminated on December 31, 1974 and who had had maximum covered earnings since January 1, 1956, when his governmental employer had first elected coverage. When he attained age 62 at the beginning of 1976, his Social Security retirement benefit for himself and his wife (of the same age) was $387.00 per month, whereas if coverage had not been terminated it would have been $419.50. The additional value of the Social Security taxes that he and his employer together would have paid for 1975 if coverage had not terminated would have been $1,650, but the actuarial value of the additional benefits foregone as a result of termination would have been about $5,300 (making allowance for the automatic-adjustment feature by using a 3 percent interest rate), or $3,650 more than the taxes.

## A Profit "On Average" Means Losses for Some

Even though in some cases a government entity can, on the average, profit—or else its employees can, on the average, get more benefits—by opting out of Social Security, there is considerable question as to whether this is desirable.

Generally, any gain so involved (if there really is any) will be relatively small, and it may not be worth the extra effort and administrative expenses to take such action. This is especially so considering that the administrative expenses under such a large group operation as Social Security will necessarily be less than under a small, separate plan. Moreover, some employees will be disadvantaged.

## LIKELY NEGATIVE LEGISLATIVE REACTION

Furthermore, if the gain from withdrawing arises from a manipulation or taking advantage of the Social Security system (due to its generous treatment of short-service workers), there is a very considerable question as to whether this is morally and ethically proper, even though it may be legal. The cost of the windfall does not come from some ethereal source, but rather must be paid by the general work force of the nation. Moreover, if much of this manipulation occurs, Congress might crack down on the offenders.

## "OPTING OUT" COSTLY IF GENERAL REVENUE FINANCING IS INTRODUCED

Another possible disadvantage of a state or local government withdrawing from Social Security (applicable also to non-profit employers) is in the event that a government subsidy from the General Treasury is injected into Social Security. I should first say that I am completely opposed to this financing method. I believe that this indirect procedure dishonestly hides the fact that, in the long run, the persons covered under Social Security really do pay the general revenues involved.

In any event, if a government subsidy to Social Security should be initiated, those not under the program would be paying part of the cost thereof, but would not be getting any return from it. In other words, in the event of a government subsidy to Social Security, the only hope of "breaking even" on the taxes that a person pays to provide such a subsidy is to be covered under Social Security!

*Editor's note: The next several paragraphs assume that New York City will, in fact, withdraw from Social Security (i.e., fail to revoke its withdrawal notice).*

New York City has apparently decided to withdraw *solely* on the basis of the immediate cash-flow savings, and not because it believes that Social Security is a bad buy or is in dangerous financial condition. It is seeking all ways that it can to reduce expenditures, and this seems to be an attractive short-term way, especially since the employees will have higher net incomes because of not paying the Social Security taxes.

There will probably be no attempt by New York City to provide similar benefit protection elsewhere, because its existing pension plan that supplements Social Security is a very liberal one all by itself.

Next, let us consider the effect of the New York City withdrawal on Social Security. From a cash-flow standpoint, there will immediately (at the end of the 2-year period) be less income to the trust funds, and this will augment the declining balance already likely. Over the long range, however, the removal of New York City from the coverage of the system will mean less benefit obligations, so that the long-run effect, although probably averaging somewhat adversely, is not nearly as much so as the short-range effect.

## LEGISLATIVE PROPOSALS

Finally, let me turn to what I believe should be done about the matter of optional coverage for state and local government employees and for non-profit organization employees. It should be noted that the same situation also exists for the relatively small category of American employees of foreign subsidiaries of American corporations.

As a broad, general principle, I am strongly in favor of complete compulsory coverage of state and local employees and of non-profit employees. I have the same belief also with regard to federal employees who are under the Civil Service Retirement system. It is an essential characteristic and requirement of a democratic national social insurance system that all employment in the country should be covered thereunder.

This is desirable from the standpoint of all parties concerned—the workers, the employers, and the nation as a whole. Social Security is not a magic machine that produces benefits at substantially less cost than any other mechanism. But neither is it a high-cost, low-benefits system. There can really be no substitute for a good Social Security system supplemented by a well-coordinated private pension plan.

Accordingly, my first choice as to coverage conditions for state and local government employees and for non-profit employees would be completely compulsory coverage. There would have to be opportunity for some delay, so as to permit the organizations to adjust their private plans downward, so that the combined benefit level (and the resulting costs) would not be excessive. Naturally, the new plan, combined with Social Security, should not be less liberal than the old plan.

**Overcoming the Constitutional Problem**

The constitutional problem as to taxing the state and local governments could be solved in any of several ways. There is no question that it is constitutional to tax the employees.

One approach would be to tax the employees at the self-employed rate if the employer does not agree to pay the employer tax. For this, there is the precedent of American-citizen employees working in the United States for foreign governments or international organizations.

Another approach would be to tax the employees at the full combined employer-employee rate if the employer does not agree to pay the employer tax. Admittedly, this would be very strong medicine and is unlikely to be feasible of adoption.

Still another approach would be to credit the employees with only half of the taxed earnings if the employer does not agree to pay the employer tax. A precedent for this is the action that the House of Representatives took in connection with nonprofit employees in the 1950 Amendments.

At the very least, there should be compulsory coverage of all present employees who are *not* under an existing retirement system and of all new employees entering in the future, regardless of whether or not they are covered under a retirement system.


**SITUATION WILL WORSEN; REMEDIAL LEGISLATION IS ESSENTIAL**

Finally, it is most important to note that the anti-selection problem associated with the Social Security coverage of state and local employees and of non-profit employees will get worse and worse as time passes. This is because of the current-cost or pay-as-you-go financing basis of the Social Security system, as against the actuarially-funded nature of supplementary pension plans (or at least, as they should be). As the Social Security contribution rates rise over time under the current-cost basis, there will be *increasing* financial advantages to withdraw and substitute a private plan. Accordingly, in the interest of all parties concerned—and to produce equitable results—prompt resolution of this problem by Congress is essential.

If it is not possible to have compulsory coverage of state and local government employees and of non-profit employees, the next best procedure would be to require that, once coverage has been elected, withdrawal should not be allowed. The precedent for this is the manner in which ministers are covered. Under this approach, the problem arises as to what to do about those employing organizations who have already served notice of withdrawal. If it is not feasible to prevent them from exercising this option when the 2-year notice period expires, then at least no organizations which have as yet not filed for withdrawal should be permitted to do so. In other words, the right to withdraw should be eliminated prospectively, and once election to be covered has been made, it will be irrevocable.

As another possible alternative, if withdrawal continues to be allowed insofar as the employer is concerned, it could be provided that the employees would nonetheless remain covered compulsorily—in one of the manners described previously.

## AN "ADJUSTMENT" SOLUTION TO THE WINDFALL BENEFIT

Yet another approach would be on the benefits side, so as to prevent or ameliorate the windfalls that employees may get in the cash-benefits program when coverage is terminated. This would be a much more complex procedure. One way would be to compute (1) the Social Security benefit based on the actual service with the organization that withdrew and (2) such benefit based on the actual service plus all service with the organization after the termination date and up to age 62 (or prior death or disability, as the case may be) at the same salary rate as prevailed at the termination date—in both cases without regard to insured-status requirements or minimum-benefit provisions. Then, the "earned benefit" would be computed as: item (2) times the ratio of (3) the total covered wages with the organization before its withdrawal to (4) such total wages plus the presumed ones for service after the termination date. The "windfall benefit" would be the excess of item (1) over the "earned benefit," and it would be deducted from the computed total Social Security benefit (based on all covered employment).